Reform Responsa
for the Twenty-First Century

Sh'eilot Ut'shuvot

VOLUME 2

1999–2007/5759–5767

Reform Responsa
for the Twenty-First Century

Sh'eilot Ut'shuvot

VOLUME 2

1999–2007/5759–5767

Edited by Mark Washofsky

Central Conference of American Rabbis
New York, New York

Library of Congress Cataloging-in-Publication Data

Reform responsa for the twenty-first century : sh'eilot ut'shuvot / edited by Mark Washofsky.
    v. cm.
  Responsa on topics related to holiday observance, life cycle events, synagogue life, bio-medical ethics, Jewish ethics, and personal status.
  Includes bibliographical references and index.
  Contents: v. 1. 1996–1999 (5756–5759)—v. 2. 1999–2007 (5759–5767)
    ISBN 978-0-88123-162-5 (pbk., set ; alk. paper)—ISBN 978-0-88123-160-1 (paper, v. 1 : alk. paper)—ISBN 978-0-88123-161-8 (paper, v. 2 : alk. paper)
  1. Responsa—1948- 2. Reform Judaism. I. Washofsky, Mark. II. Title.

BM522.A1R44 2010
296.1′8541—dc22

                           2010030577

CCAR Press, 355 Lexington Avenue, New York, NY 10017
(212) 972-3636
www.ccarpress.org

CONTENTS
VOLUME 2

Choshen Mishpat: The Life of the Community

ORACH CHAYIM: WORSHIP, SHABBAT, AND FESTIVAL OBSERVANCE

May a Non-Jew Wear a Tallit?
5765.5

Sh'eilah

A certain congregation family has asked whether or not the non-Jewish grandfather of a bar mitzvah may wear a tallit during the Sabbath morning service when the bar mitzvah will lead the congregation in worship. If he wears the tallit, he may wear it on the *bimah*. In our congregation, the non-Jewish parent or grandparents stand on the *bimah* but do not pass the Torah when the Torah is passed from one generation to another.

This question is the subject of two existing Reform responsa. Rabbi Solomon B. Freehof[1] allows a non-Jewish clergy to wear a tallit in an ecumenical service in a synagogue. He reasons that since the tallit, and especially the *tzitzit*, are of lesser sanctity than the Torah and its accouterments, and since they may be discarded when worn out, unlike the Torah and its accouterments, which must be stored away, then we may deal with them differently. He continues that we may offer the tallit to the non-Jew "for the sake of peace." However, Rabbi Walter Jacob[2] mentions that wearing the tallit is a mitzvah from the Torah and requires a *b'rachah* that specifically mentions the chosenness of Israel and so may be recited only by a Jew.

So, may a non-Jew wear a tallit during the Sabbath morning service? (Rabbi Harry D. Rothstein, Utica, New York)

T'shuvah

This *sh'eilah* asks us to decide between two conflicting *t'shuvot*, each authored by an eminent *poseik* and teacher of the Reform Movement. We therefore state at the outset our profound debt of gratitude to our teachers, even though we may disagree with them on one issue or another. Although our interpretations of text and our religious stance may diverge from those of our predecessors, we are able to conduct this discussion solely because they taught us the art and the process of Reform responsa and halachic thought. We stand on the shoulders of giants, and that very fact, ironically, accounts for the different angle of vision that we bring to this and to other questions.[3]

With that in mind, let us consider the responsum of Rabbi Freehof. He bases his permissive ruling upon the distinction between *tashmishei k'dushah*, "appurtenances of sanctity," and *tashmishei mitzvah*, "appurtenances of a mitzvah." Ritual articles belonging to the former category, including "the Torah and its accouterments," are of a higher degree of sanctity than those belonging to the latter category, such as the *tzitzit*. Thus, if a Torah mantle has become worn and is no longer suitable for use, it must be stored away (placed in a *genizah*), while the fringes of a tallit that are broken or no longer used may, in the words of the *Shulchan Aruch*, "be thrown onto the ash heap because it is an appurtenance of a mitzvah and not inherently holy."[4] Indeed, Rabbi Freehof continues, the halachah even permits one "to go to the toilet wearing the tallit."[5] This leads him to the following *kal vachomer* argument: "If, therefore, the tallit may be worn in all sorts of places, and if its fringes (when separated) may even be tossed upon the ash heap, there is no question that one may lend it to a Gentile minister who will handle it reverently."[6] He adds that in allowing the minister to wear the tallit "we will thus fulfill the basic mitzvah of acting 'to follow the paths of peace' (*mipnei darchei shalom*)," which, he notes, our tradition also states as "to avoid ill will" (*mishum eivah*).

In our view, Rabbi Freehof's *t'shuvah* is somewhat less than persuasive. This is true, in part because of some of the debatable points of halachah that it contains,[7] but primarily because we do not think it is a helpful way to frame the question. The tallit's inherent ritual sanctity (or lack thereof) is not the point. Even a Torah scroll, which possesses much more sanctity that a tallit, is hardly "defiled" if a non-Jew should touch it, yet this does not mean that we may or should call a non-Jew to the

Torah for an *aliyah*. The relevant issue in all these matters is whether it is *appropriate* for a non-Jew to participate in a particular public ritual observance. In the case of being called to the Torah, our answer is "no,"[8] and we would say the same here. To wear a tallit is to perform the mitzvah "to remember to observe all My mitzvot and be holy to your God" (Num. 15:40); it is, in other words, a material expression of one's membership in the community of Israel, a people sanctified through the mitzvot that characterize its covenant with God. The Rabbinic tradition understands the *tzitzit* as a physical sign that marks Israel as a separate people, "made distinct by the mitzvot."[9] A gentile may wish to wear a tallit for his or her own reasons, but the tallit is *our* symbol; it does not belong to the non-Jew, and it is not for him or her to define. The tallit, as *our* symbol, functions *for us* as a declaration that the one who wears it is a Jew, who bears the title *Yisrael*, who partakes with the rest of us in the covenant that distinguishes us as a unique religious community. The grandfather in our *sh'eilah* may well feel a deep sense of familial pride in his grandson's becoming a bar mitzvah, and his desire to participate in this special event is understandable. He is not, however, a Jew, a member of our covenant community. He should not wear a tallit.

We also hesitate to apply here the categories "to follow the paths of peace" and "to avoid ill will."[10] While we certainly want to maintain good relations with our non-Jewish neighbors and to avoid causing family strife, we doubt that these principles are the *appropriate* way to frame the issues at stake in this question. We are dealing, after all, with matters of deep religious principle, with observances that define us as a Jewish community and that therefore set us apart from others. By calling ourselves a *Jewish* community, we necessarily draw lines and establish boundaries that flow from and reinforce our identity as Jews. To do so inevitably limits the role that non-Jews, those who do not partake in that identity, may play in our communal ritual life.[11] After all, we do *not* argue that a gentile ought to be called to the Torah, recite *Kiddush*, or lead the synagogue service on the grounds that this would help preserve friendly relations with non-Jews. Indeed, our *sho-eil*'s congregation places clear limits upon the role that the non-Jewish grandparents play at the service marking bar mitzvah. The non-Jew should understand the need of the Jewish community to assert the right—a right that belongs by every self-identified community, religious or otherwise[12]—to define itself, its patterns of life, and its qualifications for membership. This is especially true in democratic and pluralistic societies such as our own, where this right is acknowledged and where Jews are proud and equal citizens. It is good to preserve peace and to avoid hostility, but these goals, worthy as they are, do not convince us of the need to compromise our basic religious principles.

For these reasons, we endorse the position taken by Rabbi Walter Jacob in his responsum. We do so not exclusively because the wearing of a tallit is preceded by the recitation of a *b'rachah* that stresses the nature of this act as a mitzvah. We frequently invite our gentile neighbors to participate in activities—for example, attending a Passover seder,[13] sitting in the sukkah—over which we recite *birchot mitzvah*. Since it is obvious to all that they join with us as guests and not as Jews, we would not think to regard their participation as improper. Yet for a gentile to don a tallit at a public worship service, something he or she need not do in order to take part in that event, is to identify physically as one of us. Again, our position is based primarily upon the symbolic function of the tallit as a statement of Jewish identity and of membership in the covenant community. The gentile cannot make this statement; therefore, he or she should not wear a tallit at our synagogue services.

NOTES

1. R. Solomon B. Freehof, *Reform Responsa for Our Time*, no. 5.

2. R. Walter Jacob, *Halakhah* (a publication of the Freehof Institute of Progressive Halakhah), Spring/Summer 1996.

3. The classic statement—"we are dwarfs, standing on the shoulders of giants"—seems to have originated with the twelfth-century Scholastic philosopher Bernard of Chartres. R. Yeshayahu di Trani (d. ca. 1250) is apparently the first Jewish author to use the

phrase, which he calls "a saying [*mashal*] of the philosophers" (*Resp. RYD*, no. 62). R. Yeshayahu learns from this saying that although the dwarf certainly lacks the great stature of the giant, he nevertheless can see farther, precisely because the giant enables him to do so. This explains how we *acharonim*, or "later" sages, are permitted to disagree with our predecessors (the *rishonim*), even though the *rishonim*, according to traditionalist ideology, are by definition greater and wiser than we. On this subject, see Yisrael Ta-Shema, *Halachah, Minhag, Um'tziut B'ashkenaz* (Jerusalem: Magnes, 1996), 70–71; Avraham Melamed, *Al Kitfei Anakim* (Ramat Gan: Bar Ilan University Press, 2003); and Robert K. Merton, *On the Shoulders of Giants: A Shandean Postscript* (Chicago: University of Chicago Press, 1993).

4. *SA, OC* 21:1. Actually, the passage reads "because no sanctity attaches to its physical substance" (*she-ein b'gufah k'dushah*); i.e., the *tzitzit* is holy only because it is whole and attached to a four-cornered garment. A *tzitzit* that is detached from the tallit is mere thread; no mitzvah is performed with it, and it thus may be discarded. We wonder whether a proper analogy can be drawn from a detached *tzitzit* to a fringed tallit with which a mitzvah is indeed performed.

5. *SA, OC* 21:3. The commentators on that passage, however, notably the *Magen David* and the *Mishnah B'rurah*, write that this refers to the *tallit katan*, the fringed undergarment that one may wear all day long, and not to the *tallit shel mitzvah* that is worn specially during prayer. The latter, they declare, should *not* be worn in the toilet.

6. The precise *sh'eilah* addressed by Rabbi Freehof concerns a Christian minister who is to participate in a joint service at the synagogue and who wishes "to wear a *talit* as the rabbi does."

7. See notes 4 and 5, above.

8. On the general question of gentile participation in synagogue services, see *Teshuvot for the Nineties*, no. 5754.5, pp. 55–75.

9. *P'sikta D'Rav Kahana* 16:3 on Lam. 2:13; *Sifrei D'varim*, chap. 36 (to Deut. 6:9).

10. *Mipnei darchei shalom* is the justification cited for a number of *takanot* (Rabbinic legislative ordinances) during tannaitic times. See M. *Gittin* 5:8–9 and M. *Sh'vi-it* 4:3, among other places. *Mishum eivah* appears during the later, amoraic period; see, for example, BT *Bava M'tzia* 32b and *Avodah Zarah* 26a.

11. This Committee has spoken to the issue on a number of occasions. Non-Jews are not called to the Torah, do not read the haftarah, do not receive important "honors" surrounding the Torah service, and do not lead the central rubrics of our liturgy

(*Teshuvot for the Nineties*, no. 5754.5, pp. 55–75; *Reform Responsa for the Twenty-first Century*, no. 5758.11, vol. 1, pp. 195–204; *American Reform Responsa*, no. 6, pp. 21–24; *Current Reform Responsa*, no. 23, pp. 91–93; and *New Reform Responsa*, no. 7, pp. 33–36).

12. For example, as one member of our Committee puts it, "How would we feel about a Jew attending a Catholic mass for a relative's confirmation and taking communion?" The members of that Catholic church would surely question whether the Jew had acted appropriately with regard to their sacrament.

13. Many traditionally observant Jews will not invite non-Jews to a seder or to any other *Yom Tov* meal. This is because the permission to cook on a Festival day (so long as it does not fall on Shabbat) is interpreted to apply only to food that is cooked for Jews; therefore, "it is forbidden to invite the non-Jew, lest one cook extra food on the Festival day specifically for him" (*SA, OC* 512:1; see BT *Beitzah* 21b on Exod. 12:16). We Reform Jews clearly do not observe this restriction. Moreover, so long as it is clear that one will complete the cooking prior to the onset of the holiday, there is no reason why Orthodox Jews should refrain from inviting non-Jews to the meal.

Sh'eilah

A congregant has asked that a Sabbath morning service, during which her daughter will lead the congregation in worship as a bat mitzvah, will read Torah, haftarah, and offer a *d'var Torah*, begin as late in the morning as possible, perhaps as late as 11:30 A.M. or even noon. She makes this request so that her elderly and ill father, the grandfather of the bat mitzvah, will be able to participate and to fully appreciate the service and the efforts of his granddaughter, as she demonstrates her commitment to Judaism as a young Jewish adult. He is suffering from a severe illness and is not fully aware until late in the morning or early afternoon. The family and the bat mitzvah want to participate in a Sabbath morning service, as they feel that it is more rewarding than the shorter *Minchah,* afternoon service.

Our congregation does not normally have a Sabbath morning or afternoon service. The Friday eve service is the "flagship" service of our temple. Sabbath morning services are held only when a bar mitzvah or a bat mitzvah leads our congregation in worship. Such Sabbath morning services have begun as early as 10:00 A.M. or as late as 11:00 A.M. (Rabbi Harry D. Rothstein, Utica, New York)

T'shuvah

This *sh'eilah*, in addition to the particular case it addresses, raises a more general issue. It is the common custom (*minhag*) for Reform congregations in North America to begin their Shabbat morning services (*Shacharit*) at 10:00 A.M. or later. This custom is no accident, and it did not emerge for reasons of mere convenience. We have established it in order to facilitate a larger attendance at worship services, which enables more people[1] to fulfill the mitzvah of *t'filah b'tzibur*, the traditional Jewish preference for public over private prayer.[2] Yet alongside this positive goal, our late starting times ensure that the congregation will recite the central rubrics of the morning liturgy—the *Sh'ma* and the *T'filah*—at an hour later than is prescribed for them according to the codified halachah. This fact might lead to two conclusions. On the one hand, it might suggest that our prayers, because we say them "late," are invalid in the eyes of Jewish law. On the other hand, it might raise the suspicion that Reform Judaism is indifferent to the question of proper times for prayer, which would mean that it is of no consequence whether this synagogue schedules its morning service at 11:30 A.M., at noon, or even later.

Both these conclusions, in our view, are erroneous. To establish this point, we want first to consider the general issue: does the Jewish legal and liturgical tradition offer support for our *minhag* to begin services late in the morning? We will then turn to the case at hand: given that we do begin our services during the late morning, do we nonetheless recognize a time limit, a *terminus ad quem* beyond which a morning service should not begin? And if so, should we insist upon that time limit in a difficult case such as this one?

1. THE MORNING *SH'MA*

The *Sh'ma*, according to our Rabbinic tradition, is to be recited "when you lie down and when you rise up" (Deut. 6:7), that is, in the evening and in the morning.[3] Although the precise time for the recitation of the morning *Sh'ma* is the subject of a dispute in the Mishnah,[4] the settled halachah is that one must recite it by the end of "the third hour" of the day, the time by which the vast majority of the community have "arisen" from sleep.[5] The hour to which our sources refer is a "temporal hour" (*shaah z'manit*), that is, a segment consisting of one-twelfth of the period of daylight on a particular day. Thus, the "end of the third hour" is equivalent to the first quarter of the daylight period.[6] As we note above, few Reform congregations ever recite the *Sh'ma* before that time.

The tradition, however, is more complex than the above might indicate. For one thing, although one *should* recite the morning *Sh'ma* before the end of the third hour, it is not forbidden to recite it afterwards. The Mishnah states that "one who recites it (after the third hour) loses nothing; he is as one who reads [the *Sh'ma*] in the Torah," fulfilling the mitzvah of Torah study if not the mitzvah of reciting the *Sh'ma* at its proper time.[7] Moreover, one is encouraged to recite the *Sh'ma* even though one has missed its "deadline," for "it is good to accept upon oneself the yoke of the Kingdom of Heaven" at any time of day.[8] Maimonides declares that if one has not recited the *Sh'ma* before the end of the third hour, one may recite it along with its accompanying blessings (*Yotzeir Or, Ahavah Rabbah*, and *Emet V'Yatziv*)[9] throughout the day.[10] Other scholars do not go so far, but they nonetheless allow the recitation of the *Sh'ma* and its accompanying blessings until noon, the latest acceptable time for the recitation of the *T'filah* (see below).[11] Although these rulings are controversial,[12] they raise the possibility that the entire day is the "proper time" for the fulfillment of the mitzvah.[13] This interpretation is suggested by R. Yosef Karo, the author of the *Shulchan Aruch*, in his commentary to Rambam's *Mishneh Torah*. In Karo's view, Rambam holds that the "by the end of the third hour" rule is a Rabbinic stringency imposed upon the basic Toraitic (*d'oraita*) standard, which requires only that the *Sh'ma* be said during the daytime, the time of "rising up."[14]

Most authorities do not accept this interpretation of Maimonides; for them, the "proper time" for reciting the morning *Sh'ma*, even according to the Torah, is the first quarter of the day.[15] Yet the undeniable existence of this interpretation, along with the fact that it is not forbidden to recite the *Sh'ma* and Its Blessings after the end of the third hour, offers support for our Reform practice to recite the *Sh'ma* after 10:00 A.M. Given the positive reasons for which we schedule our services later in the morning, we believe that we stand upon solid traditional ground.

2. THE MORNING *T'FILAH*

The Mishnah records the following dispute: "The morning *T'filah* [*t'filat hashachar*] is recited until noon; R. Y'hudah says it is recited until the end of the fourth hour."[16] The argument centers over a disagreement as to when the *tamid shel shachar*, the public morning sacrifice brought daily in the Temple, was offered, whether at noon or by the end of the fourth hour.[17] The halachah is decided according to R. Y'hudah;[18] hence, the morning *T'filah* must be recited before the end of the first third of the daytime. Again, many Reform services would miss this deadline, reciting the *T'filah* later than its set time. On the other hand, one who recites the *T'filah* after the fourth hour but before noon—the midpoint of the daylight hours—fulfills the mitzvah of prayer, even though he or she does not achieve the merit of praying at the set time.[19] Reform congregations *do* recite the *T'filah* prior to noon.

Further, we would note that the traditional set times for the *T'filot* are not relevant in a Reform Jewish context. Each of the fixed prayers—*Shacharit*, *Minchah*, *Arvit*, and *Musaf*—is scheduled to correspond to a sacrifice or a related event at the ancient Temple.[20] Reform Judaism has long since abandoned this connection.[21] We have instead returned to a different, earlier understanding of prayer times,[22] one that schedules prayer not according to activities in the Temple but according to "astronomical" criteria, to the time of day. The Talmud itself cites Daniel's custom to pray three times daily and suggests with the Psalmist that these times are "evening, morning, and afternoon."[23] We pray at these times of day, in other words, not because our ancestors brought sacrifices at those hours but because they are regarded as natural and proper times to turn to God with words of praise and supplication. If morning is one of those times, then we should define it in the way it is customarily defined in our culture, not by its association with the *tamid shel shachar*: "morning" is that part of the day prior to noon. And as we have noted, we begin our services later in the morning in order to enable more people to attend them and to fulfill the mitzvah of public prayer.

3. SERVICE TIMES AND EXCEPTIONAL CIRCUMSTANCES

Our Reform custom to hold services in the late morning is therefore a valid expression of Jewish liturgical tradition, reflecting both its letter and its spirit. Our discussion implies, however, that our morning service at any rate be held *in the morning*, a requirement that would seem to pose a hardship to the family at the center of our *sh'eilah*. Can their special needs be satisfied within a principled understanding of our own Reform liturgical practice? We offer the following comments and suggestions.

a. The set schedule for synagogue services should not be altered for the convenience of individual members. It is especially important to make this point in connection with the observance of bar/bat mitzvah, a *minhag* that tends to overwhelm the regular weekly observance of Shabbat in our congregations. The Shabbat service is a *synagogue* service, a communal event, and not a private *simchah*.[24] To change the starting time for the benefit of the bat mitzvah's family would tend to give the opposite impression.

b. In this case, however, the congregation does not have a regular Shabbat morning service. The community assembles on Saturday mornings, at either 10:00 A.M. or 11:00 A.M., only when the service is held in conjunction with a bar/bat mitzvah observance. Given that these services by their nature are special events, there would be no objection to scheduling them later than the usual starting time, provided that they remain *morning* services, that is, the congregation should be able to recite both the *Sh'ma* and the *T'filah* before noon. This suggests a starting time of no later than 11:30 A.M.

c. If the grandfather cannot be brought to the synagogue by that hour, the service might pause briefly between the *T'filah* and the Torah reading in order to give him time to arrive.[25]

d. Alternately, the bat mitzvah observance might be scheduled at *Minchah*.[26] Although the family feels that a Shabbat morning service is a more "rewarding" experience, a bit of liturgical creativity can lend a similar feel to the *Minchah* service. The young person might read a bit more Torah than is normally read at *Minchah*,[27] and she may also recite her haftarah, albeit without the blessings.[28]

e. Finally, all the above applies only if it is truly impossible or unfeasible for the grandfather to be awakened early to be brought to the synagogue. In the event that he can arrive by the normal starting time, we should not delay the beginning of services.

This last point deserves emphasis. We want to do everything we can to respond to this family's special situation. At the same time, a large part of becoming a bat mitzvah is the acceptance of Jewish communal responsibilities. One of those responsibilities is to participate in the religious rituals of the community, observances that are created by our tradition and defined by a set of rules. Among these rules are the set times for the recitation of the *Sh'ma* and the *T'filah*. There is flexibility in the way we interpret and apply these rules, but because the rules possess substance and meaning for us, there are limits to that flexibility. This is a reality that should be recognized by all members of the community, including the bat mitzvah and her family on her special day.

NOTES

1. "A numerous people is the glory of the king" (Prov. 14:28). From this, the Sages infer that it is better to pray in a larger rather than in a smaller assembly. See BT *B'rachot* 53a and *M'gillah* 27b; *Magen Avraham*, OC 90:15; *Mishnah B'rurah*, OC 687: 7.

2. "'May my prayer to You be at a time of favor' (Ps. 69:14). When is this 'time of favor'? When the community prays together" (BT *B'rachot* 7b–8a). Thus, "one must join the community to pray, and one must not pray alone when one is able to pray with a congregation" (*Yad, T'filah* 8:1). See also SA, OC 90:9.

3. See M. *B'rachot* 1:3. As we shall see, the word "morning" may not be precise; it may be permissible to recite the *Sh'ma* at any time during daylight hours. Still, the sources all speak of *k'riat Sh'ma shel shacharit*, that is, the *morning Sh'ma*.

4. M. *B'rachot* 1:2. The other opinion in the Mishnah holds that the *Sh'ma* must be recited by sunrise. This is now recognized as the standard of the *vatikin* (i.e., those who are particularly stringent in their observance of the mitzvot; Bartenura to M. *B'rachot*

3:5 and *M. D'mai* 6:6) rather than the standard applied to all. Since sunrise is the earliest time that the *T'filah* may be recited, those who are particularly strict seek to recite the *Sh'ma* right at sunrise, so that the two rubrics may be recited together (BT *B'rachot* 9b: *k'dai sh'yismach ge'ulah l'tefilah*).

5. BT *B'rachot* 10b (Sh'muel declares that the halachah follows the viewpoint of R. Y'hudah in the Mishnah); *Yad, K'riat Sh'ma* 1:11; *SA, OC* 58:1.

6. *SA, OC* 58:1. On the *shaah z'manit*, see Rambam's commentary to *M. B'rachot* 1:2. Some authorities rule that we begin to measure these twelve temporal hours at dawn (see *Magen Avraham, OC* 58:1), while others say that the daytime for this purpose begins with sunrise (*Biur HaGra, OC* 459:2).

7. *M. B'rachot* 1:2; *Yad, K'riat Sh'ma* 1:12 and *Tur, OC* 58.

8. *Mishnah B'rurah, OC* 58:27.

9. *M. B'rachot* 1:4. *Ahavah Rabbah* is the name of the second *b'rachah* in the Ashkenazic rite; Sephardim begin that benediction with the words *Ahavat Olam*, as they (and all other rites) do in the evening.

10. *Yad, K'riat Sh'ma* 1:13. The Talmud (*B'rachot* 10b) explains the Mishnaic phrase "one who recites it [after the third hour] loses nothing" as: one does not lose the opportunity to say the benedictions that accompany the *Sh'ma*. Rambam cites this explanation in his *Commentary* to *M. B'rachot* 1:2. See also *Sefer HaChinuch, mitzvah* 420.

11. *Chidushei HaRashba, B'rachot* 10b, citing *Tosafot*, and *Mishnah B'rurah, OC* 58, in *Biur Halachah*, s.v. *korah b'lo birchoteha*.

12. Most authorities hold that it is forbidden to recite the accompanying blessings of the *Sh'ma* after the end of the fourth hour—i.e., one-third—of the day. This ruling is attributed to Hai Gaon; see *Hil. HaRosh, B'rachot* 1:10 and *Chidushei HaRashba, B'rachot* 10b, who explain that Hai arrives at his "fourth hour" limit by linking the *Sh'ma* to the *T'filah*, which according to the accepted halachah (see below) is to be recited by the end of the fourth hour. The *Tur* and *SA, OC* 58:6 adopt this position as well, as do "most of the *acharonim*" (the authorities who have flourished since the publication of the *Shulchan Aruch*); see *Mishnah B'rurah, OC* 58, in *Biur Halachah*, s.v. *korah b'lo birchoteha*.

13. The theory is that, were it *unacceptable* to recite the *Sh'ma* past the third (or fourth) hour, it would be forbidden to recite the blessings. A blessing recited at an inappropriate

time is considered a *b'rachah l'vatalah*, quite possibly an instance of taking God's name in vain (see note 28, below). A number of the authorities cited in the preceding note make this very point in limiting the recitation of the blessings to the fourth hour or to noontime.

14. *Kesef Mishneh, K'riat Sh'ma* 1:13. This interpretation proceeds from a consideration of the evening *Sh'ma*. Although the settled halachah is that one must recite the evening *Sh'ma* before midnight, this is understood to be a Rabbinic stringency. As far as the Torah law is concerned, one fulfills one's obligation by reciting the *Sh'ma* at any time during the night, because the entire night is "the time of lying down" (*M. B'rachot* 1:1; *Yad, K'riat Sh'ma* 1:9). Karo posits that the same is true for the morning *Sh'ma*: if *b'shochb'cha* means "all night long," then *uv'kumecha* means "all day long." Though the Rabbis have introduced their stringency, the Torah would permit the recitation of the *Sh'ma* throughout the "time of rising up," i.e., the entire daytime period.

15. Both *Magen Avraham* (OC 58:7) and *Turei Zahav* (OC 58:4) reject Karo's interpretation of the Torah's language *uv'kumecha*, "and when you rise up." This, they say, does *not* mean "when you are awake" but rather "when you arise from sleep," i.e., during the early part of the morning. By contrast, *b'shochb'cha*, "and when you lie down," can be and is interpreted to mean "when you are in bed," i.e., the entire night. *Magen Avraham* notes that this insight is adopted by the earlier *Sefer HaChinuch*, *mitzvah* 420. See also R. Chizkiyah Da Silva (seventeenth-century *Eretz Yisrael*), *P'ri Chadash* to OC 58:1, for a detailed refutation of Karo's theory.

16. *M. B'rachot* 4:1. The phrase *ad arba sha-ot* is translated "until the *end of the* fourth hour" according to the Talmud's conclusion at BT *B'rachot* 27a.

17. BT *B'rachot* 26b; *Tosefta B'rachot* 3:1.

18. BT *B'rachot* 27a: the halachah follows the individual opinion of R. Y'hudah against the anonymous viewpoint because *M. Eduyot* 6:1 supports his position. See *Yad, T'filah* 3:1 and SA, OC 89:1.

19. See *Yad* and *Shulchan Aruch*, ibid.

20. According to the *baraita* in support of R. Y'hoshua ben Levi in BT *B'rachot* 26b and *Tosefta B'rachot* 3:1. Although no sacrifice was offered at night, the *baraita* notes that the internal organs that had been placed upon the fire for the *minchah* offering were consumed at that time. The *N'ilah* prayer on Yom Kippur corresponds to the "closing of the gates" of the Temple at the end of the day (*M. Taanit* 4:1; *Tosefta B'rachot* 3:2).

21. Witness to this is our omission of the *Musaf* prayer. *Musaf*, more than any other prayer, expresses the traditional link between *t'filah* and the sacrifices. Indeed, it is seen as the fulfillment of Hosea 14:3, "Instead of bulls, we will pay the offering of our lips" (*Tosafot, B'rachot* 26a, s.v. *i'baaya*).

22. Relevant here is a *baraita* in BT *B'rachot* 26b, cited in support of R. Yosei b. R. Chanina, who holds that "the Patriarchs established the times for prayer." This position is not the "officially" accepted narrative for the origins of the daily cycle for prayer (see *Yad, T'filah* 1:5), quite possibly because it does not account for the establishment of *Musaf*. It does show, however, that the tradition is not unanimous in determining the prayer times in accordance with the daily schedule at the Temple.

23. BT *B'rachot* 31a, on Dan. 6:11 and Ps. 55:18.

24. On this point, see our *Reform Responsa for the Twenty-first Century*, no. 5758.9, vol. 1, pp. 21–31, and no. 5762.6, vol. 2, pp. 39–48.

25. Aside from its being part of the "morning" service, there is no set hour for the reading of Torah on Shabbat. But while it would be permissible to read Torah later than noon, those organizing the service must be cognizant of *tircha d'tzibura*, the possibility that the delay will be a burden upon the congregation.

26. In most cases, we discourage the practice of holding bar/bat mitzvah observances at Shabbat *Minchah* (see the responsa in note 24, above). The reason is that most of our congregations do not hold a regular weekly Shabbat *Minchah* service, so that the bar/bat mitzvah observance would perforce be a private rather than a public, congregational event. In this case, where even the Shabbat morning service would be held only when a bar/bat mitzvah is being observed, the distinction between *Shacharit* and *Minchah* disappears.

27. The *Minchah* reading normally consists of ten verses from the *parashah* of the subsequent Shabbat (BT *Bava Kama* 82a; *SA, OC* 292:1).

28. Since the haftarah is normally not read on Shabbat at *Minchah*, the recitation of the blessings would be an instance of *b'rachah l'vatalah* or "an unnecessary *b'rachah*," and it is forbidden to recite a blessing when one is not required to do so. See *Encyclopedia Talmudit*, v. 4, 280–85. There is no objection, however, to reading from the Prophets without the *b'rachot*.

Sh'eilah

I have two questions concerning the wording of the liturgy we use in our Reform synagogues.

1. The Reform Movement has sought to include the Matriarchs in the *Avot*. Which order is appropriate: should the names of the three Patriarchs be stated first followed by the Matriarchs, or should the wives be paired with their husbands (*Avraham v'Sarah*), etc.? In my opinion the goal of reducing gender bias is best achieved with the latter approach and therefore is preferable.

2. Of the four women who bore the sons of Jacob, we mention Leah and Rachel in the *Avot*. Should Bilhah and Zilpah be included as Matriarchs? By leaving these women out, the Reform Movement gives tacit approval to the idea that woman is property. Indeed after Rachel and Leah die, Israel refers to Bilhah and Zilpah as his wives. In my opinion, it is essential to the concept of equality to add these two unsung mothers in the Matriarch listing.

As the new Reform prayer book reaches its conclusion, these two issues need immediate attention. I look forward to your responses. (Cantor Jerome Krasnow, South Windsor, Connecticut)

T'shuvah

1. THE MATRIARCHS IN THE *T'FILAH*[1]

It has become the widespread *minhag* (custom) in our congregations to add the names of the *Imahot*, the Matriarchs Sarah, Rebekah, Leah, and Rachel, to the names of the Patriarchs in the first benediction of the *T'filah*.[2] The motive for this change in the traditional prayer text was to express our understanding that *all* Jews, both male and female, participate equally in Israel's covenant with God and to give voice to the role of our Matriarchs in the transmission of that covenant to their descendants. This innovation is consistent with the liturgical tradition of the Reform Movement, which from its inception has embraced the notion that the formal, public prayer recited in our synagogues should reflect our people's most deeply held values and commitments.[3]

Our innovation is also consistent with the much older liturgical tradition of Rabbinic Judaism, the foundation of our own worship service. We say this in terms of both the history and the theory of that tradition. The history of Jewish prayer is a story of ongoing change and development, not only during the Talmudic period, a time when the formal rules of liturgical practice had not yet been established,[4] but also during subsequent centuries, when the halachah of Jewish liturgy had supposedly been set in stone.[5] In adjusting the words of the *T'filah* to the needs of our time, therefore, we are simply doing what Jews have always done with the text of their prayer. Moreover, the halachah itself, the "rules" and theory of traditional Jewish liturgy, does not prohibit liturgical innovation. On the contrary: change, fluidity, and pluralism are the essence of prayer as that term is understood in the sources of Jewish law. The Talmud defines "prayer" as *rachamei*, a heartfelt supplication to God, rather than the recitation of a fixed text; therefore, "one may pray in whatever way one wishes to pray."[6] Indeed, as Maimonides recounts the story, in its original form the Torah's mitzvah of prayer imposed no fixed text upon the worshiper; one may approach God with words of one's own choosing that reflect the content of one's mind and heart.[7] Over time, of course, the Jewish community adopted a fixed text for the *T'filah*, the "Eighteen Benedictions."[8] This text was taken quite seriously. The Talmud goes so far as to declare that "one who alters the form [*matbei-a*] of a benediction [*b'rachah*] that the Sages ordained has not fulfilled his obligation."[9] Yet even this rule does not forbid us from making appropriate adjustments in the text of the liturgy: a *b'rachah* may depart from its accepted wording provided that the content and theme of the new text correspond to those of the traditional form (*inyan hab'rachah*).[10] Our version of the *T'filah*'s first benediction does retain its traditional content and theme: that our God is also the God of our ancestors, the biblical progenitors of the Jewish people. Our text surely does not please those Jews who are temperamentally opposed to *all* liturgical innovation.[11] Nonetheless, it is in accord with the history of Jewish prayer and with the demands of liturgical halachah.

2. THE ORDER OF THE NAMES

Let us turn now to our *sho-eil*'s specific queries. Is it better, as he suggests, to recite the names of the *Imahot* along with the names of their husbands or to recite them separately, as is our custom? There is no one obviously correct answer to this question. Our *sho-eil* may be right when he says that his version—"the God of Abraham and Sarah, the God of Isaac and Rebekah," and so on—is the more egalitarian one.[12] Yet it can be argued that his text would have the opposite effect, presenting the Matriarchs primarily as wives rather than as individuals, each with her own personal relationship with God. Indeed, our "female" parallel to that formulation—"the God of Sarah, the God of Rebekah, the God of Leah, and the God of Rachel"[13]— expresses the idea that the Matriarchs are equivalent to the Patriarchs as a group as well as individually. Moreover, the current formulation—"the God of Abraham, the God of Isaac, and the God of Jacob—is taken verbatim from the Torah's narrative of God's revelation to Moses at the Burning Bush (Exod. 3:15 and 4:5). The *T'filah* is replete with biblical quotations, and preserving these expressions in our prayer can be said to reinforce the link between our present-day community and our origins as a covenant people. In short, each of these two wordings has its advantages, and we see no compelling reason to demand that one version be given preeminence over the other.

3. THE MAIDSERVANTS

Should the names of Bilhah and Zilpah, the maidservants of Rachel and Leah, be included in the *T'filah*? Again, one can argue in favor of this departure from our Reform *minhag*. As our *sho-eil* indicates, the Torah does refer to these two women as the "wives" of Jacob (Gen. 30:4, 30:9, 37:2), even though elsewhere it calls them his concubines (Gen. 35:22).[14] Moreover, there is a midrashic text that numbers Bilhah and Zilpah among the "six matriarchs" of Israel.[15] Finally, it can be argued that to include the maidservants in our prayer is to make a strong statement against social elitism and in favor of an affirming attitude toward diverse family structures.[16]

Yet much can also be said in defense of our current custom. We single out the names Sarah, Rebekah, Leah, and Rachel, not because of their legal status, but because each of them plays a pivotal role in the biblical narrative: in their relationship to their families, husbands, and children and in their influence upon the events that shaped the course of Israelite history. Each of these four women, in other words, appears to us as a personality in her own right, not simply as the wife of a patriarch. The aggadic tradition, in fact, regards them as prophets,[17] recipients of divine revelation. This suggests that it is possible to view Sarah, Rebekah, Leah, and Rachel as partners with their husbands in the establishment of the covenant. By including their names in the first benediction of the *T'filah*, we simply take this traditional Jewish conception and make it explicit. By contrast, none of these characteristics apply to Bilhah and Zilpah, who simply do not occupy such an exalted position in the biblical narrative and in the religious memory of the Jewish people.[18]

Thus, in this case as well, while Reform Jews are certainly entitled to include the names of Bilhah and Zilpah in the first benediction of the *T'filah*, we find no compelling reason to recommend that change from our current practice.

NOTES

1. It is not the function of this Committee to determine the text, structure, or wording of the new prayer book of the Central Conference of American Rabbis (CCAR). Those tasks belong to the prayer book's editors, as overseen by the CCAR Liturgy Committee. (As of this writing, the new prayer book of the CCAR, *Mishkan T'filah*,

was still in preparation.) We therefore venture no opinion here as to the appropriate text of the new siddur. We consider this *sh'eilah* rather because it touches upon a matter of Reform Jewish religious observance and, as such, does pertain to the function of this Committee.

2. This innovation appears in recent liturgical publications of the Conference, including *Gates of Prayer for Shabbat* (New York: CCAR, 1992). Our current "official" siddur, *Gates of Prayer: The New Union Prayer Book* (New York: CCAR, 1975), does not include the *Imahot* in the Hebrew texts of the *T'filah*, but it does mention them in several English renditions of those texts (e.g., pp. 229 and 356).

3. For the historical record of liturgical innovation within our movement, see Jakob J. Petuchowski, *Prayerbook Reform in Europe: The Liturgy of European Liberal and Reform Judaism* (New York: World Union for Progressive Judaism, 1968), and Eric L. Friedland, *"Were Our Mouths Filled with Song": Studies in Liberal Jewish Liturgy* (Cincinnati: Hebrew Union College Press, 1997).

4. Space does not permit us to cite the long list of scholarly works in the history of Jewish liturgy that argue this point. We content ourselves with mentioning two of them: Stefan C. Reif, *Judaism and Hebrew Prayer* (Cambridge: Cambridge University Press, 1993), and Joseph Heinemann, *Prayer in the Talmud* (New York: de Gruyter, 1977).

5. Two of our CCAR colleagues have produced groundbreaking research in this area: Lawrence A. Hoffman, *The Canonization of the Synagogue Service* (Notre Dame: University of Notre Dame Press, 1979), and Ruth Langer, *To Worship God Properly: Tensions between Liturgical Custom and Halakhah in Judaism* (Cincinnati: Hebrew Union College Press, 1998).

6. BT *B'rachot* 20b and *Sotah* 33a.

7. *Yad, T'filah* 1:1–3. Rambam derives that prayer is a Toraitic mitzvah from a midrash on Deut. 11:13, which requires that one "serve God with all your heart": "What is this 'service of the heart'? It is prayer" (BT *Taanit* 2a). Not all halachists accept this narrative. Nachmanides, for example, holds that Jewish prayer originated not as a Toraitic commandment but as a popular practice, reflecting the need and desire of human beings to communicate with God. See his *hasagah* to Rambam's *Sefer HaMitzvot*, positive commandment no. 5. Importantly, though, both authorities agree that *t'filah* was originally an utterance that had no fixed, defined text or structure.

8. *Yad, T'filah* 1:4. Rambam holds that this text was instituted by "Ezra and his *beit din* [rabbinical court]." This is his version of the Talmudic tradition that ascribes the

text of the *T'filah* to the "120 elders, including the latter prophets" (BT *M'gillah* 17b) or to "the members of the Great Assembly" (BT *B'rachot* 33a). Historians of Jewish liturgy do not take these statements literally, although some are of the opinion that the *T'filah* was in fact the product of a formal enactment by a religio-legal institution. Rambam's narrative affirms the traditional conception that the specific forms of the prayer we recite are *mid'rabanan*, established by Rabbinic ordinance (*takanah*).

9. BT *B'rachot* 40b, following the opinion of Rabbi Yosei.

10. Rambam, *Yad, B'rachot* 1:5–6. If this is the case, then what in Rambam's view *does* constitute an "unacceptable" change in the *matbei-a* of a benediction? The answer can be found in *Yad, K'riat Sh'ma* 1:7. There, Rambam writes that because Ezra and his *beit din* instituted the forms of the blessings, "one is not entitled to detract from them or to add to them. In a place where [the Sages] require that one conclude with a *chatimah* [i.e., to recite a "*baruch atah*" formula at the end of a paragraph], one is not permitted to do otherwise. In a place where they require that one *not* conclude with a *chatimah*, one is not entitled to do otherwise.... The general rule is this: one who alters the form [*matbei-a*] of a *b'rachah* that the Sages established is in error and must repeat the *b'rachah* correctly." In other words, an unacceptable change in the form of a *b'rachah* is defined as an alteration of its formulaic structure. A change in the wording of a benediction, including the wording of its *chatimah*, is *not* defined as an improper alteration of its form and is therefore halachicly acceptable, so long as the new form retains the content and theme (*inyan*) of the traditional *matbei-a*. This is the plain sense of Rambam's rulings in these passages, and it is the way that R. Yosef Karo understands him as well; see the latter's *Kesef Mishneh, B'rachot* 1:5–6.

11. For example, we imagine that Rambam himself would not have been delighted with our insertion of the names of the *Imahot*. In *Yad, B'rachot* 1:5, he writes that "it is not proper [*v'ein ra-ui*] to alter the texts of the *b'rachot*, to add to them or to detract from them." Yet as Karo notes (*Kesef Mishneh* ad loc.), Rambam pointedly does *not* say that one who changes the traditional wording of a *b'rachah* does not fulfill his ritual obligation thereby. In Rambam's view, so long as one retains the theme and content of the traditional *b'rachah*, "it is not an error [*ta-ut*]" to recite the benediction according to its altered wording, even though he would prefer that the individual not make that linguistic change. In other words, opposition to liturgical innovation per se is a matter of style and temperament rather than of liturgical law.

12. It also reflects the historical and developmental nature of our understanding of God: the covenant is handed down from *generation* to *generation*, and each generation arrives at its own appreciation of its terms.

13. The texts of our current siddur (*Gates of Prayer*) mention Leah before Rachel. Yet it is perfectly acceptable to alter that order, following the verse in Ruth 4:11.

14. See Ramban to Gen. 37:2, end: perhaps Jacob made Bilhah and Zilpah his wives following the deaths of Rachel and Leah. This elevation in their legal status can be seen as an effort to ensure that the sons they bore to Jacob (and the tribes who descended from them) are considered equal to his other sons. Rashi hints at this possibility, while R. David Kimchi states it explicitly; see their commentaries to Gen. 37:2.

15. The text in *B'midbar Rabbah* 12:17 (Vilna ed.) is paralleled in *Shir HaShirim Rabbah* 6:2 and *Esther Rabbah* 1:12.

16. Rabbi Richard Rheins, a corresponding member of this Committee, states, "I believe that it is our duty to raise awareness of the blessed role Bilhah and Zilpah played as mothers and nurturers of our people. Questions about their social status or even their ethnic origin are irrelevant. The Torah does not give us minute details about their lives. Accordingly, the text's ambivalence permits us the interpretive freedom to see Bilhah and Zilpah in roles that seem modern and familiar. In the modern era, interfaith families, new spouses, single parents, and stepchildren are not uncommon. And yet the quality of a family cannot be judged by its composition. The essence of a family is in the commitment made by each of its members to love and nurture. Those who fulfill that commitment deserve our honor, respect, and appreciation regardless of their ethnicity or social status. An inclusion of Bilhah and Zilpah would be an effective role model for those of blended families."

17. *B'reishit Rabbah* (Vilna ed.) 67:9 and 72:6. Sarah is a special case: her gift of prophecy is said to have exceeded that of her husband (BT *M'gillah* 14a; *Sh'mot Rabbah* 1:1; Rashi to Gen. 21:12).

18. We disagree with the *sho-eil*'s assertion that by omitting the names of these maidservants "the Reform Movement gives tacit approval to the idea that woman is property." By this logic, one might as well say that by mentioning the names of Leah and Rachel we give our tacit approval to the idea of polygamy. That conclusion, of course, would be absurd.

Sh'eilah

A member of the congregation would like an *aliyah* to the Torah but objects to the use of masculine God language in the traditional *b'rachah* (blessing or benediction). She wishes to use an alternative *b'rachah* that is gender feminine (something along the lines of "*B'ruchah at Yah*"). The custom of our congregation has been to use the traditional Hebrew for the Torah blessings. Is the Torah blessing a private blessing or a blessing made on behalf of those gathered? If it is private, it would seem meritorious to permit the blessing as a way of encouraging the mitzvah of reading Torah and as a way of honoring the various conceptions of God held by members of the community. Should a member called to the Torah be permitted to use the blessing of his or her choice? (Rabbi David Thomas, Sudbury, Massachusetts)

T'shuvah

1. INTRODUCTION

At first glance, the answer to this *sh'eilah* might seem clear and obvious. The reading of the Torah is indeed a public act, the fulfillment of a communal obligation.[1] Thus, it is formally called *k'riat haTorah b'rabim*, "the public reading of the Torah," and traditionally must take place in the presence of a "public," that is, a minyan.[2] The person who receives the *aliyah* (the *oleh/olah*) enables the community to fulfill its obligation to hear the Torah reading. Thus, when he or she recites the customary *b'rachot*, the *congregation* must respond, "*Amen*," since the Torah reading is a communal, rather than an individual mitzvah.[3] On this basis, the individual is not entitled to depart from the communal *minhag* (custom). Acting as the representative for the congregation when called to the Torah, he or she must recite the *b'rachot* in accordance with the congregation's pattern of observance.

In another sense, though, the answer is not obvious at all. A congregation is empowered to alter its *minhag*, and implicit in this *sh'eilah* is the request that the congregation formally permit this individual to recite alternative *b'rachot* when she is called to the Torah. Should the congregation grant her that permission? There are good arguments on both sides of the issue.

On the one hand, the congregant might cite the long record of liturgical innovation in Reform Judaism. We Reform Jews have always been ready to amend our inherited liturgical forms in favor of new structures of prayer that reflect our contemporary religious values.[4] One of these values is our commitment to gender equality, our insistence that women be included with men as equal partners in all aspects of communal life.[5] This congregant objects to the male-gender form of the traditional *b'rachah*, perhaps because its presentation of God as a commanding Lord and King "has reinforced forms of patriarchal power and male privilege in the world."[6] We do not wish our liturgy to convey such a message, and we would therefore find this to be a strong Reform Jewish argument in her behalf.

On the other hand, that very same history indicates that, alongside our record of innovation, we Reform Jews have also maintained much of traditional Jewish liturgical practice. For example, it is the *minhag* of this congregation, and of every Reform congregation with which we are familiar, to begin and to conclude each *aliyah* (section of the Torah reading) with the customary *b'rachot*. In doing so, the congregation has accepted upon itself the discipline of a particular liturgical form. That is to say, a *b'rachah* is not simply a "blessing," a lyrical utterance of praise. It is a formal ritual act, and like all such acts it is defined by the *halachah*, traditional Jewish law. It is the *halachah* that tells us what a *b'rachah* is, how it should be formulated, and the circumstances under which it may be recited. These details cannot be dismissed as mere "Orthodox" minutiae. Given that we Reform Jews have adopted the traditional Jewish practice to recite *b'rachot* at appropriate ritual moments, the rules that govern that practice are not "Orthodox" rules but *Jewish* rules; they are *our* rules as well.[7] This does not mean, of course, that we are constrained to interpret the halachah as do other Jews.[8] It does mean, however, that the form of a *b'rachah* is acceptable only when it meets the specifications that the halachah—as we understand it—demands of that ritual act.

In addressing this *sh'eilah*, therefore, we want to focus upon two lines of inquiry. First, we will ask whether the halachah, the rules and principles that define the structure of Jewish liturgy, can accommodate the sort of innovation that this congregant seeks. And second, we want to consider the question in light of our movement's history of liturgical innovation and, as well, its continuing attachment to Jewish tradition.

2. HALACHIC CONSIDERATIONS

Our halachic discussion begins with this Talmudic passage:[9]

> Rav says: A benediction that does not include the mention of God's name [*hazkarat HaShem*] is not a valid benediction.

> R. Yochanan says: A benediction that does not include the mention of God's sovereignty over the world [*malchut*] is not a valid benediction.

> Abayei says: Rav's position is the correct one, for it is supported by a *baraita*:[10] "'I have neither transgressed nor neglected any of Your commandments' (Deut. 26:13). 'I have neither transgressed' means that I have not failed to recite the proper *b'rachah*,[11] while 'nor neglected' means that I have not forgotten to include the mention of God's name in the benediction." And this *baraita* says nothing about "sovereignty."

How would R. Yochanan respond? He would read the *baraita* thus: "Nor neglected" means "I have not forgotten to mention God's name and God's sovereignty in the benediction."

The authorities hold that the law follows R. Yochanan's position:[12] a valid benediction must include *shem umalchut*, the mention of God's name *and* of God's sovereignty over the world.[13] According to universal custom, "God's name" is the Tetragrammaton, the ineffable four-letter *yod-hei-vav-hei*,[14] which in its pronunciation *Adonai* signifies "Lord" or "Master." "Sovereignty over the world" refers to the words *Melech haolam* (literally "King of the universe").[15] There are some exceptions to this rule, the most obvious of which is the *T'filah*, where none of the *b'rachot* mention God's sovereignty (*malchut*).[16] Halachists account for these exceptions in various ways. For example, the *b'rachot* that conclude each paragraph of the *T'filah* (*chatimot*) do not require *malchut* because they are part of a series (*seder*) of benedictions, and each benediction in such a series "relies" upon the mention of God's sovereignty in the first *b'rachah*.[17] As for the first benediction of the *T'filah* (the *Avot*), which also omits the word *Melech*, the phrases "the God of Abraham" (*Elohei Avraham*) and "the great, mighty, and awesome God" (*ha-El hagadol hagibor v'hanora*) in that benediction serve as substitute expressions of God's sovereign power in the world.[18]

Given that there are exceptions to the rule of *shem umalchut*, we should ask if other deviations from the traditional version might meet halachic standards? The answer, apparently, is "yes." For one thing, the halachah accepts as valid a blessing recited in translation.[19] From this fact, the estimable twentieth-century authority R. Yisrael Meir Kagan (author of the *Mishnah B'rurah*) learns[20] that a benediction recited in Hebrew can be valid even if it does not include the Tetragrammaton, so long as it substitutes in its place any of God's proper names—i.e., the *azkarot*, the names of God that, when written in Hebrew, must never be erased.[21] His point is that if a translation of God's name may substitute for the Tetragrammaton, then surely any of these Hebrew *azkarot* must be just as acceptable.[22]

Jewish law, therefore, suggests two ways of meeting this congregant's request. She could, first of all, say the benediction in gender-neutral English: "Praised are You, Eternal our God, Sovereign of the universe...."[23] Should she prefer to recite it in Hebrew, she might replace the name *Adonai* (to which she objects because it connotes "Lord") with one of the other *azkarot*, such as *Elohim* (God). *Yah*, a shortened form of *yod-hei-vav-hei*, is not listed among those *azkarot* and would not, therefore, be halachicly acceptable as a name of God in a *b'rachah*. For "sovereignty" she might replace *Melech* with the expression *Elohei Avraham v'Sarah*, which as we have seen functions as the symbolic equivalent of *malchut* in the first benediction of the *T'filah*.[24] The rest of the *b'rachah* formula could be feminized (*B'ruchah at, asher bachrah banu*, etc.). This language, of course, would not agree grammatically with the *azkarot*, which are all masculine in form (for that matter, so is the name *Yah*).[25] Yet if we conceive of God as being above and beyond all considerations of gender, we can with integrity decide that God might accurately be addressed by way of masculine *or* feminine nouns, verbs, and adjectives.[26]

3. TRADITION, THE HEBREW LITURGY, AND REFORM JUDAISM

We have discovered that a benediction structured along the lines suggested in our *sh'eilah* might meet the minimal[27] requirements for a *b'rachah* under Jewish law. Yet we should not confuse "minimal" with *optimal*; the fact that a particular act might be valid under the rules does not, in and of itself, mean that it is a good thing and that we should adopt it. In this particular case, in fact, we believe the opposite conclusion is warranted. The synagogue should insist upon the traditional version of the *b'rachah* in its congregational worship services.

We base this statement, first and foremost, upon our reverence for Jewish tradition. It is true, as we have said, that Reform Judaism is accepting of liturgical innovation, particularly innovation that reflects our commitment to gender equality. Yet along with this we have noted that "we Reform Jews have also maintained much of traditional Jewish liturgical practice." This includes, in particular, the accepted *minhag* among our congregations to recite the traditional *b'rachah* formula during the Torah ritual and, indeed, throughout their public worship. Let us understand clearly what that *minhag* represents. When we maintain traditional forms of observance, we do so *intentionally*, not out of simple habit or inertia but as a conscious act of Jewish identification. By adopting such observances, we make the explicit statement that our Reform Jewish religious life is an identifiably *Jewish* one. With all our embrace of ritual creativity, our practice is not exclusively our own invention, a collection of behaviors meaningful only within the context of the North American Reform synagogue. Our forms of practice are "Jewish" to the extent that they affirm our roots in the Jewish past and our ongoing connection with the religious life of Jews throughout the world. In defining Reform Judaism to ourselves and to others, therefore, it is not sufficient to point to our love of "innovation." We must also emphasize the opposite side of the coin: our recognition that "Judaism is the historical religious experience of the Jewish people"[28] and our desire to give voice to our faith through ritual forms that evoke our sense of that experience.

The history of our religious practice, including our liturgical practice, is therefore in large part the record of our efforts to draw a proper balance between these goals, to reach a satisfying accommodation between our dedication to Jewish tradition and to our liberal ethical and cultural values. In our prayer books, we now compose both the translations and the stand-alone sections in gender-neutral English.[29] We have also introduced changes into some of the Hebrew texts, such as the names of the Matriarchs in the first benediction of the *T'filah*.[30] Yet we have not seen fit to redraft the entirety of our Hebrew liturgy to remove any and all references to God in the masculine gender. Thus, even in that introductory *b'rachah* of the *T'filah* we continue to address God in the second person masculine singular (*Baruch atah*) and to describe God in the third person masculine singular (*hagadol hagibor v'hanora*). In the *Sh'ma Yisrael*, we continue to declare God to be "One" in the

masculine form of that word—*echad*—rather than in the feminine
achat. To repeat: our preservation of the traditional liturgical forms
should not be interpreted as accidental or as evidence of negligence
on our part. Rather, these texts *as they are*, taken from the Bible, the
Rabbinic literature, and the siddur, are the very substance of Jewish
prayer. Through centuries of use they have come to play a central and
indispensable role in our religious lives. We have therefore preferred to
leave largely intact the language of the prophets, the poets, the psalmists,
and the sages who wrote them.

We do not believe that our decision to retain much of the traditional
Hebrew liturgy, even when it is expressed in masculine language,
compromises our commitment to gender equality. We say this for two
reasons. The first has to do with the nature of Hebrew grammar: the
so-called "masculine" formulation is in fact an inclusive one, since
Hebrew uses the masculine to describe persons or things of unspecified
gender or groups of mixed gender. The second has to do with our own
liberal Jewish outlook, which determines how we think about and talk
about the words we pray. We hold that God is above and beyond all
considerations of gender, and no traditional liturgical text or formula,
no matter how "masculine" its literal formulation, should call that
commitment into question.

And therein lies our difficulty with this congregant's request. If the
concern is that our liturgy be gender-neutral and inclusive, then the
formula *B'ruchah at* fails, since it is unequivocally feminine and cannot
be construed as neutral. To allow its recitation would be to say, in
effect, that there is *only* gender and *no* neutrality: God is either "male"
or "female," and we must choose between those two alternatives. This
would necessarily imply that the traditional *b'rachah* is a "masculine"
and not a neutral one. It would send the unmistakable message
that those Reform Jews who say *Baruch atah Adonai*—that is, the
overwhelming majority of our people—are promoting a masculine
conception of God. We do not believe this. We believe that when we
recite the traditional liturgy, we are identifying our own prayer with that

of our people in ages past, who authored these words and bequeathed them to us. We do *not* believe that we are reinforcing "forms of patriarchal power and male privilege in the world." Our Reform Jewish teaching, preaching, and record of liturgical creativity contradict that message; they establish beyond a doubt our movement's devotion to the concept and practice of gender neutrality. We should avoid taking actions that suggest otherwise.

CONCLUSION

The form of *b'rachah* that this congregant wishes to recite meets the minimum standards that Jewish law sets for a benediction, provided that the rules governing the mention of God's name and of God's sovereignty are properly observed. For this reason, she may certainly use it in private worship or as part of ritual observances in her home. The synagogue service, however, as a communal, public setting, is another matter. For the reasons we have outlined—our devotion to the linguistic tradition of traditional Jewish prayer and our commitment to gender neutrality in our liturgy—we would discourage the congregation from permitting the use of this alternative *b'rachah* form in its public worship.[31]

NOTES

1. The tradition ascribes the institution of the public Torah reading to enactments (*takanot*) of Moses and Ezra; see BT *Bava Kama* 82a and *Yad, T'filah* 12:1.

2. *M. Megilah* 4:3; *Yad, T'filah* 12:3; *SA, OC* 143:1.

3. BT *Sotah* 39b; *Yad, T'filah* 12:6; *SA, OC* 143:5 and *Mishnah B'rurah* ad loc., no. 17.

4. For example, Reform prayer books have excised traditional liturgical passages that petition God for the rebuilding of the Temple, the re-institution of sacrificial worship, the resurrection of the dead, the advent of a personal Messiah, and the like. On the history and development of Reform Jewish liturgy, see Jakob J. Petuchowski, *Prayerbook Reform in Europe: The Liturgy of European Liberal and Reform Judaism* (New York: World Union for Progressive Judaism, 1968); Eric L. Friedland, *"Were Our Mouths Filled with Song": Studies in Liberal Jewish Liturgy* (Cincinnati: Hebrew Union College Press, 1997); and the two volumes of *Gates of Understanding*, ed.

Lawrence A. Hoffman (New York: CCAR Press, 1977; and New York: CCAR Press, 1984).

5. Our prayer books, for example, now commonly use gender-neutral English, and we have also altered the traditional Hebrew text in various places to reflect this commitment. The most notable example of such a change is the insertion of the names of the Matriarchs (*Imahot*) in the first benediction of the *T'filah*, or *Amidah*. For an argument that this innovation accords with traditional liturgical halachah, see *Reform Responsa for the Twenty-first Century*, no. 5763.6, vol. 2, pp. 19–25.

6. Marcia Falk, *The Book of Blessings* (New York: HarperCollins, 1996), xvii (explaining her view that the traditional *Adonai Eloheinu, Melech haolam* "is an example of dead metaphor").

7. For a more extended version of this argument, see *Teshuvot for the Nineties*, no. 5755.4, pp. 91–96; and *Reform Responsa for the Twenty-first Century*, no. 5760.3, vol. 2, pp. 59–70.

8. On the contrary: all Jewish communities interpret the halachah from the standpoint of their own particular social and theological perspective. This is precisely what the Responsa Committee—and indeed the entire Reform halachic process—has done throughout its history. When we interpret the traditional Jewish legal sources, we do so consciously and explicitly from the perspective of contemporary Reform Jews. Our point here is that *all* Jews must interpret the sources from their own perspective, for the activity of interpretation must begin from the standpoint of the particular community of interpretation. On this view Orthodoxy is but one of several possible vantage points from which to read and understand the sources. We therefore should not fall into the common misperception of identifying the Orthodox interpretation of the halachah as *the* halachah.

9. BT *B'rachot* 40b.

10. That is, a text dating from the period of the *Tannaim*, roughly the first two centuries of the Common Era. Rav, R. Yochanan, and Abayei are *Amoraim*, the name given to the Rabbinic scholars during the period of the Talmud (ca. 200–500 C.E.). If a tannaitic source can be cited in support of the viewpoint of an *Amora*, then that counts as a strong proof on behalf of that viewpoint.

11. The benediction over the separation of tithes from one's agricultural produce.

12. On the grounds that the Talmud has successfully defended that position from the critique offered by Abayei. See as well JT *B'rachot* 9:1 (12d), where Rav is quoted

as requiring *malchut* in the formula for the benediction. *Tosafot* (*B'rachot* 54a, s.v. *haro-eh*), in turn, cites this passage from the *Y'rushalmi* in support of its ruling that "all these *b'rachot* (i.e., the ones mentioned in *M. B'rachot* 9:1) must include the mention of God's name and of God's sovereignty." See also *Sefer HaEshkol, Hil. Birchot HaShachar*, 5a.

13. The geonic compilation *Halachot G'dolot* (ed. Hildesheimer, v. 1, 82) explains that the Talmud's defense of R. Yochanan's position is an indication that it decides in accordance with his view. See also Alfasi to *B'rachot* 40b; *Yad, B'rachot* 1:5; *Tosafot, B'rachot* 40b, s.v. *amar*; Nachmanides, *Torat HaAdam, Inyan HaR'fuah*, Chavel ed., p. 4; *Shibolei HaLeket, Seder B'rachot*, chap. 165; *Hil. HaRosh, B'rachot* 6:23; *Sefer Kolbo*, chap. 25; *SA, OC* 214.

14. "Universal," at least, since tannaitic times. See *Tosefta B'rachot* 6:20 (ed. Lieberman; 6:26 in the traditional printed editions) and Saul Lieberman, *Tosefta Kifshutah* ad loc.: some sects shied away from reciting the Tetragrammaton in the *b'rachah*, and their practice was branded "heretical" by the Rabbis.

15. On the early history and development of the *b'rachah* as a liturgical form, see Yosef Heinemann, *Hat'filah b'tekufat hatanaim v'ha'amoraim* (Jerusalem: Magnes, 1978), 52–66. At pp. 61–62, he suggests that while *Baruch atah Adonai* is quite ancient (the formula is already present in the Qumran texts), *Melech haolam* comes later (hence the disagreement between the third-century *Amoraim* Rav and R. Yochanan in BT *B'rachot* 40b; see at note 9, above). The decision to mention God's sovereignty in the *b'rachah* (and, for that matter, to recite *Malchuyot* verses in the *T'filah* on Rosh HaShanah (*M. Rosh HaShanah* 4:5) may therefore have been an act of protest against the deification of the emperor in Roman cultic practice.

16. Historians have their own explanations for this fact. Heinemann (see note 15), for example, notes that the *T'filah* is a creation of the *Tannaim* and therefore predates the amoraic dispute over whether *malchut* must be included in the *b'rachah*.

17. *Yad, B'rachot* 1:5. The technical term for these benedictions is *b'rachah has'muchah l'chavertah*, literally "a benediction that relies/rests upon the one preceding it." The benedictions recited over *k'riat haTorah* are good examples of this rule, as are the benedictions that precede and follow the recitation of *Sh'ma* and the *Kiddush* blessing. Each *b'rachah* begins with the full formula, a phrase that mentions both God's name and God's sovereignty, and concludes with a shorter phrase that mentions God's name but not God's sovereignty. The *Sefer HaRokeach* (chap. 363), a thirteenth-century Ashkenazic compilation, suggests a reason for this distinction: in the beginning blessings we follow the opinion of R. Yochanan (BT *B'rachot* 40b), who requires

malchut, and in the concluding benedictions we follow the opinion of Rav, who does not.

18. Tosafot, *B'rachot* 40b, s.v. *amar*; *Hil. HaRosh*, *B'rachot* 6:23; R. Yosef Karo, *Beit Yosef*, OC 214.

19. See BT *B'rachot* 40b, several lines above the passage quoted at note 9. Rav accepts as valid a blessing recited in Aramaic, even though it does not mention the Tetragrammaton, because it does refer to God as *Rachamana*, "the Merciful One." The Talmud derives the rule that a *b'rachah* may be recited in any language from M. *Sotah* 7:1. Rambam (*Yad, B'rachot* 1:6) codifies this as follows: "All the *b'rachot* may be recited in any language…[provided that the translated *b'rachah*] includes a proper name of God [*azkarah*] and the mention of God's sovereignty and that it maintains the substance of the original *b'rachah*."

20. *Mishnah B'rurah* 214:4.

21. Rambam (*Yad, Y'sodei HaTorah* 6:2) identifies these as *Adonai* (written either as the Tetragrammaton or as it is pronounced—*alef-dalet-nun-yod*), *El, Eloah, Elohim, Elohai, Shaddai*, and *Tz'vaot*. The provision that these names never be erased applies only when they are written in Hebrew. On this, see *Reform Responsa for the Twenty-first Century*, no. 5762.1, vol. 2, pp. 71–83.

22. *Mishnah B'rurah* 214, in *Shaar HaTziyun*, no. 3. The argument is a classic *kal vachomer*, an *a fortiori* inference.

23. "Eternal," used here as a substitute for *Adonai*, appears in some English translations of Jewish prayer texts. It is a suggested rendering of the written form of the Tetragrammaton, which may be related to the Hebrew root *hei-vav-hei*, "to be." The translation "the Lord," by contrast, renders the meaning of the Tetragrammaton in its spoken form, *Adonai*.

24. See above at note 5: it has long been our Reform practice to add the names of the Matriarchs to those of the Patriarchs in this *b'rachah*. Alternatively, she could convert the expression to its feminine form: *Malkat haolam*, "Sovereign of [literally, 'Queen of'] the universe." The difficulty here, as one member of our Committee notes, is that in normal usage a queen is "sovereign" only in the absence of a legitimate king. Thus, the word *malkah* or "queen" does not express the concept of "sovereignty" in a sense as complete as that of *melech* or "king."

25. See, for example, Exod. 15:2 and Pss. 118:18 and 135:4, where the name *Yah* is used with masculine verbs and adjectives.

26. A partial analogy to this is the fact the names *Elohim* and *Eloheinu* are plural in form, even though since biblical times they have been read as singular nouns when referring to the God of Israel (see, most obviously, Gen. 1:1, where *Elohim* is paired with *bara*, a singular verb). Since we have long accepted that the God of Israel is One, such grammatical curiosities do not trouble us. The same might apply here, when we recognize gender as being irrelevant to our conception of God.

27. We use the word "minimal" because the author of the *Mishnah B'rurah*, whom we follow here, undoubtedly did not intend his ruling as a "permit" for such *b'rachot* in practice. He is speaking to a situation of *b'diavad* (after the fact), in which a person has already recited such a benediction. This is evident from the wording in *Mishnah B'rurah* 214:4: one who mentions an *azkarah* other than the Tetragrammaton has fulfilled his obligation (*yatzah*). His point is that should one recite this "deviant" benediction one need not repeat it in its "correct" form inasmuch as it meets the minimum liturgical requirements. It is not, however, in principle "permitted" to construct the *b'rachah* in that manner. Were that the case, Kagan would have used a word that definitely signifies permission (such as *mutar*, "it is permitted").

28. See the CCAR's Columbus Platform of 1937 http://ccarnet.org/documentsandpositions/platforms/), section A.1, "Nature of Judaism."

29. When translating the traditional Hebrew, this is generally accomplished through the use of the gender-neutral second person. Thus, "Praised are You, O God" avoids the masculine language of *Baruch atah Adonai*. Our prayer books will frequently translate a Hebrew third-person usage ("He") into the English second person ("You"). A good example is *Hu Eloheinu ein od* in the *Aleinu*, which often appears in our liturgy as "You are our God, there is none else."

30. See above, note 5.

31. A postscript: given that, as we have noted, one may recite a benediction in gender-neutral English and meet the halachic requirements for a valid *b'rachah*, one member of our Committee suggests that the congregation permit an individual called to the Torah to say the benediction in English. The majority do not join in this recommendation, on the grounds that we wish to encourage Hebrew literacy among our congregants and the use of Hebrew in our worship services.

Sh'eilah

A family in my congregation wishes to schedule a bat mitzvah service on either October 11 or October 18, 2003. Each of these dates is a Shabbat, and both coincide with a *Yom Tov*, a Festival day: October 11 is the first day of Sukkot, and October 18 is Sh'mini Atzeret. Is there any reason these services should not be scheduled on *Yom Tov*? (Rabbi Scott Gurdin, Newport News, Virginia)

T'shuvah

1. THE OBSERVANCE OF BAR/BAT MITZVAH

The bar/bat mitzvah "service" is the synagogue observance that marks a young person's reaching the age of Jewish majority. The classical Rabbinic literature does not mention such an observance, although the Sages do note that a father recites the blessing *Baruch shep'tarani mei-onsho shelazeh* ("Blessed be the One who has exempted me from legal liability for this one's actions")[1] when his son reaches the age of thirteen.[2] Later sources record the custom for the young man to lead worship services or to deliver a sermon or lesson (*d'rashah*) at a festive meal (*s'udat mitzvah*) held in honor of the occasion.[3] The bat mitzvah "service" for young women is an innovation of twentieth-century liberal Judaism,[4] although a nineteenth-century Iraqi authority writes that it was customary in his community to arrange a *s'udat mitzvah* in celebration of a girl's reaching the age of majority.[5] The central liturgical element of bar/bat mitzvah is the calling of the young person to the Torah. Thus, bar/bat mitzvah is observed during regularly scheduled services at which the Torah is read.

2. A RITUAL PROHIBITION?

Given that we read from the Torah at Festival *Shacharit* (morning) services, is there any reason to prohibit bar/bat mitzvah observance on those days? We might derive such a prohibition from the rule that one does not marry during *chol hamo-eid*.[6] The Talmud explains this rule on the grounds that "we do not mix our celebrations of joy" (*ein m'arvin simchah b'simchah*): as we are already commanded *v'samachta b'chagecha*, "you shall rejoice in your Festival" (Deut. 16:14), we should not allow the private wedding celebration to interfere with the public, communal celebration of the Festival week.[7] Our bar/bat mitzvah celebration is, like the wedding, a private *simchah*, or celebration, surrounded by parties and festivities (although on this, see below). We might therefore draw an analogy between the two celebrations: just as weddings are not held on days set aside for a different sort of rejoicing, it is similarly inappropriate to schedule bar/bat mitzvah on a Festival day.

We reject this argument, however, for several reasons. First, the principle "we do not mix our celebrations of joy" knows of numerous exceptions. We Reform Jews, for example, do schedule weddings during *chol hamo-eid*,[8] and even the traditional halachah hedges that prohibition with various leniencies.[9] Second, the principle applies only to weddings. Festive meals for other religious occasions may be scheduled during *chol hamo-eid*, because "only the wedding feast is considered a *simchah*" for this purpose.[10] Third, it is our long-standing practice (*minhag*) to schedule other religious celebrations on *Yom Tov*. Many of our communities hold confirmation services on Shavuot[11] and consecration on Sh'mini Atzeret/Simchat Torah,[12] and the Central Conference of American Rabbis has declared that these services, rather than distracting from the holy day, actually serve to strengthen its significance in the minds of our people.[13] We might also mention in this connection the universal Jewish observance of Simchat Torah on the second Festival day of Sh'mini Atzeret.[14] From its beginnings, this observance troubled the rabbis, because it involves certain kinds of *simchah* that have nothing to do with the original meaning of the

Festival and that seem to conflict with the standards of halachah. These standards, though, have been relaxed in order to permit the "new," innovative celebration.[15] In short, we Jews have long been in the habit of "mixing our celebrations," of associating different kinds of joy with the *simchah* of *Yom Tov*.

Our central objection to this argument, though, is the analogy that lies at its foundation: the bar/bat mitzvah is emphatically *not* to be compared to the wedding. The analogy does not work, first of all, because Jewish tradition reckons the wedding as a kind of "Festival" for the bride and groom, lending that celebration an exalted ritual status that the bar/bat mitzvah observance does not share.[16] We also reject the comparison on grounds of religious policy: the tendency for today's bar/bat mitzvah celebration to resemble that of a wedding is one of the more regrettable features in contemporary Jewish life. Our concern is not simply with the inordinate extravagance and expense of the parties associated with some bar/bat mitzvah celebrations, an emphasis upon the material side of the *simchah* that can crowd out its religious significance.[17] We are also disturbed that, in many of our congregations, the bar/bat mitzvah observance has become a private celebration, much like the wedding, to the point that few if any worshipers other than the invited guests will attend the service. Reform Judaism, by contrast, teaches that bar/bat mitzvah be observed as a public event. An observance that proclaims the child's readiness to assume a full and active role in the religious life of the community ought to take place at a regularly scheduled congregational service in the presence of the regular worshiping community.[18] We have therefore criticized the custom of scheduling bar/bat mitzvah at the Shabbat *Minchah* service (the inaccurately named "*Havdalah*" bar/bat mitzvah).[19] This service, especially if it is not a regularly scheduled time of worship for the congregation, will likely turn into the sort of private celebration that we should avoid.[20]

Thus, because there is no ground on which to base a ritual prohibition, we conclude that Jewish tradition does not forbid the scheduling of a bar/bat mitzvah observance at a Festival service.

3. FESTIVAL OBSERVANCE IN REFORM JUDAISM

Yet the absence of a formal halachic prohibition does not necessarily imply that there is *no* objection to observing bar/bat mitzvah on *Yom Tov*. The fact that our tradition does not explicitly forbid a practice does not by itself mean that we ought to adopt that practice. Before we draw such a conclusion in this case, we need to consider another factor: the quality of our Festival observance.

The duty to rejoice on the Festival is, as we have seen, a Toraitic mitzvah. The *simchah* of which this mitzvah speaks is not primarily an inner, emotional state. It is defined rather by a set of ritual duties and prohibitions[21] that focus our attention upon the meaning of the holiday in the history of Israel. Thus, Pesach is "the season of our liberation from bondage" (*z'man cheiruteinu*); Shavuot is "the season of the giving of the Torah" (*z'man matan Torateinu*); and Sukkot–Sh'mini Atzeret, called simply "the season of our joy" (*z'man simchateinu*), is linked in our memory to our forty-year sojourn in the wilderness (Lev. 23:42–43). The *simchah* of *Yom Tov*, in other words, is "ours," a collective joy and not a personal one. The agenda of the day is a *Jewish* agenda, a celebration of God's redemptive power in the national experience of our people. That collective Jewish agenda should dominate our celebration of the day; we should therefore avoid scheduling events that distract our attention from it. We have already made this point concerning Shabbat, which, we have written, "is not simply a day on which we do good deeds. It is *Shabbat kodesh*, a holy day, a refuge from many of the activities associated with the weekday world of building and planting, sowing and reaping, getting and spending. We do not trespass upon Shabbat, even for the sake of mitzvot, unless those mitzvot must be performed on that very day."[22] Such is our best understanding of how Shabbat ought to be observed. We would say the same about the observance of *Yom Tov*.

Let us not, therefore, be content to say merely that Jewish law does not prohibit the celebration of bar/bat mitzvah on a Festival day.

We ought to aspire to a higher standard of practice and to a higher conception of our tradition than that. Let us instead ask ourselves a deeper, more complex question: is bar/bat mitzvah truly compatible with our best understanding of the significance of *Yom Tov* and of how the Festivals ought to be observed in our communities? Having posed this question, we acknowledge that it has no single, indisputably correct answer. One could argue that bar/bat mitzvah celebrations, especially the extravagant celebrations that all too frequently occur in our congregations, cannot but distract our attention from the significance and theme of the holiday. Yet one could also argue that there is no necessary conflict between the observance of this important moment in the life of a young Jew and the observance of an important moment in the life of our people. Our own precedents point in both directions. Our teacher R. Solomon B. Freehof permitted a congregation to schedule a bar mitzvah observance on Sh'mini Atzeret, even though it is a Festival and even though it is customary to recite the memorial service (*Yizkor*) on that day.[23] He clearly did not believe that the spirit of the observance violated the requirements of the *Yom Tov*. On the other hand, he ruled that bar mitzvah should not be scheduled on Yom Kippur, because the celebration "is in jarring disharmony with the spiritual affliction of" the Day of Atonement.[24] It seems to us that either of these decisions could have gone the other way. R. Freehof could just as easily have said that the celebration of bar/bat mitzvah "is in jarring disharmony" with the somber nature of *Yizkor*.[25] He could also have ruled bar/bat mitzvah especially appropriate on Yom Kippur, a day on which we rejoice in our spiritual purification and rededication to God's service.[26] Our point is not to dissent from R. Freehof but to observe that both of these rulings are based upon judgments concerning the nature of bar/bat mitzvah and the nature of the specific holiday. Such judgments may not admit of an obvious answer. When we make them, we can often imagine good arguments in support of more than one conclusion. Yet make them we must, and we must make them on the basis of our best understanding of the nature of both observances, that of bar/bat mitzvah and that of *Yom Tov*.

CONCLUSION

What judgments do we make in *this* case? The best solution, we think, is *not* to schedule bar/bat mitzvah on *Yom Tov*. While it may not be prohibited "to mix our celebrations of joy," we ought not to mix the very different messages that these celebrations teach. Though it should be observed as a public event, bar/bat mitzvah is about a particular young person. It brings friends and family together to celebrate his or her "big day" and to rejoice in the *simchah* of *this* family. This personal and family *simchah* cannot help but be a major, indeed predominant theme of the day. *Yom tov*, meanwhile, is about all of us. It brings a community together[27] to celebrate a defining event in Jewish history and to rejoice in the *simchah* of the entire family of Israel. We would prefer that these messages be kept separate and distinct, to teach that just as there is a proper time to celebrate as a family unit, so too is there a proper time to join as one, to celebrate with the Jewish people *as* the Jewish people.

At the same time, we recognize that some congregations will find it difficult if not impossible to avoid scheduling bar/bat mitzvah on *Yom Tov*, particularly (as in this *sh'eilah*) when the Festival day coincides with Shabbat. Given that our tradition does not *forbid* the observance of bar/bat mitzvah on *Yom Tov*, we would permit it, provided that the family understands that the predominant theme of the service is the Festival and *not* their own celebration. Bar/bat mitzvah, we stress again, is a *public* event; the family does not "own" the synagogue service on any day, much less on *Yom Tov*. We should take care to emphasize the Festival through the liturgy in the sanctuary and at the *s'udat mitzvah* and through the symbols associated with the day. On Sukkot, for example, the congregants can be encouraged to take the *lulav* and to visit the congregational sukkah.[28] In such ways we can see to it that the congregation experiences the service as a *Festival* observance and not simply as the celebration of bar/bat mitzvah.

NOTES

1. Isserles cites this form of the *b'rachah*, which omits *shem* and *malchut* (i.e., the name of God and the mention of God's sovereignty over the world) as the preferred wording

(*SA, OC* 225:2). This is ostensibly because the *b'rachah* is not mentioned in the Talmud and therefore lacks the status of an "official" benediction (i.e., one ordained by the Sages). He notes, however, that other authorities hold that *shem* and *malchut* should be mentioned in this *b'rachah*. To these authorities we should add the Gaon of Vilna (*Biur HaGra* to OC 225:2). See *Mishnah B'rurah, OC* 225:8.

2. *B'reishit Rabbah* 63:10, s.v. *v'yigdelu hane-arim*. That thirteen is the age at which a young man becomes responsible for fulfilling the mitzvot is expressed by the Mishnah in *Avot* 5:21. However, we should be careful before recognizing that age as the point of adulthood in all respects. See Yitzchak Gilat, *Perakim behishtalshelut hahalakhah* (Ramat Gan: Bar-Ilan, 1992), 19–31, who argues that the earliest halachic sources do not know of a fixed "age of majority." Rather, the obligation to observe the mitzvot either depended upon the child's physical ability to perform a particular required act or was determined by biological criteria (the onset of puberty). The tendency to view the age of thirteen as the transition point into adult status developed during the amoraic period, but even then there were exceptions: according to some authorities, certain public functions, such as the eligibility to sit in judgment of capital cases or to sell one's land, require that the individual in question be at least twenty years old.

3. *Magen Avraham* (seventeenth century) to *SA, OC* 225:4; R. Sh'lomo Luria, *Yam shel Sh'lomo* (sixteenth century), *Bava Kama* 7:37.

4. The first such ceremony is thought to be that arranged by R. Mordecai M. Kaplan for his daughter Judith on March 18, 1922, at the Society for the Advancement of Judaism in New York. See Mel Scult, *Judaism Faces the Twentieth Century: A Biography of Mordecai M. Kaplan* (Detroit: Wayne State University Press, 1993), 301–2.

5. R. Yosef Chayim b. Eliyahu of Baghdad, *Ben Ish Chai*, v. 1, *R'eih*, par. 17.

6. M. *Mo-eid Katan* 1:7. This rule is codified as halachah in *Yad, Ishut* 10:14 and *SA, OC* 546:1 and *EHE* 64:6.

7. BT *Mo-eid Katan* 8b. It is important to note that this rule applies only to the intermediate days of Pesach and Sukkot and not to the Festival day itself. Weddings are indeed prohibited on *Yom Tov*, but this is for the same reason that they are prohibited on Shabbat: the fear that one might have to write a marriage document on a day when writing is forbidden (M. *Beitzah* 5:2; BT *Beitzah* 37a; *Yad, Shabbat* 23:14). In addition, marriage is the formation of a contract and the creation of financial obligations, legal acts that do not take place on Shabbat or *Yom Tov* (*Mishnah B'rurah, OC* 339:22).

8. R. Solomon B. Freehof, *Reform Jewish Practice and Its Rabbinic Background* (New York: UAHC Press, 1963), 1:72–73; *Questions and Reform Jewish Answers (QRJA)*, no. 216.

9. See *SA, OC* 546:1–3. It is permitted to betroth (to arrange *eirusin*, as opposed to *nisuin*) during *chol hamo-eid* and to celebrate with "dancing and singing"; a man is permitted to remarry his divorcee on the intermediate days of a Festival; and weddings may be held on the day before a Festival (*Erev Yom Tov*), even though the wedding feast will extend past sundown into *Yom Tov* itself.

10. See *Tosafot, Mo-eid Katan* 8b, s.v. *mipnei bitul*; *SA, OC* 546:4; *Magen Avraham, OC* 546:5; *Turei Zahav* ad loc., no. 4; *Biur HaGra* to OC 546:4; *Mishnah B'rurah, OC* 546:11; *Aruch HaShulchan, OC* 546:6.

11. *Gates of the Seasons*, ed. Peter S. Knobel (New York: CCAR Press, 1983), 77–78; Freehof, *Reform Jewish Practice*, 1:25–26.

12. *Gates of the Seasons*, 85; Freehof, *Reform Jewish Practice*, 1:26–27.

13. See the resolutions in *CCAR Yearbook (CCARY)*, 37 (1927): 209–10; *CCARY* 65 (1955): 114; and *CCARY* 67 (1957): 110.

14. Reform Jews who observe but one day of *Yom Tov* observe Simchat Torah on what other Jews in the Diaspora reckon as the first Festival day of Sh'mini Atzeret. See *Reform Responsa for the Twenty-first Century*, no. 5759.7, vol. 1, pp. 49–64.

15. It is prohibited, for example, to dance on *Yom Tov* (*M. Beitzah* 5:2). Nonetheless, says Rav Hai Gaon, we are permitted to dance on Simchat Torah *lichvod Torah*, "for the honor of the Torah" (*Otzar HaGeonim, Beitzah*, no. 63, pp. 28–29).

16. See BT *K'tubot* 3b–4a; *Yad, Aveil* 11:7–8; *SA, YD* 342:1. Since the seven-day wedding feast is considered "as a Festival" for the couple, they are forbidden public displays of mourning during that time. Should a relative die during the feast week, mourning is delayed until the conclusion of the feast, just as is the case when a relative dies during *chol hamo-eid*. Bar/bat mitzvah does not postpone mourning. R. Sh'lomo Luria (see note 3) does refer to the coming-of-age celebration as a "Festival" (*yama tava*) for the young man. This, however, seems to be a homiletical point, connected to a statement of R. Yosef in BT *Bava Kama* 87a and elsewhere. R. Luria (the Maharshal) does not suggest that the bar mitzvah has a status akin to that of a wedding vis-a-vis the laws of mourning.

17. *QRJA*, no. 37; *Divrei Benei Mitzvah* (New York: CCAR Press, 1990), 3.

18. Thus, we have insisted that other events that we mark at public worship services, such as baby namings and blessings of couples about to be married, be allowed to take place at the bar/bat mitzvah "service"; such events are not to be regarded as intrusions upon a private family celebration. See *QRJA*, no. 33.

19. The Torah is read at the *Minchah* service on Shabbat; the ritual of *Havdalah* occurs during the *Maariv* service on Saturday night.

20. *American Reform Responsa*, no. 36; *Reform Responsa for the Twenty-first Century*, no. 5758.9, vol. 1, pp. 21–31, section 2. Our responsa have noted that special circumstances may require that a bar/bat mitzvah be scheduled outside the synagogue or at a private service. Still, we emphasize that these circumstances are *special*; they should not reflect the congregation's regular practice.

21. Among these are the festive meal; the recitation of *Hallel* and the blessing *Shehecheyanu*; and the outward expressions of mourning. See *Gates of the Seasons*, 62–63; *Gates of Mitzvah*, ed. Simeon J. Maslin (New York: CCAR Press, 1979), 60; *Rabbi's Manual* (New York: CCAR Press, 1988), 252.

22. *Reform Responsa for the Twenty-first Century*, no. 5756.4, vol. 1, pp. 33–40. See also the following responsa: *Teshuvot for the Nineties*, no. 5755.12, pp. 165–68, no. 5753.22, pp. 169–70, and no. 5751.5, pp. 97–100; *Contemporary American Reform Responsa*, nos. 176 and 177; and *Reform Responsa for the Twenty-first Century*, no. 5757.7, vol. 1, pp. 41–48.

23. *Reform Responsa for Our Time* (*RRT*), no. 3.

24. *Reform Responsa*, no. 5. The quotation is at p. 40.

25. A point that Freehof indeed allows for. See *RRT*, no. 3, pp. 18–19: "It is only in modern times, when the Bar Mitzvah celebrations have become so elaborate, that some might feel a contradiction between the Bar Mitzvah joy and the memorial *Yizkor*." He goes on to note that a family who does feel that sort of contradiction is free to postpone the bar mitzvah observance to another date.

26. See *M. Yoma* 8:9: "R. Akiva said: Happy are you, Israel! Before whom are you purified? And who purifies you?" Similar considerations lead many halachic authorities to permit weddings during the Days of Awe between Rosh HaShanah and Yom Kippur: this period of solemnity may be an especially good time for the couple to begin to build a Jewish home and family. See R. Ovadyah Yosef, *Resp. Yechaveh Daat* 1:48, and R. David Zvi Hoffmann, *Resp. Melamed Leho`il* 3:1.

27. It will be noted, no doubt, that the entire community does *not* attend our regular Festival services but that it would be more likely to do so if bar/bat mitzvah were scheduled on those days. One could argue, therefore, that bar/bat mitzvah observance would enhance the experience of *Yom Tov* as a community event. The difficulty with this argument, of course, is that the larger crowd would not be attending the service in order to "experience" the Festival. Indeed, the celebration of bar/bat mitzvah would tend to overwhelm the very different atmosphere of the holiday observance.

28. Traditional practice forbids the taking of the *lulav* on Shabbat, lest one be tempted to carry the *lulav* through a public thoroughfare and thereby violate the prohibition against carrying on Shabbat. This is the same reasoning that forbids the sounding of the shofar when the first day of Rosh HaShanah falls on Shabbat (BT *Rosh HaShanah* 29b). Reform Jewish practice permits both the sounding of the shofar and the taking of the *lulav* on Shabbat. See R. Solomon B. Freehof, *Recent Reform Responsa*, no. 6. For additional argumentation, see Mark Washofsky, *Jewish Living* (New York: URJ Press, 2001), pp. 120 and 403.

YOREH DEI-AH: RITUAL OBSERVANCE

MAY NON-JEWS PARTICIPATE IN THE WRITING OF A TORAH SCROLL?

5765.1

Sh'eilah

Our congregation has commissioned a *sofer* to write a new Torah scroll. Although he is Sephardi Orthodox he is being very flexible on the issue of who can help him "write" a letter in the Torah scroll by allowing women and children to participate. (The practice is to schedule "scribing" appointments where people fill in a letter that the *sofer* has already outlined. People make a donation to the project and fill in a letter while the *sofer* holds their hand, etc.) Assuming our *sofer* would allow it, the question is: is it appropriate to allow non-Jewish adults involved in raising Jewish children to participate in the mitzvah of writing a Torah scroll? Our initial inclination is to permit it for a number of reasons: (1) *Shalom bayit*: the individual is committed to raising a Jewish family and working to maintain Jewish survival. (2) Ritual consistency within a diverse congregation: given that we allow a non-Jewish parent to hold a Torah scroll or open the ark at a service or *b'nei mitzvah*, etc., it seems logical to allow/encourage this form of participation as well. (3) Learning/*keiruv* (nearness): by participating in this activity we are giving the individual an opportunity to learn about Judaism and to increase their love of Torah by sharing in this mitzvah. (4) Shared tradition of Scripture: assuming the individual's religion of origin or active faith is Christianity, then the Five Books of Moses is holy to them as well. (Rabbi David Wirtschafter, Burlingame, California)

T'shuvah

Our tradition teaches that the very last of the Torah's 613 commandments[1] is "the mitzvah incumbent upon every Jew to write a Torah scroll,"[2] derived by way of a midrash on Deuteronomy 31:19.[3] It is this mitzvah that these congregants seek to fulfill by taking part in the project our *sho-eil* describes. And fundamental to this mitzvah is the fact that a gentile does *not* take part in it. A Torah scroll written by a non-Jew is *pasul*, disqualified for the purpose of *k'riat haTorah*, the public reading of the Torah at worship services.[4] The non-Jew cannot act as a *sofer* precisely because he does not partake of the covenant of Israel; he is not a member of the Jewish community, a people defined by its obligations to the mitzvot.[5] Since it is likely that the congregation will use this particular Torah scroll for public reading, it would be inappropriate under Jewish tradition to allow non-Jews to participate in this project.

Various objections might be raised against this conclusion on halachic grounds. One could argue, for example, that it is the *sofer* who does the actual "writing" when he holds the member's hand; therefore, strictly speaking the gentile family members would not be "writing" the scroll at all. Yet this is not persuasive, since the *sofer*, engaged by the congregation, is acting as the agent (*shaliach*) for each member who participates in the project. The general rule in the halachah is that one's agent acts with power of attorney, so that the agent's acts in fulfilling the assignment are considered to be the actions of the one who engages him or her.[6] In this specific case, moreover, we learn that "when one employs a *sofer* to write a Torah scroll, it is as though one has written it by oneself."[7] Since such is the case here, we conclude that the congregants fulfill in this manner the mitzvah to *write* a *sefer Torah*.

It might also be objected that, if it is indeed "incumbent upon every Jew to write a Torah scroll,"[8] then no mitzvah is being performed here, because no one person is writing the entire *sefer Torah* or commissioning a scribe to write it. If there is no mitzvah taking place, then arguably there is no reason to prevent gentiles from taking part in the activity. The halachic literature does discuss at length the question whether one may successfully fulfill this mitzvah by contracting with others to write a Torah scroll. Yet though opinions are divided, the fact remains that "it is the general custom [*minhag haolam*]" for individuals to write a Torah scroll in partnership (*b'shutafut*) with others and to presume that each member of that group, as an individual, has fulfilled the mitzvah thereby.[9] We would note, as well, the statement of tradition that when one writes a single letter of a *sefer Torah* "it is as though he has written the entire scroll."[10]

Each member of the congregation, then, fulfills the mitzvah to write a Torah scroll by taking part in this project. Accordingly, it is inappropriate for gentiles to participate in it, just as it is inappropriate for them to be called to the Torah and to perform other important ritual mitzvot on our behalf.[11] The *sefer Torah* is the most visible and powerful symbol of Israel's covenant with God. The writing of the scroll enables us to read it in public, an act by which we reenact the giving of the Torah at Sinai and rehearse our identity as a covenant people. A gentile does not partake of Jewish identity. He or she bears no obligation under the mitzvot, the terms of the covenant, and therefore cannot perform this mitzvah for us. Our case, it is true, involves "non-Jewish adults involved in raising Jewish children." We deeply appreciate the love and devotion with which the non-Jewish parents in our midst help see to it that their children receive a Jewish upbringing and education. Yet so long as they remain outside the covenant of Israel, they bear no *responsibility* to bring their children into that covenant. That responsibility, that obligation, is precisely what we Jews bear *as* Jews.[12] If the non-Jews in our midst wish to accept these responsibilities and obligations upon themselves, they may do so through the process of conversion, a path that is freely open to them. Many individuals who came to our congregations as non-Jewish spouses or partners have chosen to take this step, and they now participate fully and equally in the public life of our Jewish community. If others choose not to convert (or not *yet* to convert), we respect their choice, and we believe that they will recognize the obvious implications of that choice. We believe, that is, that they will respect our need to maintain the lines and definitions that preserve our distinctness as a *Jewish* community.

With these considerations in mind, we would respond to the arguments cited by our *sho-eil* in favor of permitting non-Jews to take part in the *sefer Torah* project.

1. *SHALOM BAYIT*

Although these individuals are "committed" to raising Jewish families, they are not, as we have seen, *obligated* to do so under the terms of the covenant. The obligation to respond to God's call to Israel is what we term *mitzvah*, and this obligation, which the gentile by definition does not share, is the key factor in our case. A non-Jew cannot perform on our behalf ritual mitzvot by which we constitute ourselves as a covenant community.

2. RITUAL CONSISTENCY WITHIN A DIVERSE CONGREGATION

Our position, which we have expressed elsewhere,[13] is that non-Jews should not participate in the Torah service or lead the central rubrics of our communal liturgy. This view, again, is based upon the fact that non-Jews are not members of the Jewish people and therefore cannot lead or perform on our behalf those rituals that affirm our identity as a Jewish community. The same reasoning applies to the question before us.

3. LEARNING/*KEIRUV*

It is important to afford individuals the opportunity to learn about Jewish life and to draw them closer to it. As we note below, there are appropriate ways in which the congregation might design this project toward that end. Yet *keiruv*, or "outreach," has its proper limits, a reality that all congregations accept and understand. For example, the wording of our *sh'eilah* indicates that this congregation does impose some restrictions upon the participation of non-Jews in its ritual life. The reason for these limits, we would think, is the felt need to preserve the nature of the congregation as a *Jewish* religious community, one in which the performance of defining constitutive rituals is reserved for Jews. The writing of a *sefer Torah* is just such a ritual act.

4. SHARED TRADITION OF SCRIPTURE

Although the Five Books of Moses are holy to Christians, they mean something very different to them than they mean to us. For Christians, these books are not "Torah"; they are the "Old Testament," the first part of a record of revelation in which the climax is the incarnation of God in the person of Jesus Christ. Christian theology traditionally holds that the Hebrew Bible has been superseded by the "new covenant" established through Jesus, and it reads Jewish Scripture in large part as a prophecy of his advent and ministry. This interpretation, obviously, contradicts the most fundamental tenets of our own faith. Thus, while we may "share" some scriptural traditions with Christians, they do *not* share our Jewish understanding of the covenant. For that reason, they should not participate in the creation of the scroll that embodies and symbolizes that understanding.

We emphasize that our objections to the participation of non-Jews in this project focus specifically upon the writing of the *sefer Torah*. At the same time, non-Jews might take part in related activities that are not, strictly speaking, mitzvot.[14] Non-Jewish family members might craft ornaments and coverings for the Torah scroll, participate with the *sofer* in writing a certificate to be presented at the dedication of the *sefer*, and so forth. Thus, if the congregation so wishes, it can design its project in a way that would include all family members, thereby serving the goal of *keiruv*, a vital task in our communal life.

CONCLUSION

The writing of a *sefer Torah* is a mitzvah, a constitutive ritual of Jewish religious life, a powerful symbolic expression of Israel's covenant with

God. It is a duty that only Jews can fulfill; others cannot do it on our behalf. Non-Jews may take part in other activities surrounding the creation of a Torah scroll.

NOTES

1. See BT *Makot* 23b–24a. The number 613 is derived from the verse "Moses commanded us [the] Torah" (Deut. 33:4). The numerical value of the letters of the word *Torah* equals 611; hence, we received 611 mitzvot from Moses's intercession with God. We heard two other commandments ("I am *Adonai* your God" and "You shall have no other gods besides Me" [Exod. 20:2–3]) directly from God. *Sefer HaChinuch*, which lists the mitzvot according to their appearance in the text of the Torah, counts this one as mitzvah number 613.

2. The wording is that of Rambam, *Yad, Sefer Torah* 7:1, repeated by R. Yosef Karo in *SA, YD* 270:1.

3. BT *Sanhedrin* 21b. In the verse, God tells Moses to "write down this poem"; the Rabbis interpret this as an instruction to each Israelite to write an entire *sefer Torah.*

4. BT *Gittin* 45b; *Yad, T'fillin* 1:13; *SA, YD* 281:1. Although our printed texts use the phrases *oveid kochavim* (idolator), *kuti* (Samaritan), or *k'naani* (Canaanite) in place of "gentile," the evidence of manuscripts and early commentators to the passage is that it properly reads *goy,* or "non-Jew." That word was often removed from Talmud texts by copyists and printers under pressure from censorship, especially in Christian Europe. Moreover, as the midrash that supports this rule makes clear (see below), the principle objection to a gentile scribe is precisely that he is a non-Jew and not that he worships other gods.

5. See BT *Gittin* 45b. The specific midrash that supports the disqualification is a *hekeish* (comparison) drawn from two nearly adjacent verses: just as a non-Jew is not commanded to "bind them as a sign upon your hand" (Deut. 11:18), he is also excluded from the community of those who "write these words…" (Deut. 11:20).

6. *Sh'lucho shel adam* (M. *B'rachot* 5:5; BT *Kiddushin* 41b and parallels).

7. BT *M'nachot* 30a; Isserles, *SA, YD* 270:1. See also *Yad, Sefer Torah* 7:1.

8. R. Asher b. Yechiel, a preeminent halachic authority of the thirteenth to fourteenth century, argued that this mitzvah is no longer incumbent upon Jews, since we no longer use Torah scrolls for the purpose of study. Instead, "it is a positive commandment

for every Jew…to write *Chumashim* and texts of the Mishnah and Talmud and their commentaries, in order that he and his sons might study them" (the quotation is from the *Tur*, written by Asher's son Yaakov, *YD* 270). Subsequent authorities disagree over the precise meaning of this statement. Some argue that R. Asher did not mean to exempt us from the requirement to write a *sefer Torah* but simply to note that in our time it is *also* a mitzvah to write other sacred texts (R. Yosef Karo, *Beit Yosef* to *Tur*, *YD* 270 and *SA, YD* 270:2; *Turei Zahav* and *Biur HaGra* ad loc.; R. Aryeh Lev b. Asher [eighteenth-century Lithuania], *Resp. Shaagat Aryeh*, no. 36). Others read R. Asher literally, concluding that there is no specific mitzvah in our day to write a *sefer Torah* (*P'rishah* to *Tur*, *YD* 270; *Siftei Kohein* to *SA, YD* 270:5). We do not wish, at this point, to take a position on this *machloket*. We would merely observe that both sides of the dispute would undoubtedly agree that when a person writes a *sefer Torah* he or she does fulfill a ritual duty (after all, we *do* have to produce Torah scrolls for the purpose of public reading), whether or not there exists a specific requirement that each and every Jew perform the act of writing.

9. On all of this see *Pitchei T'shuvah*, *YD* 270:1.

10. BT *M'nachot* 30a; *Yad, Sefer Torah* 7:1; Isserles, *SA, YD* 270:1. The verb that these sources use is *magiah*, which means "to correct"; it applies in our case because a Torah scroll that lacks even a single letter is *pasul* (unfit for public reading) until it is corrected. Hence, one who writes a single letter is correcting a defective scroll.

11. See *Teshuvot for the Nineties*, no. 5754.5, pp. 55–75. These mitzvot are roughly equivalent to *t'filat chovah*, "obligatory prayer," those sections of the service that most closely reflect the public, corporate (as opposed to personal and private) elements of Jewish worship. These include the *Sh'ma* and Its Blessings, the *T'filah*, the Torah service (*aliyot* and other honors), and the recitation of public benedictions (*b'rachot*) at public gatherings.

12. See *Reform Responsa for the Twenty-first Century*, no. 5762.2, vol. 2, pp. 251–56, section 2.

13. See above at note 11.

14. Is the crafting of appurtenances to the Torah scroll not a mitzvah in itself? The issue may be clouded somewhat by the fact that the word *mitzvah* enjoys several layers of definition. Some mitzvot are ritual acts that are constitutive of Jewish identity and community; therefore, they can be fulfilled only by Jews. That is the case with the rituals of public worship (see note 11, above) and with the writing of a *sefer Torah*. Other mitzvot are duties that are incumbent upon Jews but not necessarily restricted

to them. Donations to *tzedakah* and to the synagogue fall into this category; see our discussion *Reform Responsa for the Twenty-first Century*, no. 5761.2, vol. 2, pp. 241–46, at notes 5–7. Although Jews, as members of the covenant, have an obligation to give to *tzedakah*, non-Jews are not prohibited from doing so.

A Defective "Holocaust" Torah Scroll
5760.3

Sh'eilah

Our congregation possesses one of the Czech Torah scrolls that
were taken by the Nazis and then rescued and cared for by London's
Westminster Synagogue Memorial Trust. There are over one thousand
scrolls now on "permanent loan" to synagogues around the world. Ours
comes from the town of Kolin, near Prague. Some synagogues have
scrolls that are fragmentary or incomplete. Our scroll is a complete *sefer
Torah*, but sections of script have flaked away. A *sofer s'tam* (i.e., a scribe
qualified to write Torah scrolls, *t'fillin*, and mezuzot) has told us that the
parchment will not hold new ink. The scroll, since it cannot be repaired,
is technically *pasul*, disqualified for public reading.

Our congregation has decided to use the scroll for Shabbat Torah
readings, in places where the script is perfect or at least very clear. In
addition, we have allowed many *b'nei mitzvah* to read their *parashah*
from the scroll. This enables our youngsters to make a tactile connection
between themselves and the vanished community of Kolin. We have
taken synagogue and youth trips to Kolin and have prayed at its
synagogue, which still stands. The scroll and its history have therefore
become a significant part of our congregation's life.

A question has been raised: is it proper for us to read from this scroll,
inasmuch as it has been declared *pasul*? How shall we answer this
question, in light of both our tradition and the value we have found as a
congregation in the public reading of the scroll?

T'shuvah

This *sh'eilah* poses a conflict between two profoundly important Jewish
religious values. On the one hand, the honor due to the *sefer Torah* is

a matter of great consequence in our tradition,[1] which as we shall see demands that the formal public reading of the Torah (*k'riat haTorah*) be performed from a *sefer Torah kasher*, a scroll that meets the strict requirements of ritual fitness. On the other hand, the events of the Shoah have left a profound imprint upon the Jewish mind and heart, and the remembrance of that tragedy has taken on for us the character of a religious duty.[2] Many congregations have acquired Torah scrolls that were rescued from the Nazis, and by reading from these scrolls they demonstrate in a concrete and moving way the continuity of the Jewish people and faith. How do we accommodate these two religious values, both of which make powerful claims upon our attention?

1. THE READING OF THE TORAH FROM A RITUALLY UNFIT SCROLL

In his great code of Jewish law, Maimonides (Rambam) offers a list of twenty defects that render the scroll *pasul*.[3] The fifteenth item reads: "If the form of one letter should be diminished to the point that it cannot be read at all or so that it resembles another letter, whether this occurred at the original writing or through a perforation, a tear, or fading [of the text]." The Czech Torah scroll described in our *sh'eilah* is clearly *pasul* according to this definition. The proper response would be to repair the scroll and to restore it to kashrut, a ritually acceptable condition.[4] Since this is not possible in our case, tradition prescribes that the scroll be buried or stored away in a *genizah*.[5] In any event, it may not be used to fulfill the required ritual reading (*k'riat haTorah*). As Maimonides writes, "Should any one of these defects be present, the scroll is reduced to the status of a *Chumash*[6] that is used for the teaching of children; it is not to be read before the congregation."[7] The reason for this prohibition, according to the Talmud, is that to perform the reading from a *Chumash*—that is, from a scroll that is anything less than a complete *sefer Torah*—is an affront to the dignity of the congregation.[8]

The issue, however, is not as cut-and-dried as it seems. The very same Maimonides is the author of a responsum that rules to the opposite effect.[9] His correspondents ask whether a community that does not possess a *sefer Torah* may perform the public reading from *Chumashim* and recite the blessings before and after the reading, or should they abstain from reading the Torah altogether? Similarly, may the blessings be recited over a *sefer Torah* that is ritually defective? Rambam answers without hesitation: *mutar l'vareich*, it is permitted to recite the blessings over the reading from a *sefer Torah pasul*. This is because we recite the blessings over the *reading* itself and not over the scroll; thus, one may recite the blessings whether the reading is performed from a scroll that is *kasher*, from a scroll that is *pasul*, or even if one recites without reading from a text at all.[10] Rambam offers two proofs for this theory. He first refers us to the beginning of the morning service (*Shacharit*), where one recites the blessing *asher bachar banu mikol haamim*—the same blessing recited prior to the reading of the Torah—before reciting passages of Scripture and Rabbinic literature.[11] The worshiper says this *b'rachah* even though he does not recite the passages from a *sefer Torah*. "Thus, the actual mitzvah is the pronunciation [*hagayah*] of the words of Torah, and the blessing pertains to that pronunciation." Second, Rambam cites the Talmudic passage, mentioned above, that forbids congregational reading from *Chumashim*.[12] A *Chumash*, he notes, is the supreme example of a defective Torah scroll;[13] still, it is not prohibited *because* it is defective but rather because to read from it is an affront to "the dignity of the congregation." This suggests that a defective scroll is not disqualified per se for the congregational reading, but simply that it would be unseemly to use such a scroll for that purpose. The reading itself is therefore not invalid, and to recite a blessing over such a scroll is not an instance of *b'rachah l'vatalah* (a misplaced or unnecessary benediction).

This permissive ruling remains very much a minority view. Other leading authorities reject Rambam's arguments outright.[14] First, they write, Rambam's permit cuts against the grain of accepted Talmudic and halachic thought, which holds that a defective *sefer Torah* is not to be used for public reading even if no other Torah scroll is available.[15] Second, the benedictions are in fact recited over the scroll and *not* (as Rambam suggests) over the reading itself. Otherwise, we would be able to fulfill the requirement of *k'riat haTorah* by reciting the Torah portion orally; yet the ancient Rabbinic ordinance that established the practice[16] requires that the portion be read from a scroll and not from memory.[17] Third, while the Talmud's language might support Rambam's leniency with respect to a *Chumash*—that is, one of the Torah's five books written correctly on a separate scroll—the disqualification of a scroll whose writing is defective or worn away appears to be absolute.[18] Indeed, it is arguable that a scroll lacking even one letter is not considered a *sefer Torah* at all,[19] so that the reading from it does not "count" toward the fulfillment of the mitzvah of *k'riat haTorah*.[20]

These are serious objections. Rambam's ruling seems to contradict everything the tradition has to say on the use of ritually unfit Torah scrolls. It most certainly contradicts the position of his own *Mishneh Torah* on the subject. It is therefore not surprising that some subsequent authorities sought to account for this problematic responsum by questioning its validity or authenticity.[21] Still, we think it possible to explain this *t'shuvah* without excising it from the literature of Jewish law. Near the conclusion of the responsum, Rambam declares, "It is proper for every community to possess a Torah scroll that is *kasher* in all respects, and it is preferable [*l'chat'chilah*][22] to read from that scroll. If this is not possible, however, let them read in public even from a *pasul* scroll and recite the blessings, on the basis of the reasoning I have supplied." In other words, Rambam holds that the preferable, optimal standard of observance demands a *kasher* scroll, and the ruling in the *Mishneh Torah* reflects that view.[23] The responsum, meanwhile, conveys Rambam's understanding of the minimally acceptable standard of observance: when the optimal standard cannot be met, the reading from a *sefer Torah pasul* suffices to fulfill the mitzvah of *k'riat haTorah*.[24] A community that does not possess a *sefer Torah kasher* may perform the reading from a *pasul* scroll, presumably so that (in the words of a later authority) "the practice of reading the Torah not be forgotten" there.[25]

2. THE ISSUE FROM A REFORM JEWISH PERSPECTIVE

We could make a good case to support this congregation's desire to
conduct its Shabbat Torah readings from the Czech scroll. We have seen
that Jewish law does not clearly forbid the reading from a *pasul* scroll;
the responsum of Maimonides may be a minority opinion, but it is not
necessarily "wrong" on that account.[26] We Reform Jews, at any rate,
certainly see nothing wrong with adopting a minority opinion as the
basis of our own practice, particularly when that opinion expresses an
uplifting and "liberally affirmative" interpretation of Jewish tradition.[27]
In the present case, we might say that there is no reason to forbid the
use of this scroll. To read from it most certainly does not offend the
dignity of the congregation. On the contrary: reading from this *sefer
Torah*, which symbolizes the horrific events of the Shoah and our
people's determination to survive all attempts to destroy us, is a deeply
meaningful religious experience. Thus, just as Rambam and others were
concerned that the practice of Torah reading would not be "forgotten"
in small communities, we are motivated to use this *pasul* scroll by our
determination that the Shoah never be forgotten.

Yet this "good" case is insufficient, for it fails to consider the central
role that the reading of the Torah plays in our practice. *K'riat haTorah*
is more than simply one religious observance out of many. It is the
reenactment of the drama of Sinai, a reaffirmation of the covenant
that binds God and Israel. We observe this mitzvah, as do all other
Jews, by reading from a Torah scroll. By this we mean that we use
a *scroll*, not a printed book,[28] a scroll, moreover, that is written and
constructed according to the requirements set forth in Jewish law for
a proper *sefer Torah*. These requirements, it must be stressed, are not
mere technicalities, nor are they standards of "Orthodox" practice
that we Reform Jews are free to ignore. Rather, they are standards
of *Jewish* practice, the rules that define what a *sefer Torah* is, rules
universally observed in all Jewish communities, including our Reform
congregations. If Rambam permits the reading from a scroll that does
not meet these requirements, he does so as a temporary measure; he is

speaking, after all, to a community that has no *kasher* scroll available. To exalt this stopgap device to the status of a permanent and weekly observance is to say that it makes no difference to us that a Torah scroll is defective rather than *kasher*. It is to suggest that we are satisfied with an ersatz standard of Jewish practice, that appearances count more than reality, that we are perfectly content to read from a scroll that looks like—but is not—a real *sefer Torah*.[29] This is not the sort of statement that *any* Jewish community, Reform or otherwise, ought to make;[30] we should consider it an affront to the dignity of our congregation. Let us keep in mind, too, that the Czech synagogue from which this *sefer Torah* originates would never had read it publicly in its ritually unfit state. Like observant Jews everywhere, they would have done the proper thing: either to repair the scroll or to consign it lovingly to a *genizah*. It is not a little ironic that we should seek to perpetuate the memory of that community by means of an act that they themselves would have rejected as an affront to the dignity of *their* congregation.

It might be argued, of course, that our duty to remember the Shoah outweighs the need to adhere to the rules and regulations concerning the *sefer Torah*. Yet the reading from this scroll is by no means the only way for us to remember the Shoah in our ritual observance. References to the victims and the events of the Nazi persecutions figure prominently in our liturgy, in our liturgical calendar, and in our synagogue architecture and furnishings. We have frequent opportunity, in other words, to remember the Shoah, even if we do not read from this scroll. More than that: we must take great care *how* we remember the Shoah. In particular, we must not allow that memory to supersede our devotion to the laws, customs, and practices that comprise our Judaism. That the Nazis murdered millions of our brothers and sisters is a fact that has seared its way deeply into our collective consciousness, but it is no reason—indeed, it is precisely the *wrong* reason—to alter the contours and content of our religious practice. To change, detract from, or abandon essential religious observances *because* of the Shoah, to read from a *pasul* Torah scroll—something we would otherwise not do—*because* the Nazis murdered the Jews who once possessed it, is to proclaim that the crimes of Hitler take precedence over the "voice of Sinai," the proper conduct of Jewish religious life. This, too, is a statement we should not make. It is surely the wrong message to send to our young people on the day when, called to the Torah for the first time, they symbolically accept the responsibilities and commitments of Jewish adults.

We should insist, instead, that our regular weekly, Shabbat, and holiday Torah portions be read from a *sefer Torah kasher*. This is the standard bequeathed to us from Jewish tradition. This was the standard observed by the Czech community from which the scroll in question originated. And it remains the standard that informs Reform Jewish life, the standard to which we educate our children and to which we ought to aspire.

The above does not mean that the congregation should *never* read from its Czech *sefer Torah*. The point is that we should not allow the Shoah to cause us to detract from or alter the nature of our most important observances; the regular, statutory reading of the Torah, therefore, should not be accomplished from a scroll that is ritually unfit for that purpose merely because that scroll survived the Nazis. On the other hand, it is entirely permissible to *add* to the body of our observance in response to the Shoah. The institution of Yom HaShoah, a special day of memorial for the victims and the survivors of the death camps, is an obvious example of such a creative endeavor. We therefore may read from the *pasul* scroll *after* we have read the regular Torah portion for that day from a *kasher* scroll. This should be done in such a way as to distinguish it from the reading of the first scroll. The rabbi should announce that this is an additional reading, and the appropriate benedictions should *not* be recited over the *pasul* scroll. In this manner, the traditional objections to the reading from a *pasul* scroll are removed.[31] The congregation can observe the laws and customs that define the mitzvah of the reading of the Torah while at the same time honoring the memory of those who perished in the Shoah.

An overriding concern for all the members of this Committee is that the reading from the *pasul* scroll should be seen as an exceptional occurrence. The too-frequent use of this scroll would likely upset the careful balance we seek to draw between commemorating the Holocaust and focusing our people's attention upon the enduring content of Jewish life. Most of us urge that the *pasul* "Holocaust" scroll be read only on special occasions that have an obvious connection to the Shoah; the Shabbat closest to Yom HaShoah, Kristallnacht, and the *yahrzeit* (i.e., the date of the destruction) of the community from which the scroll originates are possible examples.[32] On those occasions, some of us feel that the *pasul* scroll may be used for the regular reading, with no distinctions; thus, the *b'rachot* may be recited over it.[33] Others among us hold that even on these special occasions the *pasul* scroll should be used only for an "additional" reading (i.e., not the statutory portion for the day) and that no *b'rachot* should be recited over it.[34] All of us agree, however, that the *pasul* scroll should not be read every week.

CONCLUSION

A congregation may read from a *sefer Torah pasul* in remembrance of the Shoah. This should be done, however, only on appropriate special occasions, and then in such a way as to emphasize that the reading of the Torah ought to be accomplished from a scroll that is, in all respects, a proper *sefer Torah*.

NOTES

1. The rules concerning the honor due to the *sefer Torah* are summarized in *SA, YD* 282.

2. The chief expression of this duty is the observance of Yom HaShoah. "It is a *mitzvah* to remember the six million Jews who were murdered in the *Shoah* by attending special memorial services" (*Gates of the Seasons*, ed. Peter S. Knobel [New York: CCAR Press, 1983], 102–3). See *CCAR Yearbook* 87 (1987): 87.

3. *Yad, Sefer Torah* 10:1.

4. BT *K'tubot* 19b; *Yad, Sefer Torah* 7:12; *SA, YD* 279:1.

5. BT *M'gillah* 26a; *Yad, Sefer Torah* 10:1; *SA, YD* 282:10.

6. A *Chumash* here refers to one of the five books of the Pentateuch, written as a separate scroll; BT *Gittin* 60a, and Rashi s.v. *bachumashin*; *Yad, Sefer Torah* 7:14 and *Kesef Mishneh* ad loc.

7. *Yad, Sefer Torah* 10:1.

8. BT *Gittin* 60a: *ein kor in bachumashin b'veit hak'neset mishum k'vod tzibur.*

9. The responsum is found in the traditional collections of Rambam's *t'shuvot* (*P'eir HaDor*, no. 9, and *Kovetz T'shuvot HaRambam*, no. 15) as well as in both of the two twentieth-century critical editions: *T'shuvot HaRambam*, ed. A. Freimann (Jerusalem: Mekitzei Nirdamim, 1934), no. 43; and *T'shuvot HaRambam*, ed. Y. Blau, vol. 2 (Jerusalem: Mekitzei Nirdamim, 1960), no. 294.

10. The blessings surrounding the Torah reading, Rambam writes, differ from those we recite over such mitzvot as sukkah and *lulav*. In those instances, should the object itself be *pasul* we would not recite the appropriate *b'rachah*, because "the mitzvah is the taking of a *lulav* or the dwelling in a sukkah, and the blessing is recited over those objects. Should they be ritually unfit [i.e., should they not meet the requirements for a valid *lulav* or sukkah], one does not perform the mitzvah [when using them]." The blessing would therefore be an improper one, a *b'rachah l'vatalah*. By contrast, the blessings surrounding the Torah reading are said over the reading and *not* over the Torah scroll itself.

11. See *SA, OC* 47:5, which lists the three *b'rachot* recited during the beginning of the morning service (*Birchot HaShachar*) over the study of Torah. Our own prayer book omits the third of these blessings, *asher bachar banu*; see *Gates of Prayer* (New York: CCAR Press, 1975), p. 52.

12. BT *Gittin* 60a.

13. Rambam's reason for saying this is not altogether clear. Presumably, he means that a *Chumash*, unlike other "defective" scrolls, does not even resemble a proper *sefer Torah*.

14. This is especially true of R. Sh'lomo b. Adret (Rashba; Barcelona, d. 1310), whose ruling is not found in the extant collection of his responsa but is cited at length in two early-fourteenth-century works—*Orchot Chayim, Hil. Sefer Torah*, no. 5 and *Kol Bo*, p. 13b–c—and referenced by the fifteenth-century R. Yosef Kolon (*Resp. Maharik*, no. 69) and R. Sh'lomo b. Shimon Duran (*Resp. Rashbash*, no. 11) and the sixteenth-century R. Yosef Karo (*Beit Yosef, OC* 143).

15. This, says Rashba (see note 14), is derived by the Talmud's language concerning the defective scroll: *ein korin bo*, "it is not to be read (before the congregation)"; this, he

argues, implies an absolute disqualification and not, as Rambam thinks, a provisional disqualification to be waived when no other scroll is available. See also *Resp. Rashba* 1:487. Moreover, the same language—*ein korin bo* or *al yikra bo*—is used in Tractate *Sof'rim* with respect to a *sefer pasul*, and the disqualification there appears to be absolute. See, e.g., *Sof'rim* 3:7 and 9.

16. Rabbinic tradition holds that the formal, public Torah reading was established by Moses and Ezra through a series of *takanot*, or legislative enactments. See BT *Bava Kama* 82a and *Yad, T'filah* 11:1.

17. This argument is less than airtight. Maimonides could respond that, if the reading is *supposed* to be carried out from a scroll *mishum k'vod tzibur*, "due to the dignity of the congregation," this does not imply that a reading done without the scroll is not valid *b'diavad*, or "after the fact." Yet Rashba makes the point that if the Rabbis ordain that blessings be recited over the performance of a mitzvah, they should be said *only* when that mitzvah is carried out in its intended form; thus, the *b'rachot* should not be said over anything but a proper (*kasher*) Torah scroll.

18. See BT *Gittin* 60a: while *Chumashim* are not read in the synagogue because of "the dignity of the congregation" (implying that the congregation may waive its "dignity" and allow the reading to take place), a defective scroll is simply "not read" (*ein korin bo*), presumably even if the reading would not offend the congregation's dignity.

19. See BT *Bava Batra* 15a, on Deut. 31:26, and R. Yosef Karo, *Kesef Mishneh* to *Yad, T'fillin* 1:2.

20. Thus, according to "most" opinions (*daat rov haposkim*; *Mishnah B'rurah* 143:13), when an error is discovered in a *sefer Torah* during the congregational reading, the reading must be repeated from a *kasher* scroll from the beginning of that day's appointed section. See R. Asher b. Yechiel, *Resp. HaRosh* 3:8; and *Migdal Oz* to *Yad, T'fillin* 1:2, in the name of R. Meir Abulafia, R. Avraham b. David of Posquierres, Ramban, and Rashba. This rule is not universally accepted; see below, note 26.

21. Thus Rashba (cited at note 14) proposes that the responsum represents the opinion of Maimonides "in his youth," while the *Mishneh Torah* expresses his more considered and mature viewpoint. Rashbash (cited at note 13) raises the possibility that Rambam is not the actual author of the responsum. He writes that, inasmuch as we cannot be certain that the *t'shuvah* was in fact written by Rambam ("is his signature upon it?"), it is wiser to follow the opinion of the *Mishneh Torah*, of which his authorship is not doubted.

22. The word *l'chat'chilah*, a technical term of Jewish law, signifies the optimal standard of observance, the practice that *ought* to be followed if one has a choice. Yet if an individual or community cannot adhere to that standard, they can still fulfill the requirements of the mitzvah provided that they have met the minimally acceptable standard of observance (*b'diavad*).

23. That is, although a congregation's "honor" dictates that it should not read from a ritually unfit Torah scroll, the reading therefrom is not invalid; otherwise, it would be unacceptable even *b'diavad*, as a "minimally acceptable" standard. The wording of *Yad, Sefer Torah* 10:1 suggests that Rambam, unlike Rashba, draws no distinction between the *Chumash* and the defective scroll on this point; see at note 18.

24. This line of thought is indicated by none other than Rashba in a responsum (1:805). The Talmud (BT *Gittin* 60a) declares that we do not read from *Chumashim* on the grounds that to do so affronts the dignity of the congregation. This implies that, as a matter of technical law, it is permitted to perform the public reading from a *Chumash* (*min hadin mutar*), though by all means a proper *sefer Torah* ought to be used. See also R. Yoel Sirkes (seventeenth-century Poland), *Resp. HaBach HaChadashot*, no. 42.

25. See *Magen Avraham* to SA, OC 143:2, and see note 31, below.

26. In addition, Rambam's "rejected" *t'shuvah* retains a great deal of influence over Jewish ritual practice. See *SA*, OC 143:4 and YD 279:2: if an error is found in the text of a *sefer Torah* during the reading, another scroll is brought from the ark and the reading continues from the place in the text where the error was found. In other words, that part of the reading already performed from the *pasul* scroll "counts" toward the fulfillment of the mitzvah. This ruling is, on the surface, a curious one: if a Torah scroll is ritually unfit, it stands to reason that none of its text can be utilized for the performance of the mitzvah. That, indeed, is the opinion of "most" authorities (see note 19). R. Yosef Karo, who notes that this custom originated with his colleague R. Yaakov Berav of Safed, justifies it on the basis of Rambam's *t'shuvah*: "even though we do not follow Rambam's ruling, we rely upon it after the fact in order to accept the reading" that was already performed from the *sefer Torah pasul* (*Beit Yosef*, YD 279).

27. On the tendency of Reform responsa to seek the "liberally affirmative" answer, see R. Solomon B. Freehof, *Reform Responsa* (Cincinnati: Hebrew Union College Press, 1960), 23. For a more recent, systematic account of the principles of liberal halachah, see R. Moshe Zemer, *Evolving Halakhah* (Woodstock, VT: Jewish Lights Publishing, 1999).

28. This is not to say that we are forbidden to read the Torah portion from a printed *Chumash* during our services. Sometimes, there is no alternative to doing so; see note

31, below. But the act of reading from a printed *Chumash*, however valuable in and of itself, does *not* meet the definition of the act of *k'riat haTorah*. That mitzvah, a ritual observance that meets its own particular requirements, is accomplished only through the reading from a *sefer Torah*.

29. See at note 19, above.

30. On the use of "substitutes" for ritual observance, see our responsum "Non-Traditional Sukkah," *Teshuvot for the Nineties*, no. 5755.4, pp. 91–96.

31. It is not forbidden to read in public from a non-*kasher* Torah scroll; the point is that such a reading does not fulfill the mitzvah of *k'riat haTorah*. The blessings, which pertain to that mitzvah, are therefore inappropriate. It follows that to read from the scroll without pronouncing the blessings is permitted, so long as we do not think we are fulfilling the mitzvah thereby. See Isserles, OC 143:2 and *Magen Avraham* ad loc.: a community that does not possess a *sefer Torah kasher* may read from a printed *Chumash* provided that the blessings are not recited. And see *P'ri Megadim* to OC 143, Eshel Avraham no. 2: "In a community too small to gather a minyan, perhaps it is proper to read from the *sefer Torah* without the accompanying *b'rachot*, so that the practice of *k'riat haTorah* not be forgotten."

32. There are others. Our colleague Rabbi David Lilienthal, of the Liberal Jewish congregation in Amsterdam, reports that his community reads from its own *pasul* "Shoah" Torah scroll on two occasions during the year: Shabbat Zakhor (Deut. 25:17–19, "Remember what Amalek did to you...") and Shabbat Shuvah (Deut. 32, *Parashat Haazinu*).

33. Here following the theory of Rambam's responsum: the reading from a *sefer Torah pasul* does fulfill the mitzvah of *k'riat haTorah*, and the reading from it on these special occasions is not to be considered an affront to the congregation's "honor."

34. On the grounds that even on these special occasions the congregation should respond to the Shoah by observing this mitzvah in the form that we generally think proper. The *pasul* scroll though used for the "additional" reading, will still leave a moving impression upon the congregation.

Sh'eilah

In an era of better and more widely available recycling resources, my congregants and I are curious as to how we might properly dispose of religious books in the twenty-first century. With so much emphasis being placed on the heightened need for us to dramatically decrease the amount of waste we throw away, we can't help but wonder if it would be more Jewishly responsible to recycle old prayer books rather than to bury them. (Rabbi William Dreskin, White Plains, New York)

T'shuvah

Concern for the environment is, without question, a profound Jewish ethical value. We Reform Jews believe that when we act to protect the cleanliness of our air and water and to preserve our natural resources we fulfill the mitzvah that warns us against the wanton destruction of our surroundings.[1] In particular, we recognize recycling as one of the most effective measures we can take to protect and replenish the natural world.[2] We ought to make every possible effort to institute programs of recycling in our homes and institutions.[3] This is certainly the case with the large quantities of paper that our synagogues and schools consume. To recycle this paper is both an act of environmental responsibility and a means by which those institutions can practice the Judaic values that they preach.

This *sh'eilah*, however, presents us with a conflict between the mitzvah of environmental stewardship and another important Jewish value: the care we take in the treatment and disposal of our sacred texts. As we shall see, Jewish tradition prohibits us from destroying written texts containing any of the *azkarot*, one of seven proper names of God. The recycling of old prayer books, which are replete with these names, would seem to transgress this prohibition. Our task, therefore, is to resolve this conflict of Jewish principles, each one making its powerful and legitimate claim upon our attention.

1. THE PROHIBITION

The Torah's prohibition (*isur*) against erasing or otherwise destroying an inscription containing the name of God is based upon Deuteronomy 12:2–3, which commands the Israelites to dismantle, burn, and destroy the altars of idolatry they would encounter in the land that they were about to inherit: "you shall destroy [the names of the foreign gods] from that place" (12:3, end). Verse 4 then instructs that "you shall not do thus [*lo taasun kein*] to Adonai your God." Although the contextual meaning (*p'shat*) of this verse seems to address the words that follow in verse 5 (namely, that the Israelites must not sacrifice to their God at the pagan holy places but do so only at the place God shall choose), the traditional halachic understanding (*d'rash*) of this verse reads it as a prohibition against erasing or destroying of God's name; that is, you are not to do to God's name that which you have just been commanded to do to the names of the idols.[4] As Maimonides formulates the law, "Whosoever effaces one of the pure and holy names of the Holy Blessed One violates a prohibition of the Torah."[5] This prohibition applies to the "seven [Hebrew] names that are never to be blotted out."[6] (It is important here to emphasize the word *Hebrew*: the prohibition does not apply to the name of God when it is translated into any other language.[7]) It applies even when these names of God are inscribed upon implements of glass or metal rather than written upon parchment or paper.[8] It applies to printed texts[9] and to texts that are produced photographically.[10] For this reason, our tradition would forbid us from recycling old or worn prayer books. We dispose of them in the same manner that we dispose of old and worn Torah scrolls: by storing them away in a *genizah* or by burying them in the ground.[11]

Some might argue that, as a matter of social concern, the mitzvah to protect the environment takes precedence for Reform Jews over the purely ritual prohibition of defacing the divine name. We categorically reject that argument. "Social" mitzvot do not always and necessarily override "ritual" ones. While ethics and social justice are central to Reform Jewish thought, they are not on that account more "important" than the ritual acts by which we worship God, celebrate the seasons of the year and of our lives, and sanctify the world around us. Holiness, the goal of Jewish life, requires both sorts of behavior; ritual acts, no less than ethical ones, play an indispensable role in the construction of our religious world. That Reform Judaism has done away with a number of ritual mitzvot is a fact of our history; it does not mean that ritual obligations must automatically yield in the face of conflicting ethical or social obligations.[12] This is rather a judgment that we must make in each specific instance. We should not discard any aspect of our religious behavior until we have carefully considered its place in our experience and the demands that it makes upon us. In the present case, the prohibition against defacing sacred texts is a mitzvah that we take in all seriousness and that retains its relevance for us. The traditional rules concerning the treatment of our sacred texts, which teach us how to find God and to live Jewishly, are as valid for us as they are for other Jews.[13] We cannot answer this question, therefore, merely by saying that the "ethical" act trumps the "ritual" one. Both are mitzvot, and we must seek another way to resolve the conflict between them.

2. EXCEPTIONS TO THE PROHIBITION

One way to do just that is to consider the exceptions that Jewish law recognizes to the prohibition against effacing *azkarot*. As we examine these exceptions, let us ask whether any of them might offer a justification for the recycling of old prayer books.

a. Indirect Causation. The Talmud records an opinion that permits one "upon whose flesh the name of God is written" to immerse in a *mikveh*, even though the water will erase the name, so long as he himself does not rub away the writing.[14] The reason is that Deuteronomy 12:4 prohibits us only from taking direct action to destroy the name of God;

the law does not forbid destruction by means of indirect causation (*g'rama*), that is, by putting the text in a place where some other factor, such as water, will erase the name. Although the leading codifiers omit this opinion,[15] the halachah does posit that activities otherwise prohibited (e.g., those involving labor on Shabbat) might be permitted when accomplished by indirect causation.[16] On this basis, some leading authorities rule that there is no prohibition against taking an action that leads indirectly to the effacement of the divine name.[17] This in turn has led at least one contemporary Israeli halachist to permit the recycling of sacred texts: since the recycling process involves a complicated chain of steps, the act of placing the texts in a recycling bin does not directly cause their destruction.[18]

To us, however, this line of thinking is not persuasive. *G'rama* is a flimsy basis upon which to justify the destruction of sacred texts.[19] As a matter of substance, we see no difference between the direct and the indirect effects of our action. We are surely responsible for any outcome that is the inevitable, planned result of our action, whether we were the immediate cause of that outcome or simply the first in a chain of causes.[20] Since, in our case, the effacement of the divine name is the inevitable and planned result of the recycling process, it makes no substantive difference that we do not efface it directly, with our own hands. By placing the books in a recycling bin, we knowingly set off a chain of events that leads inevitably to their destruction; thus, we are responsible for that outcome. If, therefore, we would refrain from destroying a sacred text with our own hands, then we should be equally reluctant to destroy it through indirect means.

b. Destruction for the Sake of Repair. It is not forbidden to erase the divine name when the goal is to correct the text. For example, should the letters of the name come into contact with each other, or should ink spill across them, it is permitted to scrape the ink from that spot; "this is a correction [*tikkun*], not an erasure."[21] Might we permit the recycling of old prayer books as a different sort of *tikkun*, as *tikkun haolam*, an act undertaken in order to "repair the world"?[22] This argument, too, falls short, because it makes the erroneous assumption that a sacred text we no longer use ought to be sacrificed to serve a "higher" purpose. As we have already suggested, we cannot say that concern for the environment necessarily outranks the reverence for sacred texts on our scale of Judaic priorities. Both of these values are exalted purposes; we have no calculus by which we can declare that one must automatically give way to the other.

c. Destruction to Save the Text from Disgrace. If neither of these two exceptions to the "no-destruction" rule offers a remedy for us, there is a third exception that does. The eighteenth-century sage R. Yaakov Reischer ruled that it is at times permissible to dispose of worn sacred texts by burning them. If a community has run out of space in which to store their rapidly accumulating texts, these might well be shoved into "filthy places" or trampled underfoot; in such a case, one is permitted to consign them to the flames as the only way to save them from contemptible, disgraceful treatment (*bizayon*).[23] While some disagree sharply with Reischer's conclusion,[24] similar considerations led two outstanding nineteenth-century authorities, R. Naftali Tzvi Y'hudah Berlin of Volozhyn[25] and R. Yitzchak Elchanan Spector of Kovno,[26] to permit Jewish printers to burn the galley proofs and spoiled pages of Bibles and prayer books. Here, too, the large quantity of these proofs and pages, the unavoidable products of the printing process, made it virtually impossible to store them away or to bury them, so that destroying them was the only sure means to protect them from *bizayon*. These scholars, we should note, were reacting to the challenges posed by the new technology of printing, which by increasing the number of sacred texts had also increased the problem of their proper disposal. At the same time, they recognized this new technology, which had made prayer books and works of Torah widely available and affordable, as a most positive contribution to the quality of Jewish spiritual and intellectual life. None of them calls upon the community to abandon the printing of sacred texts, even though such a course would have greatly reduced the number of texts that required disposal. They opted instead for a different means of disposal as the best available response to the problems associated with this new technology.

The situation we face today in our schools and synagogues is not at all dissimilar to theirs. Thanks to new technologies—in our case, photocopying and electronic publishing—we, too, produce a tremendous quantity of texts for study and worship. As did our ancestors, we regard our new technologies as a blessing, because they do much to help us fulfill the mitzvot of study (*talmud Torah*) and prayer (*t'filah*). Yet like the Jews of those days, we find that limitations on space make it virtually impossible for us to store away or to bury all of these papers once they have served their purpose. And we worry, as did they, over what will happen to these texts if we do not find some acceptable alternative means of disposing of them. *Bizayon*, the contemptible and disgraceful treatment of sacred texts, is as much a concern for us as it was for our ancestors. The very holiness of our texts demands that we treat them with respect when we use them *and* in the means we choose to dispose of them when the time comes; we do not wish to toss them into the trash heap or dump them out with the garbage. We could address the disposal problem, of course, by abandoning these new technologies so as to produce less material. But given their very real usefulness to us in our study and our worship, we are as reluctant to do that as our ancestors were reluctant to turn their backs on the printing press. Therefore, just as leading authorities could countenance the destruction of printed sacred texts in order to save them from disgraceful treatment, we can do the same with the texts that we produce by photocopying and electronic publishing. And if it is permitted to destroy these texts as a means of preserving their honor, we think that it is even more proper to recycle them, since in doing so we act to fulfill the mitzvah of environmental responsibility.

We add this caveat, however: the above reasoning applies only to texts that exist in the form of loose pages, pamphlets, or in any other way that suggests their temporary or ephemeral function in our religious activity. It does *not* apply to prayer books, *Chumashim*, and Bibles, for two reasons. The first reason is that we are willing to countenance the rapid destruction of sacred texts if and only if such disposal is required to save them from *bizayon*, disgraceful treatment. This may be the case with texts produced by copier and computer, which accumulate so rapidly that were we not to adopt this remedy, we would quickly run out of space to bury or store them. The same cannot be said about bound books, which we tend to acquire in rather fixed quantities. It is difficult to imagine that most of our congregations cannot find the means to dispose of these books in the traditional way, by burying them, by storing them away, or by donating them to other communities. The second reason has to do with the nature and function of these books. Prayer books, Bibles, and *Chumashim* are intended for our permanent or long-term use. They therefore embody a degree of *k'dushah* and lasting worth that other printed and photocopied pages do not attain. We encounter and express this *k'dushah* in the careful and reverent way that we treat—or at least ought to treat—these books. That sense of reverence and devotion testifies to the fact that these bound volumes occupy a status in our religious life quite unlike that of photocopied pages and computer printouts. These books are our constant companions in worship and study, guiding us through the yearly cycles of daily, Shabbat, and Festival observance. They symbolize in physical form the very message that their words would teach us: namely, the enduring values of human and Jewish life, that which is eternal and lasting over against that which is temporary and evanescent. Given what these books mean to us as individuals and as communities, it is inappropriate to dispose of them in the same way that we permit ourselves to dispose of more ephemeral texts.

It might be argued that burying or storing away our worn religious books is a senseless and wasteful misuse of space. It might be argued that, as long as these books no longer serve a useful purpose for us, it is better to recycle them so that they may serve the mitzvah to protect the environment. To this, we respond: yes, we *are* committed to preserving the environment. In the name of that commitment, our communities ought to recycle all their reusable waste products. Yet we are committed to other values as well. One of these is the respect we owe to our sacred books, and that value precludes us from defining our old and worn prayer books, *Chumashim*, and Bibles as "waste products." It is the essence of "sanctity" that we treat a sacred object *not* in a way that we find useful and not even in a way that, to our mind, serves some "higher" purpose. Rather, we treat that object in the manner prescribed by our tradition, the very source of knowledge and value that declares its true purpose, that defines it as "sacred" in the first place.[27] Therefore, if we can no longer use our sacred books, or if we cannot donate them to individuals or institutions that can, we should retire them as our tradition teaches us to do so, putting them away in a *genizah* or burying them in the earth. By doing this, we acknowledge their holiness as well as their usefulness. By doing this, we render them the honor they deserve. By doing this, moreover, we can teach an important lesson about the need to focus our attention upon the things in our world that are of permanent worth. And that lesson, too, in a throwaway culture such as ours, is part and parcel of our environmental ethic.

CONCLUSION

The traditional Jewish teachings concerning the proper treatment of our sacred texts continue to speak to us today. We should strive to dispose of worn sacred texts in the traditional manner, through *genizah* or burial, whenever possible.[28] We may recycle them if that is the only practical way of preserving them from disgraceful treatment, provided that these texts are intended for our temporary and ephemeral use. Prayer books, *Chumashim*, and Bibles, books that enjoy a status of permanence and *k'dushah* in our religious lives, should not be recycled; we should dispose of them by the traditionally prescribed procedures.

NOTES

1. This mitzvah, often referred to by its technical Rabbinic designation *bal tashchit*, is rooted in Deut. 20:19–20, a prohibition against destroying fruit-bearing trees as part of a military siege. The Rabbinic tradition, summarized by Maimonides in *Sefer HaMitzvot*, negative commandment no. 57, extends this prohibition to the wanton

destruction of manufactured articles such as clothing. ("Wanton" is our rendering of the Rambam's term *larik*, which might also be translated as "vain," "senseless," or "for no good purpose.") See also *Yad, M'lachim* 6:10, where Rambam numbers tools, clothing, buildings, natural springs of water, and foodstuffs among the items that may not be destroyed *derech hashchatah*, in a wanton and purely destructive manner. The "wanton" aspect of this definition is significant, in that the halachah permits us to destroy natural and manufactured items for a variety of acceptable human purposes (e.g., economic benefit and medical need; BT *Bava Kama* 91b–92a, BT *Shabbat* 105b, 128b–129a, and 140b). The fact that the prohibition seems to cover only those items that are of use to human consumption and that it is waived in numerous cases might lead us to conclude that destruction of the environment is unobjectionable so long as some human need can be cited to justify it. Yet we should remember that the protection of the environment is itself a vital "human need." Environmental pollution and wasteful consumption of natural resources portend the most serious consequences for our future on this planet; they therefore constitute a clear example of what Rambam calls "wanton" (*larik; derech hashchatah*) destruction. See also *Sefer HaChinuch*, mitzvah no. 529, which explains that destructiveness is a characteristic associated with evil; careful treatment of the world around us teaches us the habits of righteous people.

2. We refer the reader to *Too Good to Throw Away: Recycling's Proven Record*, published in 1997 by the National Resources Defense Council and available at http://www.nrdc.org/cities/recycling/recyc/recyinx.asp (accessed August 14, 2009). The report, written to counter a backlash against recycling among some conservative political and business interests, establishes beyond any serious doubt that recycling conserves natural resources, prevents pollution caused by manufacturing from virgin resources, saves energy, reduces the need for landfilling and incineration, helps protect and expand manufacturing jobs, and engenders a sense of community involvement and responsibility.

3. In its 1990 resolution entitled "Environment," the Central Conference of American Rabbis resolved to "encourage institutions, congregations, families, and individuals to take it upon themselves to recycle as much of their waste as possible" (*CCAR Yearbook* 100 [1990]: 160–61). For the text of the resolution, see http://data.ccarnet.org/cgi-bin/resodisp.pl?file=environ&year=1990.

4. BT *Makot* 22a; *Sifrei D'varim* 61:3.

5. *Yad, Y'sodei HaTorah* 6:1.

6. These are listed in BT *Sh'vuot* 35a; *Yad, Y'sodei HaTorah* 6:2; SA, YD 276:9.

7. We follow here the ruling of the *Siftei Kohein*, the great seventeenth-century commentator to the *Shulchan Aruch*: "The name of God in Hebrew is properly considered a holy name. The name of God written in any other language, however, is not a 'holy name' at all. You will understand this when you consider that it is permissible to erase a name written in some other language, such as the word *Gott* in Yiddish or German" (to *YD* 179:11). For this reason, Rabbi Yosef Dov Soloveitchik used to say that "those who write the English word 'God' in the form 'G-d' do so out of 'total ignorance' [*am haaratzut g'murah*]...since the English word 'God' is not one of the formal divine names but merely a literary device that refers to the Holy One, blessed be He" (R. Zvi Schachter, *Nefesh HaRav* [Jerusalem: Reshit Yerushalayim, 1994], 161). True, there are authorities who dispute the *Siftei Kohein* (see R. Avraham Danzig, *Chochmat Adam* 89:9) and who support the custom of writing the divine name as "G-d" (see R. Chaim Ozer Grodzinsky, twentieth-century Lithuania, *Resp. Achiezer* 3:32). We, however, following Maimonides and the other scholars we have mentioned, regard that custom as an unnecessary stringency.

8. *Yad, Y'sodei HaTorah* 6:6.

9. This issue touches upon the question whether "printing" (*hadpasah*) is the legal equivalent of writing (*k'tivah*). Some authorities who flourished during the early days of printing were of the opinion that the new technology was perfectly acceptable "for all texts that require writing" (R. Yom Tov Lipmann Heller [Moravia, sixteenth to seventeenth century], *Divrei Chamudot* on R. Asher b. Yechiel, *Halachot K'tanot, Hil. T'fillin*, chap. 8, no. 23). Others accepted printing for some texts but not for all; thus, R. Menachem Azariah of Fano, Italy (sixteenth to seventeenth century), ruled that a *get* might be printed although a Torah scroll must be written (*Responsa*, no. 93), as did R. Yair Bachrach (Germany, seventeenth century; *Resp. Chavat Yair*, no. 184). See, in general, Yitzchak Z. Kahana, *Mechkarim b'sifrut hat'shuvot* (Jerusalem: Mosad Harav Kook, 1973), 274–76. Given that most authorities require that the holiest texts (Torah scrolls, *t'fillin*, mezuzot) be written rather than printed, one might draw the conclusion that printed texts are of a lesser degree of sanctity with respect to the prohibition against destroying the divine names contained in them. Yet this conclusion has been overwhelmingly rejected. See R. Binyamin Selonik (Poland, d. 1610), *Resp. Mashat Binyamin*, no. 99–100; *Turei Zahav, YD* 271:8; R. David Zvi Hoffmann (Germany, nineteenth to twentieth century), *Resp. Melamed Leho`il, YD*, no. 89; and R. Avraham Karelitz (Israel, d. 1953), *Chazon Ish, YD*, chap. 164.

10. Some authorities seem to draw a distinction between printing and the photo-offset method of publication: the former is much more akin to "writing" than the latter. Still, "we must not be lenient with the disposal of these texts, for that would be prohibited

as the contemptible treatment of holy writings [*bizayon kitvei kodesh*]" (R. Shalom Schwadron [Galicia, nineteenth century], *Resp. Maharsham* 3:357). R. Moshe Feinstein (USA, twentieth century) notes that photocopying, though it cannot produce acceptable Torah scrolls, *t'fillin*, and mezuzot, nonetheless "performs the work of writing" because it makes the letters visible (*Resp. Ig'rot Moshe*, OC 4:40).

11. See *Reform Responsa for the Twenty-first Century*, no. 5757.4, vol. 1, pp. 83–88.

12. We have reached this conclusion several times, for example, with respect to Shabbat observance. We have said that *tzedakah* projects involving physical labor, monetary transactions, or other violations of what we consider to be proper Shabbat observance ought not to be permitted on that day. Although *tzedakah* is a great mitzvah, Shabbat is also a mitzvah, an indispensable feature of Jewish religious life. Shabbat makes legitimate demands upon our attention, and it cannot be set aside merely because its observance would tend to interfere with the performance of *tzedakah*. See *Reform Responsa for the Twenty-first Century*, no. 5757.7, vol. 1, pp. 41–48, "The Synagogue Thrift Shop and Shabbat," and no. 5756.4, vol. 1, pp. 33–40, "Presenting a Check for *Tzedakah* at Shabbat Services"; *Teshuvot for the Nineties*, no. 5755.12, pp. 165–68, "Delayed *Berit Milah* on Shabbat" ("The fact that Shabbat 'conflicts' with another *mitzvah* or worthy cause does not mean that it is *Shabbat* which must give way," and no. 5753.22, pp. 169–70, "Communal Work on Shabbat"; and *American Reform Responsa*, no. 52, pp. 53–55, "Substituting for Christians on Christmas."

13. See *Reform Responsa for the Twenty-first Century*, no. 5760.3, vol. 2, pp. 59–70 (as well as no. 5757.4, cited in note 11).

14. BT *Shabbat* 120b; the opinion, cited in a *baraita*, is that of R. Yosei.

15. *Yad, Y'sodei HaTorah* 6:6, rules that it is forbidden to immerse without covering the inscription. The *Tur* and the *Shulchan Aruch* do not address this issue at all.

16. The classic source for this rule is M. *Shabbat* 16:5 and BT *Shabbat* 120b: while it is forbidden to extinguish a fire on the Sabbath, one is permitted to place vessels containing water in the path of a fire, so that when the heat of the flames causes them to break, the water will quench the fire. See *Yad, Shabbat* 12:4–5; SA, OC 334:22; and Y. Noivirt, *Sh'mirat Shabbat K'hilchatah* 41:16–17. From this rule, most halachic opinion draws an analogy to all acts of labor (*m'lachot*) normally prohibited on Shabbat: the law does *not* forbid actions that bring about the desired effect in an indirect manner (*Mishnah B'rurah* to 334:22 in *B'ur Halachah*; R. Shaul Yisraeli in *Torah Shebal Peh* 24 [1983]: 21).

17. Among these is R. Moshe Sofer (Hungary, eighteenth to nineteenth century), *Resp. Chatam Sofer*, OC, no. 32. For a summary of opinions on both sides of the issue, see R. Chaim Chizkiah Medini (*Eretz Yisrael*, nineteenth century), *S'dei Chemed, k'lalei ha-mem*, nos. 11–12.

18. R. Shabetai Rappaport, *Alon Sh'vut* 86 (Adar, 5741/1981): 68–77. See also R. Uri Dasberg, *T'chumin* 3 (1982): 319–21.

19. As a matter of technical halachah, a number of authorities hold that the permit to cause indirectly (through *g'rama*) the destruction of a sacred text applies only to such works of Rabbinic literature that do not contain *azkarot* (e.g., Mishnah, Talmud, midrashim) but *not* to Bibles, *Chumasim*, and prayer books that do contain those names. See, for example, R. Moshe Feinstein (USA, twentieth century), *Resp. Ig'rot Moshe*, OC 4:39.

20. This, in fact, is how Professor Shalom Albeck explains the Jewish legal rule that one who causes damage through indirect means is exempt from liability. "A person is liable for damages that he brought about as the first of a chain of causes *if* he should have known that his act would inevitably result in that damage"; in other words, indirect causation is exempt from liability only when no actual negligence is involved. See *Pesher Dinei Nezikin Batalmud* (Tel Aviv: Devir, 1965), 44. We think that the same should apply in other areas of the law: one should not be absolved from responsibility for the indirect results of one's action if one should have known that the action would lead to that result.

21. *SA, YD* 276:11. See Tractate *Sof'rim* 5:7.

22. This is not the place to chart the history of the term *tikkun haolam* in Jewish practice. Suffice it to say that the term serves in Mishnaic halachah as a justification for Rabbinic legislative enactments designed to correct abuses in the law, i.e., instances where the literal application of the Toraitic legal standard would lead to a socially undesirable result (see especially *Mishnah Gittin*, chaps. 4 and 5). The contemporary use of the term as a synonym for "social action" is related to, though not identical with, its original usage.

23. *Resp. Sh'vut Yaakov* 3:10.

24. R. Yechezkel Katznelbogen (Germany, eighteenth century), *Resp. K'neset Yechezkel*, YD, no. 37; R. Shaul Nathanson (Galicia, nineteenth century), *Resp. Sho'el Umeshiv*, v. 3, part 2, no. 15.

25. *Resp. Meshiv Davar* 2:80.

26. *Resp. Ein Yitzchak* nos. 5–7.

27. See *Reform Responsa for the Twenty-first Century*, no. 5757.4, vol. 1, pp. 83–88.

28. One member of our Committee suggests that when we print or reproduce sacred texts, we should attempt to substitute *kinuyim*, traditional substitutes for the divine name (such as the letter *hei* for the Tetragrammaton) so as to avoid the necessity of destroying texts that contain *azkarot*. We repeat here that *azkarot* are the seven specified *Hebrew* names of God and that this category does not include any of the renderings of God's name in any other language; see note 7, above.

A Convert's Hebrew Name

5760.6

Sh'eilah

A Jew-by-choice in my community does not wish to accept the customary Hebrew name *bat Avraham avinu v'Sarah imeinu*. She objects to this name for two reasons. First, since the name advertises her status as a convert, she finds it to be embarrassing and thus a possible violation of the rule that one is not to remind a *ger/giyoret* of his/her past. Second, this name ignores the identity of her actual parents, who though they do not join her in conversion nonetheless have raised her and loved her from birth. She wants her Hebrew name to include the names of her parents. Is this permissible? If so, should we find Hebrew equivalents for her parents' names? (Rabbi Gerald Raiskin, Burlingame, California)

T'shuvah

1. THE CONVERT'S NAME IN JEWISH TRADITION

By long-standing practice, we refer to the Jew-by-choice as "the son/daughter of Abraham our father" (*ben/bat Avraham avinu*).[1] R. Yosef Karo, who mentions this practice in his *Shulchan Aruch*,[2] identifies as its source a responsum of R. Asher b. Yechiel (thirteenth- to fourteenth-century Germany and Spain).[3] R. Asher tells us that the *ger* (convert) is called "the son of Abraham" because Abraham is called "the father of many nations" (Gen. 17:4–5). This suggests a Talmudic debate concerning the mitzvah of *bikurim*, or "first fruits." The Torah instructs that an offering of the "first fruits" of the harvest be brought to Jerusalem, to the priest in authority in those days, and that the person who brings the offering recite a "confession" (*vidui*), a litany expressing our gratitude for having been brought forth from Egypt and for having inherited a "land flowing with milk and honey" (Deut. 26:1–11). The question:

does a convert recite this confession when he brings his *bikurim* to the Temple? The Mishnah answers "no": the *ger* may not recite the *vidui* because, as his ancestors were not Jewish and did not inherit the Land of Israel, he cannot truthfully give thanks for "the land that God swore to our ancestors to give to us" (Deut. 26:3).[4] The *Talmud Y'rushalmi*, however, cites the conflicting view of Rabbi Y'hudah: the *ger* does recite the confession, because Abraham, "the father of many nations," is the spiritual ancestor of converts as well as of born Jews.[5]

How does the halachic tradition decide between these conflicting interpretations? Some authorities follow the Mishnah and even extend its rule, declaring that a convert cannot lead either the *Birkat HaMazon* (Blessing after Meals) or the synagogue service (i.e., as *sh'liach tzibur*) because those liturgies, too, contain words that seem to exclude the *ger*.[6] Yet over time, the *Y'rushalmi*'s more inclusive view came to predominate.[7] A proselyte may therefore lead the worship service and recite any portion of the liturgy that speaks of "*our* ancestors," because they are his or her ancestors as well.[8]

This insight has never been communicated so clearly and forcefully as by Maimonides, in a *t'shuvah* to a Jew-by-choice named Ovadyah:

> You ask whether you may recite privately and publicly the words "our God and the God of our ancestors," "who has sanctified us by the mitzvot and commanded us," "who has chosen us," "who performed miracles for our ancestors," and similar statements in the liturgy. You may recite them all; you are not to change any of the wording; you are to recite the blessings and prayers according to the same formulae used by born Jews.... The essential point is that our father Abraham taught Judaism, the faith in the one God, and the rejection of idolatry to all the people, bringing many under the wings of the Divine Presence.... Therefore, whosoever converts to Judaism, from now until the end of time... is a disciple of our father Abraham... the father of every proselyte.... There is no difference between us and you in any of these matters.[9]

The *ger*, in other words, is called *ben Avraham avinu* in order to proclaim that he is one of us and part of our family, to affirm that the Jew-by-choice and the Jew-by-birth enjoy the same religious status in the eyes of God and of the Jewish people.[10]

2. THE CONVERT'S NAME: A SOURCE OF EMBARRASSMENT?

According to our tradition, therefore, the name *ben/bat Avraham v'Sarah* is a powerful symbol of inclusion, of the proselyte's full and equal membership in the covenant of Israel. How disappointing, then, that for the person mentioned in our *sh'eilah* the name has become a cause of discomfort. Does the embarrassment she feels warrant the changing of her name? It is true that the Torah warns us not to oppress the *ger* (Lev. 19:33) and that the tradition understands this oppression as *onaat d'varim*, "verbal embarrassment": that is, we must not scorn the proselyte by mentioning his or her gentile origins.[11] Yet this prohibition has always referred to the gratuitous insult, the conscious, intentional attempt to shame.[12] It has never been understood as an argument for changing the proselyte's traditional name, nor could it be, since to ascribe a person's spiritual lineage to Abraham and Sarah is among the highest compliments we can pay him or her. We are indeed forbidden to embarrass the Jew-by-choice, but to call him or her "the child of Abraham and Sarah," however, is most definitely *not* a matter of embarrassment or shame.

One could respond, of course, that shame is in the eye of the beholder, that this Jew-by-choice would feel a sense of embarrassment when her Jewish name is read in synagogue, and that she is therefore entitled to alter that name. Yet such a course, we think, is precisely the wrong solution for her problem. While we do not question the sincerity of her feelings, we suspect that her embarrassment has less to do with her Jewish name than with some unresolved doubts she may still harbor over her decision to convert and its effect upon the members of her family. If so, then our response should be a pastoral one. Her rabbi should work with her to help resolve the tensions associated with that choice.

Alternately, her embarrassment may be rooted in external factors; perhaps the community has not been as welcoming and as accepting of her as it could and should be. If so, the proper response is again a pastoral one. The rabbi should work with the community to explore why this is happening and to remind them of our duty to love the Jew-by-choice as one of our own.[13] Altering the name, by contrast, does nothing to help her confront these issues. It merely allows her to hide the fact of her conversion, an act that contributes in no way to her healthy adjustment to her Jewish status. It is an act, moreover, that has the most negative connotations for us as Jews and particularly as Reform Jews, members of a movement that is committed to outreach and to the full inclusion of the Jew-by-choice in our community. We do not believe that conversion is something to hide, a source of embarrassment. We believe, rather, as tradition teaches us, that the name *ben/bat Avraham avinu v'Sarah imeinu* is a badge of honor and respect, bestowed with love and admiration, a badge that ought to be worn with satisfaction and pride.

3. THE JEW-BY-CHOICE AND HER PARENTS

May the Jew-by-choice replace *Avraham* and *Sarah* with the names of his or her actual parents, even though they remain non-Jews? It is true that the proselyte is obligated to render honor to his or her parents as an expression of love and of gratitude for all they have done to raise, care for, and educate their child.[14] Yet this duty does not touch upon the question of name. The "Hebrew name" by which one is called in synagogue is more appropriately called a *Jewish* name.[15] It is a *covenantal* name, a declaration that the one who bears it is a member of the community that stood at Sinai to receive the Torah. In this covenantal name, the names of one's parents do not testify simply to one's biological lineage. Rather, they register the fact that it was through these parents that this person was brought into the *b'rit* (covenant) between God and Israel. The parents of this Jew-by-choice surely gave her love and care and taught her many of the values by which she lives. But they did not teach her Torah; they did not bring her into the covenant. As an adult,[16] this is a decision she made on her own, and for that reason her *covenantal* parents, the ones from whom she legitimately claims her Jewish descent, are Abraham and Sarah, who we are told brought many seekers like her under the wings of God's presence.[17]

CONCLUSION

When a person chooses to become a Jew, he or she receives the name *ben/bat Avraham avinu v'Sarah imeinu*, signifying that he or she is one of us and at one with us, a full partner in the community of Israel and its covenant with God. It is an important statement of our religious belief, of our understanding of the meaning of conversion and of the Jewish experience. It is a mark of respect and honor. It is not a cause for embarrassment, nor is it a sign that the proselyte has broken ties with his or her gentile family. Any and all difficulties that the Jew-by-choice encounters upon joining our people should be faced squarely and seriously, but it would be a serious mistake to try to address those problems through altering his or her Jewish name.

NOTES

1. The addition of "and Sarah our mother"—*v'Sarah imeinu*—is an innovation of recent decades. Nonetheless, support for this innovation may be found in *Tosafot, Chagigah* 9b, s.v. *bar*: Bar He He was, according to some opinions, a convert, "that is, the son of Abraham and Sarah, for whom the Hebrew letter *hei* was appended to his name."

2. *SA, EHE* 129:20. The issue there is the correct name for a *ger* in his bill of divorce (*get*).

3. *Resp. HaRosh* 15:4. Karo provides this identification in his longer work, the *Beit Yosef* to *Tur, EHE* 129 (in the section *Hil. Gittin*, fol. 29b, near the end of the first column).

4. *M. Bikurim* 1:4 and Bartenura ad loc. See also *Sifrei D'varim*, chap. 299.

5. JT *Bikurim* 1:4 (64a), and see Bartenura to *M. Bikurim* 1:4. Compare as well Maimonides, *Commentary* to *M. Bikurim* 1:4: Abraham taught faith in God to the world and is thus the father of all.

6. The second blessing of *Birkat HaMazon* contains the words "You have bequeathed to our ancestors a good land...," and the first benediction of the *T'filah*, the central prayer of the worship service, reads "our God and God of our ancestors." The authorities include Rabbeinu Tam (*Tosafot, Bava Batra* 81a, s.v. *lema`utei*), the *Or Zarua, Hil. T'filah*, chap. 107, and the rabbis of medieval Würzburg, Germany, who prevented converts from serving as worship leaders (*Mordechai, M'gillah*, chap. 786).

7. *Yad, Bikurim* 4:3. The *Y'rushalmi* itself goes out of its way to reject the position enunciated in the Mishnah, citing a teaching by R. Y'hoshua b. Levi that the halachah follows Rabbi Y'hudah and a ruling to that effect by R. Abahu in an actual case (involving prayer, it would seem, since *bikurim* were no longer offered at that time).

8. See *SA, OC* 53:19: the view that the *ger* may not serve as *sh'liach tzibur* has been "rejected." Among those who take this position are R. Yitzchak of Dampierre (*Tosafot, Bava Batra* 81a, s.v. *lema`utei*); Nachmanides (*Chidushei HaRamban* to *Bava Batra* 81a); R. Sh'lomo b. Adret (*Chidushei HaRashba* to *Bava Batra* 81a); R. Yom Tov ibn Ishbili (*Chidushei HaRitva, Makot* 19a); R. Nissim Gerondi (*Chidushei HaRan, Bava Batra* 81a).

9. *Resp. HaRambam*, ed. Blau, no. 293 (no. 42 in the Friedman edition). In this responsum, Rambam repeats the decision reported in his *Commentary* to M. *Bikurim* 1:4: the halachah does not follow the Mishnah but rather the ruling of the *Talmud Y'rushalmi*.

10. See R. Ben Zion Meir Hai Ouziel, *Resp. Mishp'tei Ouziel* II, YD, no. 59: the name *ben Avraham avinu* functions to establish the halachic ruling (*l'horot*) that the proselyte is entitled "to lead the prayer service and the *Birkat HaMazon*, to say 'our God and God of our ancestors' and 'we thank you O God for having bequeathed a good land to our ancestors.'"

11. BT *Bava M'tzia* 58b–59a; *Yad, M'chirah* 14:12–13; *SA, CM* 228:1–4.

12. Examples (see the sources cited in the preceding note): "see how one who once ate impure things seeks to fill his mouth with words of Torah!"; "remember the deeds [i.e., the idolatry] of your ancestors."

13. Deut. 10:19; *Yad, Dei-ot* 6:4.

14. See BT *Y'vamot* 22a: although considered in principle a "newborn child," a *ger* must not ignore those moral duties that he or she observed as a non-Jew, "lest it be said that [the *ger*] has descended from a higher degree of holiness to a lower one" (*Yad, Mamrim* 5:11; *SA, YD* 241:9). On the nature of the mitzvah to honor one's parents as

an expression of gratitude for their having raised and cared for the child, see *Teshuvot for the Nineties*, no. 5753.12, pp. 201–7.

15. See, for example, the service for *b'rit milah* and the covenant service for a daughter in the CCAR *Rabbi's Manual* (1988), pp. 12 and 21 respectively: the child's name is bestowed by the formula *v'yikarei sh'mo/sh'mah b'Yisrael*, "his/her name in Israel shall be...." See as well at p. 208, the service for conversion: "and from this time forth you shall be known in the Jewish community as _____ Ben/Bat Avraham veSara."

16. This is an important distinction: if a minor child converts along with the parent(s), the child may be called the son or daughter of the parent(s), since it is the latter who actually teach Torah to the child. See the responsum of R. Ouziel cited in note 10, and R. Gedalyah Felder, *Sefer Nachalat Tzvi* (Toronto, 1978), 1:124–25. This is not the case in our *sh'eilah*, which deals with an adult proselyte who did not learn Judaism from her parents.

17. See *B'reishit Rabbah* 39:14 and Rashi to Gen. 12:5, on "all the souls they had gotten in Haran": to bring people to Judaism is equivalent to creating them, to giving them life.

Sh'eilah

A woman has asked a congregational rabbi to sponsor and guide her through the conversion process. After a thorough initial interview, the rabbi discovers that her husband, a Roman Catholic, has no intention of converting to Judaism along with her. Although the rabbi judges her character and motives to be sincere in every way, he cannot agree to be her sponsor because her conversion will result in an interfaith marriage. If she were single or married to a Jew, there would be no question of her qualifications as a potential Jew-by-choice. Should this woman's love of Judaism and her sincere desire to convert be impacted by the religious identity of her partner? If an interfaith marriage is the result of this conversion, is the sponsoring rabbi held responsible? (Kathy Kahn, UAHC Commission on Outreach)

T'shuvah

Should we accept for conversion a married person whose gentile spouse does not share the desire to become a Jew? Orthodox rabbis would likely respond in the negative. The conversion of one spouse would create a mixed marriage, which is prohibited under Jewish law.[1] Orthodox halachists would interpret the potential convert's desire to remain in what would become a mixed marriage as a lack of commitment on his or her part to "accept the mitzvot" and to live a fully Jewish life; such a lack of commitment is a serious impediment to the acceptance of a conversion and to its subsequent validity.[2] Even those authorities who are generally lenient with regard to accepting proselytes would presumably reject *this* conversion.[3]

Should we Reform rabbis respond in the same way? On the one hand, we certainly view the phenomenon of mixed marriage as a matter of deep

concern, in that it calls into question the Jewishness of home and family
life and the very survival of the Jewish people. We teach that "it is a
mitzvah for a Jew to marry a Jew so that the sacred heritage of Judaism
may be transmitted most effectively from generation to generation."[4]
Our Conference has formally declared "its opposition to participation
by its members in any ceremony which solemnizes a mixed marriage."[5]
Even though many of our members will, under certain circumstances,
officiate at ceremonies of mixed marriage,[6] they do so not to lend Jewish
religious sanction to those unions but rather in the hope that their act
might increase the possibility that the couple will create a Jewish life
for themselves and for their children. Even though we do our utmost to
reach out to religiously mixed couples and their families and even though
we want them to feel fully at home in our synagogues, we do not see
mixed marriage as a proper *religious* choice for a Jew. Given this stance,
it might be argued that we should deny this woman the opportunity to
convert to Judaism, on the grounds that converting her would create a
mixed marriage in this case and give the impression that we condone
mixed marriage in general.

Yet there is another side to this argument. In presiding over this
conversion, the rabbi and the *beit din* do not "create" a mixed marriage.
The couple are already married to each other in the eyes of the state,
and the conversion does nothing to affect that status in either Jewish or
civil law. The ritual of conversion (*giyur*) is emphatically *not* a wedding
or some other "ceremony which solemnizes a mixed marriage." Nor
does the conversion signal that we somehow "condone" mixed marriage.
Although a mixed marriage will be the result of the conversion, it is not
its *intended* result, the goal or purposeful outcome of the action of the
beit din. The *giyur* centers not upon the couple—indeed, the husband is
not a participant in the ceremony—but upon the individual who chooses
Judaism. It concerns itself with her, with the motivations that have led
her to Judaism and with her readiness to enter the covenant of God and
Israel. Far from condoning mixed marriage, the conversion does not
address that subject at all; it does not alter in the least our teaching that
"it is a mitzvah for a Jew to marry a Jew."

The new Jew-by-choice, it is true, will be living in a situation in which she does not fulfill the mitzvah of Jewish marriage. This fact, however, is not a sufficient cause to deny her request to become a Jew. We do not demand of a *ger* or *giyoret* that he or she observe "all" the mitzvot (however we understand that term) as a condition for conversion. For that matter, it is far from certain that even the traditional halachah makes that demand.[7] This person, to be sure, has come to Judaism at a time and from a place in her life that present special challenges to her as she undertakes to "find satisfaction and joy in the fulfillment of Your sacred *mitzvot*."[8] Yet each of us, it must be said, travels a unique path to Jewish commitment. All of us struggle to overcome the obstacles that stand in our way to a more complete Jewish life. None of us is perfect (however we understand *that* term) in his or her Jewish observance, and we do not require perfection from this proselyte. All we ask of her—and this is no little thing—is that she make a sincere and informed decision to adopt the Jewish faith as her exclusive religious expression and that she identify her fate and destiny with that of the people of Israel.[9] Who are we, who do not know this person, to say that she has *not* made such a commitment? Who are we to say that she is not one of those who, according to our aggadic tradition, has come to discover that she, too, stood at Sinai and entered the covenant?[10]

How do we determine whether this person is in fact fully and sincerely prepared to accept the faith of Israel and to join the Jewish people? That decision, our sources teach, is left to the judgment of the local rabbi.[11] Our point is simply that, given that her motives are "sincere in every way," the fact that this woman's husband will remain a gentile does not constitute in and of itself a reason for us to turn her away. The rabbi, we think, is entitled to accept her as a Jew-by-choice.

At the same time, however, it should be abundantly clear that the rabbi is not *required* to accept her. We say this because, though her marriage does not automatically disqualify her from conversion, it most certainly signals the rabbi to proceed with caution. Again, we emphasize that we do not know this person and that we have no reason to doubt the sincerity of her decision. Yet we cannot overlook the fact that a conversion in a case such as this creates a mixed-religion household, and this raises serious questions as to the capacity of even the most devoted proselyte to construct a Jewish life. Our ceremony for *giyur* requires that the Jew-by-choice answer "yes" to the following, among other questions: "Do you promise to establish a Jewish home?" and "If you should be blessed with children, do you promise to raise them as Jews?"[12] Even with the best of intentions, a proselyte whose spouse remains a gentile will face enormous difficulties in achieving these goals. For example, does the spouse identify strongly with his or her own religion? A household in which some other religion is practiced on an equal basis with Judaism cannot be called a "Jewish" home in any plausible sense of that term. If children are born to the couple after one of them converts, does the gentile spouse support him or her in raising those children *exclusively* as Jews? Children raised in more than one religious identity do not qualify for Jewish status under the CCAR's Resolution on Patrilineal Descent.[13] All of this testifies to the fact that Judaism is not simply a matter of personal spirituality, restricted to the worship service. Judaism is a complete and all-encompassing religious way of life; it must be practiced in the home as well as in the synagogue, in the family as well as in the heart. No matter how sincere a potential convert's personal commitment to the Jewish faith, he or she is not yet ready to become a Jew unless that commitment is realized in the arena of home and family life. It is up to the rabbi to determine that such is the case.

Finally, we must raise the issue of the stability of the marriage and the family relationship. A decision to choose Judaism is a life-transforming event, a matter of ultimate seriousness. From this point forward, the Jew-by-choice is committed to new patterns of worship, of ritual behavior, and of personal consciousness. "The proselyte," we are taught, "is like a new-born child";[14] making a significant break with all that is past, he or she from now on seeks religious fulfillment as a member of the community of Israel. What does this transformation do to the spouse who does not join in it? How will it alter the common fabric of the marriage? Does it reflect a separation between the couple, a coming apart? As a matter of pastoral responsibility, the rabbi must inquire as to the psychological sources of this decision and as to its effects upon the marriage and the household.

CONCLUSION

A person who wishes to become a Jew should not be rejected merely because his or her spouse will remain a gentile. In dealing with conversion, our primary responsibility is toward the individual proselyte. If the rabbi determines, through careful examination, that the decision to convert is "sincere in every way," then he or she may be accepted as a Jew-by-choice. On the other hand, the spouse's decision not to become a Jew may be an indication of serious obstacles to the proselyte's creation of a Jewish life and of problems in the marriage. The rabbi must be satisfied that these difficulties are *not* serious before proceeding with *giyur*. In any event, both the rabbi and the prospective proselyte are well advised to proceed slowly, deliberately, and with all caution. No arbitrary time limit can or should be set. Let them rather take all the time they need to determine whether this decision is the right one, both for the Jew-by-choice and for the Jewish people.

NOTES

1. The prohibition is derived from Deut. 2:13; see BT *Kiddushin* 68b. Another possible source is Deut. 7:3, which ostensibly forbids marriage only with members of the seven Canaanite nations. Maimonides, however, reads the prohibition as covering all gentiles; see *Yad, Isurei Biah* 12:1.

2. On the requirement that the *ger/giyoret* accept the mitzvot (*kabbalat hamitzvot*), see BT *Y'vamot* 47a–b; *Yad, Isurei Biah* 13:4 (where he speaks of accepting the yoke of the Torah); *SA, YD* 268:3. That this acceptance must be complete, without any reservations whatsoever, is indicated in BT *B'chorot* 30b: a gentile who comes to accept the Torah except for one precept is not accepted for conversion. Although this statement is not codified in either the *Mishneh Torah* or the *Shulchan Aruch*, it does reflect the thrust of contemporary Orthodox halachic opinion, which suggests that the proselyte's failure to observe *all* the commandments is retroactive evidence that the conversion was null and void *ab initio*. See, for example, R. Avraham Yitzchak HaKohein Kook, *Resp. Daat*

Kohein, nos. 154–55, and R. Yitzchak Halevy Herzog, *Resp. Heichal Yitzchak, EHE* 1:1, nos. 19–21. Yet not all Orthodox halachists take this position; see at note 7, below.

3. A case in point is R. Ben Zion Ouziel, *Resp. Mishp'tei Ouziel, EHE* 18. In this *t'shuvah,* he demonstrates his generally lenient approach by accepting conversion for the sake of marriage, even though this is generally considered an improper motivation for conversion, on the grounds that this step is necessary to combat the plague of mixed marriage that afflicts the Jewish community. In the same responsum, however, he addresses a second question: is it permissible to convert a gentile woman who is already married to a *kohein?* Here his answer is no: since a *kohein* is prohibited to marry a proselyte (*giyoret*), to convert this woman would mean that he would transgress that prohibition. R. Ouziel says this, even though the *kohein* is already violating the prohibition against intermarriage. Based on his reasoning, it seems clear that he would also rule strictly in our case, in which a conversion would lead to a transgression (intermarriage) in a place where, at the moment, no transgression exists.

4. *Gates of Mitzvah,* ed. Simeon J. Maslin (New York: CCAR Press, 1979), 36. And on page 37: Judaism resists mixed marriage because it weakens the fabric of family relationship and the survival potential of the Jewish community, and because it makes it more difficult to establish the *mikdash m'at* that should be the goal of every Jewish marriage.

5. See *CCAR Yearbook* 83 (1973): 97, for the text of the resolution. An expansive argument on behalf of the resolution is found in *American Reform Responsa,* no. 149.

6. As indicated in the second paragraph of the resolution cited in note 5.

7. See note 2. Although the preponderance of contemporary Orthodox opinion requires that the proselyte accept "all" the mitzvot—which is tantamount in their eyes to a requirement that he or she become an Orthodox Jew—some authorities hold otherwise. Some understand the requirement of *kabbalat hamitzvot* as the *ger/giyoret's* self-imposed obligation to undergo circumcision and/or immersion before a *beit din* (*Chidushei HaRamban, Y'vamot* 46b; R. Meir Posner, *Resp. Beit Meir,* no. 12). Others see it as a general commitment "to forsake his people and its gods, to take refuge beneath the wings of the *Shechinah,* to accept the religion of Israel, and to enter the Jewish community" (R. Sh'lomo Lifschitz [eighteenth- to nineteenth-century Poland], *Resp. Chemdat Sh'lomo, YD* 29:22–23). R. Ben Zion Ouziel sees *kabbalat hamitzvot* primarily as the proselyte's acceptance of the obligation to keep the mitzvot; this acceptance is valid even if we know in advance that he or she will *not* observe them (*Resp. Mishp'tei Ouziel* II, *YD* 1:58). In other words, the *giyur* "takes" even though the proselyte does not live a thoroughly "Orthodox" lifestyle following the conversion. On

all this in detail, see Zvi Zohar and Avraham Sagi, *Giyur Uzehut Yehudit* (Jerusalem: Mosad Bialik, 1997), 171ff.

8. *Rabbi's Manual* (New York: CCAR, 1988), 200, from the "*Giyur* Service in the Synagogue."

9. See BT *Y'vamot* 47a, the *ger*'s declaration of his readiness to accept the vicissitudes of Jewish existence; and see Rashi ad loc., s.v. *v'eini k'dai*.

10. The teaching that all future converts were virtually present at Sinai, a midrash on Deut. 29:14, is found in BT *Shabbat* 146a.

11. In matters of conversion, "everything is left to the judgment of the court" (R. Yosef Karo, *Beit Yosef*, YD 268, based upon *Tosafot*, *Y'vamot* 24b, s.v. *lo*).

12. *Rabbi's Manual*, 201.

13. The text of the resolution itself (see *Rabbi's Manual*, 226) speaks of the performance of "timely public and formal acts of identification with the Jewish faith and people"; these are "mitzvot leading toward a positive and *exclusive* Jewish identity" (emphasis added). See also *Teshuvot for the Nineties*, no. 5755.17, pp. 251–58; *Questions and Reform Jewish Answers*, no. 109; and *Contemporary American Reform Responsa*, no. 61.

13. BT *Y'vamot* 22a and parallels.

Sh'eilah

A woman came to me for the purposes of conversion and told me that she is in the United States illegally. Am I obligated to treat her like any other potential proselyte (with an open heart), or would it be against our Jewish tradition to work with someone who I knew was here illegally? (Rabbi Michelle Missaghieh, Los Angeles, California)

T'shuvah

In framing an answer to this question, we draw guidance from two principles of Jewish tradition. The first of these may be summarized by Deuteronomy 10:19: "You shall love the *ger*, for you were *gerim* in the land of Egypt." The second is expressed by the halachic principle that, in matters of conversion, "the decision is left to the discretion of the court."[1]

1

It would be a sad irony were we to reject this potential Jew-by-choice on the grounds that she is an illegal immigrant. The word *ger*, which we translate as "proselyte," in biblical times carried the meaning of "resident alien,"[2] the "stranger" or foreigner who dwelled alongside the Israelite community but was not *of* the community.[3] The biblical connotation of the word has never disappeared from the Hebrew language.[4] Thus, when the Torah notes that we were once *gerim* in a foreign land, it reminds us that we once shared the fate and experience of the individual in question here. As the Torah puts it, we "know the soul of the stranger" (Exod. 23:9); we of all people must not subject her to the sort of oppression and injustice that was once our lot (Lev. 19:34 and Exod. 22:20). Indeed, the *mitzvah* to love and to care for the stranger lies at the root of our Reform Jewish commitment to social justice.[5] And a fundamental aspect of this commitment has been our demand that the immigrant—the *ger*—receive fair and ethical treatment in our society.[6]

For these reasons, one's status as an illegal immigrant should not in and of itself disqualify him or her from conversion to Judaism. Why would we think otherwise? True, this individual has violated the laws of the United States by residing in the country without the proper legal permit. The government of the United States is entitled to prosecute or deport her, both according to its own law *and* according to Jewish law: under the principle *dina d'malchuta dina*, Jewish law accepts the validity of all legislation that pertains to the legitimate rights and powers of the civil government, and it is clear that a state enjoys the right to control its borders and to regulate matters of immigration and citizenship.[7] Yet while a government may set and enforce such laws (provided that it do so in a fair and equitable manner), this enforcement is a matter for the state and not for religious communities. On the contrary, we have always held that *dina d'malchuta dina* applies only to the area of monetary law (*dinei mamonot*) and that it has no bearing upon matters of ritual practice (*isur v'heter*).[8] Conversion to Judaism is just such a "ritual" matter, properly the concern of the Jewish people and not of the United States government. Obviously, the rabbi and the congregation will want to consult with an attorney knowledgeable in the area of immigration law in order to determine their legal responsibilities in this case. But from the standpoint of Jewish law and tradition, this woman's immigration status does not bar her from entering our community. When we look at her, we do not see an "illegal immigrant"; we see a stranger, a reflection of our own history. She has every right to seek to join us and to take refuge "under the wings of the *Shechinah*."[9]

2

At the same time, the decision in any particular case of conversion is left to the discretion of the supervising rabbi. This authority has traditionally exerted a lenient influence upon the law, empowering rabbis to accept proselytes in cases where the circumstances might have argued for rejection.[10] Yet it also allows the rabbi to say "no" when, in his or her considered judgment, an apparently valid request for conversion is hasty, not well thought out, or based upon improper motivations. Conversion, we should remember, is an *institution*, an aspect of organized community life, and not simply a personal and private religious concern. As we have written before:

> Conversion... is not a decision left to the heart and mind of the proselyte but a formal and public matter. One who seeks to convert seeks to join our community as a full and participating "citizen" thereof. It is accordingly for the Jewish community, acting through its acknowledged rabbinical representatives, to determine in each and every case whether an individual who wishes to convert is in fact ready to do so, for reasons that we find persuasive and compelling.[11]

As we have said, the rabbi should not turn this woman away simply *because* she is an illegal immigrant. On the other hand, it is the rabbi's task to inquire as to the reasons that motivate an individual to seek conversion,[12] and it is reasonable to presume that this individual's immigration status is a factor, an aspect of her life story, that must be explored. Indeed, it would be irresponsible for the rabbi *not* to explore it. Such an inquiry might lead the rabbi to conclude that the status issue functions as an improper or unacceptable influence in the decision to convert; perhaps this person believes that conversion will improve her prospects for remaining in the country. Similarly, the rabbi might find that the individual's immigration status is an element or a symptom of a deeper issue that, in the rabbi's opinion, augurs against conversion. The members of this Committee do not and cannot know, of course, whether such possibilities apply in this particular case; if, however, they do apply, then the rabbi may properly decide that "no" or "not yet" is the best response to this request for conversion.

CONCLUSION

The fact that one is an illegal immigrant does not constitute valid, objective grounds for denying his or her request to become a Jew. Yet immigration status can be one important factor in the rabbi's inquiry into a candidate's readiness to take the fateful step of joining the Jewish people. The decision, in all cases, lies within the rabbi's discretion. If this individual is accepted for conversion, the rabbi should certainly counsel and assist her in resolving her immigration status as soon as possible. The mitzvah to love the *ger* implies a duty to help her relieve her distress: we do not want her to remain in violation of the laws of the United States. Whatever the rabbi's course of action, we trust that it will be undertaken with perception, sensitivity and, as our *sho-elet* puts it, with an open heart.

NOTES

1. *Hakol l'fi r'ut einei habeit din*; R. Yosef Karo, *Beit Yosef* to *Tur*, YD 268, and R. Shabetai Kohein, *Siftei Kohein* to SA, YD 268:23.

2. The *Targum* of Onkelos preserves this bivalence. In each of the verses cited above, the *ger* whom we are required to love or forbidden to oppress is rendered as *giyora*, "proselyte," while the word *gerim* as a description of our status in Egypt is translated as *dayarin*, "temporary residents."

3. See Bernard J. Bamberger, *Proselytism in the Talmudic Period* (New York: Ktav, 1968), 16: "In the Bible the word *ger* means a foreign resident in Palestine. It is frequently joined by 'and' to the word *toshab*, meaning the same thing, and usually translated 'sojourner.'" See also his comment to Lev. 19:34 in W. Gunther Plaut, *The Torah: A Modern Commentary* (New York: UAHC Press, 1981), 899. On the legal distinctions between the *ger* and the native-born Israelite (*ezrach*), see Moshe Weinfeld, *Deuteronomy and the Deuteronomic School* (London: Oxford University Press, 1972), 229–32; and Jacob Milgrom, "Religious Conversion and the Revolt Model for the Formation of Israel," *Journal of Biblical Literature* 101, no. 2 (1982): 169–76. See also Milgrom's remarks in *The JPS Torah Commentary: Numbers* (Philadelphia: The Jewish Publication Society, 1990), Excursus 34, 398–402.

4. See, for example, Rashi to Exodus 22:20: "The word *ger* refers to a person who was not born in that particular community but came from another community to dwell [*lagur*] there."

5. For example, the obligation to protect the *ger* is cited in support of the CCAR's "Statement on Our Economic Commitment to America's Poor," *CCAR Yearbook* 105–6 (1997): 326–27; its resolution on "Sweatshops and Child Labor," *CCAR Yearbook* 107 (1998): 78–79; and others.

6. In 1997, citing Exod. 22:20 ("You shall not wrong a stranger or oppress him, for you were strangers in the land of Egypt"), the Central Conference of American Rabbis called upon the United States Congress not to reduce welfare benefits to immigrant families and to facilitate their acquisition of citizenship. In addition, the resolution urged Reform congregations to undertake efforts to provide vital services to immigrants, including those immigrants who for one reason or another are unable to attain citizenship. See *CCAR Yearbook* 107 (1998): 65–67.

7. On the subject of *dina d'malchuta dina*, see *Reform Responsa for the Twenty-first Century*, no. 5757.1, vol. 1, pp. 347–56.

8. On the conditions for and limitations upon the principle *dina d'malchuta dina*, see ibid. at notes 13–15.

9. See BT *Shabbat* 31a, the statement of the three proselytes: "Shammai's strictness would have expelled us, but Hillel's patience brought us under the wings of God's presence."

10. See *Tosafot*, *Y'vamot* 24b, s.v. *lo*, referring to the decisions by Hillel (BT *Shabbat* 31a) and Rabbi Chiya (BT *M'nachot* 44a) to accept proselytes whose motivations to become Jewish were not considered to be religiously sincere. In each case, the rabbi believed that the individual would one day be a good Jew (*sofo laasot l'shem shamayim*) and was therefore "worth the risk."

11. *Reform Responsa for the Twenty-first Century*, no. 5758.7, vol. 1, pp. 129–37. See also no. 5760.5, vol. 2, pp. 93–99, at the conclusion: "A person who wishes to become a Jew should not be rejected merely because his or her spouse will remain a gentile.... On the other hand, the spouse's decision not to become a Jew may be an indication of serious obstacles to the proselyte's creation of a Jewish life and of problems in the marriage. The rabbi must be satisfied that these difficulties are *not* serious before proceeding with *giyur*."

12. *SA*, *YD* 268:12: when a prospective *ger* or *giyoret* comes before us, we examine him or her to determine whether the motivation for the conversion is religiously sincere and—in our eyes—acceptable.

Sh'eilah

Our congregation has a policy that children who have not received the standard immunizations will not be admitted into our religious school. Recently, this policy has been challenged by several member families, who object to some of these immunizations as excessively risky and who have therefore not immunized their children. Attempts to reach a compromise have failed, and these families have now left the congregation. Is our immunization policy correct and justifiable according to Jewish tradition? (Professor Marc Bernstein, Ann Arbor, Michigan)

T'shuvah

1. THE MITZVAH OF MEDICINE

Any discussion of our *sh'eilah* must begin with this fundamental fact: Jewish tradition regards the practice of medicine as a mitzvah, a religious obligation.[1] It is an aspect of *pikuach nefesh*, the preservation of human life,[2] a mitzvah that takes precedence over virtually every other requirement of the Torah.[3] Even the rules of Shabbat and Yom Kippur are superseded in order to save life, and medicine falls under this instruction. Should an expert or competent physician (*rofei uman* or *rofei baki*) prescribe a remedy for a patient with a serious illness, the patient must accept the remedy even if its preparation and application would normally violate the prohibitions of those holy days.[4] One who refuses this treatment on the grounds that he or she prefers to observe the laws of Shabbat is a pious fool (*chasid shoteh*). This is not an act of piety but of suicide. He is compelled to do what the physicians prescribe.[5] Although our tradition speaks of a variety of acts that might be undertaken by and on behalf of the sick, such as *t'shuvah* (repentance), *t'filah* (prayer), and *tzedakah* (giving to the poor),[6] we are nonetheless required to follow the law of nature and to call the physician when we fall ill.[7] Whoever refuses medical treatment in favor of the other, nonnatural responses is guilty of the sin of arrogance, of assuming that one deserves to be healed by way of a miracle.[8]

It follows from all this that we are obliged to accept appropriate medical treatment and to provide it to our children, for their health and well-being are our responsibility. The key word here is "appropriate": we are *not* required to accept medical treatment that serves no legitimate therapeutic purpose. If a course of medical treatment is not therapeutic—that is, if it does not contribute to the successful treatment of disease—it does not qualify as "healing" (*r'fuah*) as Jewish tradition understands that term. It ceases to partake of the mitzvah of *pikuach nefesh*, and hence it ceases to be obligatory. The precise definition of terms such as "therapeutic" and "successful treatment," as we have written elsewhere,[9] is difficult to establish with precision. Still, our tradition does distinguish between therapies regarded as "proven" (*r'fuah vada-it* or *r'fuah b'dukah*), which offer a reasonably certain prospect of successful treatment, and those that are experimental or untested, which offer but an uncertain therapeutic benefit. We are required, the authorities tell us, to accept "proven" remedies; they are *pikuach nefesh*, and we have no right to refuse them. On the other hand, we are *not* required to accept medical treatments that are "unproven," of dubious therapeutic value.[10]

This distinction is of critical importance to the case before us. The parents in question claim that the immunizations required by their congregation pose excessive risks to the health and safety of the children who receive them. If this claim is correct, then Jewish tradition may well support the refusal of these parents to immunize their children, for excessively risky treatments might not be regarded as legitimate medicine. Indeed, a therapy that poses an unacceptable danger to life can hardly be said to fulfill the mitzvah of *pikuach nefesh*.[11]

The questions we must answer are these. Do immunizations qualify as
r'fuah b'dukah, as proven remedies? Do they offer a reasonably certain
prospect of successful treatment, in this case the prevention of dangerous
diseases, or are their therapeutic benefits dubious at best? Granted that
no medical therapy can be entirely free of risk, do vaccines pose a level
of danger that outweighs their benefits? And even if we regard vaccines
as a clear and positive good, is it the proper concern of a synagogue (or
any public body for that matter) to require that children be immunized?

2. IMMUNIZATION AS *R'FUAH*

"Immunization" is the process of artificially inducing immunity
or providing protection from disease. There are two forms of
immunization: "active immunization," by which the body is stimulated
to produce antibody and other immune responses through the
administration of a vaccine or toxoid; and "passive immunization,"
the provision of temporary immunity through the administration of
preformed antibodies derived from humans or animals.[12]

Not so long ago, infectious disease was counted as the most serious
threat to human life. Its effect upon children was devastating: of every
1,000 children born in 1900, 160 died of an infectious disease before
the age of five.[13] Today, by contrast, "parents in the developing world
no longer fear these diseases."[14] This welcome change, surely one of
the great success stories of the twentieth century, is largely due to
vaccines, which "are among the most effective means of preventing
disease, disability, and death."[15] The ultimate goal of immunization
is the eradication of disease, and the model for this eradication is the
experience with smallpox. This once deadly killer was eliminated from
the world in 1980 through a combination of a worldwide campaign
of immunization, surveillance, and adequate public health control
measures.[16] This experience has been repeated time and again. Prior
to the development of the Salk vaccine in 1955, paralytic poliomyelitis
claimed up to 18,000 victims in the United States during epidemic years;
today, this number is down to 5 to 15 cases per year, primarily among

those who for some reason have not been immunized. Diphtheria was once a common respiratory illness, with a 5 to 10 percent fatality rate; today, fewer than 100 cases are reported in the United States each year. Before the 1960s, well over 500,000 cases of measles occurred each year in the United States, and one out of every fifteen children who contracted the disease during the large epidemics died from it. Today, the incidence of measles has been reduced by 99 percent.[17] Worldwide, it is estimated that at current levels of immunization, 3.2 million deaths from measles and 450,000 cases of paralytic polio are prevented each year and that another 1.2 million measles deaths and 12,000 cases of paralytic polio might be prevented if full immunization is achieved.[18] During a rubella epidemic in 1964–65, 20,000 infants born to mothers infected during pregnancy suffered from blindness, heart disease, and mental retardation. "Today, thanks to nearly universal use of an effective vaccine, the rubella virus poses virtually no threat to the children of expectant mothers."[19] In addition, immunization has brought with it an enormous economic benefit, for it is far more efficient to prevent a disease than to treat it. Recent studies in the United States suggest that each of the traditional vaccines is cost saving in terms of direct medical costs alone and that an integrated immunization program saves seven to nine dollars for each dollar spent.[20] It is true, of course, that immunization is not the only factor to be credited in the successful battle against these diseases. Other measures, such as improved nutrition and sanitation, play an important role as well. Yet in the absence of effective vaccines these other measures would not have produced the impressive lifesaving results that we have witnessed in our time. Thus, in addition to all other disease-fighting tools, "every health authority with responsibility for child health must have a well-organized program of immunization as locally appropriate."[21] These programs are often made compulsory for the residents of the particular community. In the United States, the schedule of immunization for children is determined by the Advisory Committee on Immunization Practices of the U.S. Public Health Service and the Committee on Infectious Diseases of the American Academy of Pediatrics.[22] All states require immunization of children at the time of entry into licensed child care and entry into school. In addition, many states have regulations requiring immunization of older children in upper grades as well as those entering college.[23]

The parents of whom our *sh'eilah* speaks fear that some or all of the vaccines administered on the required immunization schedule pose unacceptable risks to their children. These risks are not imaginary ones. The Committee on Infectious Diseases of the American Academy of Pediatrics states openly that "although modern immunizing agents are generally considered safe and effective, they are neither completely safe nor completely effective. Some vaccines may have an untoward reaction, and some will not be protected."[24] It is hardly a surprise that vaccines may cause "untoward reactions." Medical therapies, many of which carry the potential for harmful side effects, are inherently risky; as our own tradition so starkly puts it, "that which heals one patient may kill another."[25] Yet this unhappy reality does not mean that we should refuse to go to the doctor or that the practice of medicine is not a mitzvah. Rather, we measure the risks against the benefits offered by the therapy in question. When we do this with respect to vaccines, we find that the risks they pose are far outweighed by the prospect of infection, morbidity, and mortality from the diseases they are intended to prevent.[26] For example, each year in the United States, eight to ten people will develop paralytic polio as a result of immunization with the oral polio vaccine (OPV) or through contact with a person who has received that vaccine.[27] This number is tiny compared to the many thousands of cases of polio that occurred each year prior to the development of the first successful vaccine. Another instructive case is that of the whole-cell pertussis vaccine, the subject of great controversy during the late 1970s and early 1980s. Due to claims that some children had been injured by the vaccine,[28] many parents in Japan, Sweden, and the United Kingdom chose not to immunize their children against the disease. The result was a return of pertussis in those countries to epidemic proportions.[29] The risks of the pertussis vaccine are real enough: grave complications (encephalopathy and permanent neurological damage) occur in one out of one hundred thousand and one out of three hundred thousand cases, respectively. Still, the risk of death or encephalopathy from pertussis infection in an unimmunized child is much higher. Projections from the recent epidemics indicate that the risk of pertussis-related death is ten times greater in an unimmunized population than in an immunized population of children.[30]

The risks associated with immunization are of vital concern to the medical profession and the scientific community, which have developed various means to monitor the safety of vaccines. The American Academy of Pediatrics issues recommendations that attempt to minimize risk by providing specific advice on dose, route, and timing of the vaccine and by delineating circumstances that warrant precaution in, and abstaining from, administering the vaccine.[31] In the United States, the Food and Drug Administration and the Centers for Disease Control and Prevention manage a program called the Vaccine Adverse Event Reporting System (VAERS), which like similar programs in other countries maintains surveillance over vaccine safety.[32] Improved and safer versions of the vaccines are constantly tested and made available. These surveillance and testing measures are not perfect; they do not reduce the risk factor of the vaccines to zero. Yet with all that, "the overwhelming view of the medical/public health community is that the risks of vaccine reactions, both the common mild reactions and the rare, more serious reactions, are very much outweighed by the public health benefit conferred by current vaccination practices and policies."[33]

All of this leads to the conclusion that immunization qualifies as r'fuah b'dukah or vada-it, a medical therapy of proven effect. As such, Jewish tradition would define immunization as part of the mitzvah of healing and recognize it as a required measure, since we are not entitled to endanger ourselves or the children for whom we are responsible by refusing proven medical treatment. Immunization, moreover, is a matter of social ethics and responsibility as well. Scientists recognize that protection of individuals from serious diseases depends not only on their own immunization but on the immunization of others in the community. Vaccines are not 100 percent effective; even in a fully immunized population, the vaccine will not succeed in conferring immunity upon every single person. Our chance of contracting disease is lower, therefore, if those around us remain healthy—that is, if they are immunized—than if they carry the disease. The concept here is "community immunity" or "herd immunity," the level of immunity achieved when there is a sufficient level of vaccine protection in the population to prevent the spread of the disease to those who remain biologically susceptible. "With herd immunity, the likelihood of two susceptible individuals being within the range for transmission is very, very small."[34] Immunization, therefore, is not a purely private matter but one of social ethics: our decision to vaccinate or not to vaccinate directly affects the lives and health of our neighbors.[35]

For these reasons, we would endorse programs of compulsory immunization in our communities, with exemptions granted to those individuals whose medical conditions place them at particular risk of injury or untoward side effects.[36] Aside from those individual cases, there are no valid Jewish religious grounds to support the refusal to immunize as a general principle.

3. A NOTE ON SCIENTIFIC EVIDENCE

The preceding section draws heavily upon expressions of scientific opinion, particularly those of researchers associated with the universities, professional societies, governmental agencies, and other institutions that comprise the mainstream of the scientific community. As noted above, it is "the overwhelming view" of this community that immunizations are both safe and effective. This view has been challenged, however, by critics whose arguments have provoked a controversy that rages in print, on Internet sites, and before government bodies.[37] The critics charge that many of the vaccines currently in use are ineffective or dangerous to the lives and health of children. These criticisms, in turn, are rebutted by the representatives of "the overwhelming view" who insist that vaccines prevent disease and that the risks they pose are either nonexistent or minimal.[38]

As rabbis, we are not competent to render judgments in scientific controversies. Still, we do not hesitate to adopt "the overwhelming view" as our standard of guidance in this and all other issues where science is the determining factor.[39] True, the scientific consensus is not infallible; history teaches us that the "predominant viewpoint" among scientists has often been wrong. The conclusions we reach in this responsum would therefore change were we to be convinced that the scientific information on which they are based is faulty. Yet we rely upon "the overwhelming view" of scientists, not because scientists are immune to error, but because today's science is a discipline defined by a rigorous methodology that leads to the recognition and correction of mistakes. The findings of any researcher are tested and retested carefully; they are subject to close scrutiny and peer review. Questions concerning the safety of any vaccine are vigorously examined by the medical community, and these examinations can and do lead to changes in the recommended schedules of vaccines.[40] It is precisely because scientists acknowledge that they *can* be wrong and precisely because the medical community trains such a watchful eye upon the issue of vaccine safety that "the overwhelming viewpoint," the consensus opinion among practitioners, is worthy of our confidence.

4. MAY A CONGREGATION REQUIRE IMMUNIZATION AS A REQUIREMENT FOR RELIGIOUS SCHOOL ADMISSION?

Jewish tradition recognizes the right of the community to make legislative enactments made by a community for the maintenance of its vital institutions and the governance of its public affairs. These enactments are called *takanot hakahal* (communal ordinances), a concept we have cited as the basis for our own community's power to determine its destiny and to adopt rules that bind its members.[41] In terms of substance, moreover, the community may adopt any rule it sees fit, even if the rule is not supported by formal Talmudic halachah, so long as it does not constitute an egregious violation of conscience or a clear religious prohibition.[42] This congregation is therefore entitled to require

that its students be immunized against disease prior to their admission
to religious school. Such a rule violates no prohibition of Jewish law
or tradition. On the contrary: inasmuch as this rule would reinforce a
policy of immunization that medical opinion accepts as a vital measure
in the battle against life-threatening disease, it reflects our understanding
of medicine as a mitzvah and our ethical responsibility to those who live
alongside us.

CONCLUSION

1. Immunization is in the category of *r'fuah b'dukah* or *r'fuah
   vada-it*, "proven" medicine, and as such is part and parcel of the
   traditional obligation to practice and to avail ourselves of medical
   treatment.

2. Because it can create the conditions that lead to "herd immunity"
   or "community immunity," compulsory immunization is a vital
   aspect of the medical policy of society. So long as exemptions to
   vaccination requirements are granted to those individuals to whom
   the vaccines pose a particular medical risk, neither Jewish tradition
   nor our own Reform understanding of that tradition would object
   to compulsory immunization against disease.

3. A congregation is entitled, should it so choose, to adopt a rule
   that requires immunization of students before their admission to
   religious school.

NOTES

1. SA, YD 336:1, drawn from *Tur, YD* 336. The wording of that passage indicates how
this concept developed over the centuries. The Torah itself never states explicitly that
medicine (*r'fuah*) is a mitzvah. The Sages, for their part, were decidedly ambivalent
as to the value of medical practice, with some even condemning it as evidence of
lack of faith in the power of God to heal the sick; see the discussion in *Teshuvot for
the Nineties* (TFN), no. 5754.18, pp. 373–75. Rabbinic halachah did recognize that
the physician was *permitted* to practice medicine (BT *Bava Kama* 85a, based upon

a midrash of Exod. 21:19); thus, the *Shulchan Aruch* begins by declaring that "the Torah grants the physician the permit [*r'shut*] to practice medicine." The passage adds immediately, however, that this permit is in fact "a mitzvah, in the category of *pikuach nefesh*." See note 2.

2. It was Nachmanides (Ramban) who developed this connection in his *Torat HaAdam*, Chavel ed. (Jerusalem, 1964), 41–42. He notes that the prohibitions connected with Shabbat and Yom Kippur are set aside when their observance would endanger human life and that we rely upon the diagnosis of a physician to determine that a situation of danger exists. The *Tur* and the *Shulchan Aruch* (see note 1) adopt this theory to justify the assertion that medicine is an integral element of the mitzvah of *pikuach nefesh*.

3. On *pikuach nefesh* see BT *Yoma* 85b and *Sanhedrin* 74a (and parallels); BT *Yoma* 82a ("nothing stands in the way of *pikuach nefesh* except for [the prohibitions of] idolatry, adultery and incest, and murder [which may not be violated even in order to save one's life]"); *Yad, Y'sodei HaTorah* 5:1ff.; *SA, YD* 157.

4. For the details of the halachah, see *Yad, Shabbat* 2 and *SA, OC* 328 and 618.

5. *Resp. R. David ibn Zimra* 1:1139.

6. See especially BT *Shabbat* 32a and *Bava Batra* 116a (on Prov. 16:14).

7. See Nachmanides to Lev. 26:11. Although Ramban seems to give only a grudging assent to medical practice in that passage (one that is very much at odds with the halachic formulation in *Torat HaAdam* [see note 2]), he does conclude that while in an ideal world we might be able to rely upon prayer and repentance as remedies to disease, in *this* world we are forbidden to rely upon miracles. See *Turei Zahav, YD* 336:1.

8. R. Chaim Yosef David Azulai, *Birkei Yosef, YD* 336:2, cited by R. Sh'lomo Ganzfried, *Kitzur Shulchan Aruch* 192:3.

9. For a more complete discussion, see TFN, no. 5754.14, part 3, pp. 346ff.

10. The classic statement of this distinction is R. Yaakov Emden, *Mor Uk'tziah* 328.

11. Much here depends upon the medical condition of the patient. A treatment that is "excessively risky" for one patient might well be in order—that is, therapeutically appropriate—for another patient who would likely or surely die without it. See Moshe Raziel, "Kefi'at Choleh Lekabel Tipul Refu'i," *T'chumin* 2 (1981): 335–36.

12. Stephen C. Hadler (director, National Immunization Program, Epidemiology and Surveillance Division, Centers for Disease Control and Prevention) and Walter A.

Orenstein (director, National Immunization Program, Centers for Disease Control and Prevention), "Active Immunization," in *Principles and Practice of Pediatric Infectious Diseases*, ed. S. Lang, L. Pickering, and C. Prober (New York: Churchill Livingstone, 1997), 49.

13. R. H. Waldman and R. M. Kluge, eds., *Textbook of Infectious Diseases* (New York: Medical Examination Publishing Co., 1984), 4.

14. Susan S. Ellenberg, PhD (director, Division of Biostatistics and Epidemiology, Center for Biologics Evaluation and Research, U.S. Food and Drug Administration) and Robert T. Chen, MD (chief, Vaccine Safety and Development Activity, Epidemiology and Surveillance Division, National Immunization Program, Centers for Disease Control and Prevention), "The Complicated Task of Monitoring Vaccine Safety," *Public Health Reports* 112, no. 1 (1997): 11.

15. Hadler and Orenstein, "Active Immunization," 49.

16. Committee on Infectious Diseases, American Academy of Pediatrics, *1994 Red Book: Report of the Committee on Infectious Diseases* (Elk Grove Village, IL: American Academy of Pediatrics, 1994), 7. The smallpox vaccine, developed in England by Edward Jenner in 1796, was the first successful immunization measure.

17. The figures for polio, diphtheria, and measles are taken from John H. Dorsett (professor of pediatrics, Pennsylvania State University College of Medicine), "Immunizations," in *Primary Pediatric Care*, 3rd ed., ed. R. A. Hoekelman et al. (St. Louis: Mosby, 1997), 182–94.

18. R. Kim-Farley and the World Health Organization Expanded Program on Immunization Team, "Global Immunization," *Annual Review of Public Health* 13 (1992): 223–38.

19. David Satcher, MD, PhD, Surgeon General of the United States, Statement before the U.S. House of Representatives Committee on Government Reform, August 3, 1999.

20. Hadler and Orenstein, "Active Immunization," 49. And see Satcher: every dollar spent on measles-mumps-rubella vaccine (MMR) results in thirteen dollars total savings.

21. Eva Alberman (emeritus professor of clinical epidemiology, University of London) and Peter O.D. Pharoah (professor of public health, Department of Public Health, University of Liverpool), "Children," in *Oxford Textbook of Public Health*, ed. R. Detels, W. W. Holland, J. McEwen, and G. S. Omenn (New York: Oxford University

Press, 1997), 1379–96. See also Roger Detels (professor of epidemiology, School of Public Health, University of California at Los Angeles) and Lester Breslow (professor of public health, School of Public Health, University of California at Los Angeles), "Current Scope and Concerns in Public Health," in ibid., 3ff.: before 1981, with the spread of AIDS, it appeared that pandemics of infectious disease other than influenza had been eliminated as a major problem in developing countries. This was due to provision of safe drinking water, better handling of sewage, effective vaccine campaigns, improved personal hygiene, and improved nutrition, especially among children.

22. Hadler and Orenstein, "Active Immunization," 52.

23. *1994 Red Book*, 623.

24. Ibid., 29. See also Dorsett, "Immunizations," 184: "*No vaccine is perfectly safe and always effective*" (italics in original).

25. Nachmanides, *Torah HaAdam, inyan hasakanah* (Chavel ed., 43).

26. Dorsett, "Immunizations," 187.

27. D. R. Prevots, R. W. Sutter, P. M. Stickel, et al., "Completeness for Reporting Paralytic Poliomyelitis, United States, 1980–1991," *Archives of Pediatric Adolescent Medicine* 148 (1994): 479–85.

28. See H. Coulter and B. Fisher, *DPT: A Shot in the Dark* (New York: Warner Books, 1985).

29. M. Kimura and H. Kuno-Sakai, "Developments in Pertussis Immunization in Japan," *Lancet* 336 (1990): 30–32; D. Miller et al., "Pertussis Immunization and Serious Acute Neurological Illnesses in Children," *British Medical Journal* 307 (1993): 1171–76; I. Krantz, J. Taranger, and B. Trollfors, "Estimating Incidence of Whooping Cough over Time: A Cross-Sectional Recall Study of Four Swedish Birth Cohorts," *International Journal of Epidemiology* 18 (1989): 959–63.

30. Dorsett, "Immunizations," 187.

31. The protocols are summarized in *1994 Red Book*, 35–39.

32. The system is described in Ellenberg and Chen, "Complicated Task."

33. Ibid., 19.

34. Phyllis Freeman, JD (professor and chair of the Law Center, MacCormick Institute, University of Massachusetts), "The Biology of Vaccines and Community Decisions to Vaccinate," *Public Health Reports* 112, no. 1 (1997): 21.

35. In its publication, *Six Common Misconceptions about Vaccination* (Atlanta, 1999), the Centers for Disease Control and Prevention expresses the concept as follows: "A successful vaccination program, like a successful society, depends on the cooperation of every individual to ensure the good of all. We would think it irresponsible of a driver to ignore all traffic regulations on the presumption that other drivers will watch out for him or her. In the same way we shouldn't rely on people around us to stop the spread of disease; we, too, must do what we can."

36. See *1994 Red Book*, at note 30.

37. See, e.g., Coulter and Fisher, *DPT*, at note 25. For a sharp critique of the "anti-immunization" movement, see A. Allen, "Injection Rejection," *The New Republic*, March 23, 1998, 20–23. The proliferation of anti-immunization Internet sites has spawned a number of other sites in response; these are simply too numerous to detail. A representative "pro-vaccination" page is www.vaccinesafety.edu, Institute for Vaccine Safety at Johns Hopkins University (accessed August 12, 2009).

38. Thus, Dr. Neal Halsey, director of the Institute for Vaccine Safety at Johns Hopkins University, speaks of "misperceptions" regarding causality: that is, many in the public believe that a number of vaccines are causally related to specific diseases, even though no evidence exists to prove such an association (N. Halsey, "Ensuring the Safety of Immunizations," *Programs and Abstracts from the 39th Interscience Conference on Antimicrobial Agents and Chemotherapy* [San Francisco: September 26–29, 1999], Abstract 486). See, in general, the text at notes 12–23.

39. Reform Judaism, in particular, has taken a positive stance toward modern science as a guide to making religious decisions in matters that can legitimately be defined as "scientific." See *Reform Responsa for the Twenty-first Century*, no. 5757.2, vol. 1, p. 131: "Given our positive attitude as liberal Jews toward modernity in general, it is surely appropriate to rely upon the findings of modern science, rather than upon tenuous analogies from traditional sources, in order to render what we must consider to be scientific judgments."

40. See the text at notes 31 and 32, and Satcher (note 19, above). See also *Morbidity and Mortality Weekly Report* (published by the Centers for Disease Control and Prevention) 48, no. 27 (July 16, 1999): 590: the Advisory Committee on Immunization Practices (ACIP) now recommends that the oral polio vaccine (OPV) be replaced by

inactivated poliovirus vaccine (IPV). OPV has tended to cause "vaccine-associated paralytic polio" (VAPP) in one case out of every 2.4 million distributed doses of the vaccine. While this level of risk was regarded as justified, given the lifesaving effects of OPV, it has been decided that given the success of worldwide polio eradication efforts, the safer vaccine ought to be administered.

41. See *Reform Responsa for the Twenty-first Century*, no. 5758.1, vol. 1, pp. 311–18, section 2, for sources and discussion.

42. R. Chaim Yair Bachrach, *Resp. Chavat Yair*, no. 57. For analysis, see Jacob Katz, *Halachah V'Kabbalah* (Jerusalem: Magnes, 1984), 244–46.

Sh'eilah

Recently, scientists have reported some important findings from experiments conducted upon human stem cells. These results, we are told, signal the potential discovery of treatments for a number of dreaded diseases. Yet the stem cells used in these studies are usually taken from aborted fetuses or from embryos (zygotes) created in the laboratory. According to Jewish law and tradition, is it permissible to utilize human embryos and aborted fetuses in stem cell research?

T'shuvah

1. THE SCIENTIFIC BACKGROUND[1]

Stem cells are a type of cell found in the human body at all stages of development: embryonic, fetal, and adult (in this context, an "adult" stem cell refers to a stem cell that occurs in the human organism after birth). While all other cell types, such as heart cells or skin cells, are specialized or committed to conducting specific biological functions, the stem cell is unique in that it is uncommitted to any specific function and remains so until it receives a signal to develop into a specialized cell. All stem cells are capable of renewing themselves and of becoming specialized or differentiated to yield the cell types of the particular tissues from which they originate; when the tissues become damaged or destroyed, the stem cells enable the body to restore them. Yet there are some important differences among these stem cells. Some stem cells are "pluripotent": that is, they have the capacity to develop into almost all of the more than two hundred different known cell types. Stem cells that display this characteristic come from embryonic or fetal tissue.[2] Adult stem cells do not have this capacity. Adult stem cells do possess to some extent a characteristic called "plasticity," the ability of a cell type derived from one tissue to develop into specialized cell types of another tissue. To date, however, it has not been demonstrated that the adult stem cell can be directed to develop into *any* cell type of the body.

During the past few years, researchers have succeeded in isolating pluripotent stem cells from the early (four- to five-day) human embryo (called the blastocyst) and in growing them in a laboratory setting.[3] This is a dramatic development, one that may well portend some significant advances in medicine and health. A number of deadly illnesses—among them Parkinson's disease, Alzheimer's disease, diabetes, chronic heart disease, liver failure, cancer, multiple sclerosis, and spinal cord injury—ravage the body by destroying organs and cell tissue. Scientists hope either to cure or to control these diseases by manipulating stem cells to generate new tissue to replace that which the diseases have destroyed and to restore vital bodily functions. In addition, as this technology becomes more advanced, it is possible that whole organs might be created for use in transplantation, a critical desideratum given the ongoing shortage of donor organs available for this purpose. Finally, the study of embryonic stem cells can help us gain a better understanding of genetics and human development, including the causes of birth defects, and consequently aid us in the effort to correct or prevent them.

2. THE MORAL CHALLENGE

Stem cell research, therefore, is fast emerging as one of the most hopeful fronts in our age-old battle against disease, and we are properly encouraged by its progress. Our happiness, however, is tempered by our concerns over the nature of this research, particularly as it involves fetal and embryonic stem cells. (The derivation of adult stem cells does not pose similar concerns; as we have noted, however, fetal and embryonic stem cells offer much better prospects for research.) In order to derive fetal stem cells, scientists must utilize aborted fetuses. In order to derive embryonic stem cells, they must destroy the embryo; that is, they must kill the human organism at its earliest stage of development. Such laboratory manipulation of human fetuses and embryos raises questions of great moral seriousness, and we must not ignore these questions even when that research carries the prospect of important medical breakthroughs. On the contrary: the demand that we behave in an ethical manner, a demand that is central to our concern as religious people, does not cease to apply to us when we enter the laboratory. In our scientific lives, no less than in our social or political lives, we are required to ask whether our acts, no matter how well-intentioned, pass muster before the bar of morality. As Jews, in particular, we ask these questions from the standpoint of our participation in a tradition that has a great deal to say concerning the ethics of science and medicine.[4]

What, then, should be our stance with regard to stem cell research? Is this procedure coherent with the duties imposed upon us by our Jewish moral tradition as we Reform Jews best understand it? Are we permitted to abort the human fetus and to destroy the human embryo for the purpose of medical experimentation? If so, are we permitted to create embryos and fetuses intentionally in order to use them subsequently in this manner?

These, as we shall see, are not easy questions to answer. While the answers we have arrived at represent in our view the best and most persuasive response to these questions, we do not claim to have resolved all problems with absolute certainty. Our chief hope, therefore, is that our *t'shuvah* will suggest a fruitful way for us as Reform Jews to think and to talk about the moral issues connected with stem cell research. In that way, it may prove helpful to us as we continue our discussions and debates over this latest development in medical technology.

3. THE MITZVAH OF MEDICINE

Jewish tradition holds the practice of medicine to be a mitzvah, a religious duty. The Torah, to be sure, does not explicitly enjoin us to practice medicine, and though the Rabbis deduce from Exodus 21:19 that the physician is *permitted* to ply his craft,[5] they do not suggest that the verse *obligates* him to do so. That conclusion is left to the great post-

Talmudic authorities, the *rishonim*, among them R. Moshe b. Nachman (Nachmanides or Ramban, thirteenth-century Spain).[6] In his *Torat HaAdam*[7] Ramban writes that the "permission" of which the Rabbis speak is in fact a mitzvah, because medicine falls under the category of *pikuach nefesh*, the saving of life, an act that according to all opinions is most certainly a mitzvah and that takes priority over almost all other religious obligations set forth under the Torah.[8] This understanding, which has been adopted by the leading halachic compendia,[9] reflects the predominant[10] Jewish attitude toward the practice of medicine. Our tradition requires that we utilize our knowledge and our power to their utmost in order to heal the sick; "when one who delays in doing so, it is as if he has shed blood."[11]

When we speak of the mitzvah of medicine, we have in mind more than just the dispensing of treatment to patients by physicians and other health care professionals. "Medicine" as we understand it today is a scientific discipline, defined by the canons and practices of a scientific community. Among these canons and practices is the insistence that medicine is an *experimental* science, founded upon extensive, carefully controlled laboratory and field research. It is this body of research, a continuing process of testing, verification, and discovery subject to the critical review of peer scientists, that commands our respect for the practice of medicine[12] and that empowers physicians to speak and to act with authority. For these reasons, it is difficult to draw firm distinctions between the "pure" and "applied" aspects of medical science. The scientist who tests and develops a therapy is engaged in the mitzvah of healing just as surely as is the physician who administers it to the patient; the work of each is just as essential to the saving of human life as is the work of the other.[13] If we define the administration of lifesaving medical therapy as *pikuach nefesh*, we should not forget that physicians could not save lives were it not for the extensive scientific research upon which our contemporary practice of medicine is based. Since research into human stem cells partakes of the mitzvah of healing, surely our society ought to support it.

4. JEWISH TRADITION AND RESPECT FOR HUMAN LIFE

Medicine, however, is not the only relevant aspect of the mitzvah of
pikuach nefesh. The commandment to save life reflects our tradition's
demand that we respect life and honor it. This implies an obvious
limitation upon the way we are permitted to practice medicine: we are not
allowed to commit murder, even if the shedding of one person's blood will
lead to healing for another.[14] This idea is linked in our classical texts to
the concept of *yehareg ve'al yaavor*:[15] we recognize that there are certain
actions we must *never* perform, even at the cost of our lives, because our
covenant with God requires no less. In the present context, it teaches us
that we may not practice medicine in such a way that is destructive of
human life. For example, under certain carefully specified conditions it
is morally permissible to conduct medical experimentation upon human
subjects. Yet it is clearly forbidden to sacrifice the life of the subject, even if
the therapy being tested has the potential to save many lives in the future,
for we may not use murder as a means of healing.[16] Does this rule hold in
the case before us? Does the prohibition against murder, which protects
the day-old infant,[17] apply as well to the human organism in its prenatal
stage? If it does, then it is difficult to imagine how stem cell research could
be deemed moral from the standpoint of Jewish law.

Even if the destruction of the fetus or the embryo is not considered
an act of murder under Jewish law, we cannot automatically conclude
from that fact that the destruction is "permitted." The principle we call
"respect for human life" is not identical with the prohibition against
bloodshed. It reaches beyond the scope of specific prohibitions to touch
upon our more general moral commitment to the *sanctity* of human
life.[18] To say that human life is sacred is to say that, at some definable
point, it is *inviolate*, that it is protected and preserved from our power
to control, to manipulate, and to destroy. How does this commitment
inform our attitude toward prenatal life? Is our belief in life's sanctity
compatible with laboratory experimentation upon—and the concomitant
destruction of—the fetus and the embryo, even if that experimentation
may lead to the discovery of lifesaving medical therapies?

5. THE STATUS OF THE PRENATAL HUMAN BEING

We are asking, therefore, whether and under what circumstances we may destroy the prenatal human organism for the advancement of medicine and, ultimately, the goal of *pikuach nefesh*. To answer this question, we must determine the status of the fetus and the embryo under Jewish law. Since we would never imagine that it is permissible to sacrifice the day-old infant "in the interests of science," we must ascertain whether the fetus and the embryo possess a status that is legally inferior to that of the infant. If its status indeed is a lesser one, then perhaps we are morally justified, under certain circumstances, in sacrificing the prenatal human being for the sake of medical research.

a. The Fetus. The traditional Jewish discussion of the status of the fetus customarily begins with the following Mishnah:

> If a woman experiences life-threatening difficulty giving birth,
> the fetus is dismembered in her womb and removed limb from
> limb, for her life comes before its life [*mipnei shechayeha kodmin
> l'chayav*]. Once the major part of [the fetus] has emerged, it may
> not be harmed, for one person [*nefesh*] is not sacrificed on behalf of
> another.[19]

The text clearly mandates abortion in this case, but the authorities disagree as to the grounds on which it does so. Maimonides sees the fetus as a *rodeif*, a "pursuer" that threatens the life of the mother; like all pursuers, the fetus may be killed if necessary to save its victim from death.[20] Rashi offers another interpretation:[21] so long as the fetus has not emerged from the womb, it is not a *nefesh*, a full legal person, and the mother's life therefore takes precedence over its own. Once it has emerged, it acquires the status of a legal person; therefore, "one *nefesh* is not sacrificed on behalf of another." Rashi, in our view, provides the better and more coherent reading of the Mishnah's text.[22] And while others may differ on that point, there is general agreement that Jewish law does not regard the fetus as a *nefesh*, a full legal person. For this reason, the killing of a fetus is not considered or punished as an act of murder under the halachah.[23] And since the fetus possesses a legal status inferior to that of the mother, a number of halachic authorities permit abortions in situations where the mother's life is not endangered by the birth of the child but where the abortion is necessary for her physical or mental health.[24] Given that the fetus does not enjoy the entire range of protections that Jewish law accords to the full legal person, we might conclude that it is permitted to abort the fetus in order to utilize its tissue for experimentation aimed at the development of lifesaving treatments.

That conclusion, however, would be a hasty one. Though the fetus does not qualify as a *nefesh*, the halachah nonetheless accords it a high degree of protection. We see this protection at work in both a negative and a positive context. The negative context is that Jewish law prohibits feticide in the absence of serious cause. Virtually all authorities hold this view, although they vigorously dispute the nature of the prohibition[25] and the definition of the "serious cause" that overrides it.[26] The positive context is that the laws of *pikuach nefesh* apply to the fetus: we are required to violate the laws of Shabbat or Yom Kippur if necessary in order to save its life.[27] Even though the fetus is not technically a *nefesh*, it is in any event a *potential* person, a "*nefesh* in becoming," so that "we violate one Sabbath on its behalf so that it may one day keep many Sabbaths."[28] The fetus may occupy a lower legal status than other human beings, but it *is* a human being; it partakes of the sanctity of human life, and it deserves our honor and respect.

Taken together, these two elements of Jewish teaching concerning the fetus can serve as a guide to our own conduct. Because the fetus is not a *nefesh* and because the mother's life and health take precedence over it, we can confidently permit abortion in circumstances other than mortal danger to her. Yet because the fetus is a human organism, a "potential *nefesh*," we condone abortion only for truly weighty justifications; "we do not encourage abortion, nor favor it for trivial reasons, nor sanction it 'on demand.'"[29] Specifically, abortion is indicated in order to safeguard the health of the mother or to spare her great physical or emotional pain.[30] It is difficult to define a set of abstract rules governing the decision for or against abortion. That decision requires a careful consideration of the facts and circumstances of the particular case. Yet we have written that abortion should *not* be performed for reasons other than "serious maternal anguish," that is, a real set of difficulties faced by a particular woman.[31] The destruction of fetal life for any other reason stands in direct conflict with our commitment to the sanctity of that life. We therefore cannot sanction abortion for the purpose of harvesting fetal tissue for use in medical experimentation, even though the goal of that experimentation is the advancement of science toward new lifesaving therapies. On the other hand, if a pregnancy has been terminated for a reason that we would regard as morally sufficient, we are permitted to use the aborted fetus in medical experimentation. We have long approved of autopsies for scientifically valid purposes;[32] the use of fetal tissue and organs would clearly qualify for the same approval, so long as the research is not the actual motivation for the abortion.

b. The Embryo. What is the legal status of the embryo, the fertilized egg that does not reside in utero? This question poses a special difficulty for the halachist. The classical sources certainly did not envision the possibility that a human embryo might exist and develop in a petri dish; how then can they speak to the legal status of that embryo? Contemporary authorities, however, note that while the sources do not discuss the embryo, they do discuss the case of the fetus at its earliest stages of development and that we can learn much from those discussions. The Talmud holds that prior to its fortieth day of gestation the fetus, lacking form, is to be regarded as "mere water" (*maya b'alma*).[33] This determination has some significant legal consequences[34] and, most importantly for our purposes, figures prominently in the Jewish law of abortion. A number of decisors agree with the stance of R. Eliezer Y'hudah Waldenberg that "when an abortion is indicated for medical reasons, it is best to perform it prior to the fortieth day of gestation. The law is much more lenient at that point inasmuch as the fetus prior to forty days is *maya b'alma*."[35] We should be careful not to read too much into the forty-day distinction. The fact that abortion is easier to permit prior to the fortieth day does not mean that it is not prohibited at all.[36] And the law of *pikuach nefesh*, which as we have seen applies to the fetus, presumably applies to *any* fetus, even one that is less than forty days old.[37] The distinction does indicate, though, that while we respect and honor human life from its conception, the human organism at this earliest stage of its development is seen as having a lesser or inferior legal status than that possessed by the fetus at a later stage. Its lesser legal status, in turn, suggests that it exercises a lesser claim to protection than it does subsequently.

How might this insight inform our understanding of the status of the embryo? An important ruling on this subject is that of R. Sh'muel HaLevi Wosner,[38] who considers a question arising from the IVF procedure: does the law of *pikuach nefesh* apply to the zygote? Are we permitted to violate the laws of Shabbat if this is necessary to "save" the embryo and to allow it to continue its development in the petri dish? Wosner responds that, while we are required to do just that for the fetus, and apparently even for the fetus prior to its fortieth day of gestation,[39] we are forbidden to violate Shabbat on behalf of the embryo that has not yet been implanted into the womb. He writes that the law of *pikuach nefesh* applies to the fetus, even though it is not a full legal person, because most fetuses will survive, be born, and *become* full legal persons. In Jewish terms, the fetus will likely become a *ben mitzvah*, a person subject to the obligations of Torah; accordingly, we apply to it the principle "we violate one Sabbath on its behalf so that it may one day keep many Sabbaths." We cannot say the same of the zygote. We cannot say that most of these embryos will "likely" develop into persons (*n'fashot*), because they lack the minimum qualification—implantation into the womb—that would enable us to make that statement. The embryo, therefore, possesses a legal status inferior to that of the fetus, and one element of this lesser status is that Jewish law imposes no positive duty to "save" its life.

If we have no duty to protect the embryo from death, it might follow that the halachah does not explicitly prohibit its destruction. And if destruction is not explicitly prohibited, it might well be *permitted* under particular circumstances. For example, the procedure of in vitro fertilization (IVF) requires the creation of many more embryos than can be implanted into the womb of the woman who donated the eggs or of a "host mother." What shall we do with the "excess" embryos, those not used for implantation? Must we preserve them ad infinitum, or may we discard them? Two leading contemporary halachists rule that it is indeed permissible to discard these excess embryos: not only are they not "likely" to become full *n'fashot*, there is no possibility that they will do so, since there is no intention to implant them. We owe no moral duty to these embryos, in other words, that would forbid us from discarding them.[40]

This Committee has previously reached a similar conclusion.[41] We hold that it is permissible to destroy excess embryos for two reasons. First, we accept the Jewish legal doctrine of the *nefesh*. "Personhood," according to this teaching, is a characteristic possessed exclusively by members of the human community, that is, by men, women, and children; the human organism does not become a full legal person until birth. This does not mean that we owe no moral duty toward the human organism prior to its birth; we most certainly do. We believe, however, that these obligations exist precisely because the fetus and embryo are "persons in becoming." The excess embryo, unlike the fetus or the embryo that is intended for implantation, has *no* potential to become a *nefesh*; therefore, while we would not condone its wanton destruction, we would permit it for causes of lesser gravity than those we would ask in the case of abortion. Second, the discarding of excess embryos is positively indicated as an important element of IVF. Were we to require that every one of these embryos be preserved, we would place a cumbersome burden upon hospitals and laboratories. Under such conditions, many of these institutions would likely refuse to perform IVF, thus rendering the procedure intolerably expensive or simply unavailable to many of those who seek it. The destruction of the excess embryos therefore serves to make possible the fulfillment of the mitzvot of healing and procreation.[42] Moreover, we have extended this

permit to cover medical experimentation: if Jewish tradition allows us
to destroy these excess embryos, we think it would surely allow us to
use them in experimentation aimed at the advancement of medicine, to
the fulfillment of the mitzvah of *pikuach nefesh*.[43] These embryos may
therefore be utilized in human stem cell research. This opinion, we might
add, is shared by other leading scholars in the field of Jewish medical
law and ethics.[44] The permit for the destruction of "excess" embryos for
research purposes would obviously extend to the use of existing stem
cell lines, that is, stem cells that have already been derived and that are
currently preserved in laboratories.

c. The Creation of Embryos for Medical Experimentation. The human
embryo is largely "unprotected" by Jewish law. There is no explicit
halachic prohibition against its destruction, and partly for this reason
we feel morally confident about permitting the destruction of "excess"
embryos created as part of the IVF procedure and about permitting the
use of these embryos in medical research. Let us take our inquiry to its
next logical step: would it be also permitted to *create* embryos explicitly
for purposes of medical research? It is not difficult to sketch an argument
in favor of a "yes" answer. Newly created embryos, after all, are destined
for the laboratory and not for the womb. Like excess embryos, they
have no potential to develop into full human persons. If the lack of that
potential leads us to permit the use of excess embryos in medical research,
why shall we not say the same for embryos that are created for no other
purpose than medical research? The analogy between the two sorts of
embryos, however, is not tight enough to support that conclusion. We
do not create excess embryos with the explicit intention to destroy them.
They are the necessary and unavoidable by-product of the procedure of in
vitro fertilization, which requires the creation of more embryos than can
be utilized in the initiation of pregnancy. If we could perform IVF without
creating excess embryos, we would do that; if we could use these embryos
for other purposes or store them in an economically feasible manner so
as to obviate the need for their destruction, we would do that. We permit
the discarding of excess embryos, not because of their "inferior" legal
status (though that low status does remove a major moral obstacle to their

destruction), but because in order to make IVF available to those who seek it we have no choice *but* to discard them. Given that the excess embryos will in any event be destroyed, we think it is entirely proper that their destruction be accomplished as part of the research that might lead to the discovery of lifesaving therapies. None of this requires the conclusion that we are permitted to create human embryos *explicitly in order to* destroy them, even for medical purposes. The analogy, in short, does not work.

On the other hand, we could argue for an affirmative response without resorting to analogies at all. We might reason in a more deductive fashion: if the mitzvah of *pikuach nefesh* overrides virtually all other religious and moral obligations imposed in the Jewish tradition, then surely it justifies the creation—and destruction—of human embryos in the name of medical science, particularly given the lack of any concrete prohibition against killing the embryo. This argument does have persuasive force, but that force lies in the sheer power of calculation. It depends upon the assignment of relative values to the human organism at different stages of its development: the *nefesh* receives a higher score than the not-yet-*nefesh*. It then imagines a conflict between the life of the *nefesh* and the life of the embryo, a conflict that the *nefesh* automatically wins. This mathematical approach is elegant in its simplicity, but in our judgment it is *too* simple, for it ignores some vital moral issues raised by the destruction of embryonic human life.

We repeat: embryonic human life. Let us not mince words. Although the fertilized egg may be called an "embryo," a "zygote," or a "blastocyst," these labels can mask the fact that we have here a human *being*, an organism that contains all the genetic material that would, under the proper conditions, develop into a full legal person. As a leading medical text puts it: "The time of fertilization represents the starting point in the life history, or ontogeny, of the individual."[45] The embryo may not have attained the status of a *nefesh*, a legal person, a member of the human community, and its unwarranted killing may not be defined as "murder." It *is*, however, a human being, and by that token it partakes of the sanctity of all human life.

Rather than attempt to calculate the value of one human being against that of another, let us instead ask ourselves what this sanctity means. Before we say "yes" to the creation and destruction of human embryos, with all the marketing, trafficking, and commercialization that would inevitably accompany their widespread use in laboratory research, let us consider what our commitment to the essential humanity of the embryo ought to demand of us. We Reform Jews might well answer that question in various ways. Yet even in its most minimal definition, sanctity requires the recognition that human life is at some point inviolate, that it lies beyond our reach and our manipulation. This inviolability is the single greatest moral distinction between human and all other forms of life. We accept the notion that animals can be brought into the world with the express purpose of being killed to serve our purposes. We do not apply that notion to human life, because our sense of the sanctity of human life calls forth from us a response of awe and reverence rather than dominion and utility. There is no reason to assume that this awe and reverence do not apply to human life even at the embryonic stage, for even there, in the microscopic fertilized egg, lies the supreme potential for humanity.

Differences in legal status do help us to make difficult choices. This is particularly true in the matter of abortion. It is precisely because the fetus is not classified as a *nefesh* that we are permitted to make the otherwise unjustifiable decision to sacrifice its life on behalf of the life, health, or extreme anguish of its mother. Yet that decision is made in light of the actual and direct danger that the continuation of the pregnancy poses to a particular woman. As we have suggested, the fetus's lower status would not justify its destruction for the sake of medical research that *might* yield results that *might* be helpful to some as-yet unknown persons in the distant future. We think that the same considerations apply to the embryo. The zygote's status under Jewish law may be lower even than that of the fetus;[46] for this reason, we can countenance the destruction of excess embryos created as part of the IVF procedure and their use in medical research. We do not accept, however, that this lower status would permit us to create embryos for no other purpose than to destroy them in furtherance of research that might well not lead to therapeutic benefits for some unknown person in a far-off future. To permit that action would be to stretch the definitions of *pikuach nefesh* and *r'fuah* beyond plausible boundaries. To permit that action, indeed, would be incompatible with our commitment to the sanctity that inheres in these embryonic human lives.

We should emphasize, finally, that we speak here exclusively to the current scientific situation. The question before us has to do with *experimentation*, with the destruction of human embryos as part of a research protocol that might some day lead to discoveries that would offer therapeutic benefit to actual patients. It is because any such benefit is many steps and quite possibly many years removed from medical reality that we cannot apply to that research the designation of *pikuach nefesh*. Were that reality to change—specifically, were science to develop from stem cell research real therapies to treat life-threatening illnesses like those mentioned at the outset of this *t'shuvah*—then our answer would quite possibly change as well. In that case, we might well conclude that the need to derive the necessary stem cell material overrides our concern for the life of the embryo We might say this for two reasons: first, because there is no Jewish legal prohibition against the destruction of the embryo at any rate; and second, because the real prospect that this material would provide therapeutic benefit to an actual patient would easily qualify the therapy as *pikuach nefesh*. The matter requires further careful study, not only by this Committee, but by all who are concerned with Torah and its application to the fateful moral choices that we are called upon to make.

CONCLUSION

In summary, we hope to have made the following points:

1. The practice of medicine is a mitzvah, partaking of the duty to save life. Because medicine is an experimental science, the mitzvah of medical practice includes medical research as well as the direct

treatment of patients. For this reason, we are encouraged by the dramatic therapeutic prospects offered by research into human stem cells.

2. All human life, including prenatal human life, possesses an inherent sanctity that requires our respect and honor and that conflicts with the demand that we destroy it for our own purposes, even medical purposes.

3. The fetus is not a *nefesh*, a full legal person. Abortion is therefore permitted for reason of the life or health of the mother. It is *not* permitted in order to obtain fetal tissue for medical research. The tissue of fetuses that have been aborted for morally justifiable causes, however, may be utilized in that research.

4. The legal status of the embryo that exists outside the womb is inferior to that of the fetus. There is no duty to save it from death; nor is there an explicit prohibition against its destruction. For this reason, it is permissible to discard the excess embryos created as part of the procedure of in vitro fertilization and, by extension, to use them for purposes of stem cell research. If we may destroy some embryos in order to derive stem cells for the sake of that research, it is certainly permissible for scientists to make use of the already existing lines of stem cells in possession of scientists.

5. It is not permissible to create embryonic human life for the purpose of destroying it in medical experimentation. It *might* be permissible, however, to create and destroy embryonic human life in order to derive stem cell material that would be used as medical therapy for actual patients. The development of such therapies, if it ever occurs, lies in the distant future. In the meantime, it is incumbent upon all of us to continue to study, consider, and debate the moral implications of this promising new avenue of medical research.

NOTES

1. The following account is based upon the report entitled *Stem Cells: Scientific Progress and Future Research Directions*, prepared by the National Institutes of Health of the U.S. Department of Health and Human Services, June 2001. Our description draws especially upon the report's "Executive Summary," numbered as pp. ES-1 to ES-10. We take this opportunity to state the obvious (which, though obvious, deserves emphasis): we are rabbis, students of Torah and Jewish text. We are *not* scientists, and we claim no particular expertise on scientific and technological matters. What follows is by no means intended to serve as a comprehensive explanation of the nature and the current state of human stem cell research; readers seeking such an explanation are encouraged to consult the report and the literature it cites. Rather we offer a basic, broad-outline sketch of the current state of the science. We hope that this account will provide sufficient background for the discussion of the Jewish religious and moral issues that are raised by this research and that are the proper focus of our *t'shuvah*.

2. Embryonic stem cells are derived from a group of cells called the inner cell mass, part of the early embryo, or blastocyst. Fetal stem cells are found in fetal tissue that was destined to be part of the gonads. See *Stem Cells*, ES-2.

3. The breakthrough study is that of James A. Thompson, et al., "Embryonic Stem Cell Lines Derived from Human Blastocysts," *Science* 282 (1998): 1145ff. A similar study concerning fetal stem cells (also called germ cells) is M. Shamblott et al., "Derivation of Pluripotent Stem Cells from Cultured Human Primordial Germ Cells," *Proceedings of the National Academy of Sciences* 95 (1998): 13726ff.

4. The scope and depth of this tradition can be seen in the proliferation of books with titles such as "Jewish Medical Ethics" and the like. Most of these are published by Orthodox rabbis. Among the best are Fred Rosner and J. David Bleich, *Jewish Bioethics* (New York: Sanhedrin Press, 1979); and Fred Rosner, *Modern Medicine and Jewish Ethics* (Hoboken, NJ: Ktav, 1986). A particularly useful work is A. S. Avraham, *Nishmat Avraham* (Jerusalem: 1982–), a six-volume compilation of halachic analysis and decisions on medical matters, keyed according to the order of the *Shulchan Aruch*. An important work emanating from the Conservative Jewish camp is Elliot N. Dorff, *Matters of Life and Death* (Philadelphia: Jewish Publication Society, 1998). In the Reform context, our own responsa tradition has produced numerous decisions and essays on medical topics, ranging from birth control and abortion, to genetic engineering, the treatment of the terminally ill, organ donation and transplant, the social responsibility of the medical profession, and more. This tradition is summarized and annotated in Mark Washofsky, *Jewish Living* (New York: UAHC Press, 2001), 220–68 and 445–56.

5. BT *Bava Kama* 85a, a midrash on the words *rapo yirapei.*

6. Mention should also be made of the theory of Maimonides (*Commentary to the Mishnah, N'darim* 4:4), who learns that medicine is a mitzvah from Deut. 22:2 (*vahasheivoto lo*), which the Talmud (BT *Sanhedrin* 73a) reads as implying a duty to rescue. Medicine, again, becomes an obligatory and not merely a permitted practice.

7. *Torat HaAdam*, ed. H. D. Chavel (Jerusalem: Mosad Harav Kook, 1964), 41–42.

8. That we have a positive duty to save the lives of those who are in danger is derived from Lev. 19:16 ("Do not stand idly by the blood of your fellow"); see BT *Sanhedrin* 73a; *Yad, Rotzei-ach* 1:14; *SA, CM* 426. That this obligation outweighs virtually all other duties imposed by the Torah is derived in BT *Yoma* 85b, from a midrash on Lev. 18:5; see *Yad, Y'sodei HaTorah* 5:1, and *SA, YD* 157:1. Even if the Talmud does not explicitly identify medicine with *pikuach nefesh*, Ramban notes that the halachic literature does require that the laws of Shabbat and Yom Kippur be set aside when, in the opinion of a physician, their observance would endanger life. See *M. Yoma* 8:5–6 and BT *Yoma* 83b; these rules are summarized in *SA, OC* 328–29 and 618.

9. *Tur* and *SA, YD* 336:1.

10. We say "predominant" because one stream of thought in the classical and (to a lesser extent) the medieval Jewish texts condemns the practice of medicine as an affront to God's sovereignty and a demonstration of lack of faith in God's power to dispense healing. For discussion, see *Teshuvot for the Nineties* (*TFN*), no. 5754.18, pp. 373–74, at notes 1–6. This position, fortunately, has been rejected by the halachic mainstream; see ibid. at notes 7–9, as well as the above discussion.

11. *SA, YD* 336:1.

12. On the attitude of Reform Judaism toward science and its procedures, see *Reform Responsa for the Twenty-first Century*, no. 5759.10, vol. 2, pp. 107–20, section 3, "A Note on Scientific Evidence."

13. This is true even though many medical research studies "fail," that is, they do not yield the positive results toward new discoveries and therapies for which those who conduct the studies may have hoped. In fact, such "failures" are not failures at all. If medicine is a science, it is an *experimental* science, and fundamental to the concept of experimentation is the notion that some experiments will fail to confirm or will disprove particular hypotheses. This "failure," no less than "success," is therefore an integral part of the procedures of science.

14. "We may do anything in order to heal disease, provided that we do not violate thereby the prohibitions against idolatry, sexual immorality, or murder" (BT *P'sachim* 25a–b; *Yad, Y'sodei HaTorah* 5:6). "Sexual immorality" is traditionally identified with the list of prohibited acts of intercourse in Leviticus 18.

15. "One must submit to death rather than violate this prohibition" (BT *Sanhedrin* 74a–b).

16. See *TFN*, no. 5755.11, pp. 381–89.

17. *M. Nidah* 5:3; *Yad, Rotzei-ach* 2:6.

18. This term—"the sanctity of human life"—is not native to the Jewish tradition. We do not find its probable Hebrew equivalent, *k'dushat hachayim*, in the classical Talmudic or halachic sources. On the other hand, it reflects the conviction, most certainly present throughout Jewish thought, that human life possesses supreme value and is therefore inviolate: human life may never be taken or destroyed, save for those circumstances under which the Torah permits or mandates that outcome. One major expression of this commitment is the notion that one's life is not one's personal property, to dispose of as one wishes; rather, human life belongs to God, to whom we are obliged to render an account for the way in which we have used it. Thus, writes Maimonides, the *beit din* is not permitted to accept a ransom from a murderer in order to spare him from execution, "for the life of the victim is not the property of the avenger [or of the court] but of the Holy One" (*Yad, Rotzei-ach* 1:4). In a similar vein, under Jewish law we cannot execute a wrongdoer on the evidence of his own confession. The reason for this, explains one scholar, is that "the life of the human being is not his own property but the property of God, who said 'all lives are Mine' (Ezek. 18:4). Therefore, a person's own confession has no power to dispose of that which does not belong to him" (commentary of R. David ibn Zimra to *Yad, Sanhedrin* 18:6). This insight is applied in contemporary halachic writing to the issue of suicide: Jewish law cannot abide the act of suicide (and indeed presumes that the one who takes his own life has acted under supreme duress) because the human being has no right to dispose of his own life—the possession of God—in this manner (R. Ovadyah Yosef, *Resp. Yabia Omer* 8, OC 37, sec. 5). And, in fact, some present-day Orthodox writers do use the term *k'dushat hachayim* or "sanctity of life" as a way of expressing these ideas; see *Piskei Din Rabaniim* 1, p. 164; and J. David Bleich in *Jewish Bioethics*, ed. Fred Rosner and J. David Bleich (Brooklyn: Hebrew Publishing Co., 1985), 273. We think, therefore, that the term "sanctity" conveys an accurate description of the Jewish belief that life possesses inestimable value and must be protected as though it belongs to the God who created it.

19. *M. Ohalot* 7:6. Some texts, including the printed version of BT *Sanhedrin* 72b and Rashi ad loc., read *rosho* (its head) in place of *rubo* (the major part of it).

20. *Yad, Rotzei-ach* 1:9. On the law of the *rodeif*, which the Rabbis derive from Lev. 19:16 ("do not stand idly by the blood of your fellow"), see *M. Sanhedrin* 8:7 and BT *Sanhedrin* 73a.

21. BT *Sanhedrin* 72b, s.v. *yatza rosho.*

22. A point we have made in *TFN*, no. 5755.13, pp. 171–76. This conclusion is shared by the *Sefer Mei-irat Einayim*, CM, no. 8; *Tiferet Yisrael* to M. *Ohalot* 7:6; *Chidushei R. Akiva Eiger*, M. *Ohalot* 7:6; and *Aruch HaShulchan*, CM 425:7. Rashi's is the better interpretation because it fits with the Mishnah's use of the word *nefesh* to describe the infant upon its emergence from the womb and not prior to that point; clearly, the fetus in utero is not a *nefesh*. Rambam's *rodeif* explanation is difficult: If it is permissible to destroy the fetus because its birth endangers the mother's life, why are we no longer permitted to destroy it when its head or major part has emerged from the womb? Does it not continue to endanger her life? Rather, the distinction must be based upon a difference in status between fetus and mother. So long as it is in utero, the fetus is not a full legal person; hence, in a conflict between fetus and mother, the latter, who *is* a *nefesh*, takes precedence ("her life comes before its life"). Once it has emerged, the fetus becomes a *nefesh*—i.e., a day-old infant, a full legal person—and has a claim to life equal to that of the mother.

23. See Exod. 21:22 and *Sefer Mei-irat Einayim*, CM, no. 8. M. *Nidah* 5:3 and its Talmudic commentary at BT *Nidah* 44b (on Lev. 24:17) establish that "murder" applies only to the killing of a *nefesh*, i.e., the day-old infant and *not* the fetus; see *Torah T'mimah* to Lev. 24:17, no. 47.

24. See *TFN*, no. 5755.13, pp. 171–76, which discusses the line of halachic rulings (beginning with R. Moshe Trani [d. 1639], in *Resp. Maharit*, no. 99) that permit abortions for purposes of the mother's "health" or "need," i.e., in cases that fall short of mortal danger to her. All these rulings base their legal reasoning upon Rashi's interpretation of *M. Ohalot* 7:6: the fetus is not a *nefesh* and thus may be sacrificed on behalf of its mother's overriding need. In Maimonides' view, by contrast, the only warrant for abortion would seem to be the necessity of the procedure to save the mother's life.

25. See A. S. Avraham, *Nishmat Avraham* 3:220–22, for a summary of views. Most Orthodox *poskim* during the preceding century and more have taken the position that abortion is forbidden *d'oraita*, as a matter of Torah law. Among these is R. Isser Y'hudah Unterman, *Resp. Shevet Mi'hudah* 1:29, who defines feticide as an "appurtenance" (*avizraiya*) of murder, that is, as murder in all but name. Others, however, see the prohibition as *d'rabanan*, based upon Rabbinic law; see, for example, R. Ben Zion Ouziel, *Resp. Mishp'tei Ouziel*, CM 46.

26. See above in text and notes 20–24. Those authorities who follow Maimonides' line of reasoning tend to restrict abortion to cases in which the mother's life is endangered by the birth of the fetus, defined as a *rodeif*. Those who follow Rashi, as we have seen, are more likely to permit abortion in cases where the danger to the mother is less than mortal.

27. This is a complicated yet vitally important point of halachah. The Talmud (BT *Arachin* 7a–b) reports in the name of Sh'muel that when a woman dies during labor on Shabbat, a knife may be carried through the public thoroughfare (an otherwise prohibited act) in order that we may use it to cut open her womb and save the fetus. This statement is cited as halachah by Rambam (*Yad, Shabbat* 2:15) and the *Shulchan Aruch* (OC 330:5). The eighth-century geonic work *Halachot G'dolot* extends this provision to earlier stages of the pregnancy: "It is proper to allow a pregnant woman to eat on Yom Kippur if we know that she might miscarry if she does not eat" (*Halachot G'dolot*, ed. Hildesheimer, 319; Venice ed., 31c). Nachmanides writes that this permit to violate the Yom Kippur prohibitions applies when the fetus, and not necessarily the mother, is endangered by fasting. "Even though the laws of *pikuach nefesh* do not in principle apply to the fetus [for the fetus is not a *nefesh* at all], we set aside the laws of Shabbat and Yom Kippur in order that it may survive to perform mitzvot in the future." Ramban stresses that we are obliged to override the laws of Shabbat and Yom Kippur even on behalf of the fetus that is less than forty days old, "when it possesses no vitality [*chayut*] at all" (*Torat HaAdam*, ed. H. D. Chavel, 28–29). It should be noted that not all *rishonim* agree with Ramban's interpretation of the *Halachot G'dolot*. R. Nissim Gerondi (Ran) declares, "These deductions are unnecessary. There is no case of danger to the fetus that is not also a case of danger to the mother" (*Commentary of Ran* to Alfasi, *Yoma*, fol. 3b). In other words, we set aside the laws of Shabbat and Yom Kippur *not* on behalf of the fetus (which is not a *nefesh*) but on behalf of the mother.

28. BT *Yoma* 85b and *Shabbat* 151b, on the verse "The Israelites shall keep the Sabbath…throughout their generations as an everlasting covenant" (Exod. 31:16). The Talmudic references apply this midrash to persons (i.e., *n'fashot*) and not to a fetus in utero. The extension of the rule "We violate one Sabbath on its behalf" is Ramban's innovation; see *Torat HaAdam*, 29.

29. *Contemporary American Reform Responsa* (CARR), no. 16, p. 27.

30. *TFN*, no. 5755.13; CARR, no. 16 (ibid.); *American Reform Responsa* (ARR), no. 171.

31. *TFN*, no. 5755.13 (ibid.), end.

32. *ARR*, no. 82; *Rabbi's Manual* (New York: CCAR Press, 1987), 247.

33. BT *Y'vamot* 69b. We should note that this designation is made by the halachah in accordance with its own categories and frames of reference. It is not a scientific designation, i.e., it is not based upon scientific observation as we understand that term today.

34. See, e.g., ibid. and *Yad, T'rumot* 8:3. The halachah holds that the daughter of a priest (a *bat kohein*) who marries a non-priest forfeits her right to eat of the priestly *t'rumah* once she becomes pregnant with her husband's child. The question is raised: why do we not forbid her to eat the *t'rumah* from the time of the marriage, on the grounds that she *might* be pregnant? The answer is that the law ignores the first forty days of the pregnancy, when the fetus is but "mere water" and lacks legal (if not physical) substance.

35. R. Waldenberg's quotation is from his *Resp. Tzitz Eliezer* 7:48, chap. 1 (pp. 190–91). See also R. Yaakov Emden, *Resp. Chavat Ya-ir*, no. 31; R. Chaim Ozer Grodzinsky, *Resp. Achiezer* 3:65 (end); and R. Yechiel Yaakov Weinberg, *Resp. S'ridei Eish* 3:127 (p. 341).

36. Some *poskim*, in fact, reject the notion that the law concerning abortion is more lenient when the fetus is not yet forty days old. See R. Isser Y. Unterman (*Noam* 6, 1–11) and R. Moshe Feinstein, *Resp. Ig'rot Moshe, CM* 2:69.

37. Ramban (*Torat HaAdam*, ed. H. D. Chavel, 29) makes this very point.

38. *Resp. Shevet HaLevi* 5:47.

39. Wosner notes that the permit to violate Shabbat for the less-than-fortieth-day fetus is "according to the opinion of the *Halachot G'dolot*"; he does not indicate whether he accepts that opinion as halachicly authoritative.

40. R. Chaim David Halevy, *Sefer Assia* 8 (1995): 3–4, and R. Mordechai Eliahu, *T'chumin* 11 (1991): 272–73. The latter writes explicitly that it is forbidden to destroy embryos that are intended for implantation; we may discard only those embryos that will *not* be implanted and therefore have no possibility of further development.

41. See *Reform Responsa for the Twenty-first Century*, no. 5757.2, vol. 1, pp. 159–68.

42. But see *Reform Responsa for the Twenty-first Century*, no. 5758.3, vol. 1, pp. 169–83. Although we do see procreation as a "mitzvah" and although those who desire children are certainly encouraged to make use of new techniques and procedures such as IVF, they are under no obligation to do so.

43. *Reform Responsa for the Twenty-first Century*, no. 5757.2, vol. 1, pp. 159–68, section 4.

44. See the testimony of Rabbi Elliot Dorff and Rabbi Moshe Dovid Tendler in National Bioethics Advisory Commission, *Ethical Issues in Human Stem Cell Research: Volume Three, Religious Perspectives* (Rockville, MD: June 2000).

45. Bruce M. Carlson, *Patten's Foundations of Embryology* (New York: McGraw-Hill, 1996), 3.

46. It is crucial to note that the reason for the embryo's inferior status is the very fact that it lacks the essential quality—implantation in the womb—that would allow us to view it as a "person in becoming" (see the responsum of R. Wosner, note 38). Let us consider, however, the following hypothetical. Suppose it were possible for scientists to develop the fertilized egg for a full nine months in a laboratory environment, without having to implant it into a womb at all. This embryonic human life would skip the fetal stage entirely. Would we say then that it lacks even the minimal status possessed by the fetus? We do not have to address ourselves to hypothetical situations, of course. But the very fact that such a prospect is imaginable suggests to us that we should take great care before dismissing the human embryo as something not worthy of a significant level of moral concern.

LIVE LIVER TRANSPLANTATION
5763.2

Sh'eilah

My question concerns the medical procedure known as live liver
transplantation, in which a significant part of a donor's liver is removed
and transplanted into the body of a recipient. This is unlike the case
of live kidney donation. There, an individual who donates one of two
healthy kidneys places him- or herself in no serious danger aside from
the risks normally associated with major surgery (e.g., from anesthesia),
so that the lifesaving benefit to the recipient far outweighs the risk
incurred by the donor. In the case of live liver donation, the donor
faces a much greater degree of danger. This means that the risk-benefit
comparison, which is so favorable with respect to live kidney donation,
is much more difficult to assess.

According to our understanding of Reform Judaism, is it ethical to
conduct this procedure? Should we permit an individual to risk his or her
life and health by donating a large section of his or her liver, even if this
would save the life of the recipient? How does this procedure comport
with the basic medical ethic of "do no harm"? And how do we evaluate
this procedure in light of the concept of "informed consent," a standard
so much a part of the current medical environment? Can there really
be "informed consent" when a person is asked to put his or her life in
danger? Can there be "informed consent" when it is a family member in
need and when "no" is not an answer easily lived with? (Rabbi Deborah
Pipe-Mazo, New York, New York)

T'shuvah

Before we begin our *t'shuvah*, we should acknowledge the principle
that stands behind it and that guides it throughout: the mitzvah of
healing, *r'fuah*.[1] The practice of medicine is the most common means

by which we fulfill the obligation to preserve human life (*pikuach nefesh*), a duty that takes precedence over virtually every other core Jewish value. All Jews, we would think, agree on this general point. Where we disagree is on the specifics: what, in any particular situation, constitutes an acceptable practice of "medicine"? That is the case here, with our *sh'eilah*. Our generation has long since accepted the proposition that organ transplantation from donors dead or living is a valid form of medicine, of the healing arts. Yet as our questioner notes, some transplantation procedures seem to pose an unacceptable risk to the living organ donor, thus constituting an example not of medicine but of the "harm" that physicians must not inflict upon their patients. In framing our response, we shall first consider the issue of organ transplantation in general: what are the circumstances under which Jewish law, according to our understanding of it, permits the donation of a human organ from a dead or a living person to help save the life or health of another? How does the element of risk, the danger to the living organ donor, affect the calculation of these circumstances? At that point, we will be in a position to ask whether our tradition forbids, permits, encourages, or even requires an individual to donate part of his or her liver to another human being.

1. CADAVERIC ORGAN DONATION

As of this writing, nearly eighty percent of all organs transplanted in the United States are taken from deceased donors.[2] Given the large number of potential organ recipients who currently await transplantation[3] and the efforts by governments and other institutions to encourage individuals to become organ donors upon death,[4] it is clear that cadaveric organ donation is a critically important resource in the struggle against disease. For this reason, we might suppose that Jewish law, which places such great emphasis upon the mitzvah of healing, would raise no objections to this practice. Yet it is far from obvious that this is so. The harvesting of organs from deceased persons might well conflict with another central Judaic value, that of *k'vod hameit*, the obligation to respect the dignity of the dead. This respect entails that human remains are to be quickly and properly buried; we are not to utilize or manipulate them for our own purposes, even for the fulfillment of the mitzvah of *r'fuah*.[5] "The dead," it has been noted, "are not obligated to fulfill the commandments…and we are [therefore] not empowered to deny them the honor that is their due."[6] In particular, the use of cadaver organs for transplantation would seem to conflict with three separate ritual prohibitions:[7] the ban against deriving benefit or profit from the dead (*isur hanaah min hameit*),[8] the disrespectful treatment of the corpse (*nivul hameit*),[9] and the delay in burial of the remains (*m'niat hak'vurah*).[10]

Halachic authorities, however, have come to recognize organ donation as an exception to each of these prohibitions. For example, Rabbi Isser Y'hudah Unterman, a former chief rabbi of Israel, rules that the positive duty to preserve human life (*pikuach nefesh*) outweighs the prohibition against deriving benefit from the dead. As additional support, he offers the novel argument that the prohibition ceases to apply "when these organs are 'resurrected' [i.e., through the process of transplantation]" and can be considered "alive" rather than "dead."[11] Various *poskim* waive the proscription against "disrespectful treatment" when the otherwise forbidden act is undertaken for a good and appropriate reason.[12] And once an organ has been transplanted into the body of the recipient, it is no longer part of the body of the deceased and thus no longer subject to the requirement of burial.[13]

Reform Jewish tradition concurs with this permissive view. Indeed, we teach our people that organ donation is a mitzvah,[14] and we are not so concerned in this regard with the various prohibitions concerning the handling of the remains of the deceased. This is not to say that we do not believe that the dead deserve respectful treatment, but simply that the traditional definitions of *k'vod hameit* and *nivul hameit* came into being long before medical science developed the technologies of organ transplantation. Now that physicians and surgeons can save many lives through these procedures, they have become an integral feature of the legitimate practice of medicine. In this new scientific reality, the operative rule is the dictum that "any and all measures, with the exception of idolatry, sexual immorality, and murder, may be utilized for the sake of healing."[15] Cadaveric organ donation is included in these measures. It is a mitzvah, and it must not in any way be associated with the acts that our tradition condemns as disgraceful treatment of the dead.

2. ORGAN DONATION BY LIVE DONORS

When a suitable cadaveric organ is not available for transplantation, doctors may take an organ from a live volunteer. From the standpoint of Jewish tradition, an organ donor fulfills one of the most profound duties recognized by the Torah: the mitzvah to rescue a person from mortal danger. As the Talmud states:

> From where do we learn that if one sees his fellow drowning in the river, attacked by wild beasts, or endangered by robbers that one is obligated to save him? "You shall not stand idly by the blood of your neighbor" (Lev. 19:16).[16]

This obligation, however, may conflict with another requirement, the duty to preserve one's own life, which stems from the obligation to preserve human life in general (*pikuach nefesh*). The Rabbis learn this obligation from Leviticus 18:5: "These are the mitzvot... that a person shall perform and live by them," to which the midrash adds: "and not *die* by them."[17] This implies that a person should not perform a mitzvah if that act endangers his or her life. Thus, the prohibitions against work (*m'lachah*) on Shabbat and the commandment to fast on Yom Kippur are waived when the observance of these mitzvot would jeopardize an individual's life or health.[18] It follows that the mitzvah of rescue is also annulled when that action would endanger the life of the potential rescuer.

We shall examine this question in some detail below, because it is central to every halachic discussion concerning the propriety of organ donation. For the moment, let it suffice to say that, in Jewish terms, the ethical issue demands a measurement of the degree of risk in each particular case. While halachah forbids suicide and does not require us to risk mortal danger in order to fulfill the commandments (including Lev. 19:16), halachic authorities are generally willing to permit a living person to donate an organ when physicians judge the operation to pose no serious risk of death or injury to the donor.[19]

3. LIVE LIVER TRANSPLANTATION: THE PROCEDURE

What degree of risk does live liver donation pose to the donor? The surgery[20] usually involves the taking of the left lateral part of the liver from the donor. The principal arteries, veins, and biliary ducts of the donor organ are connected to the corresponding vessels and ducts of the recipient. The cut vessels and ducts on the surface of the donor liver are sealed to minimize leakage of blood or bile. The incision is then closed. Those who perform the surgery argue that it is safe, on the basis of several facts: (a) an individual with a normally functioning liver can survive a 75 percent loss of liver tissue; (b) no more than 30 percent of the donor liver mass is excised; (c) in the above case, the donor's liver should regenerate in one month; (d) the donor will recover most, if not all, of his or her liver function. The above applies to donation of the left lobe of the liver; some researchers have obtained similar results when taking the donor's right liver lobe, a more difficult and potentially dangerous procedure.[21] A team of Japanese physicians, surveying 470 cases of live liver transplantation at Kyoto University hospital from 1990 to 1999, found no donor deaths and concluded that "the morbidity of living donors is low or minimal even for right lobectomy, the most extended procedure, and complete recovery can be expected in all cases."[22] An American survey published in 2000 estimated that donor death occurs in 0.2 percent of cases of adult donors and 0.13 percent for pediatric donors; among other cases, "all donors returned to predonation activities," most by the end of three months following the surgery and all by the end of one year.[23]

Yet some observers are more cautious in their evaluation of the data. In the opinion of one expert, although "formidable success appears to have been attained with the adult-to-adult procedure thus far," the world "still awaits center-specific and compiled data to determine whether the procedure truly reduces adult waiting list times for liver transplant recipients with minimal donor risk."[24] The director of a live donor program in Massachusetts states frankly that "adult living liver donation is much riskier [than living kidney donation], and there is little published data on rates of complications and mortality among the donors."[25] A recent study finds that while the mortality rate for live liver donations is low, the rate of complications (morbidity) is "significant": 65 of the 449 donors surveyed (14.5 percent) experienced one or more complications of donation, including bile leak (in 27 donors), the need for blood transfusion, and the need for a subsequent operation.[26]

The evidence, therefore, presents a decidedly mixed picture. Live liver donation is "safe" in that many medical practitioners believe its risks to be manageable: the overwhelming majority of liver donors survive the operation and recover full function. Yet the procedure is definitely a serious one; liver donors do risk more significant medical complications than those posed by donors of other organs.

4. LIVE LIVER TRANSPLANTATION: THE ETHICS

In addressing this question, our *sho-elet* refers to two separate and distinct ethical traditions: the philosophical discourse known as "secular medical ethics" and the tradition of Jewish thought and lore that we generally designate as halachah. Concerning the former, she asks whether the procedure transgresses against the guiding medical-ethical principles of nonmalfeasance ("above all, do no harm"[27]) and of informed consent. The response in the first case depends, we think, upon one's definition of "harm." For example, some argue that organ donation is not "harmful" so long as "the benefits to both donor and recipient...outweigh the risks associated with the donation and transplantation of the living donor organ."[28] This general standard may very well apply to live liver transplantation, which is a clear benefit to the recipient and which, it can be argued, may not pose an unacceptably high degree of risk to the donor.

The second principle, on the other hand, presents a greater difficulty. "Informed consent" means, first, that a patient agrees to a suggested medical procedure only when he or she has been supplied with all material information that a reasonable medical layperson would consider significant with regard to that decision, and second, that the patient make his or her decision in an autonomous manner, free of coercion.[29] Yet, as our *sho-elet* notes, "autonomy" and "informed consent" may not apply in a situation such as ours, where the potential donor is likely to be a family member operating under powerful emotional pressures to agree to the surgery. This is a telling point. Research indicates that decisions concerning organ donation are often made quickly, as soon as the possibility is raised to the potential donor, and *not* on the basis of deliberation or informed consent.[30] Indeed, concludes one study, "informed consent in living donation is a myth," because the context in which the donor must choose guarantees that the decision cannot be made in a coercion-free manner.[31]

The Jewish ethical tradition, as we have seen, would analyze our *sh'eilah* in accordance with the conflicting duties of rescue and of self-preservation: if the attempt to rescue would endanger the life of the would-be rescuer, then he or she is not required—indeed, is forbidden—to make the attempt. The logic of this prohibition is as stark as it is elegant: since each human being is created in God's image, then each human life possesses the same intrinsic value. No life is more "worthy" of preservation than another; although my blood is no redder than yours, neither is your blood any redder than mine. One who risks mortal danger in order to rescue another is thereby making the ethically unacceptable calculation that the value of the other's life surpasses that of his or her own. In the event that we must choose between saving one life or another, the only sure course is to make no "choice" at all, to allow events to take their course, even if that means that the endangered person will die.[32]

Does this rule govern our case? Although the live liver donor does undertake a certain degree of risk, that risk is much less than the danger to the life of the patient who needs the transplant. To put this into traditional halachic terminology, the donor enters a situation of *safeik sakanah* (possible, but less-than-mortal danger), while the patient is in a situation of *vadai sakanah* (mortal danger). We would therefore ask: does *vadai* outweigh *safeik*? Granted that one need not risk mortal danger to save the life of another, is one permitted—or even required—to accept a lesser degree of risk in order to fulfill the duty of rescue, the obligation imposed by Leviticus 19:16?

We begin our answer with what must be considered the predominant view in the halachah. Most halachic authorities who have considered this question rule there is *no* obligation to rescue when the attempt would involve even *safeik sakanah* to the life of the rescuer.[33] Their analysis tends to being with the words of Maimonides, who codifies the rule of rescue as follows: "*One who is able to rescue [kol hayachol l'hatzil] and does not do so* violates the commandment 'you shall not stand idly by the blood of your neighbor.'"[34] Some suggest that by these italicized words, which do not appear in the Talmudic source of the rule, Rambam seeks to place limits upon the requirement when the element of risk is present. R. Menachem HaMeiri, for example, writes that one is required to attempt the rescue "if one is *able* to do so [*yachol l'hatzilo*] in the absence of danger [*b'lo sakanah*]."[35] HaMeiri, of course, might be referring here to *vadai sakanah*, mortal danger. R. Yoel Sirkes, however, reads less-than-mortal risk into Maimonides' words: "When Rambam writes 'one who is *able* to rescue,' he refers to a situation in which one is certain [*b'de'ein safeik*] that he will be successful in the attempt. One is not, therefore, obligated to risk potential danger [*safeik sakanah*] in order to rescue another."[36] A leading commentator interprets the *Shulchan Aruch* to the same effect.[37] Many authorities go farther, ruling that one is *forbidden* to enter into a situation of potential danger to save a person whose life is in mortal danger.[38] They base this conclusion upon various passages of the Talmud[39] as well as a strictly literal (and eminently logical) reading of Leviticus 18:5: if one is commanded to live and not die by the mitzvot, then one is forbidden to place one's life in any jeopardy whatsoever, to risk even the possibility of death [*safeik*

mitah] in order to perform any mitzvah, including the duty to rescue.[40]
R. David ibn Zimra (Radbaz, sixteenth- to seventeenth-century Egypt)
offers a somewhat different line of reasoning in a famous responsum.
Suppose, he was asked, that the sultan were to give a Jew the following
choice: either let me cut off one of your limbs, or I will kill one of
your fellow Jews. Is the first Jew obligated to undergo the "surgery,"
inasmuch as he faces a lesser degree of danger than does the second
Jew? Radbaz answers that such a demand would offend against reason
and common sense (*haseichel v'has'vara*). Since the Torah's ways "are
ways of pleasantness,"[41] we cannot imagine that it would impose such a
moral obligation upon us. Whoever enters a situation of *safeik sakanah*
in order to fulfill the mitzvah of Leviticus 19:16, concludes Radbaz, is a
"pious fool" (*chasid shoteh*).[42]

With these considerations in mind, contemporary *poskim* arrive at their
decisions concerning organ transplantation. R. Yitzchak Yaakov Weiss,
basing himself in large part upon the responsum of Radbaz, forbids
live kidney donation on the grounds that the surgery and the possible
subsequent complications place the donor in a state of *safeik sakanah*.[43]
While other authorities permit live kidney donation, they tend to do so
because physicians report that the surgery has become routine to the
point that it poses no risk, not even *safeik sakanah*, to the donor.[44] If, on
the other hand, kidney donation did pose such a risk, these authorities,
too, would likely prohibit the surgery. Given that, according to the
medical data we have surveyed, live liver donation surgery is regarded as
significantly "riskier" than kidney donation, it surely constitutes *safeik
sakanah*. If so, then in light of the position we have just described, an
individual is not obligated—and may well be forbidden—to donate part
of his or her liver for transplantation.

The foregoing, however, is but one side of an old dispute in Jewish law.
There is another side, a different voice that emerges from our source.
It is a voice that declares, against the predominant view we have just
described, that we are obliged to rescue our fellow human being even
when the attempt would place us in potential danger (*safeik sakanah*).

This interpretation is supported by several arguments. First, none of the passages from the Babylonian Talmud that are usually cited on this question clearly state that one is forbidden to risk *safeik sakanah* in order to save another. True, it is possible to *derive* that conclusion from those passages, but an interpreter need not do so.[45] In fact, one can just as easily arrive at the opposite decision on the basis of those very sources[46] and others.[47] Second, none of the major halachic compendia, such as Maimonides' Code, the *Tur*, or the *Shulchan Aruch*, rule that the obligation to rescue is annulled in the face of *safeik sakanah*. Again, it is possible to read these works in such a way as to support that ruling, but one is not compelled to do so by the logic of the texts.[48] Finally, commentators have for centuries cited a passage from the *Talmud Y'rushalmi* as evidence that one is indeed obliged to accept a lesser degree of danger in order to rescue a person whose life is in mortal danger.[49] Although that passage, like those in the Babylonian Talmud, is hardly free of difficulty,[50] some *poskim* do rely upon it for purposes of halachic decision.[51]

The "other" view, a more stringent interpretation of the duty to rescue, has never been completely vanquished by its opponents. It has, in fact, exerted a constant and considerable influence upon the *p'sikah* (halachic decision) of a number of authorities who hold to the predominant halachic position. In his *Arukh HaShulchan*, R. Yechiel M. Epstein (nineteenth- to twentieth-century Lithuania) writes:[52]

> The *poskim* cite the *Talmud Y'rushalmi* to the effect that a person is obligated to risk *safeik sakanah* in order to rescue his fellow. This passage has been omitted from the earlier codes, since our [i.e., the Babylonian] Talmud takes the opposite position. Each instance, however, must be judged on its own merits. One should weigh one's decision carefully and not protect himself more than is necessary [*yoter m'dai*]...for when a person saves one Jewish life, it is as though he has saved an entire world.[53]

A commentator to the *Shulchan Aruch* states the point as follows:

One should in any event weigh the situation carefully, to determine whether it is in fact a case of *safeik sakanah*, and not to be overly strict [*shelo l'dakdek beyoter*] in the matter. As we have learned elsewhere, one who is overly strict in insisting upon his own rights will one day lose that which he seeks to protect.[54]

These remarks express a tension between what the authors perceive as the letter of the law and what we might call the law's higher aspirations. The authors are aware that a too-literal application of the halachah's minimum standard, the mitzvah of self-preservation, will allow the individual to exempt him- or herself in virtually all cases from the mitzvah of rescue. Yet such an outcome sharply conflicts with the Torah's vision of the just and compassionate society. Nowhere is this tension more evident than in the words of Rabbi Isser Y'hudah Unterman:

Since the leading codes do not rule explicitly [that one is obligated to assume potential danger in order to rescue], the uncertainty in the law requires that we apply the rule "your own life takes precedence." Yet we must define what we mean by *safeik sakanah*. Not every fear or concern on the part of the would-be rescuer deserves to be called "danger." For example, if a person is drowning in a river, and a man is present who knows how to swim, but this man worries lest he catch cold on account of the chilly water—can this really be called *safeik sakanah*? Suppose that a person hears his neighbor cry for help against men who are attacking him. Is this person exempt in any such case from offering assistance, simply because he fears that the attackers may harm him?[55]

We agree: a literal application of the predominant halachic viewpoint—if, indeed, that viewpoint is the "correct" understanding of the Jewish law of rescue—can lead to absurd and intolerable consequences. A community whose citizens press the mitzvah of self-preservation to its legal and logical extreme is a community defined by selfishness, where none will reach out to aid their endangered brothers and sisters.[56] It is a community where the qualities of personal courage, nobility, and selflessness do not exist. It is the sort of community in which none of us would wish to live. Our understanding of Torah, of Jewish tradition, and of our ethical responsibilities to our fellow human beings demands that we balance the predominant viewpoint, which grants us the necessary right to safeguard our own lives from danger, with the minority viewpoint, which reaches beyond this bare minimum standard of conduct toward a higher aspiration for our lives. What this means in practice is that those who teach and interpret Jewish tradition must find a way to say "yes" to the decision to become a live organ donor, even when that decision involves a degree of risk to the one who makes it.

Various *poskim* do just that. In addressing the question of live kidney donation, Rabbi Moshe Feinstein notes that the commandment to preserve one's own life supersedes virtually all other obligations; under its terms, we are even forbidden to place ourselves in a situation of possible danger. Still, he rules that the duty to rescue may be an exception to this rule. Since the purpose of rescue is to save a human life that is equal in God's eyes to our own, then although one cannot be required to endanger himself to rescue, "it is obviously permissible to risk potential danger [*safeik*] to save a person who faces mortal danger [*vadai*]."[57] In dealing with the same question, Rabbi Ovadyah Yosef writes that "it is a permissible act and a mitzvah [*mutar v'gam mitzvah*] for a person to donate one of his kidneys to his fellow."[58] By mitzvah, Rabbi Yosef clearly means that the donation of a kidney is a meritorious and praiseworthy act though not an obligatory one, for which he would have used the word *chovah*.[59] A mitzvah, in this sense, is an act that is encouraged if not necessarily required of us, an act that, if performed, is worthy of our commendation and respect, an act that reaches the higher aspirations that Torah would have us set for our lives. Both these rabbis, in other words, uphold the predominant interpretation of the halachah, but they refuse to let it confine them like a straitjacket. They want the religious Jew to consider a choice that advances beyond that which the law absolutely requires. Aware that today's surgeons are not to be compared to the sultan's executioner, they know that the act of organ donation, in a procedure that is carefully supervised by medical professionals, is hardly the behavior of a "pious fool." To put this another way, they read the halachah not only according to its predominant interpretation but also according to the minority viewpoint that calls upon us to realize a more demanding standard of moral conduct.

It is the way that we, too, read our Torah and apply it to the *sh'eilah* before us. The question we consider here—the assumption of personal risk in order to save the life of another—is a difficult one that admits of two plausible answers. Accordingly, our tradition would have us address it in a way that does justice to both sides. On the one hand, the majority interpretation of Jewish tradition reminds us that undertaking a risk to one's life, even when that risk is *safeik* or potential, is a fateful decision that should not be forced upon a person. This is all the more true in the case of live liver donation, a procedure that poses a greater degree of risk than do other kinds of *safeik sakanah*. Yet the minority position, the "other voice" that emerges from our sources, teaches us that a person's free and reasonable decision to become a live liver donor and thereby save the life of a fellow human being is by no means a violation of Jewish law and ethics. On the contrary: it is a choice that reflects Judaism's highest legal and ethical standards.

CONCLUSION

All of the above leads us to the following points:

1. Jewish tradition sees the preservation of human life as a mitzvah of the highest order. By its terms, we are required to protect ourselves from danger and to rescue, if we can, the lives of those in harm's way.

2. In the event of an unavoidable clash between these two requirements, if the attempt to rescue another person would pose a

mortal danger (*vadai sakanah*) to our own lives, we are forbidden to attempt the rescue. In such a case, we learn that "your own life takes precedence" (*chayecha kodmin* [BT *Bava M'tzia* 62a]).

3. The tradition gives us no unambiguous guidance should the attempt to rescue another pose a less-than-mortal danger (*safeik sakanah*) to our lives. Most halachic authorities rule that one is not obligated, and is perhaps even forbidden, to risk *safeik sakanah* in order to save another. At the same time, the opposing viewpoint, which permits or even requires us to take on *safeik sakanah* in such an instance, is at least as well supported by our sources. That more stringent minority viewpoint reflects a higher standard for our duty to our fellow human beings, a higher aspiration for our moral conduct.

4. Since live liver donation involves a measure of risk to the donor, an individual cannot be required to undergo that procedure in order to save the life of another. Indeed, that very refusal to serve as a donor can be seen as fulfilling the mitzvah of Leviticus 18:5, the duty to preserve one's life. That decision is a valid Jewish choice, and we must not criticize a person for making it.

5. The procedure's risks, though not insignificant, are manageable, so that the donor is far more likely to recover full physical function than to suffer permanent medical complications. One is therefore permitted to serve as a live liver donor, thereby fulfilling the mitzvah of Leviticus 19:16, the duty to rescue. That person sets an example of nobility and courage worthy of our admiration and even our emulation.

6. We recognize that the value of "informed consent" is exceedingly difficult to realize in situations such as this. Potential liver donors are often family members of the patient, subject to the sorts of emotional pressure that negate the likelihood of an autonomous, non-coerced decision. Yet this does not mean that an ethical

decision for live liver donation is impossible to obtain. First, we must remember that ethical decisions are made in the real world, a world in which every one of us lives within a tight web of social connection and in which none of us is immune to the "pressures" of social and family life. The demand for total autonomy, therefore, is unrealistic. Second, while "pressures" cannot be entirely avoided, physicians, other medical personnel, and, indeed, the family's rabbi can make sure that precautions are taken to protect the would-be donor against excessive pressure.[60] They can also remind him or her that one is not obligated to say "yes," that "no" is also a legitimate decision.

NOTES

1. For sources and discussion, see *Reform Responsa for the Twenty-first Century*, no. 5761.7, vol. 2, pp. 121–42, section 3, at notes 5ff.

2. The data, covering the period from January 1, 1988–March 31, 2003, are collected by the Organ Procurement and Transplantation Network, the unified transplant network established by the United States Congress under the National Organ Transplant Act (NOTA) of 1984 (http://optn.transplant.hrsa.gov/SharedContentDocuments/NOTA_as_amended_-_Jan_2008.pdf, accessed August 16, 2009). These figures deal with the following organs: kidney, liver, pancreas, heart, lung, and intestine. Other donations (e.g., corneal tissue) are not included.

3. As of this writing, more than 82,000 persons are currently on waiting lists for organ transplantation in the United States, while 6,279 transplantations were performed in the United States during the first three months of 2003. See the data collected by UNOS (http://www.unos.org/data/default.asp?displayType'usData , accessed August 16, 2009), the nonprofit, scientific, and educational organization that administers the Organ Procurement and Transplantation Network.

4. Resources and information may be found at the website www.organdonor.gov (accessed August 16, 2009), sponsored by the United States Department of Health and Human Services.

5. R. Yechiel M. Tucazinsky (twentieth-century *Eretz Yisrael*) entitles the fifth chapter of his *Gesher HaChayim*, a treatise on the Jewish law of mourning and burial, "*K'vod HaMeit.*" The chapter begins with a one-sentence paragraph: "Whosoever takes part in

the preparation and burial of a human corpse must bear in mind that he is dealing with a holy thing."

6. R. Yitzchak Yaakov Weiss (twentieth-century England and Israel), *Resp. Minchat Yitzchak* 5:8.

7. See R. A. S. Avraham, *Nishmat Avraham* (Jerusalem, 1982), YD 349:3, pp. 261–64. On all the following, we are indebted to our colleague, Rabbi Moshe Zemer, for his article *"T'rumat Eivarim V'Hahalachah,"* in *Dilemot Be-etikah Refu'it*, ed. R. Cohen-Almagor (Jerusalem: Van Leer Institute/Hakibbutz Hameuchad, 2002), 265–82.

8. BT *Sanhedrin* 47b; *Yad, Aveil* 14:21; *SA, YD* 349:1.

9. The phrase *nivul hameit* is not found in the classical Rabbinic sources. Indeed, the word *nivul* as "disgraceful treatment" is applied twice by R. Y'hudah b. Ilai to activities with respect to *living* persons: a form of cosmetics (M. *Mo-eid Katan* 1:7) and a form of execution (M. *Sanhedrin* 7:3). On the other hand, the concept of *nivul* is used with respect to the dead in various places, including BT *Arachin* 7a, *Mo-eid Katan* 27b–28a, and *Bava Batra* 154a.

10. The mitzvah to bury the dead in the ground is derived from Deut. 21:23; see BT *Sanhedrin* 46b. The prohibition against unnecessary delay in burial is found in M. *Sanhedrin* 6:5; *Yad, Aveil* 4:8; and *SA, YD* 357:1.

11. Rabbi I. Y. Unterman, *Shevet Mi'hudah* (Jerusalem: Mosad Harav Kook, 1955), 54–55. Rabbi Unterman, who admits that his *chidush* (novel legal argument) is at first glance somewhat "strange" (*muzar*), compares organ transplantation to famous instances of resurrection (*t'chiyat hameitim*) in the Bible (e.g., Ezekiel 37; II Kings 4): just as there is never a question of forbidden *hanaah* in those biblical cases, so there should be no similar issue with respect to transplantation. Like many *chidushim*, Unterman's is forced and, we think, ultimately unpersuasive. Kidneys, corneal tissue, and other organs retrieved from corpses are in fact "dead," not "living," at the time of the transplantation. *T'chiyat hameitim*, moreover, pertains not to the realm of human science but to the miracles traditionally associated with the end of days. The argument that *pikuach nefesh* takes precedence over the prohibition against deriving benefit from the dead is more than sufficient to permit this medical procedure. Still, Rabbi Unterman's suggestion is an important example of the power of creative thinking in halachah—a trait not restricted to liberal rabbis—and of the readiness of a leading *poseik* to find a way to transcend the existing conceptual structure of Jewish law in a situation where it is vital to forge an affirmative response.

12. R. Ovadyah Yosef (twentieth- to twenty-first-century Israel), *Resp. Yabia Omer* 3, YD 23. The classic precedent is provided by R. Yechezkel Landau (eighteenth-century Bohemia), *Resp. Noda Bihudah* 2, YD 210, who permits autopsies when the procedure is needed to uncover information to save the lives of persons "in our presence," despite the fact that autopsy was generally regarded as an instance of *nivul hameit*. See as well R. Shaul Natanson (nineteenth-century Galicia), *Resp. Sho'el Umeshiv* I, 1:231, who permitted the exhumation and examination of a corpse in order to determine its identity and to permit the deceased's wife to remarry; *nivul hameit* applies only when the "desecration" is committed for no valid purpose, and sparing a woman from the fate of the *agunah* is indeed a valid purpose.

13. *Resp. Yabia Omer* 3, YD 22. R. Yosef cites the opinion of Rabbi Unterman (see at note 11) in this context.

14. For example, the "Matan Chaim" program of the Union for Reform Judaism (http://urj.org//life/health/bioethics//?syspage=document&item_id=16960) actively encourages organ donation.

15. BT *Avodah Zarah* 25a; *Yad, Y'sodei HaTorah* 5:6; *SA, YD* 155:2.

16. BT *Sanhedrin* 73a. The passage goes on to ask why the verse from Leviticus is necessary, seeing that the duty to rescue one's fellow is also derived from Deut. 22:2. It answers that the Leviticus verse adds an obligation to hire others to perform the rescue when one cannot personally perform that action.

17. BT *Yoma* 85b.

18. For details, see *SA, OC* 328 and 618.

19. See below at note 44.

20. The Responsa Committee expresses its deep gratitude to the Committee on Bioethics of the Union of American Hebrew Congregations, chaired by Harvey S. Gordon, MD, for its invaluable assistance in the collection and analysis of the relevant scientific data.

21. S. T. Fan et al., "Safety of Donors in Live Donor Liver Transplantation using Right Lobe Grafts," *Archives of Surgery* 135, no. 3 (March 2000): 336–40.

22. S. Fujita et al., "Hepatic Grafts from Live Donors: Donor Morbidity for 470 Cases of Live Donation," *Transplantation International* 13, no. 5 (2000): 333–39.

23. J. F. Renz and J. P. Roberts, "Long-Term Complications of Living Donor Transplantation," *Liver Transplantation* 6 (6 Suppl 2): S73–76.

24. D. S. Seaman, "Adult Living Donor Liver Transplantation: Current Status," *Journal of Clinical Gastroenterology* 33, no. 2 (August 2001): 97–106.

25. "Panacea or Peril? Do New Treatments Save Lives or Do They Endanger Them?" *Medical Ethics Advisor*, August 2001, citing Elizabeth Pomfret, MD, director of live donor program at Lahey Clinic in Burlington, MA.

26. Robert S. Brown, Jr., in *New England Journal of Medicine* 348 (February 2003): 818–25.

27. This maxim, most familiar in its Latin formulation *Primum non nocere*, is often attributed to Hippocrates and/or Galen. Although both those authorities do make statements to this effect, the source of the precise wording remains unclear. See Albert R. Jonsen, "Do No Harm: Axiom of Medical Ethics," in *Philosophical Medical Ethics: Its Nature and Significance*, ed. S. F. Spicker and H. Tristam Engelhardt, Jr. (Boston: Reidel, 1977), 27–41.

28. M. Abecassis et al., "Consensus Statement of the Live Donor Organ," *Journal of the American Medical Association* 284, no. 22 (2000): 2919–26.

29. This definition reflects the formulation of American law, represented especially by the leading case *Canterbury v. Spence*, 464 F.2d 772 (D.C. Cir. 1972). One of the major building blocks of the doctrine of informed consent was the decision of Judge Benjamin N. Cardozo in *Schloendorff v. Society of N.Y. Hospital*, 105 N.E. 92 (N.Y. 1914): "Every human being of adult years and sound mind has a right to determine what shall be done with his own body, and a surgeon who performs an operation without his patient's consent commits an assault for which he is liable in damages." See, in general, Ruth R. Faden, Tom L. Beauchamp, in collaboration with Nancy M. P. King, *A History and Theory of Informed Consent* (New York: Oxford University Press, 1986).

30. "Empirical studies show that most kidney donors make their decision to donate immediately after the subject of transplant is first mentioned to them, and no additional information has any effect on their decision" (J. D. Lantos and M. Siegler, "Re-evaluating Donor Criteria: Live Donors," *The Surgeon General's Workshop on Increasing Organ Donation: Background Papers* [July 8–10, 1991], [Washington, D.C.: U.S. Department of Health and Human Services, 1992], 271–90).

31. See Austern Garwood-Gowers, *Living Donor Organ Transplantation: Key Legal and Ethical Issues* (Brookfield, VT: Ashgate/Dartmouth, 1999), 67.

32. The foregoing rests upon the following sources: BT *Sanhedrin* 74a ("How do you know that your blood is redder than that of another?"); Rashi ad loc., s.v. *mai chazit*

(the requirement to do nothing when faced with a choice between two lives); BT *Bava M'tzia* 62a (in accordance with the view of Rabbi Akiva: when two men are lost in the desert, the one who holds the container of water may drink it all in order to survive— i.e., he allows the status quo to remain in effect—rather than share the water with his fellow or give it all to him).

33. See R. Ovadyah Yosef, who surveys the literature in his usual comprehensive manner and finds that "most of the later authorities" (*rov haacharonim*) hold this position (*Resp. Y'chaveh Daat* 3:84).

34. *Yad, Rotzei-ach* 1:14.

35. Meiri, *Beit HaB'chirah, Sanhedrin* 73a (ed. A. Sofer, Frankfurt, 1930), pp. 272–73.

36. *Bayit Chadash* to Tur, CM 426.

37. *Sefer Mei-irat Einayim*, CM 426:1.

38. Among these are: R. Yonah Ashkenazi (fifteenth-century Germany), *Sefer Isur Veheter, k'lal* 59, no. 38; R. Shneur Zalman of Liady (eighteenth century), *Shulchan Aruch HaRav*, OC 329:8; R. Naftali Tzvi Y'hudah Berlin (nineteenth-century Volozhyn), *HaAmek HaSh'eilah, she'lta* 147, end; R. Yosef Babad (nineteenth-century Poland), *Minchat Chinuch, mitzvah* 237, no. 2; R. Eliezer Yehudah Waldenberg, *Resp. Tzitz Eliezer* 9:45, chap. 7; R. Yechiel Yaakov Weinberg (twentieth-century Germany-Switzerland), *Resp. S'ridei Eish* 2:78; R. Yaakov Breisch (twentieth-century Germany-Switzerland), *Resp. Chelkah Yaakov*, CM, no. 33; R. Moshe Feinstein (twentieth-century USA), *Resp. Ig'rot Moshe*, YD 2:174.

39. One of these passages is the dilemma of the "two men lost in the desert" (BT *Bava M'tzia* 62a). There, Ben Petura requires the one who holds the water to share it with his fellow, even if both of them will thereby die of thirst, while R. Akiva rules that the one who holds the water should keep it for himself, ensuring his survival. R. Berlin (see the preceding note) understands Ben Petura's position as a hopeful stopgap: if the two men share the water, perhaps they can survive a day or two and someone will come along to rescue them. Thus, sharing the water does not place its owner in a situation of mortal danger but of *possible* danger; after all, he will not *necessarily* die if he shares it. Thus, by ruling that the man need not share the water, R. Akiva declares that he must not risk even *safeik sakanah* in order to save his fellow.

40. See Rashi, BT *Yoma* 85b, s.v. *d'shmuel leit leih pirka.*

41. After Prov. 3:17.

42. *Resp. Radbaz* 3:627. Radbaz does conclude that if the first Jew is certain that he will not die if the oppressors sever, say, his hand or foot, he is permitted to submit to this demand as an act of piety (*midat chasidut*). He warns, however, that if there is any danger that the severing of the organ will lead to the "donor's" death, he is forbidden even on grounds of piety from assenting to this demand.

43. *Resp. Minchat Yitzchak* 6:103.

44. R. Yosef, note 33; R. Waldenberg, *Resp. Tzitz Eliezer* 10:25, chap. 7; R. Yisrael Meir Lau (twentieth- to twenty-first-century Israel), *Resp. Yichal Yisrael*, no. 73.

45. See R. Unterman, *Shevet Mi'hudah*, 17–21. One example: the case of the two men lost in the desert (BT *Bava M'tzia* 62a). As we have seen (at note 39), R. Naftali Tzvi Y'hudah Berlin interprets the act of sharing the water as placing one's life in a state of *safeik sakanah*. Hence, because we follow Rabbi Akiva, who rules that one is forbidden to share his water, we learn that one is forbidden to risk *safeik sakanah* in order to save the life of another. Yet this reading of the case is surely forced. The Talmud never hints that the men may be rescued in a day or two. On the contrary: "If they both drink the water, they will both die [Rashi: because there is not enough water to allow them to reach the next settlement]." There is no ambiguity here: by sharing his water, the man holding the container risks mortal danger (*vadai sakanah*). The story teaches us nothing about his obligation should he run the risk of less-than-mortal danger (*safeik sakanah*).

46. See, for example, R. Yair Bachrach (seventeenth-century Germany), *Resp. Chavat Yair*, no. 146, on *B. Bava M'tzia* 62a: R. Akiva forbids the holder of the container to share his water only because if he does so he will *certainly* die (i.e., a case of *vadai sakanah*). But if by sharing the water he were to face a lesser degree of danger (*safeik sakanah*), R. Akiva would rule that he must do so in order to rescue his fellow from mortal danger.

47. R. Baruch Halevy Epstein (twentieth-century Lithuania), *Torah T'mimah* to Lev. 19:16, no. 110, learns from the stories surrounding R. Chaninah ben Dosa that one is required to risk potential danger in order to rescue.

48. On Maimonides, see above at note 34. On the *Shulchan Aruch*, see above at note 37. In the latter case, although there is no mention of the element of danger, either *safeik* or *vadai*—indeed, the author, R. Yosef Karo, merely repeats Rambam's formulation—the commentary *Sefer Mei-irat Einayim* notes that Karo omits mention of the opposing view, namely that one is obliged to risk *safeik sakanah* in order to rescue. Given that Karo does mention that opposing view in his *Kesef Mishneh* to *Yad, Rotzei-ach* 1:14 and *Beit Yosef* to *Tur, CM* 426, its omission in the *Shulchan*

Aruch is taken to imply his agreement that one must not risk *safeik sakanah*. This is an argument from silence, which however persuasive it may be to some is hardly conclusive.

49. The passage apparently is JT *T'rumot* 8:4 (46b), the story of R. Shimon ben Lakish's rescue of a kidnapped colleague. R. Yosef Karo, in his *Kesef Mishneh* (*Yad, Rotzei-ach* 1:14) and *Beit Yosef* (CM 426), claims that this passage was cited as halachicly authoritative by the thirteenth-century *Hagahot Maimoniot*, although the citation does not appear in our printed versions of that work.

50. See R. Waldenberg (note 38), who suggests that it is not clear from the *Y'rushalmi* text that the halachah in fact follows R. Shimon b. Lakish.

51. See R. Bachrach, note 46, and R. Shmuel di Medinah (sixteenth-century Italy), *Resp. Maharashdam, Y D* 204.

52. *Aruch HaShulchan,* CM 426, par. 4.

53. This is a quotation from *M. Sanhedrin* 4:5. A number of manuscript variants omit the word "Jewish" from the text; see *Dikdkei Sof'rim* to *Sanhedrin* 37a and Chanoch Albeck's *hashlamot* to *M. Sanhedrin* 4:5 in his edition of the Mishnah. We would agree that the word "Jewish" is out of place in this text: first, because the context clearly refers to a general human situation and not a specifically Jewish one; and second, because as Reform Jews we adhere to a tradition of moral thought that makes no distinction between Jews and gentiles in matters that have nothing to do with ritual law.

54. *Pitchei T'shuvah* to CM 426:2. "As we have learned elsewhere," etc. refers to BT *Bava M'tzia* 33a and *SA, CM* 264:1, on the laws of returning a lost object.

55. Unterman, *Shevet Mi'hudah,* 21.

56. See *M. Avot* 5:10: "One who says, 'What is mine is mine and what is yours is yours' is of an average level of morality. But some say that this is the characteristic of Sodom."

57. See note 38.

58. See note 33. R. Yosef, to be sure, declares that one is not permitted to risk *safeik sakanah* in order to save another person, but he insists that the term "potential risk" be reserved for substantive dangers (*safeik shakul,* a "weighty" potential risk) rather than for more tenuous, far-fetched possibilities of danger (*k'tzat safeik sakanah*). In this point, his reasoning closely follows that of Rabbi Unterman (note 55).

59. On the categories *r'shut* (a permitted act), *mitzvah* (a praiseworthy act, one that fulfills the Torah's higher aspirations but is not absolutely required), and *chovah* (a required, obligatory act), see *Reform Responsa for the Twenty-First Century*, no. 5758.3, vol. 1, pp. 169–83, at notes 47–48.

60. For example, when a relative does not wish to donate an organ, the physicians can explain to the family that "medical complications" rule out that relative as a donor. Though this is an untruth, our tradition does permit us to tell such "little white lies" in order to preserve family peace (*shalom bayit*). See tractate *Derech Eretz Zuta*, chapter "*Hashalom*," and Rashi to Genesis 18:13.

HASTENING THE DEATH OF A POTENTIAL ORGAN DONOR

5763.3

Sh'eilah

I serve on the board of the Mid-America Transplant Association. One of our committees is struggling with the issue of non-beating organ retrieval. This concerns someone who may not be technically brain dead but cannot live without life support. All concerned recognize that the person will most likely die, and the family has given consent for organ donation. The issue concerns the massive amount of anticoagulant that must be given to keep the organ viable for donation. Technically, the administration of this medicine (usually heparin) "kills" the person because it causes internal bleeding. I know that we are supposed to do nothing to hasten death. I also know that there is nothing holier than saving a life by donating an organ. (Rabbi Susan Talve, St. Louis, Missouri)

T'shuvah

This question, as our sho-elet correctly notes, arises out of our commitment to two fundamental and, in this case, perhaps conflicting Jewish ethical principles. The first principle is what we might call the sanctity or the inviolability of human life.[1] We are forbidden to take any action that shortens human life or hastens death, even in the case of the goseis, one whose death is imminent. The goseis is compared to a flickering candle; "the one who touches it and causes it to go out is guilty of bloodshed."[2] At the same time, we are commanded to preserve human life through the practice of medicine (r'fuah),[3] and the transplantation of human organs has become a major weapon in our struggle against life-threatening diseases. The critical shortage of organs available for transplantation is in large part responsible for creating the situation to which our sh'eilah alludes.[4] Our task here is to consider whether the desire to acquire organs, in the name of the preservation of life, has led to the adoption of measures that are in some way destructive of life and of our duty to preserve it.

1. THE MEDICAL CONTEXT[5]

Human organs destined for transplant can be retrieved from one of four sources: cadavers; live donors; donors who are brain dead but whose organs are maintained by life-support technology; and non-heart-beating donors (NHBDs), that is, individuals whose deaths are determined by cessation of heart and respiratory function rather than loss of whole brain function. Our *sh'eilah* deals primarily with donors in this latter category, which in some ways marks a return to the "old" cardiorespiratory criteria of death that were superseded by the general acceptance in the medical profession of neurological criteria (brain death) as the determinative indicator that death has taken place.[6] The NHBD category was reintroduced in response to two perceived needs. The first of these was the growing shortage of organs available to meet the demand for transplantation. The second was the desire among some dying patients, usually acting through their surrogates, to donate their organs upon death. To meet these needs, the University of Pittsburgh Medical Center developed a set of guidelines, commonly referred to as the "Pittsburgh protocol," to allow for "planned" organ retrieval. In the hypothetical case, a patient or the patient's surrogates make a legal and ethical decision to withdraw life support. The patient is weaned from the ventilator and is simultaneously prepared ("prepped") for organ retrieval. The patient's pulse is monitored by a femoral catheter, and the heart's electrical activity is measured by electrocardiogram (EKG). When these show a total absence of a pulse and of cardiac activity for a period of two minutes, the patient is pronounced dead and organ retrieval may proceed. If the patient spontaneously resumes breathing after the removal of the ventilator, he or she is returned to the intensive care unit.

During this process, anticoagulant drugs such as heparin are administered to the donor a few minutes before the withdrawal of life support. This is done to prevent blood clots that would render the retrieved organs useless for transplantation. Our *sh'eilah* indicates that heparin "'kills' the person because it causes internal bleeding." This assertion, as far as we can determine, is unproven. According to a report by the Institute of Medicine, an arm of the National Academy of Science, heparin *may* cause internal bleeding if administered to *some* NHBDs, especially in large doses. The report therefore concludes that it is appropriate to use heparin for the purposes described here, provided that this decision is made on a case-by-case basis and that the drug is administered carefully, so as not to harm the patient or to hasten his or her death.[7] According to the information made available to us, standard medical practice restricts the dosage of heparin administered to NHBDs to the "safe" range, so that it does not harm the donor. Indeed, given that hemorrhagic organs would be useless for transplantation, physicians have no motivation for administering these drugs in doses large enough to kill the patient by causing internal bleeding.[8] In light of these findings, there is no Jewish ethical reason to prohibit the use of heparin or other anticoagulants in this situation, provided that the drugs are in fact administered so as not to shorten the life of the donor.

2. NON-HEART-BEATING DONORS AND THE CRITERIA FOR DEATH

Beyond the specific concern of anticoagulant drugs, our *sh'eilah* raises a more general and troubling issue. The "Pittsburgh protocol" specifies that organs may be retrieved once the patient meets the cardiopulmonary criteria for death (i.e., the irreversible cessation of cardiopulmonary function),[9] and it determines that "irreversible cessation" has occurred once the patient's pulse has stopped for a period of two minutes. To wait longer than two minutes would subject the internal organs to warm ischemia (damage caused by lack of blood flow) and possibly render them useless for transplantation. This presents a serious problem for those who accept neurological criteria (brain death) as the determinative indicator of death. Put starkly, "there are no clear empirical data proving that a patient who meets the Pittsburgh protocol's criteria for cardiopulmonary death, two minutes of pulselessness, also meets the neurological criteria for death, irreversible loss of all brain functions."[10] Indeed, since "no one would claim that two minutes of anoxia is sufficient evidence that the brain has ceased to function,"[11] a patient declared dead according to the Pittsburgh protocol may not in fact be brain dead at the time his or her organs are retrieved. We must therefore address the question: are the Pittsburgh protocol's criteria for death acceptable according to our understanding of Jewish tradition?

The "classic" halachic "definition" of death (i.e., the set of criteria accepted by virtually all Jewish legal authorities prior to the late 1960s) is based upon cardiopulmonary indicators: death is established by the complete and irretrievable cessation of heartbeat and respiration.[12] This standard proceeds from *Mishnah Yoma* 8:6–7, which declares that the saving of life supersedes the laws of Shabbat even when it is not certain that an individual's life is in danger or, for that matter, that he is still alive.[13] Thus, when a building collapses upon an individual on the Sabbath, the halachah permits all necessary labor to remove the debris so that it can be determined whether he is still alive. The Talmud (BT *Yoma* 85a) cites a dispute as to how we are to ascertain that fact: do we examine his heartbeat or his respiration? The major codes rule that the cessation of respiration is the determinative criterion for death.[14] This does not mean that heartbeat is an irrelevant factor; later *poskim* realized that the cardiac and respiratory functions are inextricably linked.[15] Thus, R. Moshe Sofer, the "Chatam Sofer" (eighteenth- to nineteenth-century Hungary), established a threefold set of criteria for death: "When a person lies still as a stone [i.e., absence of reflexes], with no discernible pulse, and then his respiration ceases, he is certainly dead."[16]

Yet alongside the *Yoma* passage, we find in the halachic sources suggestions of a different "definition," namely that death is indicated by the cessation of neurological activity.[17] With the advent of the "Harvard criteria,"[18] which established testing protocols for determining that all neurological activity (including that of the brain stem) has ceased, some halachists came to accept brain death as a proper indication of death according to Jewish law. This does not, in their view, contradict the cardiopulmonary standard as promulgated by Sofer: death is still indicated by the complete cessation of independent cardiac and respiratory activity. The difference is one of diagnostic technology. In Sofer's day, death could be determined solely by the actual measurement of heartbeat and respiration. Today, when the accepted tests can establish the cessation of all neurological activity, the patient may be declared dead, since "brain death is final and irreversible and there is no possibility that autonomous respiration will begin anew."[19] The fact that the organs of a brain-dead person are kept functioning by means of life support technology does not mean that the person is still alive, because with the cessation of neurological activity autonomous, independent heartbeat and respiration cannot be restored. Those Orthodox *poskim* who accept brain death as an adequate indicator of death have ruled in favor of heart and liver transplantation surgery, which require that these organs be retrieved from brain-dead donors.[20] This stance, however, remains controversial within the Orthodox world; most noted halachists continue to insist on the literal application of the "Chatam Sofer" standard: death occurs only when heartbeat and respiration have irretrievably ceased.[21]

Liberal halachic opinion,[22] including that of this Committee,[23] accepts the brain death standard as a proper criterion for death. Brain death, again, does not replace the "older," cardiopulmonary criteria; rather, it confirms them. Since the determination of brain death signals that the body has irretrievably lost its ability to maintain cardiopulmonary functions on an independent basis, the brain death standard satisfies the demands of both Jewish tradition and simple moral sense. When clinical tests establish beyond scientific doubt that brain activity has irretrievably ceased and that circulation and respiration are maintained solely through mechanical means, the patient is dead. It is then, and *only* then, that the body's organs may be removed for transplantation.

As we have seen, the Pittsburgh protocol standard does not meet the criteria for brain death. We should also note that it does not meet the Jewish standard of establishing death according to cardiopulmonary criteria. That standard, like the brain death standard, was meant to indicate that heartbeat and respiration have *irreversibly* ceased to function. Two minutes of pulselessness are not sufficient to meet this test: cardiopulmonary functions can return spontaneously or be restored through resuscitation during a much longer period, even up to ten minutes following asystole (cardiac arrest).[24] It may be, of course, that physicians and family members have no *intention* of resuscitating such a patient. That decision can be a proper one. As we have written, there are times when it is ethically permissible to withdraw most forms of medical treatment, to "allow nature to take its course" and to let the patient die without further "heroic" measures.[25] Yet such a decision does not indicate "irreversibility." The fact that pulse and respiration *will not* be restored through medical intervention does not prove that they *cannot* be restored. Until that latter point is reached, until it is clear that "there is no possibility that autonomous respiration will begin anew," we cannot certify that the cessation of heartbeat and respiration are in fact irreversible. It is for this reason that the brain death standard, which does testify to the irreversible cessation of autonomous heart and lung activity, meets the criteria for death as set forth in the sources of our Jewish tradition.

3. TO CHANGE THE CRITERIA FOR DEATH?

Why have some hospitals and clinics adopted the Pittsburgh protocol as a standard for determining the death of non-heart-beating organ donors? Why have they abandoned the brain death standard, which is still recognized as the predominant criterion for establishing death?[26] The obvious, practical reason is the desire to increase the availability of organs for transplantation: "The number of persons eligible to donate organs who die when heart and lung functions stop is believed to be much larger than the number who are pronounced 'brain dead' while on life support."[27] This desire, to be sure, is not evidence of evil intent. The goal of organ transplantation, after all, is to save human life, to fulfill the mitzvah of *pikuach nefesh*. The donors (or their surrogates) have consented in advance to this procedure: they have asked to be removed

from life support and have permitted the removal of the needed organs
from their bodies. Nor is the acceptance of the Pittsburgh protocol
necessarily an act of cynical manipulation, the altering of the definition
of death in order to serve our own purposes, however exalted. As some
ethicists argue,[28] "death" is not a biological event that can be defined
by medical criteria. All that science can do is to identify specific clinical
situations, such as the irreversible cessation of heartbeat or of brain
activity. The decision to regard those situations as evidence of "death" is
a legal or moral decision, arrived at through discussion among scientists,
practitioners, and the community as a whole. Death "happens," in other
words, at a point in the clinical situation that is morally, sociologically,
and anthropologically acceptable. Why then is it wrong or immoral
to declare death at a moment that is consistent with the retrieval of
vital organs? Such thinking may have motivated the acceptance of
the brain death standard several decades ago,[29] and such thinking lies
behind the Pittsburgh protocol and other current proposals to accept
alternative criteria for death (e.g., higher-brain death or a diagnosis of
permanent vegetative state) so as to increase the availability of organs for
transplantation.[30]

With all this in mind, should we Reform Jews, who honor our Jewish
tradition but who are open to new ways of thinking about our moral
responsibilities, reconsider our own criteria for death? Should we
abandon the traditional Jewish standards in favor of a new definition
that, like the Pittsburgh protocol, would facilitate the retrieval of more
human organs for transplantation?

We oppose such a step. We do so out of our commitment to the principle
with which we began this *t'shuvah*: the sanctity of human life. Any
discussion of a Jewish approach to the determination of death must
proceed from that fundamental affirmation. To perceive human life
as "sacred," in Jewish terms, is to hold it *inviolate*: as the ultimate
possession of the God who has created it and given it to us, human life
may never be taken or shortened save for those circumstances under
which the Torah permits or mandates that outcome.[31] For this reason,

although we are not obligated to delay a terminal patient's impending death through the employment of therapeutically useless measures, we are forbidden to practice active euthanasia or assisted suicide, to hasten the death of that patient. The fact that there is nothing physicians can do to save the life of this patient does not entitle us to kill him or her, even out of compassion and, importantly for our *sh'eilah*, even when it would benefit others were we to do so.[32] It makes no difference that the patients or their surrogates have consented to them. The sanctity of life precludes suicide just as it forbids homicide.[33] The act, however benign or beneficent, remains an act of killing.

Since our tradition regards human life as sacred, it bids us to do everything we can to save life and to heal the sick. By that same token, however, because all human lives are equally sacred, it does not and cannot permit us to save the life of one person by shortening the life of another.[34] Yes, we have accepted new criteria for death (the brain death standard) that justify the retrieval of human organs from donors whose hearts are still beating. Yet as we have written, the neurological criteria did not represent a change but rather a reliable alternative indicator that the traditional Jewish standard for death (the complete and irreversible cessation of autonomous heartbeat and respiration) had been met. A brain-dead person is, by Jewish criteria, dead. By contrast, a medical institution that implements the Pittsburgh protocol or some of the other "alternative" criteria for death is retrieving organs from persons who, in the eyes of Jewish tradition, are likely still alive. That is a difference that makes all the difference in the world. The prospect of killing NHBDs may not trouble those who do not share the Jewish conception of the sanctity of human life. But those of us who do, who participate in a tradition that regards human life as inviolate and beyond our power to destroy even for beneficial purposes, find it a chilling thought indeed.

CONCLUSION

The administration of anticoagulant drugs to a non-heart-beating organ donor is permissible so long as it is done so as not to harm the patient or hasten his or her death. Organ retrieval is permissible when, but not before, the patient is declared to be brain dead.

NOTES

1. The term "sanctity of human life" is not native to the Jewish tradition. We do not find its probable Hebrew equivalent, *k'dushat hachayim*, in the Talmudic or halachic sources. On the other hand, it reflects the conviction, most certainly present throughout Jewish thought and discussed below in this responsum, that human life possesses supreme value and is therefore inviolate. This insight is applied in contemporary halachic writing to the issue of suicide (R. Ovadyah Yosef, *Resp. Yabia Omer* 8, OC 37, sec. 5). And, in fact, some present-day Orthodox writers do use the term *k'dushat hachayim* or "sanctity of life" as a way of expressing this commitment; see *Piskei Din Rabaniim* 1, p. 164, and J. David Bleich in *Jewish Bioethics*, ed. Fred Rosner and J. David Bleich (Brooklyn: Hebrew Publishing Co., 1985), 273. We think, therefore, that the term "sanctity" conveys an accurate description of the Jewish belief that life possesses inestimable value and must be protected as though it belongs to the God who created it.

2. *S'machot* 1:1: "The *goseis* is considered a living person in all respects"; Rambam, *Yad, Aveil* 4:5; SA, YD 339:1.

3. For sources and discussion, see *Teshuvot for the Nineties* (TFN), no. 5754.14, pp. 337–63, at pp. 346ff.; *TFN*, no. 5754.18, pp. 373–80, at pp. 373–75; and *Reform Responsa for the Twenty-first Century*, no. 5761.7, vol. 2, pp. 121–42, at notes 5–13.

4. See, in general, *Reform Responsa for the Twenty-first Century*, no. 5763.2, vol. 2, pp. 143–64.

5. We are deeply indebted to the Bioethics Committee of the Union of American Hebrew Congregations, chaired by Harvey L. Gordon, MD, for their assistance and instruction in the preparation of this part of our *t'shuvah*.

6. "Brain death" refers to the complete and irreversible cessation or stopping of all cerebral and brain-stem function. The clinical tests to determine brain death are described in "A Definition of Irreversible Coma: Report of the Ad Hoc Committee of the Harvard Medical School to Examine the Definition of Brain Death," *Journal of the American Medical Association* 205 (1968): 337–40. That brain death became a consensus standard is indicated by the statement signed by nearly all the leading American authorities in the field in *Journal of the American Medical Association* 246

(1981): 2184–87. The President's Commission for the Study of Ethical Problems in Medicine and Biomedical and Behavioral Research officially recognized the brain death standard in *Defining Death: A Report on the Medical, Legal, and Ethical Issues in the Determination of Death* (Washington: U.S. Government Printing Office, 1981). On the question of brain death in Jewish law and in the Reform responsa tradition, see below in this *t'shuvah*.

7. Institute of Medicine, *Non-Heart-Beating Organ Transplantation: Medical and Ethical Issues in Procurement* (Washington: National Academy Press, 1997); see especially pp. 4 and 52.

8. George J. Agich, "From Pittsburgh to Cleveland: NHBD Controversies and Bioethics," *Cambridge Quarterly of Healthcare Ethics* 8 (1999): 517–23. In the interests of full disclosure, we note that Dr. Agich is the chair of the Department of Bioethics at the Cleveland Clinic Foundation. The Cleveland Clinic was the subject of a controversy in 1997 over the very issue that impels this *sh'eilah*: the administration of anticoagulant drugs to non-heart-beating donors prior to the withdrawal of life support. Agich supports the procedure on the grounds indicated here, namely that the drugs are administered under the Institute of Medicine guidelines (see preceding note) and in dosages that do not cause harm to the patient. The Bioethics Committee of the UAHC, in a communication to this committee, agrees with Agich's assessment: "[We] have found nothing in the literature to substantiate the assumption of your questioner that heparin causes internal bleeding, much less that it is the cause of the donor's death."

9. University of Pittsburgh Medical Center, "Management of Terminally Ill Patients Who May Become Organ Donors after Death," 1992. A text of the protocol is included in Robert M. Arnold, et al., *Procuring Organs for Transplant: The Debate over Non-Heart-Beating Cadaver Protocols* (Baltimore: The Johns Hopkins University Press, 1995), 235–49. The quotation in the text is at p. 240, paragraph S. See also *Kennedy Institute of Ethics Journal* 3, no. 2 (1993): A-1 to A-15. The "cardiopulmonary criteria for death" referred to in the protocol match those set by the Uniform Declaration of Death Act (UDDA), sec. 1, 12 ULA 340 (suppl. 1991): "An individual who has sustained either irreversible cessation of circulatory and respiratory functions, or irresible cessation of all functions of the entire brain, including the brain stem, is dead."

10. Arnold, et al., *Procuring Organs for Transplant*, 7.

11. Joanne Lynn, "Are the Patients Who Become Organ Donors under the Pittsburgh Protocol for 'Non-Heart-Beating Donors' Really Dead?" in Arnold et al., *Procuring*

Organs for Transplant, 91–102. The quotation is at p. 99. Dr. Lynn is director of the Center to Improve Care of the Dying at George Washington University. At the time of the publication of the Arnold volume, she was a professor of medicine at Dartmouth-Hitchcock Medical Center in Hanover, NH.

12. See, in general, the article by our colleague, Moshe Zemer, "*T'rumat Eivarim V'hahalachah*," in R. Cohen-Almagor, *Dilemot Be'etikah Refu'it* (Jerusalem: Van Leer Institute, 2002), 265–82.

13. In Jewish tradition, the saving of life is called *pikuach nefesh*. The situation referred to in our Mishnah is one of *safeik n'fashot*, a case where it is uncertain that life is in fact in danger. On this subject, see *Reform Responsa for the Twenty-first Century*, no. 5763.2, vol. 2, pp. 143–64.

14. See *Yad, Shabbat* 2:19 and *SA, OC* 329:4. The ruling is based upon the statement of Rav Papa in BT *Yoma* 85a, along with the citation in that passage of Gen. 7:22 ("every creature with the breath of life in its nostrils").

15. That is to say, the *poskim* have rejected the literal reading of Rambam and the *Shulchan Aruch*, according to which cessation of respiration is the exclusive indicator of death. The nineteenth-century Galician authority Rabbi Shalom Schwadron, for example, declared that cessation of breathing indicates death only "if there is no indication to the contrary...but if any sign of vitality is detected elsewhere in the body...then it is obvious that we do not declare death on the basis of the cessation of respiration alone" (*Resp. Maharsham* 6:91). See also R. Isser Y'hudah Unterman in *Noam* 13 (1970): 1–9, and R. Eliezer Y'hudah Waldenberg, *Resp. Tzitz Eliezer* 9:46 and 10:25, chap. 4.

16. *Resp. Chatam Sofer, YD*, no. 338.

17. These include the following: (a) *M. Ohalot* 1:6: one whose head is severed from the body is immediately regarded as dead and capable of transmitting ritual impurity, even if all physical reflexes have not yet ceased (and see Rambam's commentary to that mishnah, where he speaks of an "animating force" in the body that emanates from one source, suggesting that he saw the brain as the source of all bodily reflexes, including respiration); (b) BT *Chulin* 21a: a person whose neck is broken immediately transmits ritual impurity (i.e., is dead); and (c) *Yad, Tumat Meit* 1:15, codifying the above sources: "One does not transmit impurity until the soul has departed...if the neck has been broken...or if the head is severed...he transmits impurity even though there may be some residual reflexes in one of his limbs."

18. See note 6, above.

176 • Sh'eilot Ut'shuvot

19. Dr. Avraham Steinberg, "The Definition of Death," in *Medicine and Jewish Law*, ed. Fred Rosner (Northvale, NJ: Jason Aronson, 1990), 146. Steinberg's definition of brain death parallels that of the President's Commission (note 6, above): "The heart and lungs are not important as basic prerequisites to continue life but rather because the irreversible cessation of their functions shows that the brain had ceased functioning." The "accepted tests" he lists are apnea tests, cerebral blood flow studies (e.g., radioisotope studies), Doppler tests, cerebral arteriograms, and electrophysiological examinations. "The electroencephalogram is insufficient to determine total brain death" (ibid.).

20. See especially R. Moshe David Tendler (who is both a *rosh yeshivah* at RIETS seminary and the chair of the biology department at Yeshiva University), *"Kevi'at Rega` Hamavet Ve-hashtalat Eivarim,"* in *Emek Halakhah*, ed. A. Steinberg (New York: Yeshiva University, 1989), 213–19 ("that the heart continues to beat [after brain death] is no sign of life, since the heart, when removed from the body and placed in a bucket with certain chemicals can maintain its pulse for hours or even for weeks" [p. 215]); decision of the Chief Rabbinate of Israel, *"Hashtalat Lev Be-yisra'el,"* published in *T'chumin* 7 (1986): 187–89; R. Shelomo Goren, *Torat HaR'fuah* (Jerusalem: Hemed, 2001), 82 and 112; R. Moshe Feinstein, *Resp. Ig'rot Moshe*, YD 3:132 (dated 1976) and CM 2:72 (dated 1978). The position of R. Feinstein on this issue remains a subject of controversy in Orthodox circles, largely because in earlier *t'shuvot* he explicitly forbade the heart transplantation procedure. Tendler, who is Feinstein's son-in-law, insists that Feinstein changed his view as he became more informed of the technology that measures brain death.

21. Among these are R. Eliezer Y'hudah Waldenberg, *Resp. Tzitz Eliezer* 10:25, chap. 25; R. Yitzchak Yaakov Weiss, *Resp. Minchat Yitzchak* 5:7, 9; and R. S. Z. Auerbach, cited in *Nishmat Avraham*, vol. 5, YD 339:1. See, in general, J. David Bleich, *Contemporary Halakhic Problems* (New York: Ktav/Yeshiva, 1995), 4:316–50.

22. See the responsa of R. Avram Reisner and R. Elliot N. Dorff in *Proceedings of the Committee on Jewish Law and Standards, 1986–1990* (New York: Rabbinical Assembly, 2001), 13–126.

23. *Contemporary American Reform Responsa*, no. 78; R. Walter Jacob, *Questions and Reform Jewish Answers*, no. 156.

24. See N. Zamparetti et al., "Defining Death in Non-Heart Beating Donors," *Journal of Medical Ethics* 29 (2003): 182–85, at notes 19–24.

25. On this subject, see *TFN*, no. 5754.14, pp. 337–63.

26. The Bioethics Committee of the UAHC informs us that the institutions employing the Pittsburgh protocol constitute "a small percentage" of all medical establishments and that "brain-dead donors continue to constitute the vast majority."

27. Arthur L. Caplan, in Arnold, et al., *Procuring Organs for Transplant*, 208. Dr. Caplan is director of the Center for Bioethics at the University of Pennsylvania.

28. On the following, see Zampretti et al., "Defining Death."

29. Henry Beecher, the chairman of the Harvard committee that established the brain death criteria (see note 6, above), wrote in 1971, "At whatever level we choose to call death, it is an arbitrary decision. . . . The need is to choose an irreversible state where the brain no longer functions. It is best to choose a level where, although the brain is dead, usefulness of other organs is still present" (cited in Zampretti et al., "Defining Death," at note 36).

30. Among these are James M. DuBois, "Non-Heart-Beating Organ Donation: A Defense of the Required Determination of Death," *Journal of Law, Medicine and Ethics* 27 (1999): 126–36; Robert D. Truog, "Is It Time to Abandon Brain Death?" *Hastings Center Report* 27, no. 1 (1997): 29–37; R. M. Arnold and S. J. Youngner, "The Dead-Donor Rule: Should We Stretch It, Bend It or Abandon It?" *Kennedy Institute of Ethics Journal* 3, no. 2 (1993): 263–78; Zampretti et al., "Defining Death"; and Linda Emanuel, "Reexamining Death: The Asymptomatic Model and a Bounded Zone Definition," *Hastings Center Report* 25, no. 4 (1995): 27–35. The "permanent vegetative state" criterion is a feature of Emanuel's proposal.

31. One major expression of this commitment is the notion that one's life is not one's personal property, to dispose of as one wishes; rather, human life belongs to God, to whom we are obliged to render an account for the way in which we have used it. Thus, writes Maimonides, the *beit din* is not permitted to accept a ransom from a murderer in order to spare him from execution, "for the life of the victim is not the property of the avenger [or of the court] but of the Holy One" (*Yad, Rotzei-ach* 1:4). In a similar vein, under Jewish law we cannot execute a wrongdoer on the evidence of his own confession. The reason for this, explains one scholar, is that "the life of the human being is not his own property but the property of God, who said, 'All lives are Mine' (Ezek. 18:4). Therefore, a person's own confession has no power to dispose of that which does not belong to him" (commentary of R. David ibn Zimra to *Yad, Sanhedrin* 18:6).

32. See *TFN*, no. 5754.14, pp. 337–63.

33. Jewish law forbids suicide as it forbids homicide; *S'machot* 2:1; BT *Bava Kama* 91b (and see Gen. 9:5 and Rashi ad loc.); *SA, YD* 345. The halachah as developed in

the later sources presumes that the one who takes his or her own life is driven to do so by circumstances beyond his or her control; in other words, suicide by definition is an irrational act.

34. See BT *Sanhedrin* 74a, Rabbah's classic question *mai chazit*: "How can you say that your blood is redder than that of another? Perhaps his blood is redder than yours."

Sh'eilah

The non-Jewish parent of a non-Jewish member of our synagogue has died. The non-Jewish member wishes to observe shivah and have a service each night at home. Is there any reason why he should not do so? Should we use the "Service for a House of Mourning" provided in *Gates of Prayer*, or is there something more appropriate? Is it permissible to recite *El Malei Rachamim*? (Joel Morgovsky, Chair of the Ritual Committee, Monmouth Reform Temple, Tinton Falls, New Jersey)

T'shuvah

This *sh'eilah* asks that we consider the question of boundaries in our religious communities: the boundaries that distinguish between Jews and gentiles and the boundaries that delineate our religious and communal responsibilities toward the non-Jews in our midst. These lines of definition are difficult to draw to the satisfaction of all, and since every congregation must confront this issue, it is not surprising that different versions of such boundaries exist within our movement. Our Committee is similarly divided as to the best response to the case before us. We are in full agreement, however, that boundaries must be set and that they must reflect a process of careful and thorough Judaic thinking.

The first boundary to be considered is the one that determines membership in our synagogues. We proceed from the presumption that formal membership in our congregations is reserved for persons of the Jewish faith.[1] Again, while each congregation makes its own decisions in these matters, the essential purpose of synagogues is "to promote the enduring and fundamental principles of Judaism and to ensure the continuity of the Jewish people."[2] It is therefore inappropriate for those who are not Jewish to enjoy formal membership in a Jewish congregation.³ While our *sh'eilah* speaks of a "non-Jewish member" of the congregation, this person is more accurately understood as the spouse of a Jewish member. The non-Jewish spouse of a member should not hold office in the congregation or in any of its auxiliary organizations, nor should he or she vote at congregational or committee meetings. On the other hand, the spouse may attend religious, social, and educational activities and share in the fellowship of the congregation.⁴

This brings us to our second boundary, that which distinguishes Jew from non-Jew. As we have noted, the gentile spouses in our midst are welcome to take part in the activities we offer, and we most certainly encourage them to attend and to worship at our religious services. It is therefore not surprising that those who do so may find much meaning in our religious life, to the point that they wish to adopt some Jewish observances as their own. The problem with this, to put it plainly, is that these observances are not *theirs*; they are *ours*. We do not look upon Jewish rituals and ceremonies simply as instruments for the attainment of spirituality, satisfaction, and comfort. They are rather the means through which we Jews define ourselves as a religious community, rehearse our sacred history, and express our distinct identity. Their meaning for us is primarily a *Jewish* meaning. It is by keeping these observances (and, at times, by introducing change and innovation into them) that we fully participate in the tradition that we have inherited from Jews in ages past, that binds us to all Jews today, and that we seek to pass on to future Jewish generations. It is for this reason that, though the non-Jews in our midst may attend and worship at our religious services, there are clear limits as to their participation in our synagogue's ritual life. Our rituals, again, are expressions of our Jewish identity, an identity that the non-Jews in our midst, so long as they do not choose to become Jewish, do not share. It is inappropriate for them to participate in our religious life *as though they are Jews* when in fact they are not Jews.⁵

Our *sh'eilah* is a clear and difficult test of these boundaries. This non-Jew, grieving at the death of his parent, has discovered a source of comfort in the observance of *dinei aveilut*, traditional Jewish mourning rituals. He wants to "sit shivah" and asks that we organize for him a service or "minyan" in his home each night of that seven-day mourning period so that he might say *Kaddish*.[6] We would certainly do so for a Jewish congregant; is it appropriate for us to do so for him? There are some strong arguments that would cause us to say "yes." This non-Jew violates no ritual prohibition by observing Jewish mourning rites. He is already welcome at our synagogue services, where he may say *Kaddish* along with the congregation. Moreover, though he may not be a formal member of the synagogue, he *is* a member of our congregational family. He has shared our "fellowship"; he is in a very real sense one of us. It is our human and pastoral inclination to minister to him in his time of sadness. If the customs of Jewish mourning bring him strength and solace, why would we wish to deny these to him? On the other hand, we cannot forget that *dinei aveilut* are indeed the customs of *Jewish* mourning, practices that enable Jews to express grief in a way that links them to the life and heritage of our people. For us to arrange a "minyan" for this individual is a well-intentioned act of kindness, but it also confuses the boundary between Jew and non-Jew; it blurs the distinction (central to our existence as a religious community) between *being* Jewish and *doing* Jewish.

CONCLUSION

In considering our question, therefore, we are pulled in different directions by the persuasive power of two sets of concerns, each of which makes legitimate demands upon us. How do we balance these concerns and establish the boundaries appropriate to this case?

1. One member of our Committee recommends that no service be held at the home of this non-Jewish mourner. He should be invited to attend any regularly scheduled synagogue service and to say *Kaddish* there. *El Malei Rachamim* may also be recited, but again, only at a synagogue service and not at a "shivah minyan" specially arranged for him. The strength of this approach lies in its insistence on the standards of Jewish propriety: a "shivah

minyan" is a Jewish mourning custom, a means of expression rightfully reserved for Jews. Most of us reject this suggestion, however, on the grounds that it pays insufficient attention to the personal, emotional needs of one who is, after all, part of the congregational family. He finds meaning and comfort in the rites of Jewish mourning; we want to find an appropriate way for him to participate in those rites.

2. What is the "appropriate" way for this individual to observe Jewish mourning rites? Some of us would permit the community to arrange a regular "shivah minyan" for him at his home. The liturgy for this service would be the same as used for all such services, whether the *Gates of Prayer*'s "Service for a House of Mourning," as mentioned by our *sho-eil*, or the regular weekday services.[7] *Kaddish* and *El Malei Rachamim* may be recited. There is no ritual or halachic objection to this procedure, so long as the service is led and conducted by Jews—and not by the gentile mourner—and the *Kaddish* is recited by a Jew or by the entire company, as is the custom in most Reform communities. In the absence of such objections, some of us see no reason to exclude this member of our family from an observance that will bring him strength and solace.

3. Finally, some of us feel that the "service" at this individual's home should *not* be the regular liturgy or the "service for a house of mourning." Instead, the service might consist of special readings, perhaps including the study of text, followed by *Kaddish* and *El Malei Rachamim*. To do otherwise, in this view, would give the impression that this person is participating in our religious life as though he is a Jew. Those of us who take this position believe that the boundary between Jews and non-Jews—a boundary without which we do not exist as a distinct religious community—would be more clearly marked in this way. And all of us, no matter which proposal we favor, believe as one that this boundary must be honored.

NOTES

1. See *Suggested Constitution and By-Laws for Congregations Affiliated with the Union of American Hebrew Congregations*, adopted by the Joint Commission on Synagogue Administration of the Union of American Hebrew Congregations and the Central Conference of American Rabbis, April 1984, article V, section 1.

2. *Suggested Constitution*, Preamble.

3. See R. Solomon B. Freehof, *Recent Reform Responsa*, no. 12, p. 65: "Jewish congregations consist of Jews by birth or conversion. All who wish to come into Judaism are welcome. No sincere applicant for conversion will be rejected. But we cannot allow the transformation of a Jewish congregation so that it ceases to be the family...of Israel. Our people and our faith are one, joined in a covenant with God."

4. On the gentile "member" of a congregation, see *Suggested Constitution*, article V, section 2; *Contemporary American Reform Responsa*, no. 161 and no. 162; *American Reform Responsa*, no. 10; and Freehof, *Reform Responsa for Our Time*, no. 47.

5. On the question of gentile participation in synagogue ritual, see *Teshuvot for the Nineties* (*TFN*), no. 5754.5, pp. 55–76.

6. May a person say Kaddish in the absence of a minyan, the traditional quorum of ten? That issue has been discussed at various times in Reform responsa. For the most recent treatment, see *TFN*, no. 5752.17, pp. 23–28.

7. Traditionally, the minyan gathers at the house of mourning to recite regular daily worship services (*Shacharit*, *Minchah*, and *Maariv*; on Rosh Chodesh, *Musaf* would be added). Very little in the way of "special" liturgy is added, although a number of prayers and rubrics are omitted or modified in the house of mourning. On this, see Rabbi Aaron Felder, *Yesodei Smochos* (New York: Felder, 1978), 87–90.

WHEN A PARENT INSTRUCTS A CHILD NOT TO SAY *KADDISH*

5766.1

Sh'eilah

A convert is anticipating the way in which she will mourn for her elderly and ailing father. He has never been entirely reconciled to her conversion to Judaism, and his own parents, she says, were out-and-out anti-Semites. The father plans to be buried in the family plot near his own father. He has asked his daughter not to recite *Kaddish* over his grave, citing his own parents' negative feelings toward Judaism. The daughter now faces a conflict between the obligation to honor her father's wishes (*kibud av*) and her own Jewish mourning practices. When the time comes, should she ignore her father's wishes and recite *Kaddish* at his grave? (Rabbi David Ostrich, State College, Pennsylvania)

T'shuvah

A person's choice to become a Jew should be an occasion for happiness in our community. Unfortunately, as in this case, that decision can be accompanied by family tension and lingering bitterness. Our Committee cannot directly speak to this woman's difficult family situation; that is a personal issue that must be addressed in her conversations with her rabbi. Our task is to consider the more formal question she poses: what is the Jewish religious duty of the Jew-by-choice in such a case? We do hope, though, that our words will offer some emotional support to her and to others who face a similar dilemma.

1. THE *GER'S* OBLIGATION TO MOURN NON-JEWISH RELATIVES

We begin with our tradition's discussion of the relationship between the *ger*, the Jew-by-choice, and his/her blood relatives. The Talmud declares that "the one who converts to Judaism is like a newborn child,"[1] expressing the conviction that the proselyte begins a brand-new life upon joining the Jewish people. In a legal sense, this means that all blood ties between the *ger* and his or her non-Jewish relatives are rendered null and void.[2] However, the halachah does not develop this principle to its logical extreme. For example, a Jew-by-choice is not permitted to marry any blood relative that would be forbidden to a born Jew, even though according to the halachah they are not his "relatives." Similarly, the *ger* is required to honor her gentile parents, even though she is a "newborn child" and they, technically, are no longer her mother and father. The law makes these exceptions to the rule of the convert's "newborn" status because "let it not be said that a proselyte has descended in holiness."[3] That is, conversion to Judaism should not serve as a justification for behavior considered shameful by all people, Jews and non-Jews alike. Our Reform tradition applies this reasoning to the case of the mourner as well. Thus, the Jew-by-choice observes the rites of mourning for his or her non-Jewish relatives in the same way that a born Jew would mourn his or her loved ones. This includes the obligation to recite *Kaddish* for them.[4]

2. MAY A PARENT EXEMPT A CHILD FROM THE DUTY TO SAY *KADDISH*?

The *ger* owes the same moral obligation to his or her parents as does the Jew by birth. We must now consider the following question: what is the duty of *any* Jew whose parent requests that he or she not recite *Kaddish* when the parent dies? On the one hand, as our *sh'eilah* indicates, it is a mitzvah to honor and to revere our parents,[5] which implies that we should endeavor to fulfill their wishes, especially those they communicate to us toward the end of their life.[6] On the other hand, our parents are not entitled to demand that we violate other *mitzvot*,[7] and perhaps this means that they may not require that we forego the traditional practices of mourning (*aveilut*).

The view among traditional authorities is mixed. The nineteenth-century Galician *poseik* R. Shaul Nathanson[8] rules that a child should honor a parent's instruction not to say *Kaddish* for him or her. His reason is that the recitation of the Mourner's *Kaddish* (*Kaddish Yatom*) is for the benefit of the dead. Traditionally, it is considered a *tikkun l'nefesh hameit*, an act of expiation by the son that speeds his parent's entry into paradise or the world-to-come.[9] Since a person is entitled to reject a benefit that another wishes to confer upon him, the child is not obligated to recite *Kaddish* against the parent's wishes. R. Ovadyah Yosef, the contemporary Israeli scholar, takes the opposing view: the child should *not* honor this request, for had the parent truly considered how important it was that his soul be lifted toward paradise, he never would have instructed the child not to recite *Kaddish*.[10] This dispute evokes the Talmudic discussion over the eulogy (*hespeid*):[11] do we honor the deceased's request that he not be eulogized at his funeral? Is the eulogy "an honor for the dead," in which case the deceased is entitled to forego the honor, or "an honor for the living," in which case we would say that the deceased cannot deny his mourners an honor to which they are entitled? The later authorities determine that the eulogy is "for the honor of the dead"; hence, they rule that we obey the deceased's request that no eulogy be recited.[12] Both Nathanson and Yosef regard the *Kaddish* as "an honor for the dead" that the deceased may refuse, though Yosef holds that such a refusal cannot be understood as an "informed decision."

We Reform Jews take a different approach to the theology of *Kaddish*. We do not believe that we elevate the souls of our dead to paradise by reciting *Kaddish* for them. Rather, we recite *Kaddish* because it is the primary liturgical expression of traditional Jewish mourning. For us, it evokes the unbroken link of memory that binds every Jewish generation to its past. Its recitation is the way we declare our faith, even at the darkest moments of loss, in the eternity of Israel's covenant with God, in the triumph of hope and "in the coming of the divine kingdom."[13] We no longer hold, therefore, that the recitation of *Kaddish* is "for the honor of the dead"; it is, however, vitally important for *us* that we say it. As such, this ritual indisputably serves "the honor of the living," and the dead, according to the Talmudic principle, are not entitled to deny us the "honor"—we would prefer to say "responsibility"—of mourning as Jews. Thus, we recite *Kaddish* whether or not our loved ones request us to do so, or even if they forbid us from doing so after they are gone.

3. TO HONOR ONE'S (NON-JEWISH) PARENT

A Jew is therefore obligated to say *Kaddish* and to mourn a parent even though the parent has instructed the child to the contrary.[14] Our duty to honor our parents does not empower them to demand that we cease to act as Jews. *This* parent, however, is a non-Jew who, for his own very heartfelt reasons, does not want his daughter to recite *Kaddish* over his grave. She might argue that her practice of mourning is her own business, one that flows from her sense of Jewish religious duty, and that this duty overrides any obligation to honor his wishes. Yet this non-Jewish father has every right to believe that the commandment "honor your father and your mother" prohibits his daughter from drawing him against his will into a world of religious duty and observance that is not his own. We are speaking, after all, of *his* funeral, *his* burial place in a non-Jewish cemetery. Seen from this perspective, the daughter who stands at that place and recites *Kaddish* is no longer simply "minding her own business" or "mourning in her own way"; she has invaded her father's "space" with Jewish ritual in direct contradiction to his wishes.

We think that the daughter should honor her father's request and not say *Kaddish* at his grave. We base our conclusion primarily upon two reasons.

First, to say *Kaddish* over the father's grave in violation of his explicit instruction would smack of religious coercion. As we have noted in another context, our experience as Jews in a free society has made us quite sensitive to actions that, however unobjectionable they appear to some, strike others as an unwanted intrusion of religion into their lives. We reject those actions when others perform them; we should avoid them as well.[15]

Second, since the funeral service will be a non-Jewish one, taking place in a non-Jewish cemetery, it is arguably inappropriate to introduce Jewish ritual into that setting. Such, after all, is our own policy: although we in the Reform Movement permit the burial of non-Jews in our cemeteries, we insist that the burial service be a liturgy of our own devising, that no non-Jewish liturgy be used, and that no non-Jewish religious symbolism be displayed during the service or on the tombstone.[16] We believe that this is a reasonable standard, and we also believe it to be reasonable when non-Jews apply it to their services. It is only right to accord to this father the same understanding that, were the situation reversed, we would ask of him.

Note that we are speaking of the non-Jewish funeral and the father's grave. It is there that the daughter should honor her father's wishes. Elsewhere, however, her decisions as to how she shall mourn are very much her own. If, for example, her father had requested that she *never* say *Kaddish* for him, even while observing shivah or at a synagogue service, she would be under no obligation to honor that request. In those Jewish settings, her wishes and her sense of religious duty would prevail over his. Fortunately, the father's request does not seem to extend beyond the boundaries of the cemetery in which he is to be buried.

CONCLUSION

We have argued the following points:

1. The Jew-by-choice owes the same duty of honor to his or her parents as does the born Jew. This includes the obligation to mourn them when they die.

2. A Jewish parent is not entitled to instruct his or her child not observe the rites of mourning or recite *Kaddish*. The child, though obliged to "honor" the parent, has no duty to fulfill such an instruction.

3. The Jew-by-choice should honor his or her non-Jewish parent's request that *Kaddish* not be recited and other Jewish rites not be performed at the parent's grave in the non-Jewish cemetery. At his or her home or in any other Jewish setting, however, the *ger* should recite *Kaddish* and mourn as a Jew, even if the parent had requested otherwise.

Our *t'shuvah* attempts to chart a compromise between two sets of duties: the duty of every Jew to mourn our loved ones in a Jewish manner and our duty to honor our parents. These duties usually do not conflict, since our parents are not entitled to demand that we abandon our Jewish practices in order to please them. In this case, the dying father does not ask that his daughter abandon her Judaism. He has asked her, however, not to recite *Kaddish* at his grave, because he is struggling with his own issues of filial responsibility and because he perceives the introduction of Jewish ritual into that non-Jewish setting as an encroachment upon his own religious integrity. Although his daughter does not share that perception, we think it is a reasonable one and that he is entitled to make that request.

It is indeed unfortunate, from our standpoint, that the father has never become "entirely reconciled" to his daughter's conversion. We hope that, as his death approaches, a way can be found to resolve, at least in part, the issues that have divided them. And we believe that, by honoring her father in acceding to this request, the daughter would take a significant step toward that end.

NOTES

1. BT *Y'vamot* 22a and parallels.

2. For example, a *ger* may testify in court concerning his brother; *Yad, Eidut* 13:3 and *SA, CM* 33:11.

3. BT *Y'vamot* 22a. On marriage, see *Yad, Isurei Biah* 14:12 and *SA, YD* 269:1. On honoring one's gentile parent, see *Yad, Mamrim* 5:11 and *Kesef Mishneh* ad loc.

4. *Contemporary American Reform Responsa*, no. 121. At least one Orthodox *poseik* rules likewise; see R. Aharon Walkin, *Resp. Z'kan Aharon* 2:87. The codes, it should be noted, exempt the *ger* from the obligation to mourn for a blood relative, including a parent (*Yad, Aveil* 2:3 and *SA, YD* 374:5). This stance is justified on the basis of the dictum, cited above, that "the one who converts to Judaism is like a newborn child" (*Kesef Mishneh* to *Aveil* 2:3). For our part, we would argue that this ruling conflicts with the halachah's explicitly stated desire that the *ger* live according to the same standard of holiness as the born Jew; see the sources in the preceding note. It therefore makes no religious sense to us to require the Jew-by-choice to honor his parents when they are alive but to exempt her from the requirement to mourn them when they are dead. Rather, we encourage this Jewish person to express his or her feelings at such a moment in the way that all Jews express them. We think this position is preferable to forced efforts to reconcile the halachah, as traditionally interpreted, with modern sensibilities; see, for example, Maurice Lamm, *The Jewish Way in Death and Mourning* (New York: Jonathan David, 1969), 82–83.

5. Exod. 20:12 and Deut. 5:16; Lev. 19:3.

6. "It is a mitzvah to fulfill a dying person's instructions" (BT *Gittin* 14b and parallels; *Yad, Z'chiah* 4:4–5; *SA, CM* 125:8).

7. BT *Y'vamot* 5b; *Yad, Mamrim* 6:12; *SA, YD* 240:15.

8. *Resp. Sho'el Umeshiv* v. 3, 1:259.

9. On the history of the *Kaddish*, with a discussion of the origins of the Mourner's *Kaddish*, see Ismar Elbogen, *Jewish Liturgy* (Philadelphia: Jewish Publication Society, 1993), 80–84.

10. *Resp. Yabia Omer* 6, *YD* 31:4.

11. BT *Sanhedrin* 46b.

12. *Yad, Aveil* 12:1; *SA, YD* 344:10. Whether *we* would rule that way is another question, but one that we need not address here.

13. See *Gates of Prayer* (New York: CCAR Press, 1975), 628.

14. See *SA, YD* 344:10 and commentaries. Some authorities take the view that all the rituals of *aveilut*, including shivah, *sh'loshim*, etc., are "for the honor of the dead" and that the dead may exempt the mourners from the obligation to observe these practices. Others disagree (see *Kol Bo al Aveilut*, 301, par. 7), and we side with them. We see the

practices of mourning as important religious expressions for the mourners, quite apart from what the deceased would have wished.

15. See *Questions and Reform Jewish Answers*, no. 93. The case there involved a *mohel*'s surreptitious recitation of the *b'rachot* of *milah* at a medical circumcision of a Jewish boy whose parents had explicitly requested that no religious ritual take place.

16. *Rabbi's Manual* (New York: CCAR Press, 1987), 250–51; Simeon J. Maslin, ed., *Gates of Mitzvah* (New York: CCAR Press, 1979), 57; *American Reform Responsa*, no. 99.

WHEN A PARENT REQUESTS CREMATION
5766.2

Sh'eilah

A man, who is approaching death, has instructed that his body be cremated. His children are very uncomfortable with this request. They ask whether, under Jewish tradition, they are obliged to honor it, or are they entitled to bury him intact, in contradiction to his express wishes? Rabbi Solomon B. Freehof has ruled that in such a case we apply the Talmudic dictum "It is a mitzvah to fulfill the wishes of the deceased" (BT *Gittin* 40a and elsewhere). I wonder, however, if a more nuanced approach is better suited to a case such as this, where the children have strong religious objections to their father's instruction. (Rabbi David Katz, Binghamton, New York)

T'shuvah

In the responsum that our *sho-eil* mentions, R. Freehof rules that "we should urge" the family to carry out a father's wish to be cremated.[1] He acknowledges that the principle "It is a mitzvah to fulfill the wishes of the deceased" is not absolute; we are in fact *forbidden* to fulfill the wishes of the deceased if he or she instructs us to commit a transgression against Jewish law.[2] Thus, an Orthodox rabbi would surely rule against the request: "since cremation is contrary to Jewish law, the man's wish contravenes the law and may not be carried out." However, since the question has been posed to a Reform rabbi, "the answer cannot be so clear-cut." For us, cremation does *not* necessarily "contravene the law"; the Central Conference of American Rabbis (CCAR) resolved in 1892 that "in case we should be invited to officiate" at a cremation, "we ought not to refuse on the plea that cremation be anti-Jewish or irreligious."[3] R. Freehof notes that there is no clear and obvious prohibition against cremation in the sources of Jewish law and that "the Orthodox agitation against cremation actually began about a century ago" in response to the growing movement toward cremation in Western societies. Indeed, "when one studies the (Orthodox) arguments adduced against cremation, one can see that they are forced." On this basis, R. Freehof concludes that Reform Jews can have no principled religious objections to cremation. In the instant case, unless the man's family is Orthodox, we should counsel them to honor his instruction. "Surely, if we officiate at a cremation, we cannot refrain from fulfilling or encouraging the fulfillment of a man's wish for this type of disposal of his body."

We have quoted at length from R. Freehof's responsum because we do not want to minimize the challenge that faces us. Our *sho-eil* is asking that we rule against our teacher, and we are ordinarily reluctant to do so.[4] We would argue, though, that the times demand a different response. For one thing, the situation is no longer "so clear-cut"; the Reform position on cremation is more complex today than it was when R. Freehof wrote his *t'shuvah*. We also think that our attitude toward the maintenance and encouragement of traditional forms of Jewish observance has changed quite a bit over the last several decades. For these reasons, we hold that the children in this case may well be entitled to act upon their own religious beliefs and *not* to fulfill their father's request.

In order to make this argument, we shall have to consider, first of all, the attitude of Jewish law and tradition toward cremation as a means of the disposal of human remains. We shall then look at the developing Reform Jewish attitude toward cremation as expressed in the literature of the CCAR. Finally, we shall consider this particular case in the context of Jewish tradition, Reform Jewish practice, and the ethical obligations that the children may owe to their dying father.

1. CREMATION IN JEWISH LAW

There is no explicit requirement in the biblical text that the dead be buried rather than cremated. The sources make clear that burial was the normative practice in ancient Israel,[5] but nowhere do we find an express prohibition of the burning of the corpse. The Rabbis understand burial to be a requirement of Torah law, derived from Deuteronomy 21:23.[6] Maimonides codifies the law as follows: "If the deceased gave instructions that his body not be buried, we ignore him, inasmuch as burial is a mitzvah, as the Torah says (Deut. 21:23), 'You shall surely bury him.'"[7] Yet like the Bible, the Talmud and the classical halachic literature contain no explicit prohibition of cremation. The subject seems almost never to have come up, most likely because cremation was simply not practiced by the Jews and no one thought to ask whether it was permitted or forbidden.[8] The silence lasted until the nineteenth century, "when cremation became an ideal that was agitated for through many societies in the western lands."[9] At that time, the leading halachic authorities condemned cremation as a transgression against Jewish law, an opinion that remains the consensus viewpoint.[10] This prohibitive opinion rests primarily on two halachic grounds. First, cremation does not fulfill the commandment to bury the dead, based as we have seen on Deuteronomy 21:23. Burial of the cremains would not rectify this, since the mitzvah of burial applies to the body itself and not to its ashes.[11] Second, Jewish tradition mandates *k'vod hameit*, that we treat the corpse with honor and respect, and it regards the burning of a body as an act of *nivul* (or *bizayon*) *hameit*, contemptible treatment of a corpse.[12] Other arguments include the prohibition against imitating gentile customs (*chukot hagoyim*)[13] and the contention that cremation is tantamount to an act of heresy in that it denies the belief in *t'chiyat hameitim*, the physical resurrection of the dead.[14]

These arguments may or may not be "forced," as R. Freehof describes them. Some of them may be more persuasive than others. What is certain, though, is that Orthodox authorities are united in the opinion that cremation violates traditional Jewish law, an opinion shared by Conservative[15] and Reform[16] writers.

2. CREMATION IN THE LITERATURE OF THE CCAR

Our Conference has published a number of statements with respect to cremation:

a. The 1892 resolution, referred to above, declares that "in case
    we should be invited to officiate as ministers of religion at the
    cremation of a departed co-religionist, we ought not to refuse
    on the plea that cremation be anti-Jewish or anti-religion."[17]
    The resolution followed upon the report of a special committee,
    chaired by R. Bernard Felsenthal, that had been appointed to
    study the issue. The report made two essential points. First, it
    demonstrated at some length that the practice of cremation was
    contrary to Jewish law and tradition.[18] Second, it sought to avoid
    the substantive issue of whether to endorse cremation as a method
    for disposal of human remains. "The writer of this does not wish
    to be understood that he pleads for cremation. He also does not
    oppose it." Since a rabbi is not "a competent expert" in the matter
    of whether cremation is "preferable" to burial, the only motion
    "in order in a rabbinical conference" is one that calls upon rabbis,
    whatever their position concerning cremation, to provide pastoral
    care for those of their people who do choose the procedure.[19]

b. The 1961 *Rabbi's Manual*, recounting the 1892 resolution,
    states, "Since that time, most Reform Jews have gone beyond this
    cautious tolerance and have accepted cremation as an entirely
    proper procedure. A number of leading Reform rabbis have
    requested that their bodies be cremated."[20] In its section on funeral
    liturgy, the *Manual* contains a prayer suggested for recitation when
    "the body is to be cremated."[21]

c. The 1974 responsum of R. Freehof discussed at the beginning of
    our *t'shuvah*.

d. *Gates of Mitzvah*, a guide to Reform Jewish life-cycle observance
    published in 1979, stresses that "while both cremation and
    entombment in mausoleums are acceptable in Reform Judaism,
    burial is the normative Jewish practice."[22]

e. In 1980 the CCAR Responsa Committee appended a comment
    to the 1892 resolution. It notes that the resolution "remains

unchallenged policy within our Conference," but adds, "In this generation of the Holocaust we are sensitive to terrible images associated with the burning of a body. Rabbis may, therefore, choose to discourage the option of cremation. The practice remains permissible, however, for our families."[23]

f. The current *Rabbi's Manual*, published in 1988, states, "We continue to stress that burial is the time-honored Jewish way of disposing of the dead....However, the practice of cremation has lately spread, for a number of reasons. We would reiterate that it ought to be discouraged if possible, especially in our generation which has seen the murderous dispatch of millions of our people by way of crematoria. If, however, cremation has been decided upon by the family, we should not refuse to officiate. It is suggested in such cases that the service be held at an appropriate place and not at a crematorium."

g. A 1990 responsum notes, "Reform Jewish practice permits cremation...although...we would, after the Holocaust, generally discourage it because of the tragic overtones."[24]

The record of these statements suggests a perceptible shift of attitude toward cremation within North American Reform Judaism during recent decades. While our earlier pronouncements accept cremation as permissible or even as "entirely proper," the Conference since 1979 has pulled back from that affirmative stance. Although acknowledging that the 1892 resolution remains on the books and that Reform Jewish practice "permits" cremation, our more recent statements call upon rabbis to actively "discourage" the practice. This negative position is based upon two threads of argument: that burial is the normative traditional Jewish practice and that, after the Holocaust, cremation has become associated with one of the darkest periods in Jewish and human history.

These threads of argument, in turn, reflect two important transformations in the way that many Reform Jews have come to think about their religious lives and decisions. The first has to do with the positive reevaluation of "tradition." In the past, the fact that a particular observance was "traditional" or accepted Jewish practice did not in and of itself recommend that observance to Reform Jews. Indeed, we were quite ready to dispense with any such practices that were "not adapted to the views and habits of modern civilization" and that "fail to impress the modern Jew with a spirit of priestly holiness."[25] It is for this reason that R. Felsenthal could argue *both* that cremation was a transgression against traditional Jewish law *and* that this fact was irrelevant to Reform Jewish thinking on the subject:

> Joseph Qaro's Code is of no obligatory authority to you. The Talmud is of no obligatory authority to you. Even the laws of the Bible as such are of no obligatory authority to you.... Shall we for the sake of the living inquire of the dead? Shall we for the sake of the living open the old folios, and submit to what they have said hundreds of years ago under quite different conditions of life? Shall we learn there whether or not cremation is in accord with the spirit of Judaism?[26]

R. Felsenthal's words remain an eloquent expression of a central article of Reform Jewish faith. To this day, we affirm our right to define the "spirit of Judaism" and to abandon, alter, or replace old practices that we no longer find religiously meaningful. In this view, we cannot declare to Reform Jews that cremation ought to be forbidden solely because it runs counter to the halachah or to the customs of our ancestors.

In recent decades, however, a new attitude has taken hold within our community. We have described it as follows:

> Many of us have reclaimed ritual observances abandoned by previous generations of Reform Jews, from the generous use of Hebrew in the liturgy, to the wearing of *kipah*, *talit* and *tefilin*, to the dietary laws (*kashrut*), to the ceremonies surrounding marriage and conversion. These examples—and more could be cited—testify

that our approach to traditional ritual practice differs significantly from that of our predecessors. This difference stems, no doubt, from the divergent religious agenda that we have set for ourselves. If our predecessors regarded their acculturation into the surrounding society as a predominant objective, we who benefit from the social and political gains that they achieved are more concerned with taking active measures to preserve our distinctive Jewishness. Thus, where they may have viewed many ritual observances as barriers to social integration and as obstructions to "modern spiritual elevation," we may find them an appropriate and desirable expression of our Jewish consciousness.[27]

This is what we mean by the positive reevaluation of "tradition." The point is not that traditional practices exert, to use R. Felsenthal's words, "obligatory authority" upon us. The point, rather, is that we take the Bible, the Talmud, and even "Joseph Qaro's Code" more seriously than we did in his day as positive influences upon our own religious behavior. We are now more inclined than ever before to adopt or to preserve a ritual observance precisely because it is "Jewish." We are more likely to regard a practice's traditional pedigree as a reason for maintaining it, especially when there are no compelling moral or aesthetic arguments against that practice. We are therefore today more likely—though not obligated—to oppose cremation on the grounds that burial is a mitzvah, the "normative" Jewish way of disposing of human remains.

We might in a similar way explain our differences over whether cremation constitutes an act of *nivul hameit* (contemptible treatment of a corpse). A Reform Jew is certainly entitled to define this term in a way that is "adapted to the views and habits of modern civilization." Cremation is widely accepted in Western culture as an honorable way of treating human remains. We are therefore under no obligation to regard it as an act of *nivul hameit* solely because some Rabbinic texts portray it as such. Yet to say that we are not obligated to adopt the traditional definition does not entail that we are *forbidden* to do so. It is true that concepts such as "honor" and "disgrace" do not admit of objective definition. All this means, however, is that such terms can only be defined from within a particular social context; to reach these definitions, we must choose to work within a particular culture's set of values and affirmations. The particular culture that is Jewish tradition declares the burning of the corpse to be an act of *nivul* or *bizayon*. A Reform Jew today who finds special and satisfying meaning in the values and affirmations of Jewish tradition is thus entitled—though, again, not obligated—to adopt this definition precisely because it flows from the religious and cultural heritage of our people.

The second transformation in our religious thinking concerns our sensitivity to the experience of the Shoah (Holocaust). There is, to be sure, all the difference in the world between the Nazi crematoria and the freely made choice of cremation for ourselves and our loved ones. We should, moreover, be wary of invoking the memory of the Shoah as a facile justification for decisions concerning religious practice.[28] Yet for all that, the Jewish world *is* a different place now, "after Auschwitz," than it was before. Neither we nor our religious consciousness has emerged unchanged from our confrontation with that event. And one such change, as the recent statements of our Conference affirm, has to do with our attitude toward the machinery of cremation. The images of fire, ovens, and smokestacks, which we recall so vividly when we contemplate the mass murder of our people, can and do persuade many liberal Jews that today, after Auschwitz, the consigning of our dead to the flames is not the proper Jewish way to honor them.[29]

We emphasize that we are dealing here with general trends. To speak of transformations in our religious thinking is to *describe* what is happening within large segments of the Reform Jewish community rather than to *prescribe* a correct course of action in a specific instance. Not all Reform Jews are affected in the same way by these trends, and not every Reform Jew will draw from them the same conclusions concerning his or her religious observance. As a noted jurist once remarked, "General propositions do not decide concrete cases."[30] Yet in this particular concrete case, the Conference has moved decisively away from its previous acceptance of cremation. The members of this Committee reiterate this stance. Although we, like our more recent predecessors, continue to acknowledge that the 1892 resolution remains the formal policy of the CCAR, we would continue to call upon our rabbis to discourage the practice of cremation among our people. We do so for three primary reasons. First, burial is the normative traditional Jewish practice; as such, it is a mitzvah that exerts a strong persuasive force upon us. Second, we note the absence of convincing moral or aesthetic objections to the practice of traditional burial that would move us to abandon it.[31] Finally, we concur with our predecessors that today, after the Shoah, the symbolism of cremation is profoundly disturbing to us as Jews.

3. THE QUESTION BEFORE US

How should the children of whom our *sh'eilah* speaks respond to their father's request? Considering all the above, we would counsel the following.

a. The North American Reform Movement does not regard cremation as a "sin." The 1892 resolution of the CCAR calls upon rabbis to officiate at cremation services, and despite our reservations concerning cremation, we hold that the procedure does not "contravene the law." Therefore, the children are not forbidden to honor this request, and they may arrange for cremation in response to the mitzvah to honor our parents and to the dictum that we should seek to fulfill the wishes of the deceased.

b. Nonetheless, the children are not *obligated* to honor their father's request. The CCAR discourages the choice of cremation; it supports the choice of traditional burial; and Reform thought today recognizes the right of our people to adopt traditional standards of religious practice that previous generations of Reform Jews may have abandoned. The commandment to honor one's parents does not apply in such a case, for a parent is not entitled to compel his or her children to violate their sincerely held Judaic religious principles.[32] Thus, when a Reform Jew has serious and substantive religious objections to cremation, he or she may refuse a loved one's request for it.

c. By "traditional burial," we do not mean to endorse many of the practices that, although associated with burial in the public mind, would be deemed as excessive or inappropriate by many of us. Among these are such elaborate and unnecessary steps as embalming, expensive caskets, and the like. Jewish tradition emphasizes simplicity and modesty in burial practices; individuals should not feel driven to choose cremation in order to avoid the expense and elaborate display that all too often accompany contemporary burial.[33]

d. It is essential that families speak about such matters openly, honestly, and before the approach of death. When the child fails explicitly to say "no" to a parent's request for cremation, the parent will justifiably think that the child has agreed to carry out that instruction. In such a case, the child quite likely has made an implied promise to the parent and thus bears an ethical responsibility to keep it. Therefore, if the children have objections to cremation, they should make their feelings known to their parents sooner—much sooner—rather than later.

NOTES

1. Solomon B. Freehof, "Family Disagreement over Cremation," *Contemporary Reform Responsa* (1974), no. 51.

2. See the midrash cited in BT *Y'vamot* 5b. Lev. 19:3 says, "Each of you shall revere his mother and father, and you shall keep my Sabbaths." The midrash explains that the second clause comes to limit the scope of the first: we "revere" our parents (i.e., we fulfill their wishes) so long as they do not instruct us to contravene the laws of the Torah, of which Shabbat is an example. See also *Yad, Mamrim* 6:12; and *SA, YD* 240:15.

3. *American Reform Responsa* (ARR), no. 100. A much more complete version of the debate that led to the adoption of this resolution can be found in *CCAR Yearbook 3* (1893): 53–68.

4. We have on occasion differed with Rabbi Freehof. Often, this is due to transformations in the religious outlook of Reform Jews from his day to ours. Such changes are inevitable over the course of time, so that by responding to them we do not believe that we do any dishonor to Rabbi Freehof's teachings or to his accomplishments in the field of Reform responsa, a genre he did so much to develop. In fact, we think he would be pleased that we, his successors, continue his work in the spirit of free and critical inquiry, an ideal that he always championed and to which our movement has long pledged loyalty. On the other hand, we are aware that were he with us Rabbi Freehof would no doubt offer cogent responses to our objections. We don't do this lightly; after all, as the Talmud cautions, "Do not contradict the lion after his death" (BT *Gittin* 83a–b).

5. "There is no evidence that corpses were cremated in Palestine, except in days long before the coming of the Israelites, or among groups of foreigners; the Israelites never practiced it" (Roland de Vaux, *Ancient Israel* [New York: McGraw-Hill, 1965], 1:57). See also *Encyclopedia Mikra-it*, 7:4–5: "It is clear that [cremation] was not generally practiced." This doesn't mean that it never happened. Amos 6:10 speaks of the *m'sareif* who comes to the house during time of plague to collect the bones of the dead, presumably for burning (*s-r-f*). Scholars, however, are unsure of the precise explanation of the term; see F. I. Anderson and D. N. Freeman, *The Anchor Bible: Amos* (New York: Doubleday, 1989), 572, 574. Then there is the burning of the corpses of Saul and his sons by the men of Yavesh-Gilead (I Sam. 31:12–13). This detail causes some obvious perplexity and embarrassment to later writers; the Chronicler (I Chron. 10:12) omits it entirely, and the traditional Jewish commentators are at pains to explain it away. From this, we can learn two important points: first, that cremation was not unheard of in ancient Israel, and second, that later Jewish tradition did not derive any positive support for the practice of cremation from these isolated references.

6. Although that verse speaks of the body of an executed offender, its requirement of burial is interpreted to apply to all the dead. See BT *Sanhedrin* 46b, which cites the verse as a *remez* (a hint, an indication) to the fact that burial is a Toraitic obligation.

7. *Yad, Aveil* 12:1. See also Rambam's *Sefer HaMitzvot*, positive commandment no. 231. In the Talmud (BT *Sanhedrin* 46b) we find a dispute over whether the purpose of burial is to safeguard the corpse from contemptible treatment (*mishum bizyona*) or to effect atonement (*kaparah*) for the deceased. If the latter is the case, the Talmud suggests that the deceased would be within his rights to instruct his heirs not to bury

him, since he is entitled to refuse atonement for himself. The dispute is not firmly resolved (*Hil. HaRosh, Sanhedrin* 6:2); therefore, say some authorities, we ought to rule strictly and require burial, inasmuch as the Torah mentions it (*Sefer Or Zarua, Hil. Aveilut*, chap. 422). R. Yosef Karo (*Kesef Mishneh, Hil. Aveil* 12:1; *Beit Yosef*, YD 348) arrives at a similar conclusion, which he attributes to Nachmanides. *Lechem Mishneh* (*Yad, Aveil* 12:1) argues that this dispute is relevant only for those who hold that the mitzvah of burial is of Rabbinic origin. Maimonides, quite clearly, holds that it is a Toraitic commandment. In any event, we find no evidence in the traditional halachah that one is in fact entitled to instruct his heirs not to bury him.

8. In the thirteenth century, R. Sh'lomo ben Adret permitted mourners, who wanted to transport their father to a family plot, to put quicklime on the corpse in order that the flesh be consumed rapidly and to spare it the dishonor (*bizayon*) of rotting (*Resp. Rashba* 1:369; see Isserles, YD 363:2). Does this serve as a precedent to allow cremation? Most likely, the answer is no. For one thing, not everyone would be persuaded that fire is analogous to quicklime. For another, subsequent interpreters have limited Rashba's decision to precisely this sort of case: the exhumation and transport of a corpse for permanent burial. See the eighteenth-century R. Yaakov Reischer (*Resp. Sh'vut Yaakov* 2:97), who permits quicklime in a case where the alternative to transporting the corpse would be to bury it in a place where it could not be protected and would necessarily suffer *bizayon*. See also *Aruch HaShulchan*, YD 363:2. This line of thinking, in other words, deals with exceptional circumstances and not with the use of cremation as a regular means of disposing of human remains.

9. Freehof, "Family Disagreement over Cremation," p. 230. Does this mean, as R. Freehof suggests, that cremation is considered a transgression *only* because of the nineteenth-century Orthodox "agitation" against it? Not necessarily. It is just as likely that cremation would have been explicitly prohibited had the question been raised during the seventeenth century, or the thirteenth, or earlier. The question was not considered until the practice became widespread in the West.

10. R. Yitzchak Shmelkes, *Resp. Beit Yitzchak*, YD 2:155; R. David Zvi Hoffmann, *Resp. M'lamed Leho`il*, 2:113–14; R. Chaim Ozer Grodzinsky, *Resp. Achiezer* 3:72; R. Avraham Yitzchak HaKohein Kook, *Resp. Daat Kohein*, no. 197; R. Yaakov Breisch, *Resp. Chelkat Yaakov*, YD, no. 203; R. Yekutiel Greenwald, *Kol Bo al Aveilut*, 53–54; R. Yechiel M. Tykocinski, *Gesher HaChayim* 16:9.

11. Hoffman (see note 10) learns this from JT *Nazir* 7:1 (55d): Deuteronomy's commandment to "bury him" applies to the entire body (*kulo*, or at least to the major part of the body) and not to a small portion of it (*miktzato*). He points as well to the fact that the ashes of a burnt human corpse, unlike the corpse itself, are not a source

of ritual impurity (*M. Ohalot* 2:2; *Yad, Tumat Meit* 3:9–10). In other words, burnt remains are not a "body" such as requires burial under the law. Grodzinsky (note 10) notes simply that ashes are not the "body" of the dead person. Although it may be proper (*rau'i*) to bury the ashes of those who have been accidentally burned in a Jewish cemetery, he concludes, no actual obligation is fulfilled thereby.

12. Among other proof texts, the authorities point to the law that permits the removal of a corpse on Shabbat from a courtyard in which a fire has broken out. Transferring the corpse under normal conditions would violate the rules concerning the moving of objects on Shabbat, but it is permitted in this case because it would be a disgrace (*bizayon*) to the body were it consumed in the fire. See *SA, OC* 311:1 and commentaries (the latter make it clear that the permit to remove the body extends to transferring it to another *r'shut*). Although the *Magen Avraham* commentary to that passage (no. 3) suggests that burning would *not* be a case of *bizayon hameit* (or, at least, not enough of a *bizayon* to warrant setting aside the restrictions of Shabbat), his opinion is rejected by virtually all other commentators.

13. Lev. 18:3 and 20:23. On the issue, see *Teshuvot for the Nineties*, no. 5751.3, pp. 159–64.

14. See Freehof, "Family Disagreement over Cremation," p. 230. This point does appear in the writings of some of the authorities cited in note 10. It is, however, a somewhat tangential argument. The *poskim* do not spend much time developing it, nor do they present it as the major focus of their objection to cremation. It is unfortunate, therefore, that R. Freehof cites this contention as his only example of the "arguments adduced (in the last century) against cremation," which he describes as "forced." This might give the reader the erroneous impression that Orthodox opposition to cremation is founded mainly upon a doctrine that we Reform Jews have long since rejected, at least in its literal form. In fact, the Orthodox writers invest a great deal more intellectual effort into the halachic arguments that we have noted, namely that cremation does not fulfill the mitzvah of burial and that it constitutes an act of *bizayon hameit*.

15. See the responsum authored by R. Morris N. Shapiro, "Cremation in the Jewish Tradition," issued in 1986 by the Committee on Jewish Law and Standards of the Conservative Movement's Rabbinical Assembly (http://rabbinicalassembly.org/teshuvot/docs/19861990/shapiro_cremation.pdf, accessed August 22, 2009).

16. See at notes 18 and 19, below.

17. See note 3, above.

18. This was in response to a paper delivered at a previous conference by R. Max Schlesinger (*CCAR Yearbook* 2 [1892–93]: 33–40). Schlesinger's argument, namely that cremation was "the primitive custom among the Hebrews" (p. 36), was thoroughly refuted by Felsenthal and his committee.

19. *CCAR Yearbook* 3 (1893): 67–68.

20. *Rabbi's Manual* (New York: CCAR Press, 1961), 140.

21. Ibid., 90.

22. Simeon J. Maslin, ed., *Gates of Mitzvah* (New York: CCAR Press, 1979), pp. 56–57 (C-11).

23. Found at the conclusion of *ARR*, no. 100 (http://data.ccarnet.org/cgi-bin/respdisp. pl?file=100&year=arr).

24. *Questions and Reform Jewish Answers*, no. 191.

25. The "Pittsburgh Platform" of 1885, paragraphs 4 and 5. A text is available at http:// ccarnet.org/documentsandpositions/platforms.

26. *CCAR Yearbook* 3 (1893): 66.

27. *Reform Responsa for the Twenty-first Century*, no. 5759.7, vol. 1, pp. 49–64.

28. An argument in this vein can be found in *Reform Responsa for the Twenty-first Century*, no. 5760.3, vol. 2, pp. 59–70.

29. The above paragraph reflects the ways in which the CCAR, through the publications we have cited, has described this particular "transformation in our religious thinking." R. David Lilienthal, a corresponding member of our Committee, notes that the reaction of survivors of the Shoah may be quite different. His work in Europe with many survivors and children of survivors indicates that some may be inclined to choose cremation for themselves as a sign of solidarity with murdered family members. Other members of our Committee report that they have detected no such tendency among survivors and descendants. In any event, we stress again that we are referring here to general trends and that, when it comes to the perception of the symbolic meaning of particular ritual acts, one community may well differ from another.

30. Justice Oliver Wendell Holmes, Jr., dissenting in the case of *Lochner v. New York* (198 U.S. 45, 76). He continues, "The decision will depend on a judgment or intuition more subtle than any articulate major premise."

31. This is not to say that such objections cannot be raised but rather that they do not persuade us that there is a compelling reason to adopt cremation as the standard procedure for the disposal of human remains. Individuals, of course, may be impressed by arguments to this effect, but we as a Committee are not. Although this is not the place for a lengthy discussion of specific issues, we think that the ecological and economic criticisms that are raised from time to time against traditional burial can be addressed in ways that do not entail the choice of cremation. See the article by our colleague Daniel Schiff, "Cremation: Considering Contemporary Concerns," *Journal of Reform Judaism* 34, no. 2 (Spring 1987): 37–48, and see below in the text at note 32.

32. See *Reform Responsa for the Twenty-first Century*, no. 5766.1, vol. 2, pp. 185–92.

33. See *Gates of Mitzvah*, 55. We should follow the example of Rabban Gamliel, who instructed that he be buried in simple linen shrouds rather than expensive ones to demonstrate that burial need not impose a crushing financial burden upon the mourners (BT *Mo-eid Katan* 27b).

Sh'eilah

A congregant has approached me with the following question. There is
a new veterans' cemetery opening in Palm Beach, Florida. Her husband
is buried in a Jewish cemetery further south (almost 3 hours). The area
around that Jewish cemetery, moreover, has changed and is "not safe."
The Veterans Administration (VA) will cover the costs of disinterment
and reburial in the veterans' cemetery closer to the woman and her
children. There is not a specific Jewish area, but the grave would have
a Jewish marker. The VA would also cover the cost of her eventual
burial and the plot next to her husband. Is moving from a specifically
Jewish cemetery where no one is able to visit to another cemetery that
does not have a specific Jewish area permissible in the view of the
Reform approaches to halachah? (Rabbi Michael Birnholz, Vero Beach,
Florida)

T'shuvah

The fundamental issue underlying our *sh'eilah* is that of disinterment:
under what circumstances is it permitted to remove a body from its
place of burial? Halachic literature has much to say about this question,
and our own responsa have addressed it in some detail. As we shall
also see, these writings do not lead us to a sure and certain conclusion.
This uncertainty results, in part, from the always present difficulty
of applying a general principle to a specific and necessarily unique
set of circumstances.[1] It occurs in this case, as well, for the reverse
reason: a particular solution to this specific case may have unintended
ramifications were we to apply it in general, that is, to other cases that
may resemble this one.

1. DISINTERMENT: THE PROHIBITION AND
ITS EXCEPTIONS

The prohibition against removing a corpse from its grave is found
in the *Shulchan Aruch*,[2] which draws the ruling from a number of
Talmudic[3] and earlier halachic sources.[4] Various reasons are cited for
this prohibition, among them that disinterment "is painful for the dead,
because it arouses in them the fear of the Day of Judgment."[5] Other
authorities provide what is to our way of thinking a more persuasive
explanation, namely that the opening of the grave and the removal of
the remains is an act of *nivul hameit*, contemptible treatment of the
corpse.[6] It follows that we might waive this prohibition under certain
circumstances, when the disinterment is considered honorable (rather
than contemptible) treatment of the corpse or when we can presume that
the deceased would have wanted to be moved to another burial place.
And, indeed, the tradition permits disinterment, for example, to move
the deceased to his or her family plot,[7] for reburial in the Land of Israel,[8]
if the deceased had left instructions that he be buried elsewhere, or if the
burial had taken place under the advance stipulation that the body be
moved to another location.[9] Similarly, the body may be exhumed when
there is a concern that the grave "cannot be properly protected" from
vandalism or from natural erosion; "it is a mitzvah" to bury the corpse
in another grave to spare it distress (*tzaar*) and disgraceful treatment
(*bizayon*).[10]

Based upon the above, it would be possible to construct a good
argument for permitting disinterment in this case. The ultimate intention
is the creation of a family burial place, and we have seen that the
tradition permits disinterment when the object is reburial in a family
plot. The nearness of the new cemetery means that the deceased's wife
and daughters will visit his grave more frequently, and this is surely an
act of *k'vod hameit*, rendering honor to the dead, as well as *nichum
aveilim*, a source of comfort to the mourners. It is also quite conceivable
that the husband would have agreed to the plan of disinterment, and this
might have the force of an advance stipulation such as that described

above. Finally, that the cemetery where the husband currently lies buried is "not safe" is further reason, according to our tradition, to consider disinterment.

2. OBJECTIONS TO THE DISINTERMENT

On the other hand, this argument is not without its difficulties. Let us consider some of them here.

a. The "family plot" contention is somewhat forced. For one thing, the term is our translation of the Hebrew *kever avot*, which identifies the "family" resting place with the burial site of one's parents and ancestors. Some authorities, accordingly, would limit the permit for disinterment to such instances and would not extend it to cover burial next to a spouse. We, along with other authorities, are comfortable with a more expansive definition of "family."[11] Nonetheless, we would note that when Jewish tradition speaks of disinterment and reburial in *kever avot*, it has in mind an already existing burial site.[12] In our case, the wife does not seek to rebury her husband in such an existing site (say, next to his parents) but rather to create a new "family plot." In so doing, she would uproot the existing family burial site, namely at the cemetery where her husband currently rests. None of the authorities who allow disinterment for purposes of reburial in *kever avot* refer to a situation such as this. They would likely urge the opposite course: the wife should wish to be buried next to her husband, at the existing "family plot," rather than to disturb his corpse for burial in a place where, as yet, no family members have been laid to rest.

b. The argument that the husband's cemetery is in an area that is "not safe" is a serious one, but it is difficult to measure. R. Moshe Feinstein permits the removal of all the bodies buried in a cemetery that is located in an unsafe neighborhood and where it is impossible to protect it against vandalism,[13] and our teacher

R. Solomon B. Freehof concurs that disinterment is "the optimal solution" in such a situation.[14] But just how "unsafe" is the cemetery where this woman's husband lies buried? The members of this Committee cannot make that determination. We would suggest, moreover, that the claim that the cemetery is located in an "unsafe" area raises issues of special sensitivity. That claim, to our sorrow, is sometimes used as a code-phrase to express a sentiment that we may be unwilling to utter openly, one that might call into question our Reform Jewish commitment to social justice.[15] We have no reason to believe that the congregant who brings this *sh'eilah* is motivated by such a sentiment. Still, it is up to her rabbi to judge whether and to what extent her concern over the security of the current cemetery is warranted by the facts.

c. Removing the deceased to a cemetery "closer to the woman and her children" will enable them to visit his grave more often. That is surely a good thing, but we think it is insufficient grounds to permit disinterment. Our society (we speak here principally of the United States) has for some time been an increasingly transient one. Many of us live far away from what was once our family home, and we tend not infrequently to move from place to place for purposes of education, employment, professional advancement, and retirement. In our travels we have generally not thought to uproot our dead and to bring them along with us. We have preferred, in devotion to our Jewish tradition, to leave them undisturbed in their final resting places and to visit them whenever we can. This approach certainly places a burden of inconvenience upon us, but we have thought that it better comports with the specific Jewish way of rendering honor to the deceased (*k'vod hameit*).[16] Again, we have no reason to believe that the congregant in this case is motivated primarily by considerations of personal convenience. Yet should we issue an affirmative answer to her request, that answer would rightly be cited as a precedent by others in similar circumstances who might in fact seek to disinter and to move their dead largely out of such reasons. That is a line we can ill afford to cross.

d. Finally, we would discourage the removal of the dead from a Jewish cemetery to a non-Jewish cemetery. Although Jewish law imposes no formal (i.e., Toraitic or Rabbinic) requirement that the dead be buried in a "Jewish cemetery," Jewish communities have by long-standing custom acquired land for the purpose of establishing their own burial places.[17] It is there that we ought to lay our dead to rest. We have, indeed, no objection to the burial of our dead in national military cemeteries that are not associated with any particular religion, since those burial grounds are considered the property of all the country's citizens. Yet from this absence of an "objection" we have never deduced that it is permissible to disinter a Jew from a Jewish cemetery for reburial in such a cemetery, and we have in fact decided otherwise.[18] This, too, is a weighty consideration against approval of the widow's request in our case.

CONCLUSION

Jewish tradition does not unequivocally prohibit this wife's request for the removal of her husband's remains to the veterans' cemetery closer to her home. As we have said, one could construct a good argument from the sources in support of an affirmative response. But the objections that we have cited are serious enough to give us pause, particularly because a "yes" answer to this *sh'eilah* might lead to undesirable ramifications in future cases. Given our general opposition to disinterment, we would urge the rabbi to discourage the widow and her family from taking this step. He should support their request only if he is convinced that the arguments brought in support of it—especially the concern over the lack of safety at the existing cemetery—are truly substantive and persuasive.

NOTES

1. This point parallels the famous insight of U.S. Supreme Court Justice Oliver Wendell Holmes, Jr., who wrote, "General propositions do not decide concrete cases. The decision will depend on a judgment or intuition more subtle than any articulate major

premise" (*Lochner v. New York*, 198 U.S. 45, 76). In Jewish law, too, the correct application of the rules is frequently not determinable by way of logical syllogism. It requires, instead, an act of judgment by the interpreter(s). Judgment, by its nature, is controversial in a way that logic and mathematics are not. It is established by argument, not demonstrated by proof, and in any given case a different judgment might arguably be a better one. Yet no sort of legal or religious interpretation can occur without judgment and argument. It is for this reason that rabbis write responsa to argue for their conclusions and that their readers are invited to join in discussion and debate over them.

2. *SA, YD* 363:1.

3. JT *Mo-eid Katan* 2:4 (81b); *S'machot* (*Evel Rabbati*) 13:7.

4. *Sefer Raavyah* III, *Mo-eid Katan*, chap. 832; Nachmanides, *Torat HaAdam, inyan hak'vurah* (ed. Chavel, 119); *Or Zarua* 1, responsa, no. 755, and 2:419–420; *Sefer Kolbo*, chap. 60; *Tur, YD* 363.

5. *Sefer Kolbo*, chap.114, citing Job 3:13 and I Sam. 28:15 as proof texts; R. Y'hoshua Falk Katz, *P'rishah* to *Tur, YD* 363:1; *Turei Zahav* and *Siftei Kohein* to *SA, YD* 363:1.

6. R. Yaakov Reischer (eighteenth-century Germany) refers to *nivul* as the "principal reason" for the prohibition and plays down the theme of fear of Judgment Day; *Resp. Sh'vut Yaakov* 2:103. See also R. Zvi Ashkenazi (d. 1718; Germany/Poland), *Resp. Chacham Zvi*, no. 50.

7. *SA, YD* 363:1: "It is pleasing to a person that he be buried next to his ancestors." *Siftei Kohein* ad loc.: burial with one's ancestors "is an honor to the deceased."

8. *SA, YD* 363:1. The reasons (ad loc.): burial in *Eretz Yisrael* effects atonement (*kaparah*) for one's sins (*Siftei Kohein*), and we can presume that the deceased would have wanted his final resting place to be in the Land of Israel (R. Eliyahu, Gaon of Vilna, *Biur HaGra*).

9. *Shulchan Aruch* ad loc. The theory here is that if the deceased is buried in a place not of his or her own choosing, he or she has not truly "acquired ownership" of that grave; *Resp. Chatam Sofer* 6:37 and *Resp. Maharam Schick, YD* 354.

10. *Or Zarua* 2:420; *SA, YD* 363:1.

11. R. Moshe Feinstein, *Resp. Ig'rot Moshe, YD* 1:236, allows disinterment in this sort of case only for the burial of a child next to a parent. On the other hand, he cites the

differing view of R. Meir Simchah of Dvinsk, *Or Sameach* to *Mishneh Torah, Aveil* 14:15. See as well the discussion in R. Yekutiel Greenwald, *Kol Bo al Aveilut*, 233–34.

12. See *Turei Zahav*, YD 363, no. 2; *Resp. Knesset Yechezkel* (R. Yechezkel Katznellenbogen, eighteenth-century Germany), no. 43. The Chatam Sofer (6:37) sided with those who permitted the exhumation and reburial of R. Mordechai Benet in "the burial place of his ancestors [*avotav*] and his relatives [*mishpachto*]."

13. *Resp. Ig'rot Moshe*, YD 1:246.

14. *American Reform Responsa*, no. 115 (http://data.ccarnet.org/cgi-bin/respdisp. pl?file=115&year=arr).

15. For example, the Feinstein responsum cited in note 13 refers explicitly to a Jewish cemetery located in a "black neighborhood" (*sh'chunah kushit*) where the residents "treat the place contemptibly, throwing all sorts of trash into it. The cemetery cannot be protected, because each time the fence is repaired they break through it again. The expense incurred, moreover, is greater than the community can bear." This may have been an objective and accurate description of the security situation at the graveyard (the *sh'eilah* came from New Orleans in late 1951). Yet it makes for uncomfortable reading, especially in that it assigns the responsibility for the damage not to unspecified vandals but to the fact that the cemetery lies in what is now a "black neighborhood."

16. One can argue, of course, that it is possible to show honor for the dead in ways other than those specified by Jewish tradition. We would agree, but as we have written elsewhere, "[it] is true that concepts such as 'honor' and 'disgrace' do not admit of objective definition. All this means, however, is that such terms can only be defined from within a particular social context; to reach these definitions, we must choose to work within a particular culture's set of values and affirmations" (*Reform Responsa for the Twenty-first Century*, no. 5766.2, vol. 2, pp. 199–200). The particular culture within which we choose to work is the religious tradition of the Jewish people, a choice that accounts for many of the conclusions that we reach in our work.

17. See, in general, *Contemporary American Reform Responsa*, no. 105. R. Yitzchak Elchanan Spektor (eighteenth-century Lithuania) argued that this custom stems from the concern that, should we not own the cemetery, we may one day be forced by its owners to remove our dead from there (*Resp. Ein Yitzchak*, YD, no. 34).

18. *Reform Responsa for the Twenty-first Century*, no. 575.65, vol. 1, pp. 147–49.

EVEN HA-EIZER:
PERSONAL STATUS, MARRIAGE,
AND FAMILY LIFE

Adoption, Conversion, and "Patrilineal" Descent

5767.2

Sh'eilah

Two lesbian women are expecting a baby conceived through sperm donation. One of these women is Jewish and affiliates with the Reform Movement, but the other is not, and it is she who will be the birth mother. The sperm donor is not Jewish. The two women partners will be the child's parents, and they plan to raise their child in a Jewish home. Will their baby have to undergo a formal conversion (i.e., be immersed in a *mikveh*) to confer Jewish status according to Reform Movement principles? Will the Jewishness of the non-carrying parent-partner play a role in conferring Jewish status to the child, as it could in a situation of patrilineal descent where the parents are heterosexuals? (Rabbi Andrew Vogel, Brookline, Massachusetts)

T'shuvah

We should state at the outset of our *t'shuvah* that this couple's sexual orientation is not germane to the issues at hand. Our *sho-eil*'s questions would apply as well to the case of a heterosexual couple. In either case the child, as the offspring of two gentile biological parents, would be a gentile at birth and would subsequently be adopted by the mother's Jewish partner. The critical factor here is that of adoption: how does a gentile child acquire a Jewish identity when adopted by a Jewish parent or parents? Is a formal conversion (*giyur*) necessary?

1. ADOPTION AND "PATRILINEAL" DESCENT

Our *sho-eil* asks whether this child might qualify as a Jew under the CCAR's doctrine of "patrilineal"descent. That doctrine, more properly called "the doctrine concerning the status of offspring of mixed

marriage,"[1] is set forth in a resolution enacted by the CCAR
in 1983:

> The Central Conference of American Rabbis declares that the child
> of one Jewish parent is under the presumption of Jewish descent.
> This presumption of the Jewish status of the offspring of any mixed
> marriage is to be established through appropriate and timely public
> and formal acts of identification with the Jewish faith and people.
> The performance of these mitzvot serves to commit those who
> participate in them, both parents and child, to Jewish life.
>
> Depending on circumstances, mitzvot leading toward a positive
> and exclusive Jewish identity will include entry into the covenant,
> acquisition of a Hebrew name, Torah study, Bar/Bat Mitzvah,
> and Kabbalat Torah (Confirmation). For those beyond childhood
> claiming Jewish identity, other public acts or declarations may be
> added or substituted after consultation with their rabbi. [2]

Some might argue that this doctrine applies to our case because adoption
creates a legitimate family relationship; one's adoptive parents are in
every respect one's *real* parents.[3] This child, who acquires a Jewish
parent by way of adoption, should therefore be treated in every way
as though she or he were the biological offspring of that parent. This
Committee, however, has understood the doctrine to apply exclusively
to biological offspring.[4] That is because the 1983 resolution comes
to adjust—but *not* to abolish—the traditional "biological" definition
of Jewishness, that is, descent from a Jewish mother.[5] The new
definition, though it differs from the traditional one in some important
respects, reaffirms the central importance of biological descent for
the determination of Jewishness. Thus, we continue to recognize the
biological offspring of two Jewish parents as a Jew, even in the absence
of "appropriate and timely" acts of Jewish identification, and we
continue to recognize the biological offspring of two gentile parents
as a gentile who would require conversion in order to become a Jew.
Similarly, the child of one Jewish parent enjoys a "presumption of Jewish

descent" solely because he or she is the biological offspring of that parent, and upon the performance of those "appropriate and timely" acts he or she is considered to have been Jewish *from birth.*[6] The child, that is, has never been a gentile, and no conversion is necessary to alter his or her status.

The child in our *sh'eilah* will be born to two gentile parents and, as a gentile from birth, will not begin life under the presumption of Jewish status. Our 1983 resolution on "patrilineal" descent does not apply to such a child, and it would seem that we would require conversion in this case.

2. CONVERSION IN CASES OF ADOPTION

Yet that conclusion is not at all obvious. A number of statements issued over the years by the CCAR and by this Committee declare that a gentile child adopted by a Jewish family requires no formal *giyur.* In 1947, the Conference enacted the proposal of its special Committee on Mixed Marriage and Intermarriage that adopted children should not be required "to undergo a special ceremony of conversion but should receive instruction as regular students in the school. The ceremony of Confirmation at the end of the school course shall be considered in lieu of a conversion ceremony."[7] The 1961 edition of our *Rabbi's Manual* states that "a child adopted by a Jewish family is recognized as a Jewish child."[8] And a 1989 *t'shuvah* of this Committee holds: "Among us as Reform Jews, if no formal conversion took place during infancy then the act of raising the child as a Jew is tantamount to such conversion and nothing else needs to be done."[9]

On the other hand, the Conference and this Committee have also issued statements that suggest the *opposite* position, namely that an adopted child requires conversion. A 1978 responsum writes that the adopted child's naming ceremony, performed in the synagogue once the adoption process is completed, "would be considered sufficient ritual conversion" in most Reform synagogues[10]; that is to say, a ritual *conversion* is necessary, and the ceremony of naming would be a suitable rite for that purpose. In 1984 this Committee reiterated that the adopted child should be named in the synagogue, "with a *berit* [i.e., circumcision] for a male, and if the family desires, *tevilah* [ritual immersion]." The above are defined as "ritual acts" that constitute "the conversion conducted at the time of infancy."[11] *Gates of Mitzvah* (1979), the CCAR's guide to the Jewish life cycle, tells us that "an adopted child should be named in the synagogue and entered into the *berit* as soon as the initial legal procedures for adoption have been completed." If the child is not an infant, "the rabbis should be consulted as to the procedure for formal entry into the Jewish community."[12] Here, too, a ritual of entry into the Jewish community—that is, a conversion—follows the adoption. Our current *Rabbi's Manual* (1988) recommends that all legal adoption procedures be completed "before finalizing any change of [the child's] religious status,"[13] indicating once more that the legal adoption and the establishment of the child's Jewishness are two separate processes. Finally, this Committee explicitly urged conversion for adopted children in a 1999 *t'shuvah*.[14]

3. TWO UNDERSTANDINGS OF CONVERSION

This, to put it mildly, is a confusing situation. The Conference is on record in support of two contradictory policies on whether an adopted child requires a formal conversion to Judaism. This confusion, we believe, results from the conflict between two different understandings of the nature of conversion and the acquisition of Jewish status. These understandings have appeared in our published literature and have pulled us in different directions on our subject.

The first understanding holds that conversion is primarily a spiritual rather than a legal phenomenon. This conception, which arose fairly early in the history of the American Reform Movement, led the Conference in 1893 to abolish the halachic requirement that the proselyte (*ger* or *giyoret*) undergo the traditional rites of *milah* (male circumcision) and *t'vilah* (ritual immersion).[15] In place of those rites, it was suggested that the prospective Jew-by-choice make a verbal declaration before the rabbi of "his or her intention and firm resolve" to worship the One God exclusively, to follow God's laws, and "to adhere in life and death, actively and faithfully, to the sacred cause and mission of Israel, as marked out in Holy Writ."[16] That this became the long-standing policy of the Conference is attested by the 1961 *Rabbi's Manual*, which makes no mention of *milah* and *t'vilah* in its "Conversion Service." Rather, it asks the *ger/giyoret* to declare that he or she seeks admittance into "the Jewish faith" as an act of free will, that he or she renounces all previous religious affiliations, that he or she will establish a Jewish home, raise Jewish children, and the like.[17] The ceremony of *giyur*, in other words, testifies not so much to a change in the proselyte's legal status as to the transformation in his or her religious consciousness and/or belief system. This definition of conversion obviously cannot apply to children. As the Committee on Mixed Marriage noted in 1947,[18] "A young child can hardly be examined as to motives, nor can it be well instructed in the principles of Judaism."[19] Thus, if we no longer require the traditional rites, "how are we able to convert young children or even infants?" The committee answered that, for infants, "the declaration of the parents to raise them as Jews shall be deemed as sufficient for conversion. This could apply, for example, to adopted children." Those statements of the Conference that do not require formal conversion for adopted children follow the line of thinking about conversion and the acquisition of Jewish status.

The second understanding is reflected in the pronounced recent trend within the CCAR to restore the initiatory rites for conversion. This trend, noted in a number of our responsa,[20] is part of the larger tendency in contemporary Reform practice to recover many ritual observances set aside by previous generations of Reform Jews.[21] It is also evidence of a different way of thinking about *giyur*. Conversion in this view is no longer exclusively a matter of personal religious transformation but, as well, the ritual process that signifies one's entry into the Jewish people, an act of identification with the history and traditions of Israel. It follows that a gentile who enters the covenant ought to do so through the formal procedures that have historically accompanied that transition, the same ritual process that, according to our tradition, our ancestors undertook prior to their entry into the covenant at Sinai.[22] Thus, in 1979 the *Gates of Mitzvah* could assert that "we recognize today that there are social, psychological, and religious values associated with the traditional initiatory rites, and therefore recommend that the rabbi acquaint prospective converts with the halachic background and rationale for *berit mila, hatafat dam berit*, and *tevila* and offer them the opportunity to observe these rites."[23] Citing this rationale, the 1988 CCAR *Rabbi's Manual* makes provision for *milah* and *tevilah* in its "Conversion Service."[24] In 2001 the Conference reaffirmed this position: "Rabbis should educate *gerim* concerning appropriate traditional rituals for the ceremonies of *giyur*…and should use them as appropriate."[25] This stance suggests that we are today less likely to draw sharp distinctions between the formal/ritual and the spiritual/intellectual aspects of *giyur*; both are essential parts of the concept as a whole. And if that is the case, the question posed by the 1947 committee—"how are we able to convert young children or even infants?"—loses much of its force, inasmuch as children, like adults, can enter the covenant through *milah* and *t'vilah*. Our 1988 *Rabbi's Manual*, which speaks of the conversion of children as a real and meaningful experience,[26] reflects this second way of thinking about *giyur*.

4. OUR POSITION

Faced with these profound differences in Reform practice and doctrine, this Committee has no easy task in arriving at some sort of resolution. Both of these views are well supported in the history of our movement, and we therefore cannot suggest that either of them is "incorrect." Nonetheless, we find the second understanding the more persuasive of the two and accordingly reaffirm the decision in our 1999 responsum: gentile children adopted by Jewish parents should be converted to Judaism. We do so for the following reasons:

a. Recent Reform practice favors this second understanding of conversion. Although the 1893 resolution, which abolished the requirement of the traditional rites, remains on the books, the Conference has during the last thirty years moved decisively away from the principles that lay at the foundation of that resolution. We have reclaimed the traditional conversion rites for Reform Jewish observance, and we have recommended their use to our colleagues. In so doing we have declared those rites meaningful as formal ritual acts that bind us to the historical experience of the Jewish people.

b.   Consequently, the rationale behind the 1947 report of the Committee on Mixed Marriage, which held that adopted children need not undergo conversion, no longer defines our attitudes on these questions. Our positive reevaluation of the initiatory rites indicates that conversion is for us a formal act of entry into the Jewish community as well as a transformation of an individual's religious consciousness. The conversion of children therefore serves as a ritual sign that testifies to their entry into the covenant and to their parents' commitment to raise them as Jews.

c.   As we argued in our 1999 responsum, to say that adopted children need not be converted comes perilously close to saying that the very fact of their adoption grants them their Jewish identity. While adoption does create a family, it is an act of the state, the civil legal administration, an institution that, with all our respect for *dina d'malchuta*,[27] does not possess the authority to confer Jewishness or to decide "who is a Jew."

d.   Even those CCAR statements that dispense with the requirement of conversion for adopted children contemplate ritual substitutes that, for all practical purposes, *are* conversion. The 1947 Committee on Mixed Marriage report, for example, proposes that confirmation "be considered in lieu of a conversion ceremony"; in other words, a *Jewish* ritual act is needed to stand in place of the traditional conversion ceremony. Our 1989 responsum reads, "If no formal conversion took place during infancy"—which implies that conversion would be the preferred (*l'chat'chilah*) option—"then the act of raising the child as a Jew is tantamount to such conversion." That is to say, the child's Jewish upbringing, which manifestly would include ritual acts like a naming ceremony, bar/bat mitzvah, and confirmation, is the formal equivalent of *giyur*. Even our 1961 *Rabbi's Manual*, which declared simply that "a child adopted by a Jewish family is recognized as a Jewish child," follows that statement with these words: "It is proper that such a child be named in the synagogue."[28] All of these statements concur that the state, through the legal process of adoption, does not have the authority to determine the Jewishness of the child. All of them contemplate some formal Jewish ritual act or set of acts that will testify to the transformation of his/her religious identity. Such a formal act or set of acts is the very definition of *giyur*. While some of our colleagues may not wish to apply that label to these acts, from a functional standpoint that is what they are and the purpose they serve.

CONCLUSION

The baby who is the subject of our *sh'eilah* should be formally converted to Judaism. We say this because (1) our 1983 resolution on "patrilineal" descent applies only to children of one biological Jewish parent, (2) adoption in and of itself is insufficient to bestow Jewish identity upon a gentile child, and (3) a formal Jewish process is therefore required to signify his/her transition to Jewish status. Our tradition calls that process *giyur*, and so should we.

The structure of that process is a separate question. The CCAR has never repealed its 1893 resolution abolishing the requirement of the initiatory rites; therefore, rabbis who create conversion rituals that do not include these rites can do so within the scope of the Conference's stated policy. Yet as we have noted, that policy has been significantly revised over the last several decades, both in terms of the practice of our colleagues who now insist upon these rites and in the official pronouncements by the

Conference and its constituent bodies supporting their use. We would term this new, revised policy one of "preferred option": although *milah* and *t'vilah* are not absolutely required for conversion, our colleagues *ought* to use them, for adults as well as for children, unless the exigencies of a particular case dictate otherwise. This Committee has previously declared its support for this "preferred option," and we reaffirm that stance here by quoting our earlier statement:

In general, the tendency of this Committee is to urge in the strongest terms that all proselytes undergo the traditional rites for entry into the covenant. We do so not because we suppose that Orthodox Jews will recognize the validity of our conversions, but because we regard these practices as a positive *Jewish* standard that applies to us as it does to all other Jews. This testifies to our conviction that when we accept a *ger* or *giyoret* into our midst, we convert him or her to *Judaism*. Although we presume that our proselytes will remain firm in their commitment to a Reform approach to our faith and tradition, we do not require that they do so; we do not make their conversion contingent upon their staying within our fold. We are not in the business of creating a separate sect, cut off from the rest of our Jewish family. Rather, when we accept a proselyte, we admit this person into *Am Yisrael*, the Jewish community as a whole, a living and historical enterprise of which we are an organic part. We therefore believe that it is appropriate and preferable to mark the moment of conversion not simply with liturgy of our own creation but precisely with those rituals that are and have been for centuries employed by the Jewish community as a whole.[29]

NOTES

1. The policy applies equally to the offspring of all mixed marriages, i.e., where one parent (*either* the father *or* the mother) is Jewish.

2. *CCAR Yearbook* 94 (1984): 174–79; *Rabbi's Manual* (New York: CCAR Press, 1988), 226; *Contemporary American Reform Responsa* (*CARR*), no. 38.

3. On this point, see *Teshuvot for the Nineties* (*TFN*), no. 5753.12, pp. 201–7.

4. See *New American Reform Responsa (NARR)*, no. 125.

5. That is, the biological offspring of a Jewish woman is a Jew, regardless of the Jewishness of the father, while the biological offspring of a non-Jewish woman is a gentile even if the father is Jewish. See the final clause of *M. Kiddushin* 3:12: "If a woman is legally incapable of contracting valid *kiddushin* [Jewish marriage] with this man [i.e., the father of her offspring] or with any other man, the offspring follows her status. And who is this? This is the offspring of a gentile woman or a gentile maidservant." Maimonides codifies this as follows: "This is the rule: the biological offspring [*ben haba*] of a gentile slave or a male gentile or a gentile maidservant or a gentile woman follows the mother's status; the status of the father is irrelevant" (*Yad, Isurei Biah* 15:4).

6. If the child is Jewish from birth, why do we require the performance of "appropriate and timely public and formal acts of identification" in order to establish his/her Jewish status? See *CARR* no. 38 (note 2, above): the Conference recognized that Jewish identification, in an era when mixed marriage has become a widespread phenomenon, may have more to do with one's education and upbringing than with the mere fact of one's "belonging" to the Jewish community. For this reason, we introduced a stringency into the traditional halachic definition of Jewish status, in that our position requires that the Jewishness of the child of one Jewish parent—even if that parent is the mother—be "established" (i.e., confirmed) by the performance of those "appropriate and timely" acts.

7. *CCAR Yearbook* 57 (1947): 170–71. The committee was chaired by our teacher Rabbi Solomon B. Freehof.

8. *Rabbi's Manual*, rev. ed. (New York: CCAR Press, 1961), 111.

9. *NARR*, no. 118.

10. *American Reform Responsa (ARR)*, no. 63.

11. *CARR*, no. 37.

12. Simeon J. Maslin, ed., *Gates of Mitzvah* (New York: CCAR Press, 1979), p. 18 (D-2 and D-3).

13. *Rabbi's Manual* (1988), 224.

14. *Reform Responsa for the Twenty-first Century*, 5759.1, vol. 1, pp. 121–28.

15. *CCAR Yearbook* 3 (1893): 69ff.; *ARR*, no. 68. The resolution follows a long and detailed report by a committee, chaired by Rabbi Isaac Mayer Wise, that claims to

prove that the requirements of *milah* and *t'vilah* for conversion were matters of *minhag*, customary practice, and were never truly demanded by biblical or Rabbinic law. Our Committee has subsequently shown this report to be based upon faulty scholarship and dubious reasoning; see *Reform Responsa for the Twenty-first Century*, no. 5756.13, vol. 1, pp. 99–120. Nonetheless, the resolution abolishing the initiatory rites remains on the books as the official policy of the CCAR, though this policy has been reinterpreted and modified through the years; see below in the text.

16. *ARR*, no. 68 (ibid.), end.

17. *Rabbi's Manual* (1961), 17–22.

18. For the quotations in this paragraph see note 7, above.

19. We should note that the halachic tradition encounters much the same problem with the notion of *giyur katan*, the conversion of a child, who by definition lacks the legal capacity to make a responsible decision to accept the Torah and "the yoke of the mitzvot." The solution that Jewish law offers to this difficulty is what we might call "provisional conversion." A gentile child can be converted to Judaism on the strength of the presumption that he or she would consent to receive this "benefit" were he or she old enough legally to give or withhold consent. Nonetheless, upon reaching the age of legal majority, the child does have the power to renounce this presumption, to refuse the conversion; in such a case, the *giyur* is annulled retroactively. See BT *K'tubot* 11a.

20. *ARR*, no. 69; *CARR*, no. 44, no. 45, no. 47 (dealing with infant conversion), and no. 49 (conversion of a child); *TFN*, no. 5752.2 (*hatafat dam b'rit* for a child); *Reform Responsa for the Twenty-first Century*, no. 5756.6, vol. 1, pp. 89–98, and no. 5756.13, vol. 1, pp. 99–120 (conversion of a child).

21. Much has been written about this tendency, which some call the "return to tradition" in Reform Judaism, and we cannot do full justice here to the religious, cultural, and sociological aspects of this complex phenomenon. We would simply note that many ritual observances that were once criticized as either irrelevant or counterproductive to the goal of "modern spiritual elevation" (Pittsburgh Platform, 1885; see http://ccarnet.org/Articles/index.cfm?id=39&pge_prg_id=3032&pge_id=1656) are now regarded as appropriate expressions of our unique Jewish religious consciousness. For a fuller discussion, see *Reform Responsa for the Twenty-first Century*, no. 5759.7, vol. 1, pp. 49–64, at notes 6–10.

22. BT *K'ritot* 9a and *Y'vamot* 46a–b; *Yad, Isurei Biah* 13:1–4: the Israelites entered the covenant through *milah* and *t'vilah*.

23. Maslin, ed., *Gates of Mitzvah*, 146.

24. *Rabbi's Manual* (1988), 210–14, 232.

25. Central Conference of American Rabbis, *Divrei Giyur: Guidelines for Rabbis Working with Prospective Converts*, 2001 (http://data.ccarnet.org/glgerim7.html#n13), section 8b.

26. See the responsa so indicated in note 20, above. See also *Rabbi's Manual* (1988), 233–34, on "Conversion of a Child."

27. On this subject *Reform Responsa for the Twenty-first Century*, no. 5757.1, vol. 1, pp. 347–56, section 1.

28. *Rabbi's Manual* (1961), 111.

29. *Reform Responsa for the Twenty-first Century*, no. 5756.13, vol. 1, pp. 99–120, section 3.

An Adopted Asian Child
5760.9

Sh'eilah

I've been approached by a couple who are unable to have another child (they have one already) and are interested to adopt. They are exploring the possibilities of adoption in several countries including Thailand and China. If they were to be successful in adopting a child from one of these countries, they are seeking to know whether progressive Judaism has a view on the rights of the child to be raised with knowledge of their birth (native) culture, including religious traditions. Apparently, there is considerable discussion of this topic nowadays among those officials responsible for adopted children and their welfare. More generally, how does Judaism view the welfare of adopted children in this regard: their right "by birth" to learn about their native culture, weighed against the adoptive parents' responsibility to raise their children with a sound Jewish education and sense of identity? (Rabbi Fred Morgan, Melbourne, Australia)

T'shuvah

Our responsum is based upon two earlier *t'shuvot*: no. 5753.12, "Kaddish for Adoptive and Biological Parents," and no. 5760.8, "Withholding Paternity Information."[1] The former deals with the nature of the parent-child relationship in adoptive families; the latter discusses the responsibility shared by all parents to act in accordance with the best interests of their children.

The term "best interests of the child" does not, of course, originate in Jewish literature. We borrow it from the language of other legal traditions. Yet it is a principle deeply rooted in Jewish law, which posits that along with the child's filial duty to honor and revere the parent (Exod. 20:12; Deut. 5:16; Lev. 19:3) come a set of obligations owed by parent to child.[2] To ensure that these obligations are met, Talmudic law prescribes a number of general rules concerning parental care and custody of children.[3] These rules, however, can be altered or ignored by the rabbinical court (*beit din*) when it determines that the good of the child demands other arrangements.[4] "The best interests of the child," in other words, serves as a guiding Jewish principle in matters relating to child rearing and family relationships, and we think it applies quite directly to our case. Whether adopted children enjoy a "right by birth" to learn about their native culture, it is certainly arguable that such knowledge will be beneficial or even essential to their psychological welfare. Those who study the growth and development of adopted children report that race and culture play significant roles in identity formation among adoptees whose racial and cultural heritage differs from that of their adoptive parents.[5] While we are in no position to evaluate the scientific literature in this field, much of the data seems to argue that it is important for parents to take active steps to assist their transracial and transcultural adopted children in building a positive appreciation for their ethnic origins.[6] If Judaism teaches us to work toward the "best interests of the child," it stands to reason that our tradition would encourage adoptive parents to help their children learn about their native culture.

Our responsum no. 5753.12 declares that, according to the best reading of Jewish tradition, adoption creates a *real* family and a *real* parent-child relationship.[7] When Jewish parents build their family through adoption, therefore, it is a *Jewish* family they are building, a family in which the parents teach Torah and bequeath their Jewish heritage and identity to their children. Jewish identity, as we have written on numerous occasions, is religiously exclusive. There is no such thing as a "half-Jew," a person who is simultaneously Jewish and a communicant of another religion; one is either a Jew or a non-Jew.[8] This affirmation is basic to our understanding of Jewish identity and of the task assigned by tradition to all Jewish families, however those families are created. Its implication for our *sh'eilah* is clear: Jewish parents who seek to teach their adopted child about the child's native culture must do so in a way that does not compromise the child's perception of Judaism as his or her exclusive religious identity. To put this in the language of the preceding paragraph, the "best interests" of a *Jewish* child require that he or she be raised as a Jew.

How do parents negotiate these conflicting demands? The idea that Judaism is the child's exclusive religious identity implies, at the very least, that the child should not take part in any of the overtly religious ceremonies and rituals of his or her native culture.[9] This standard, we acknowledge, is somewhat vague, perhaps unavoidably so. Religious elements are woven tightly into the fabric of everyday life in many cultures, so that it is may be impossible to distinguish with absolute clarity their "religious" from their "non-religious" aspects. Indeed, Jewish culture is a prime example of this phenomenon. Still, we can say that "overtly religious" ceremonies include worship services or rituals in which deities other than the God of Israel are invoked, as well as rituals that express theological commitments incompatible with Judaism. The child may learn about these aspects of the native culture but should not participate in them.[10] In addition, the Jewish commitments of the Jewish household take precedence over conflicting claims. For example, the family's observance of Shabbat or holidays should not be altered to accommodate events relating to the child's native culture. Similarly, if the family observes kashrut, they are under no obligation to allow their child to eat nonkosher foods associated with his or her native culture. Following these guidelines, we think, will allow the child to develop a deep and keen appreciation of the native culture while establishing a firm and sure identity as a member of the Jewish people.

NOTES

1. Responsum no. 5753.12 is found in *Teshuvot for the Nineties* (TFN), pp. 201–7. For responsum no. 5760.8, see *Reform Responsa for the Twenty-first Century*, vol. 2, pp. 333–37.

2. These are the *mitzvot haben al haav*; see M. *Kiddushin* 1:7 and BT *Kiddushin* 29a.

3. For example, a child should live with his or her mother (in the event the parents do not live together) until the age of six. Upon reaching that age, boys generally live with

their fathers, since it is the father's duty to teach Torah to his son, while girls remain with their mother, who bears the responsibility of training her daughter in the ways of Jewish womanhood. See BT *K'tubot* 65b, 102b, and 103a; *Yad, Ishut* 21:17–18; *SA, EHE* 82:7.

4. Isserles, *EHE* 82:7; R. David ibn Zimra (sixteenth-century Egypt), *Responsa* 1:123; R. Shmuel di Medina (sixteenth-century Salonika), *Resp. Maharashdam*, EHE, no. 123. This rule guides the jurisprudence of the Israeli rabbinical courts on matters of child custody; see *Piskei Din Rabaniyim* 1, pp. 61 and 157.

5. Madelyn Fruendlich, *Adoption and Ethics: The Role of Race, Culture, and National Origin in Adoption* (Washington, DC: Child Welfare League of America, 2000), 1:123. Fruendlich offers a useful, wide-ranging survey of the research in the field.

6. The following statement by D. S. Kim is representative: "It is necessary for the child to be aware of personal heritage to develop his full potential or to define his place in society. Therefore, while avoiding ethnocentricity or reverse racism, foreign children can and should be instilled with a positive ethnic identity" ("Issues in Transracial and Transcultural Adoption," *Social Casework* 5 [1978]: 477–86, at p. 485). See also R. Rios-Kohn, "Intercountry Adoption: An International Perspective on the Practice and Standards," *Adoption Quarterly* 1, no. 4 (1998): 3–32, at p. 4: adoptive families ought to pay "due regard . . . to the child's ethnic, religious, cultural, and linguistic background."

7. See *TFN*, no. 5753.12, p. 206, at the end of the responsum's text: "Children are obligated to show their adoptive parents all the deference and honor expected of Jewish children, for indeed, these have become their parents in every respect."

8. See *TFN*, no. 5754.3, pp. 263–64; *New American Reform Responsa (NARR)*, no. 88, pp. 138–39, and no. 109, pp. 173–74; *Contemporary American Reform Responsa (CARR)*, no. 61, pp. 98–99. That Judaism must be a child's *exclusive* religious identity lies at the heart of the CCAR's Resolution on Patrilineal Descent: a child brought up in a mixed-married household must be raised exclusively as a Jew in order to qualify as a Jew under the terms of the resolution. See *TFN*, no. 5755.17, pp. 251–58.

9. See also *CARR*, no. 51, pp. 97–88.

10. To use an example from a Western setting, a Jew seeking to learn about the culture of Italy would do well to witness church masses, since Roman Catholicism is such a significant element in the life and traditions of the Italian people. The Jew, however, would not worship at the mass or engage in any of the ritual behaviors particular to Catholic worship.

PRESUMPTION OF JEWISH IDENTITY
5760.2

Sh'eilah

A woman presents herself to a rabbi and states she wants to join the congregation. The woman is unknown to the rabbi, the congregation, and the Jewish community. The rabbi inquires if she is Jewish and she states that she is. Does the rabbi accept her at her word, or is the rabbi obliged to conduct further inquiry as to her Jewish status? If further inquiry is required, what threshold of proof need be met? (Rabbi Joshua Aaronson, Perth, Australia)

T'shuvah

Jewish law, in general, determines the status of persons or things in either one of two ways. The first is *eidut b'rurah*, or clear proof, whether in the form of eyewitness testimony[1] or other evidence.[2] The second is presumption, which itself can take two forms: *chazakah*, or "presumption" proper; and *rov*, the "majority" principle. The rules governing these processes are much too complex and detailed to summarize here.[3] Suffice it to say that Jewish law relies upon them as grounds for action in the absence of clear proof. There are many situations for which clear proof or documentary evidence does not exist, yet the court can determine the legal status of the things or persons at issue by means of an appraisal (*umdana*) of what *was* the case prior to the raising of the issue or of what is *likely* to be the case according to the usual behavior of persons or things. Indeed, the most fateful sort of legal decisions—that is, those dealing with capital offenses—can proceed from judgments based upon *chazakah* and *rov*.[4]

Presumption has always played a crucial role in determining an individual's Jewish status. We customarily do not ask newcomers to supply proof of their Jewishness before allowing them to join our communities.[5] This custom is based upon the rule in Jewish law that when a person we do not know comes to us and claims "I am a Jew," we accept that claim on his or her word alone.[6] This rule is explained in several ways. According to some authorities, the claim "I am a Jew" needs no proof because "the majority [*rov*] of those who come before us are Jews"; therefore, we accept this person as a member of that majority.[7] Other commentators say that we accept the claim "I am a Jew" because we presume that a person would not lie about such an easily discoverable fact.[8] In either event, the Jewish status of this person is established not by means of hard evidence but by the community's presumption that the individual is telling the truth. For this reason, it is common practice to accept as Jewish those who come to our communities and present themselves as Jews.[9]

How does this halachic standard apply to the case before us? In theory, the rabbi could follow one of the above presumptions and accept this woman as a Jew on the strength of her claim alone. Yet the matter is hardly so simple. A presumption, as we have noted, is a determination of the status of a person or thing based upon a judgment as to what the status is *likely* to be; it operates in situations where we lack firm evidence to prove what that situation actually is. We think that there is serious doubt that these presumptions concerning Jewish status, which were formulated in an era when it was quite rare for non-Jews to seek to join the Jewish people, can be applied literally to the situation in our communities. To put this bluntly, it is no longer as "likely" as it once was that those who come before us are in fact Jews. This is not to say that these persons are necessarily of malicious intent or that they knowingly lie about their Jewishness, but rather that the once sharply drawn definitions of Jewish identity are much less clear to many people today. An individual becomes a member of the Jewish people either through birth or through conversion.[10] Yet in our liberal society, where religion is often perceived as a strictly personal matter and where changing one's religious affiliation has become increasingly commonplace, many people take the position that "I am what I claim to be." In this view, religious identity is more truly established "internally," by one's heartfelt association with a particular community, than through adherence to "external," formal standards of membership. Many of us have dealt with individuals who regard themselves as Jewish but whose Jewish identity stems neither from birth nor conversion but from an emotional bond, a feeling of connection with us. Such persons might be encouraged to consider conversion to Judaism, but until they complete the conversion process they are *not* Jews. In addition, there are individuals who claim to be Jewish out of genuine misunderstanding of the rules that define Jewishness.[11] Under current conditions, to apply the old presumptions without modification—to say, in effect, that anyone who claims to be Jewish must *be* Jewish—is quite arguably tantamount to ignoring reality.

The foregoing remarks are not to suggest that these problems have reached crisis proportions. In the vast majority of cases, we are satisfied with an individual's statement that "I am a Jew." Indeed, it would be tragic were rabbis and congregations as a rule to greet newcomers with suspicion and probing questions. This would violate both our common sense of decency and the mitzvah of hospitality to strangers (*hachnasat or'chim*).[12] Yet there will be times when the rabbi, on reasonable grounds, will not be satisfied with the individual's claim of Jewishness. We will not attempt to define those "reasonable grounds"; that is a matter best left to the responsible and educated judgment of the rabbi, acting in his or her capacity as *mara d'atra* (local authority). When the rabbi feels that such grounds exist, he or she may inquire into the individual's Jewish status. Ideally, the inquiry will be restricted to questions of the "getting-to-know-you" variety. They should be unobtrusive and respectful of the person's basic human dignity; our tradition, as we know, prohibits us from causing another to suffer unnecessary shame and embarrassment.[13] Yet if the rabbi, mindful of these requirements, feels it necessary to ask for proof of the individual's Jewish status, he or she may do so. To make such determinations, however sensitive the subject matter, is quite simply part of the rabbi's job. And we trust that our rabbis will perform that task with diligence *and* with sensitivity.

NOTES

1. Deut. 19:16; *Yad, Eidut* 5:1ff.

2. The classic example is documentary evidence (*sh'tarot*). Witnesses are ordinarily required to testify orally in the presence of the *beit din* (BT *Gittin* 71a on Deut. 19:16 and *Yad, Eidut* 3:4, although Rabbeinu Tam disagrees; see *Tosafot, Y'vamot* 31b, s.v. *dechazu* and *Hagahot Maimoniot, Eidut*, chap. 3, no. 2). Still, a document such as a promissory note or a deed of sale is acceptable as evidence in legal proceedings on the grounds that "when witnesses sign a document, it is as though their testimony has been investigated by the court" (BT *K'tubot* 18b).

3. For example, the articles on *chazakah* in the *Encyclopedia Talmudit* extend from vol. 13, pp. 553–760 and then to vol. 14, pp. 1–423.

4. That is, we make judgments concerning blood and marital relationships based upon *chazakah* (BT *Kiddushin* 80a and *Yad, Isurei Biah* 1:20) and *rov* (BT *Chulin* 11a–b). These judgments, in turn, determine the application of the prohibitions against incest and adultery, both of which are punishable under biblical law with death.

5. In the words of the thirteenth-century R. Moshe of Coucy (*Sefer Mitzvot Gadol*, negative commandment no. 116): "It is common practice [*maasim b'chol yom*] that, when visitors come to our communities, we do not investigate their origins. [Rather], we drink wine with them and eat the meat that they have slaughtered" (two things that these Jews would never have done had they suspected these visitors of being gentiles).

6. This rule is based upon the Talmudic discussion of the person who comes to us and claims, "I am a convert to Judaism" (BT *Y'vamot* 46b–47a). Halachah requires this person to supply proof of conversion *only* if we know in fact that he or she was originally a non-Jew. If, however, we do not know this person's origin, we accept the claim of conversion because he or she could have said simply, "I am a Jew," a claim for which no proof is demanded. The legal principle here is *migo*: we may accept a claim as true on the grounds that this individual could have made a more advantageous claim. Since we would have accepted on face value the claim that "I am a Jew," there is no reason for us to doubt the veracity of the claim "I am a convert," which entails that he or she was born a gentile. Maimonides (*Yad, Isurei Biah* 13:10) calls this an example of the rule *hapeh sh'asar hu hapeh she-hitir*: a person who is the sole source of information that is disadvantageous to him- or herself ("I was a non-Jew") is believed when he or she gives testimony that reverses the disadvantage ("...but I have converted to Judaism").

7. Rabbeinu Tam, *Tosafot*, *Y'vamot* 47a, s.v. *b'muchzak l'cha* (and see below, note 8); *Hil. HaRosh*, *Y'vamot* 4:34. See also BT *P'sachim* 3b and *Tosafot*, s.v. *v'ana*.

8. R. Moshe ben Nachman (Ramban), R. Sh'lomo b. Adret (Rashba), and R. Yom Tov ibn Ishbili (Ritva) in their *chidushim* to *Y'vamot* 47a; R. Nissim Gerondi (Ran) in his *chidushim* to *P'sachim* 3b; and Rabbeinu Tam in *Sefer HaYashar* (ed. Schlesinger, 1959), chap. 336.

9. *Beit Yosef* and *Bayit Chadash* to Tur, YD 268, fol. 215a; SA, YD 268:10 and *Siftei Kohein*, no. 21.

10. This statement remains true even in North America, where the Reform Movement has modified the traditional standards of Jewish status with the CCAR's Resolution on Patrilineal Descent. Under that resolution, a child of *one* Jewish parent (either father or mother) may qualify as a Jew by performing "timely public and formal acts of identification with the Jewish faith and people." Yet this possibility is open to the child because he or she was born to a Jewish parent. Conversely, the child of *two* Jewish parents remains Jewish under our definition even in the absence of such "timely and formal acts." Thus, Jewishness for us continues to be established on the basis of birth or conversion. For details, see *Rabbi's Manual* (New York: CCAR Press, 1988), 225–27.

11. For example, the determination of Jewish identity under the CCAR's Resolution on Patrilineal Descent (see note 10) can be a source of uncertainty. Just *what* the resolution means by "timely public and formal acts of identification with the Jewish people" is not yet a matter of precise definition, and until that question is clarified we can expect confusion as to "who is a Jew" according to the terms of the resolution.

12. See BT *Shabbat* 127a–b, where hospitality is listed among the things "whose fruits one consumes in this world and whose principal remains available for one in the world-to-come," an example of *g'milut chasadim* (acts of loving-kindness). Maimonides classifies such acts under the rubric of "love your neighbor as yourself" (Lev. 19:18; *Yad, Aveil* 14:1).

13. BT *Arachin* 16b, based upon a midrash of the concluding words of Lev. 19:17, *lo tisa alav cheit*, "do not bear a sin on his account"; *Yad, Dei-ot* 6:8.

Sh'eilah

Our synagogue suffered a tragic fire. The community, especially the non-Jewish community, has been supportive on many levels. Local churches, some of them evangelical, have contributed to our rebuilding effort. Recently, we received a significant check from the local Messianic Jewish congregation. Do we return it, or do we accept it with gratitude in the same way we have accepted funds from other Christian groups? (Rabbi Daniel Weiner, Harrisburg, Pennsylvania)

T'shuvah

"Messianic Jews," along with the Jewish members of such similar groups as "Jews for Jesus," are apostates (*mumarim*), Jews who have abandoned Judaism for other religions.[1] The religion of the "Messianic Jews" is not a version of Judaism but of fundamentalist Christianity, and it does not cease to be Christian in essence and character merely because it is draped in the Hebrew language and Jewish religious symbolism. The Responsa Committee, basing itself upon Jewish tradition and an evaluation of the challenges that confront our community today, has long advocated that we approach apostates with a policy of strict separation tempered with openness.[2] Apostates "should not be accorded membership in the congregation or treated in any way which makes them appear as if they were affiliated with the Jewish community." They are not permitted to lead communal worship, to address the congregation, to be counted in the minyan, or to receive synagogue honors such as an *aliyah* to the Torah. This separation is necessary in order to make two points: first, that it is inappropriate for those who have renounced Judaism to participate in our religious and social life as though they remain Jews in good standing; and second, that their decision in no way constitutes a legitimate Jewish religious choice.[3] At the same time, "we can not, and should not, exclude these individuals from attendance at services, classes, or any other activity of the community, for we always hold the hope that they will return to Judaism and disassociate themselves from Christianity."[4]

How does this policy apply to the issue of gifts by apostates to our synagogues? Jewish law deals in some detail with the question of donations to our religious institutions by those outside of our community. Gentiles, for example, were permitted to donate certain sacrifices to the ancient Temple;[5] accordingly, since many of the rules relating to the synagogue are derived from those that governed the Temple,[6] the Rabbis determined that it is permissible to accept donations from gentiles to our synagogues today.[7] By contrast, the apostate (*mumar*) who rejects Judaism was not permitted to donate sacrifices to the Temple for by his actions he had separated himself from the community of Israel.[8] R. Moshe Isserles, one of the authors of the *Shulchan Aruch*, draws the analogy from Temple to synagogue: just as the *mumar* was not permitted to donate sacrifices, so we do not accept synagogue donations from apostates.[9] This comparison, however, is rejected by Isserles' sixteenth-century contemporary R. Moshe Trani, who declares that the prohibition against accepting donations from the *mumar* applied only to sacrifices and other appurtenances of the Temple and that it is therefore permissible for a synagogue to accept a gift from an apostate.[10] Subsequent halachic writers do not clearly resolve this dispute.[11] It is not certain, therefore, that the halachah would prohibit the synagogue from receiving this gift.

On the other hand, there is another perspective from which we might consider this question. That perspective is *g'neivat daat*, the prohibition against deceptive speech and behavior.[12] "Messianic Judaism" in its various guises is based upon just such a deception. It promotes the false impression that Christianity is a legitimate form of Judaism; it preaches that a Jew who adopts that religion does not abandon Judaism but rather becomes a "fulfilled" or "completed" Jew through the acceptance of Jesus as Messiah and personal savior. This false message is communicated through the very name of the group as well as through a series of deceptive practices. These congregations conduct their worship services in something of a Jewish style and structure; they celebrate the Jewish holy days; their spiritual leaders are called "rabbis," and so forth. Such practices make the "Messianic" religion "look Jewish," thereby blurring the very real distinction between Judaism—in the various forms of religious expression that partake of that experience—and Christianity. This quality of deception, moreover, sharply distinguishes the "Messianic Jews" from other Christian denominations, for while those other churches may seek to preach the Gospel to the Jews, they neither mimic Jewish practices nor present their faith as a form of Judaism. Your acceptance of this donation will be interpreted by many in the community as an acknowledgment of the religious legitimacy of the "Messianic Jewish" movement. This acknowledgment would amount to a reward paid by the Jewish community to a group whose very existence presumes a calculated deception aimed at our people.[13] We should not pay them such a reward.

We say this with no feeling of bitterness toward those Jews who have affiliated with "Messianic" congregations. Though they may have found a religious satisfaction in Christianity that for some reason seems to have eluded them in our synagogues, we do not wish to drive them away permanently. On the contrary: they remain our fellow Jews, our brothers and sisters. As we have said, we welcome them to our services and other congregational activities; our doors are always open to their return.[14] But our openness to them does not require that we affirm their religious choice, a choice that effaces the lines separating us from Christianity and that defines us as a distinct religious community. We recognize that "Messianic Jews" may sincerely believe that belief in Jesus Christ is compatible with Judaism. Yet from our perspective, a perspective born of and educated through centuries of religious life and experience, that doctrine is a falsehood, for it runs counter to everything we believe and know about the faith and tradition we profess. To present a falsehood as though it is the truth is the essence of deception. And a falsehood is still a falsehood even if those who proclaim it regard it to be true.

For these reasons, we think it best that your synagogue refuse, with all due thanks, the donation from the "Messianic Jewish" congregation.

A DISSENT

One member of this Committee disagrees with this decision and is persuaded that the synagogue may accept the donation. In this member's view, the "Messianic Jewish" congregation should be treated as other Christian evangelizing groups in this regard. The Talmud makes a distinction regarding the *intent* of gifts from non-Jews.[15] Clearly a contribution primarily designed to win legitimacy and potential converts in the Jewish community comes with idolatrous intent and would be forbidden. Since these contributions come in response to a tragic fire (possible arson) in the synagogue, however, it is possible to assume that the "Messianic Jewish" congregation gives, as do the other congregations, to demonstrate broad support for the synagogue among all religious communities in the area. The gift, if offered *mipnei darchei shalom*, to advance the cause of peace, should be accepted in that spirit. The majority of our Committee believe that the groups known as "Messianic Judaism" should be treated as "apostates" (for such is how they present themselves) rather than as "non-Jews." We also believe that, given the deceptive nature of their religious program, *any* contribution from a "Messianic" congregation would be made with the desire "to win legitimacy and potential converts in the Jewish community" and should therefore be rejected.

NOTES

1. It is true that a number of members of "Messianic Jewish" congregations are gentiles, that is, individuals who were not born as Jews but who join these communities because they like the Judaic style of their religious life. We use the word "apostates" to refer to the group in general, because they present themselves as a form of Judaism and because their message is aimed at encouraging apostasy among our people.

2. See the following responsa: *Teshuvot for the Nineties* (TFN), no. 5754.1, pp. 143–46, and no. 5753.13, pp. 81–85; *New American Reform Responsa* (NARR), no. 110

and no. 242; *Contemporary American Reform Responsa (CARR)*, no. 66, no. 67, and no. 68; and *American Reform Responsa*, no. 150.

3. Judaism and Christianity are separate, distinct, and mutually exclusive religions; one cannot simultaneously be Jewish and Christian. See *TFN*, no. 5755.17, pp. 251–58, and no. 5754.3, pp. 263–64; *CARR*, no. 61; *NARR*, no. 88 and no. 109.

4. *CARR*, no. 68, at p. 112. On our relationship to returning apostates, see *TFN*, no. 5754.13, pp. 259–60 and the sources cited therein.

5. BT *M'nachot* 73b, on Lev. 22:18; *Yad, Maaseh HaKorbanot* 3:3.

6. The analogy between Temple and synagogue is commonly based upon the designation of the synagogue as *mikdash m'at*, "the sanctuary in miniature." See BT *M'gillah* 29a, on Ezek. 11:16 ("I have become to [the House of Israel] a *mikdash m'at* in the countries whither they have gone").

7. BT *Arachin* 6a; *Yad, Matanot Aniyim* 8:8; *SA, YD* 254:2 (Isserles) and 259:4. See *Siftei Kohein, YD* 254:4, who makes the explicit connection between donations of sacrifices to the Temple and gifts to synagogues.

8. See BT *Chulin* 5a. The rule is derived from Lev. 1:2, "one *from among you* who offers a sacrifice to God...," suggesting that *others* "from among you" may not offer sacrifices. The excluded category is the *mumar*.

9. Isserles' position is registered in *SA, YD* 254:2 and *OC* 154:11. It is apparently based upon a ruling by R. Yaakov Weil (fifteenth-century Germany), *Piskei Mahari Weil*, no. 67.

10. *Resp. Mabit*, 1:214. See also *Sefer Chasidim*, chap. 687: under certain conditions it is permitted to accept donations from a *mumar* for the writing of a Torah scroll.

11. Two leading commentators to the *SA* (*Siftei Kohein, YD* 254:4, and *Magen Avraham, OC* 154:18) cite both opinions without deciding between them. See as well *Aruch HaShulchan, YD* 254:4. R. Moshe Schick (nineteenth-century Hungary) suggests that the *mumar*'s gift might be accepted under two conditions: that we not identify him publicly as a donor ("since it is a contemptible thing" to inscribe his name in the synagogue) and that his gift constitute less than half of the total donations, the rest of which would come from "legitimate" donors. In this way, the *mumar*'s gift would be "nullified" by the preponderance of other donations (*batel barov*); see *Resp. Maharam Schick, YD*, no. 231. Even were we to accept Rabbi Schick's view in principle (and one can raise serious objections to the theory upon which he bases his ruling), we could not apply it here, since the "Messianic Jewish" congregation would want to be

acknowledged as one of the donor churches; indeed, it would be manifestly unfair to accept their money and *not* to thank them publicly.

12. See BT *Chulin* 94a; *Yad, Dei-ot* 2:6 and *M'chirah* 18:1ff.; and *SA, CM* 228:6.

13. To offer "aid and comfort" to transgressors is also a transgression, even if one does not commit the prohibited act. See BT *N'darim* 22a and parallels, and *SA, CM* 266:1, 356:1, and 358:5.

14. See *D'varim Rabbah* 2:7: "The gates of repentance are always open."

15. See the sources cited in notes 5–7.

Sh'eilah

May a person who has two fathers, a stepfather who raised her and
a biological father who was a regular part of her life, be called to the
Torah with the names of both fathers? If so, which of the fathers should
be listed first? My daughter's bat mitzvah is approaching, and when I am
called to the Torah I would like my name to include the names of both of
my fathers and my mother.

T'shuvah

In our tradition, one's name follows the formula "*P'loni ben/bat
Almoni*," where *P'loni* is one's given name and *Almoni* is the name of
one's father. (In Reform Judaism, we customarily add the name of the
mother.) This custom, which the Bible dates to patriarchal times,[1] made
it possible to identify individuals for legal purposes[2] and to establish
one's lineage (*yichus*) in the community, particularly in matters related
to priestly status.[3] You ask whether it is appropriate to depart from this
custom in order to include the name of your stepfather, along with those
of your biological parents, in your Jewish name.

We certainly applaud your desire to show appreciation to one who has
loved and raised you since you were a child. It is a mitzvah to honor and
to revere one's parents,[4] and as we have argued, that obligation extends
to one's adoptive parents as well.[5] Our parents, in Jewish terms, are those
who raise us, care for us, provide for our needs, and educate us, and
adoptive parents perform these functions as surely do biological parents.
Stepparents also fill the role of parent in our lives, even though the law
does not accord them that precise status; we therefore owe a similar duty
of honor to them. As the Rabbis teach, "One who raises an orphan in his

home is regarded by the Torah as though he has given birth to that child" (BT *Sanhedrin* 19b), and "the one who raises a child is called the 'parent,' not the one who begets the child" (*Sh'mot Rabbah* 46:6).

Yet the duty to honor one's stepparent does not imply that one should alter his or her Jewish name. Our Jewish names do more than record a simple genealogical fact. They register the avenue through which we have become members of the community of Israel. If we are born into the Jewish people, we receive our Jewish status from our parents, and our name testifies to that fact. If we have chosen as adults to embrace Judaism, our name indicates that we are the "son/daughter of our father Abraham and our mother Sarah," whom our tradition recognizes as the spiritual parents of all proselytes.[6] An adopted child born of gentile parents may be named "the son/daughter of" the adoptive Jewish parents, rather than "*ben/bat Avraham avinu v'Sarah imeinu*," precisely because it is the adoptive parents who bring that child into the covenant of Israel.[7] To put this in terms of Jewish theology, we were all present at Sinai, even those of us alive today, either because we were born to Jewish parents or have converted to Judaism.[8] Your stepfather loved and cared for you, and he surely participated in your Jewish education and upbringing. But he did not bequeath to you your membership in the Jewish people; that is a status you have inherited from your biological parents.[9] Your Jewish name, which we understand as a *covenantal* name,[10] should attest to that reality.

To be sure, our tradition permits one to change his or her Jewish name under certain conditions. For example, the halachah provides that while an individual is called to the Torah by his Jewish name, he may omit his father's name (perhaps substituting the name of his paternal grandfather in its place) should the father be an apostate, that is, a convert to another religion.[11] Your biological father, however, has not done anything so grievous. He has not abandoned you or forsaken his duty as a father; indeed, you acknowledge that he has been "a regular part of [your] life." Even were we to agree, therefore, that at times one's Jewish name might be altered, this is not one of those times.

CONCLUSION

Your stepfather deserves all the respect and honor that a child owes
to a parent. There are numerous ways that you can express that
respect throughout your life and, in particular, during your daughter's
bat mitzvah observance. Our Jewish names, however, are not the
appropriate means for bestowing honor upon a stepparent or, for
that matter, upon other persons who may have cared for, taught, and
guided us through our lives. Our Jewish names are rather the symbolic
expression of our identity as Jews, the record of how each of us has
become part of the covenant of Israel.

NOTES

1. See, for example, Gen. 25:12, 25:19, 28:9, and 34:1.

2. For example, the witnesses to a divorce document (*get piturin*) must be able to
identify both the husband and the wife by name "and by the names of their fathers"; see
Beit Yosef to *Tur, EHE* 120, s.v. *v'kotvin lo*, and Isserles, *SA, EHE* 120:3. The formula
p'loni bar (or *ben*) *p'loni* appears in the text of the divorce document (*Yad, Geirushin*
4:12), the *chalitzah* document (*Yad, Hil. Yibum V'Chalitzah* 4:30), and in commercial
deeds (*Yad, Malveh V'Loveh* 22:8 and 24:3).

3. This accounts for the Torah's care in specifying the names *Itamar ben Aharon
HaKohein* (Exod. 38:21; Num. 4:28, 4:33, 7:8), *Elazar ben Aharon HaKohein* (Num.
3:32, 4:16, 17:2, 26:1), and *Pinchas ben Elazar ben Aharon HaKohein* (Num. 25:7,
25:11).

4. Exod. 20:12; Lev. 19:3; Deut. 5:16. On the definition of the "honor" and "reverence"
spoken of in these verses see *Yad, Mamrim* 6 and *SA, YD* 240.

5. *Teshuvot for the Nineties* (TFN), no. 5753.12, pp. 201–7.

6. See *Reform Responsa for the Twenty-first Century*, no. 5760.6, vol. 2, pp. 85–91.

7. Ibid., and R. Moshe Feinstein, *Resp. Ig'rot Moshe, YD* 1:161. We do not address the
question of a child born through reproductive technologies such as in vitro fertilization
whose biological parents (i.e., those who donate the genetic materials) *and* whose
adoptive parents are Jews. The issue in that case is a complex one that requires further
study; therefore, nothing we say here should be understood as conveying our position

concerning it. In the meantime, see *Reform Responsa for the Twenty-first Century*, no. 5757.2, vol. 1, pp. 159–68.

8. See Deut. 29:14, along with Rashi ad loc.; *Midrash Tanchuma, Nitzavim* chap. 3; and BT *Shabbat* 146a.

9. We note here that this affirmation is supported by the CCAR's Resolution on Patrilineal Descent; see *Rabbi's Manual* (New York: CCAR, 1988), p. 226. That resolution provides that "the child *of one Jewish parent* is under a presumption of Jewish descent. This presumption *of the Jewish offspring of any mixed marriage* is to be established through appropriate and timely public and formal acts of identification with the Jewish faith and people" (emphasis added). The resolution speaks only and explicitly to the status of a child born to one Jewish and one non-Jewish parent. By implication, the child born of *two* Jewish parents *is* Jewish; his or her Jewish status is not "presumed" but firmly fixed.

10. On the "covenantal" nature of the Jewish name, see *Reform Responsa for the Twenty-first Century*, no. 5760.6 (see note 6, above), and no. 5762.2, vol. 2, pp. 251–56.

11. R. Yisrael Isserlein (fifteenth-century Germany), *Resp. T'rumat HaDeshen* 1:21; Isserles, *SA, OC* 139:3. This ruling is limited, however, to cases where the change of name will not cause embarrassment to the son; see *Resp. Maharam Padua* (sixteenth-century Italy), no. 87.

A "Hebrew Name" for a Non-Jewish Parent
5762.2

Sh'eilah

With the influx of so many families in our congregations where there is only one Jewish parent, we have developed many new ways to appropriately welcome and engage them in the Jewish community. As a congregational rabbi, I am often asked to do baby namings or *b'rit* ceremonies for such families where there is a commitment to raise the child exclusively as a Jew. Most of the rabbis that I know will give the child a name, but the latter part of the Hebrew name (*ben/bat X and Y*) will include only the Hebrew name of the Jewish parent. It is my feeling that parents who raise a child Jewish should both be recognized as the parents of a Jewish child. To exclude the non-Jewish parent's name, I feel, is to dishonor that parent, especially since he or she has agreed to bring this infant into a Jewish covenant. Thus I would name the child with the Hebrew name of the Jewish parent and pronounce the other parent's name in Hebrew. For example, if a non-Jewish father's name is "John," I will not make it "Yonatan" but will pronounce it as John and write it accordingly.

Is it appropriate for clergy who bestow names on children with one Jewish parent to include a Hebraicized version of the name of the non-Jewish parent?

T'shuvah

We agree with "most of the rabbis" that you know: we think it is inappropriate to bestow a Jewish name upon the gentile parent of a Jewish child. You make a good argument for your point of view, but we find theirs more persuasive, for the reasons we elaborate below.

1. THE JEWISH NAME

The Hebrew name we bear is not, properly speaking, a "Hebrew" name but a *Jewish* name, the name bestowed upon us at birth or upon conversion,[1] the name by which a person "shall be called in Israel."[2] This name testifies to the manner in which that person acquired his or her identity as a Jew, whether by descent from a Jewish parent or parents or by conversion. A Jewish name, as we have written elsewhere, "is a *covenantal* name, a declaration that the one who bears it is a member of the community that stood at Sinai to receive the Torah."[3] It is therefore out of place to bestow a Hebrew name on a gentile, since that person is not a member of the covenantal community. You suggest that by transliterating rather than translating the name of the gentile parent—by writing "John" in Hebrew letters rather than "Yonatan"—we would avoid giving a false impression of Jewish identity. The difficulty is that not all Jews bear "Hebrew" names; many Jewish names have been "Hebraicized" from other cultures.[4] The distinction you draw, in other words, would not have the desired effect. The inclusion of the non-Jewish parent's name would still signify, incorrectly, that he or she is a Jewish parent.

2. BRINGING A CHILD INTO THE COVENANT

You argue that the non-Jewish parent should be given a Hebrew name because, by agreeing that the child shall be raised as a Jew, the parent acts so as "to bring this infant into a Jewish covenant." Yet this is precisely what the non-Jewish parent *cannot* do. The covenant (*b'rit*) of which we speak is a bond between the Jewish people and its God. It is a way of life, a set of common values and memories handed down from one generation to the next, from Jewish parents who are themselves parties to that covenant to their children.[5] Thus we "teach diligently" unto our children the words of Torah that *we* live by, the words that lie upon *our* heart (Deut. 6:6–7). Thus we recount to our children the foundational narrative of our history with the words "it is because of what God did for *me* when *I* went forth from Egypt" (Exod. 13:8), for we bring our children into the covenant when we incorporate them into our own experience.[6] Thus we learn that when Israel entered the covenant, those who stood there physically were joined by all Jews yet unborn, as a symbol of the passing of the covenant from parent to child, from generation to generation (Deut. 29:9–14).[7] It is for these reasons that, at ritual moments that celebrate the birth of new Jewish lives, we praise God "who hallows *us* with *mitzvot* and commands *us* to bring our son/daughter into the Covenant."[8] *We*, the Jewish people, are bound to God through a nexus of mitzvot. One of these mitzvot is the obligation to raise our children as Jews.[9] Hence, it is we Jews— and no one else—who transmit the covenant to our children. A non-Jew, who does not partake of the mitzvot, is hardly "commanded" to bring his or her child into the covenant.[10] He or she can agree that the children shall be raised as Jews. He or she can even cooperate actively in that endeavor, bringing the children to their Jewish school, attending synagogue services with them, and the like. But that parent, who is not a Jew, cannot perform these actions with *Jewish* intent.[11] The non-Jewish parent cannot transmit to his or her children the sense of belonging, of mutual obligation, and of common heritage that we mean by the word *b'rit*. A non-Jewish parent cannot bring children into the covenant of Israel.

3. A "DISHONOR" TO THE NON-JEWISH PARENT?

You write that to "exclude" the name of the non-Jewish parent would be to "dishonor" that person. This is a powerful argument. We are a liberal religious community, one that prizes the value of tolerance and openness; none of us wishes to insult the non-Jews in our midst. At the same time, we are puzzled at the use of the word "dishonor" to describe this situation. Our determination of a child's Hebrew name is based upon our conception of the proper standards of religious observance and of the definitions of Jewish identity. When we insist upon these standards and definitions—which we must be able to do if we are to exist as a distinct religious community—we do not thereby make or imply any derogatory statements concerning those who are not members of our community.

For example, our understanding of the act of Jewish communal worship leads us to place certain firm restrictions upon the role that a non-Jew may play in our synagogue services, including the services that mark life-cycle events for that person's Jewish relatives.[12] This is not meant as a slight or insult against the non-Jew. It is rather a standard we must observe in order to preserve our religious integrity as a Jewish community. Similar considerations apply to this *sh'eilah*. We think that the non-Jew, who recognizes that he or she is not a member of the Jewish religious community, can appreciate our concerns and not feel dishonored thereby. We would hope that all our congregations make it clear that we do not seek to "exclude" the non-Jewish parent from our community. On the contrary: we welcome their participation in the fellowship of our synagogue family, and we invite them to consider joining us by way of conversion. We in the Reform Movement are justly proud of our efforts at outreach to the non-Jews in our midst. We actively encourage them to choose Judaism, and we offer programs and classes to aid their journey along that path. We recognize that not every non-Jewish spouse will decide to become a Jew, and we respect whatever decision he or she makes in this highly sensitive and personal matter. In the same way, we would expect that they will respect our need to make the decisions that preserve the Jewish integrity of our communal religious practice.

4. THE PASTORAL RESPONSE

We realize that, despite our protestations to the contrary, the non-Jewish parent might nonetheless feel excluded if his or her Hebraicized name is not part of the name bestowed upon the newborn child. We do not suggest that rabbis should ignore these emotions or fail to validate them as real. We think, rather, that the situation more properly calls for a caring and sensitive response from the rabbi, acting in his or her capacity as teacher of Torah and pastor to the community. There are many appropriate and meaningful ways in which the officiant at a *b'rit* or naming can acknowledge the role of the non-Jewish parent in committing the child to Judaism. The rabbi, for example, might speak at the service about the thoughtful consideration of the parents in choosing a path and about the generosity of spirit they have shown in deciding to raise the child as a Jew, even when one of them was not raised in our tradition. By expressing these beautiful sentiments, we can declare the full parental privilege of the non-Jew without creating a Hebrew name for someone who is not *ben/bat b'rit*. In addition, the naming certificate published by the Union for Reform Judaism provides spaces in which to insert the name of the child and the names of the parents in English, as well as a space for the child's Jewish name in Hebrew. The non-Jewish parent is thus recognized in fact as the mother or father of the child, even though we do not include him or her in the child's Jewish name. The rabbi, in other words, has ample opportunity to stress that we value highly the role he or she will play in the life of the child. What the rabbi should not do, however, is to abandon a ritual practice that makes an essential statement: namely, that Jewish identity and the covenant of Israel are precious gifts to be handed down from generation to generation, from *Jewish* parents to their *Jewish* children.

NOTES

1. Conversion, in Jewish tradition, is regarded as a spiritual rebirth; "the convert is like a newborn child" (BT *Y'vamot* 22a and parallels).

2. See, for example, the service for *b'rit milah* and the covenant service for a daughter in the CCAR *Rabbi's Manual* (New York: CCAR Press, 1988), pp. 12 and 21 respectively: the child's name is bestowed by the formula *v'yikarei sh'mo/sh'mah b'Yisrael*, "his/her name in Israel shall be...." This formula is adapted from the traditional siddur. See as well at p. 208, the service for conversion: "and from this time forth you shall be known *in the Jewish community* [italics added] as _____ Ben/Bat Avraham veSara."

3. See *Reform Responsa for the Twenty-first Century*, no. 5760.6, vol. 2, pp. 85–91.

4. See SA, EHE 129 for a lengthy treatise on the proper Hebrew spelling of the non-Hebrew names of Jewish men and women (precision on this point being a necessary feature of the laws of *gittin*). And see R. Jacob Z. Lauterbach in *American Reform Responsa*, no. 59, pp. 185–86.

5. On the custom for the proselyte to take the name *ben/bat Avraham v'Sarah*, see *Reform Responsa for the Twenty-first Century*, 5760.6 (see note 3, above).

6. "In every generation, one must view himself as having personally come forth out of Egypt, as it is said, 'Because of what God did for *me* when I came forth from Egypt' (Exod. 13:8)" (*M. P'sachim* 10:5).

7. The phrase "and the one who is not here with us today" ostensibly refers to the yet-unborn generations of Israel; see Rashi to Deut. 29:14. An alternative Rabbinic tradition applies those words to all those who will one day convert to Judaism (BT *Shabbat* 146a).

8. *Rabbi's Manual* (1988), 11 and 20–21. The latter adapts the traditional circumcision benediction to the covenant ceremony of an infant girl.

9. Reform Jews differ as to the precise theological meaning of the term *mitzvah*. Still, we do not shy from using that word to describe an act or a pattern of behavior that we perceive to be an obligation stemming from our identity as Jews and our membership in the covenant. Thus, "it is a *mitzvah* to teach one's child the traditions and beliefs of Judaism" (Simeon J. Maslin, ed., *Gates of Mitzvah* [New York: CCAR, 1979], 19).

10. Relevant here is the Rabbinic dictum "the one who acts because he is commanded [*mi shemetzuveh v'oseh*] is greater than the one who acts even though he is not commanded" (BT *Bava Kama* 38a and 87a; BT *Avodah Zarah* 3a). The statement is part of a Talmudic discussion over the merit due to a non-Jew who "occupies himself with Torah." The conclusion is that while such behavior is indeed a good thing, it is purely voluntary. The non-Jew does not thereby uphold a responsibility that characterizes the covenantal relationship between God and Israel.

11. There is a famous dispute in the halachic literature over the question, do mitzvot require intention (*kavanah*)? That is, can one fulfill the obligation imposed upon him or her by simply performing an action, without at that moment formulating a specific intention that "I am about to perform a mitzvah"? See BT *P'sachim* 114b and BT *Rosh HaShanah* 28a–b. This *machloket* is generally decided in favor of the position that requires *kavanah* (SA, OC 60:4): that is, in order to fulfill a mitzvah one must perform that act with the conscious intent to fulfill it *as a Jewish religious obligation*. A non-Jew simply cannot do this. One who is not Jewish cannot perform any action with the intent to fulfill thereby a Jewish religious obligation, because the non-Jew does not partake of the covenant between God and Israel that is defined by mitzvot.

12. See *Teshuvot for the Nineties*, no. 5754.5, pp. 55–75.

Sh'eilah

A member of my congregation has sent me the following query. "In addition to belonging to our synagogue, I have also been attending Quaker meeting for several years. I would like to know if the synagogue would have a problem with me becoming a member of the Society of Friends. Granted the Quakers have a background in Christianity, the meeting for worship on Sundays is not a church service and Quakers do not have clergy. We simply sit in silent prayer for an hour and give ministry when we feel moved to speak."

What should be our response? (Rabbi David Wirtschafter, Burlingame, California)

T'shuvah

Liberal Judaism affirms the value of religious pluralism in our society. Our understanding of pluralism allows us to engage in interreligious dialogue, participate in interfaith worship that is respectful to all faiths involved, and occasionally borrow non-Jewish patterns and styles of worship and adapt them to our own distinctly Jewish worship.[1] That understanding, however, also presumes the existence of real and essential differences, distinctions, and boundaries between religious faiths and faith communities. Judaism, therefore, is different from other faiths in its commitments and practices, and it is frequently the task of rabbis to call our people's attention to this distinctiveness and the boundary lines that define our unique religious tradition.

That is exactly the rabbi's task in this case. We cannot affirm or support the desire of this congregant to join the Society of Friends.[2] Judaism makes exclusive religious demands of us: one cannot successfully be a practicing Jew and, simultaneously, a communicant of another religion.[3] The congregant might respond that Quaker worship, which lacks a verbal liturgy and contains no formal and required Christological references, is not truly Christian in nature and does not qualify as "another religion."[4] This argument fails, however, because the Quakers by virtue of history and doctrine are unquestionably a Christian sect.[5] The Society of Friends was founded in England by George Fox (1624–91), whose distinctive message was based upon the New Testament conception of the "true light."[6] Thus, "the Lord hath opened to me by His invisible power how that every man was enlightened by the divine light of Christ."[7] Quaker worship dispenses with a verbal liturgy precisely in order that the individual might contemplate this "divine light," the presence of Christ within.[8] That the Quakers conduct their worship in silence is therefore evidence of the presence of Christ—and not his absence—in their meeting. To put this another way, Quakerism is a thoroughly Christian theology even though the Quaker service makes no explicit reference to Jesus.[9]

The short answer to this question, therefore, is "yes": the synagogue most definitely *would* "have a problem" with the congregant's decision to join the Society of Friends. In saying this, we do not mean to imply that the synagogue ought to sever its ties with one who is, after all, a Jew and a member of our community. We would hope that, through continuing discussions and contact with fellow congregants and the rabbi, this individual might discover that the tradition of Jewish worship offers the very sort of spiritual satisfaction that he or she is seeking.[10] Our point, rather, is that we as a Jewish community cannot grant our explicit or implicit approval to this request.

NOTES

1. Some opinions hold that such adaptation runs counter to Jewish law. They refer to the practice of *chukat hagoyim*, the imitation of non-Jewish customs, which is prohibited under the Rabbinic interpretation of Lev. 18:3; see BT *Sanhedrin* 52b and *Avodah Zarah* 11a, along with *Yad, Avodat Kochavim* 11:1. We would note, however, that this prohibition has never been regarded as absolute. For discussion and sources,

see *Teshuvot for the Nineties* (TFN), no. 5751.3, pp. 159–64. Two important rabbinical rulings on this subject are R. Yitzchak bar Sheshet Perfet (fourteenth- to fifteenth-century Spain–North Africa), *Resp. Rivash*, no. 158, and R. Yosef Kolon (fifteenth-century Italy), *Resp. Maharik*, no. 88.

2. The term "join" does not necessarily indicate a formal act of conversion to the Society of Friends or to any other religious group. A given denomination might not require an explicit rite of passage of its new members, and it might not demand that its members regard the denomination as their exclusive religious affiliation. From our perspective, none of this matters; the difficulty begins when a Jew seeks to "become a member" of a Christian sect, however that sect defines membership.

3. We have stressed this point in a number of responsa. We do not officiate at the *b'rit milah* of a child whose parents intend to raise him simultaneously in two religious traditions (*Questions and Reform Jewish Answers* [QRJA], no. 109). Similarly, a child raised simultaneously in two religious traditions does not qualify for Jewish status under the "patrilineal descent" doctrine of the Reform Movement and therefore may not be prepared for bar/bat mitzvah (*Contemporary American Reform Responsa* [CARR], no. 61; QRJA, no. 88; and TFN, no. 5754.3, pp. 263–64).

4. The implication is that a Quaker service is more akin to an exercise in meditation, which is not necessarily antithetical to Jewish belief and practice. See *CARR*, no. 169, on the distinction between acceptable and unacceptable meditative practices within a Jewish context.

5. See, for example, *Faith and Practice: The Book of Discipline of the New York Yearly Meeting of the Religious Society of Friends* (2001 ed.), http://www.nyym.org/quakerism/fnp (accessed August 17, 2009), p. 7: "The Religious Society of Friends arose from personal experience of direct spiritual encounter with God as revealed in Jesus Christ." See also the website of the Friends United Meeting, which "commits itself to energize and equip Friends through the power of the Holy Spirit to gather people into fellowships where Jesus Christ is known, loved and obeyed as Teacher and Lord" (http://www.fum.org, accessed August 17, 2009).

6. See John 1:7–9.

7. J. L. Nickalls, ed., *Journal of George Fox* (Cambridge: Cambridge University Press, 1952), 33. Given the religious ferment in England during the days of the Protectorate and the Restoration, this was hardly a noncontroversial idea. In suggesting that every person might attain perfection by obeying the inner light of Christ, Fox set himself firmly against the Calvinist dogma of predestination, which lay at the core of Puritan

belief, as well as against Roman Catholic and Anglican practice. See Michael Watts, *The Dissenters: From the Reformation to the French Revolution* (Oxford: Oxford University Press, 1978), 186–204.

8. John Dillenberger and Claude Welch, *Protestant Christianity* (New York: Scribner's, 1954), 118–21.

9. As we have noted on several occasions, a prayer or a hymn may be authentically "Christian" even if its text makes no explicit references to Christ. Thus, it is inappropriate for a Jew to recite the "Lord's Prayer," even though the text of the prayer does not mention the name of Jesus; *CARR*, no. 171. See also *TFN*, no. 5752.11, pp. 21–22, on the hymn "Amazing Grace."

10. For example, Judaism does not reject meditation per se; see the responsum cited at note 4. Indeed, many teachers and streams of our tradition have understood prayer as a profound and intense spiritual, emotional, and intellectual experience. A case in point is the Musar movement, born in nineteenth-century Lithuania. The "Musarniks," in the words of a leading scholar of that movement, found prayer "an opportunity for comprehensive spiritual development: concentration of thought, energizing of the emotions, contemplation of the wonders of creation and the greatness of God, and the strengthening of faith and trust in God's goodness." The liturgy in some Musar yeshivot was recited very slowly, "as though one were counting out coins," so that the worshiper could mentally associate the words of the siddur with important religious and ethical concepts (Dov Katz, *T'nuat HaMusar* [Jerusalem, 1982], 2:176). We might also cite the turn toward meditative practices in some contemporary Jewish circles. Our own Union for Reform Judaism has sponsored a meditation *kallah*. This is not to say that these approaches to prayer are exact parallels to the Quaker style of worship, but instead to suggest that one need not go outside the Jewish tradition to find tendencies in worship that emphasize quiet yet intense contemplation.

COMMITMENT CEREMONIES FOR HETEROSEXUAL COUPLES; JEWISH WEDDING CEREMONY IN THE ABSENCE OF A CIVIL MARRIAGE LICENSE

5764.4

Sh'eilah

A retired heterosexual couple has approached me to perform a commitment ceremony for them in lieu of a wedding, since they wish to avoid losing Social Security benefits but still want to have a ceremony affirming their mutual love and commitment. They wish for their relationship to be validated in the eyes of our faith and also in the eyes of their family. They have cited the gay/lesbian commitment ceremonies as precedent. Should such a ceremony be conducted? (Rabbi Michael Sternfeld, Chicago, Illinois)

T'shuvah

Our *sh'eilah* raises the issue of a commitment ceremony, in lieu of a wedding, for a heterosexual couple. In this responsum, we wish to deal as well with the question of whether a Jewish wedding should be provided for a couple who, though eligible to marry under Jewish law and tradition, do not wish to obtain a marriage license from the government.[1] While these situations differ, they both involve a desire on the part of the couple to achieve Jewish religious recognition for their union and simultaneously to avoid becoming husband and wife in the eyes of civil law.

1. JEWISH WEDDING CEREMONY IN THE ABSENCE OF A CIVIL MARRIAGE LICENSE

We begin with the second question because it affords us a basis from which to analyze the first. R. Solomon B. Freehof, in a *t'shuvah* published in 1974,[2] rules that a rabbi[3] should not officiate at a wedding when the couple, seeking "to avoid reduction in the total of their Social Security," do not take out a marriage license. He bases this decision upon the Talmudic principle *dina d'malchuta dina*, "the law of the state is valid in Jewish law."[4] That is, Jewish law holds as binding upon Jews all laws enacted by the civil state that fall within its legitimate domain. By the government's "legitimate domain," as R. Freehof reminds us, the tradition means "civil matters, taxes, business law, etc., but not…ritual matters."[5] Jewish law would never countenance an effort by the civil government to restrict our freedom of worship or ritual observance, and since "marriage and divorce are deemed spiritual matters in which the law of the state does not apply,"[6] we would properly resist any effort by the government to interfere in these areas.[7] On the other hand, "if the state imposes a tax on the entire community, it is a valid mandate in Jewish law that the tax must be paid." A rabbi should not officiate at such a wedding, not because the state has the right to define rabbinical prerogatives, but because "Social Security legislation is a civil matter…valid in Jewish law." Therefore, even from the perspective of Jewish tradition, "the Rabbi may not assist in contravening the laws of Social Security."

R. Freehof also notes that it may well be a violation of state law for a clergyperson to officiate at a wedding where no license has been issued.[8] This legal prohibition is also valid under the principle *dina d'malchuta dina*, for the state has a legitimate interest in regulating the monetary and familial aspects of marriage: ownership of property, issues of inheritance, child custody, and the like. Therefore, the state may legitimately require a couple to register their marriage with the proper authorities, and we rabbis would be expected under Jewish law to honor this requirement.

This Committee affirms the decision of R. Freehof, which is also endorsed by the Central Conference of American Rabbis: we do not officiate at weddings in the absence of a valid marriage license.[9] We would simply add that the principle *dina d'malchuta dina* has been justified in halachic tradition on the theory that the residents of the community "willingly accept the king's laws and statutes upon themselves."[10] Other justifying theories are offered as well,[11] but we find this one, which emphasizes the will of the people as the basis of the law's validity, to be the most congenial to our own democratic temperament. Indeed, as citizens of the state in which we reside, *we* are the *malchut*, the state itself; its laws are *our* laws, which we as citizens have enacted by taking part in its democratic processes and which we have stipulated in advance to accept as valid and binding. Since *we* have participated in the establishment of Social Security legislation as well as the rules that enable the state to regulate the monetary aspects of marriage, it would be hypocritical for us to aid individuals or couples in the contravention of these laws.

Against this conclusion, it might be argued that when we rabbis officiate at weddings we do so primarily as representatives of the Jewish tradition and not as agents of the state. Thus, when a marriage license has not been issued, a rabbi might legitimately perform a wedding ceremony on the grounds that this is a purely "religious" ritual, so that the marriage might be valid in the eyes of Judaism even if not recognized by civil law. We disagree, because the Jewish tradition that this rabbi represents does not make such a distinction between "religion" and "state." In Judaism, the wedding is *both* a ritual and a legal ceremony, one that forges monetary bonds, as well as spiritual ones, between the couple.[12] These aspects of marriage are inseparable in our law; there is no such thing as a Jewish marriage that is valid "religiously" but not "legally," that has spiritual but not material consequences. To suggest otherwise is to distort the essential content of Jewish marriage as well as to encourage couples to "marry" while evading the law.

2. COMMITMENT CEREMONIES FOR HETEROSEXUAL COUPLES

We can now turn to the present *sh'eilah*: granted that a rabbi should not perform a wedding that is not recognized by state law, may he or she arrange a "commitment ceremony" in its stead? Such a ceremony, though "affirming" a couple's union, is emphatically *not* a wedding and therefore creates no marriage, either in Jewish or in civil law. Since the state, which would not recognize this union as a marriage, requires no license for it, no evasion of the law is involved. As our *sh'eilah* notes, rabbis may perform this non-marriage ritual for same-gender couples.[13] Why, then, should they deny it to heterosexuals?

Our answer is that the two situations are not analogous. Same-gender couples do not enjoy the legal right to marry in virtually any of the communities in which we live.[14] A commitment ceremony is their only Jewish recourse, the only ritual means available to them for affirming their union. Rabbis who perform commitment ceremonies urge the couples to take all legal steps available to them to demonstrate and enact their mutual social and legal obligations. In other words, these ceremonies are the closest possible existing equivalent to legal marriage for same-gender couples in most jurisdictions. A heterosexual couple, by contrast, need search for no "equivalent" to marriage, for marriage itself is the means by which, in our tradition, a couple establish their union and build a household together. Among all other human relationships, marriage is unique in that, through the wedding ceremony, a couple *sanctify* their bond by declaring it to be an exclusive and inviolable one, not open to other partners. It is for this reason that the ceremony of marriage is termed *kiddushin*, a word that denotes holiness and consecration, separateness and exclusivity.[15] Similarly, marriage is a union that aspires to stability and permanence. Through the ceremony of marriage, the couple commit themselves to one another, legally and financially as well as spiritually and emotionally, pledging to maintain the household they form in the face of all but the most insurmountable difficulties.

We presume that the couple in question wish to define their own relationship in these terms. They see themselves, in other words, as husband and wife, as a *couple* in the fullest, most permanent sense of that word. Yet while Judaism offers marriage as the means of establishing such a relationship, the couple have chosen to reject that option for themselves. We are not insensitive to the reason they cite for their decision. As we have written, financial duress ought not to prevent couples from fulfilling the mitzvah of marriage, and Judaism calls upon us, as individuals and as an organized community, to help remove the monetary obstacles in their path. As Jews have always done, we can offer financial assistance to couples in need.[16] If we regard the Social Security law to be unfair in its treatment of married couples, we can work to change the law. The fact remains, however, that though this couple seek to "validate" their relationship "in the eyes of our faith," our faith offers no other ritual means than marriage for "validating"—that is, sanctifying—a heterosexual relationship.[17]

We stress, again, that this couple seek to affirm a relationship that is tantamount to marriage. By arranging a "commitment ceremony" instead of a wedding, they wish to declare themselves *married* in the eyes of everyone but the state. For this reason, their device is in substance an attempt to evade the law. It also runs counter to our own Jewish tradition, which does not recognize a "marriage" that is spiritually but not legally binding. The rabbi should not arrange a commitment ceremony for them.

NOTES

1. As we will explain below, the "civil government" in question is the one in power today in the countries where we reside: a regime elected democratically and characterized by the rule of law. It is in such countries that the principle *dina d'malchuta dina* has force.

2. *Contemporary Reform Responsa (CTRR)*, no. 21.

3. Today, of course, this formulation would include the cantor and, for that matter, any *m'sadeir kiddushin*, a "celebrant" of a Jewish wedding. According to Jewish law, the presence of a rabbi or other communal official is not a requirement for a valid marriage. On a minimal basis, explains the *Shulchan Aruch (EHE* 27:1), all that is required is the performance of an act of marriage (*kiddushin*)—for example, the groom gives the bride an object of monetary value under the clear mutual understanding that this action is to effect a betrothal—in the presence of two witnesses. The marriage is valid

without clerical sanction. Still, since medieval times it has been the universal Jewish custom to prohibit weddings unless they have been approved in advance by the local rabbi, most often with the rabbi (or a designated representative) serving as *m'sadeir kiddushin*. For one example, see *Resp. Rambam*, ed. Blau, no. 348 (or ed. Freiman, no. 156), where Maimonides describes the *takanah* of 1187 in Egypt requiring that the local rabbi participate in all weddings. For a number of similar *takanot* spanning all the major centers of Jewish civilization, see Avraham Freiman, *Seder Kiddushin V'Nisuin* (Jerusalem: Mosad Harav Kook, 1964). This practice has usually been justified on the grounds that the legal and halachic issues surrounding marriage are sufficiently complicated to warrant the supervision of a recognized expert in Jewish law. The usual citation is BT *Kiddushin* 6a: "Anyone who is not an expert in divorce and marriage law should not deal with these matters." The *Shulchan Aruch* cites this statement as authoritative halachah (*EHE* 49:3). The Talmudic context of this statement does not mention the issue of rabbinic supervision of or participation in the wedding. Rashi (s.v. *lo y'hei*) interprets it to mean that a non-expert should not presume to issue authoritative halachic decisions (*horaah*) in these areas of the law. This says nothing about whether the *m'sadeir* must be an "expert." The *Turei Zahav* commentary to *Shulchan Aruch* 49:1 makes this point explicit: the Talmudic passage does *not* refer to the wedding ceremony itself and therefore does not mean that a rabbi or scholar must preside over it. On the other hand, R. Yaakov Reischer (eighteenth-century Germany) reads the passage as well as Rashi's interpretation of it to the opposite effect: the wedding itself may be conducted only by a competent scholar, either the local rabbi (*mara d'atra*) or his designate (*Resp. Sh'vut Yaakov* 3:121).

4. The principle, attributed to the *Amora* Sh'muel, is found in BT *Gittin* 10b and parallels.

5. All citations of R. Freehof in this paragraph are in *CTRR*, no. 21, pp. 101–3. For a comprehensive analysis of the nature and limits of this legal principle, see Sh'muel Shilo, *Dina D'Malchuta Dina* (Jerusalem: Defus Akademi Yerushalayim, 1975).

6. With these words, R. Freehof concedes the weakness of one of the major theories that Reform Jews have traditionally advanced in favor of the abandonment of Jewish divorce procedures (*gittin* and *geirushin*) and the acceptance of civil divorce as sufficient for remarriage. That theory, advanced during the nineteenth century by R. Samuel Holdheim in Germany and by R. David Einhorn in the United States, holds that divorce is a matter of monetary law (*dinei mamonot*) falling legitimately under the purview of civil authority according to the principle of *dina d'malchuta dina*. This Committee has concurred with R. Freehof; see our critique of the Holdheim/Einhorn theory in *Reform Responsa for the Twenty-first Century*, no. 5756.15, vol. 1, pp. 281–92. There,

we write, "In recognition of these facts our movement has created a 'Ritual of Release' which, though it does not take the place of the traditional *get*, serves as 'a form of religious divorce' for couples who desire it and 'may eventually lead us to reopen the matter of a Reform *get*'" (footnotes omitted).

7. For example, the civil government may not tell rabbis that they must officiate at a mixed marriage or at a marriage between two non-Jews. Similarly, the state may not determine the structure and content of a Jewish wedding service.

8. R. Freehof, *CTRR*, no. 21, pp. 100–101, discusses the fact that the rules on this subject will vary among local jurisdictions.

9. *Rabbi's Manual* (New York: CCAR Press, 1988), 246.

10. Rashbam, BT *Bava Batra* 54b, s.v. *v'haamar sh'muel dina d'malchuta dina*. The verb used by Rashbam (R. Sh'muel b. Meir, twelfth-century France) is *m'kablim*: that is, the people *accept* the king's laws as valid. A similar verb is used by Rambam (*Yad, G'zeilah* 5:18): *hiskimu*, that is, the people *ratify* the king and his laws. Rambam uses this same verb in the Introduction to his *Mishneh Torah* to describe Israel's willing acceptance of the Babylonian Talmud as the standard of halachah.

11. For the other theories, see *Reform Responsa for the Twenty-first Century*, no. 5757.1, vol. 1, pp. 347–56, at notes 7–12.

12. See *Yad, Ishut* 12:1ff.: the wedding ceremony is the formation of a contract by which the husband and wife obligate themselves to a series of financial rights and responsibilities. While we have yielded to the state the power to regulate and to enforce these obligations, we are not neutral towards them. There is no such thing as a Jewish marriage *without* concurrent monetary rights and duties.

13. The CCAR has resolved that "the relationship of a Jewish, same gender couple is worthy of affirmation through appropriate Jewish ritual"; see "Resolution on Same Gender Officiation" (http://data.ccarnet.org/cgi-bin/resodisp. pl?file=gender&year=2000). The resolution adds, importantly, that "we recognize the diversity of opinions within our ranks on this issue. We support the decision of those who choose to officiate at rituals of union for same-gender couples, and we support the decision of those who do not." For arguments both in favor of and opposed to officiation at same-gender commitment ceremonies, see *Reform Responsa for the Twenty-first Century*, no. 5756.8, vol. 1, pp. 213–56.

14. At this writing, the legal situation is in flux in a number of jurisdictions.

15. It is not clear why the Rabbinic Jewish tradition chose the word *kiddushin* (from the Hebrew root *k-d-sh*, "holy, to sanctify") to denote marriage. Biblical Hebrew, as the Talmud notes (BT *Kiddushin* 2b), does not use that term. The Talmud suggests that the Rabbis sought to make a point about the ritual nature of the marital union: by "consecrating" his wife, the husband "forbids her to all others as though she belonged to the Temple [*hekdeish*]." In our Reform Jewish wedding ceremonies, the bride "consecrates" the groom as well, testifying to our understanding that marriage is a *mutually* exclusive relationship. That which is holy or sacred—*kadosh*—is separate and distinct from all others. See, for example, Lev. 19:2, "You shall be holy [*k'doshim*] because I, *Adonai* your God, am holy [*kadosh*]," and Rashi and Ramban ad loc.

16. On all of this, see our responsum "Marriage and Financial Distress," *Teshuvot for the Nineties*, no. 5754.9, pp. 225–29. Providing financial assistance to couples wishing to marry is referred to by our tradition as the mitzvah of *hachnasat kallah*.

17. See *Reform Responsa for the Twenty-first Century*, no. 5756.10, vol. 1, pp. 257–68. As discussed there, Jewish law once recognized—but has long since rejected—the institution of concubinage (the *pilegesh*) as a form of nonmarital, long-term conjugal relationship.

MAY A JEW MARRIED TO A NON-JEW BECOME A RABBI?

5761.6

Sh'eilah

A resident of my community, a Jew married to a non-Jew who does not practice any other religion, wishes to become a rabbi. She has been told that, because of her marriage, she will not be admitted into the Hebrew Union College–Jewish Institute of Religion. She wishes to know why, as a believing Jew who is committed to Jewish life, she cannot be accepted into our seminary as a candidate for the Reform rabbinate. (Rabbi James Gibson, Pittsburgh, Pennsylvania)

T'shuvah

Most Reform rabbis in North America, members of the Central Conference of American Rabbis (CCAR), have attended and received their ordination from the Hebrew Union College–Jewish Institute of Religion (HUC-JIR).[1] It is the policy of HUC-JIR that a student who is married, engaged, or partnered to a non-Jew will not be ordained as a rabbi or invested as a cantor. Moreover, an individual in such a relationship will not be accepted as a student in the rabbinical or cantorial program at the College-Institute.[2] HUC-JIR is an independent institution that sets its own rules and standards for admission. It need not consult with the CCAR or with this Committee before adopting them. Still, we have been asked for our opinion as to this particular rule, and in our opinion the rule is a good one. We give it our full and unqualified support.

There was a time, not so long ago, when a sh'eilah such as this would surely not have been raised. Jewish law prohibits mixed marriage, that is, a marriage between a Jew and a non-Jew in which the non-Jewish spouse does not convert to Judaism.[3] The halachah goes so far as to declare that such unions are not recognized as marriages at all (*ein kiddushin tofsin*).[4] Until very recent times, this prohibition was strongly felt and observed by the preponderant majority of the American Jewish community. The situation has changed, however, primarily as a result of two factors. The first of these is the rise in the incidence of mixed marriage among American Jews and the acceptance of this fact within the community. Indeed, surveys indicate that many Jews today regard mixed marriage as a "normal" aspect of Jewish communal life.[5] The second factor has to do with the response that many Jewish institutions have undertaken toward this phenomenon. If the Jewish community once turned its collective back upon those who "married out," today's emphasis upon Jewish survival and continuity leads many of our organizations to open their doors to the mixed-married in an effort to "keep them within the fold." The Reform Movement in particular has instituted an energetic program of outreach, designed to help mixed-married couples and families feel welcome within our congregations and to explore and study Judaism.[6] These two factors seem to have created the impression that marriage to a non-Jew is no longer an impediment to full participation in Reform Jewish life. If that is the case, it is perhaps not so difficult to understand why a Jew might sincerely believe that her marriage to a non-Jew ought not to stand in the way of her becoming a Reform rabbi.

That belief, however, rests upon an incomplete, and therefore incorrect, perception of our attitude toward marriage between Jews and non-Jews. Although we do not use terms such as "prohibition" and "sin" to describe mixed marriage, and although we welcome mixed-married households into our community, we do not condone mixed marriage itself. As our Conference has written, "It is a *mitzvah* for a Jew to marry a Jew so that the sacred heritage of Judaism may be transmitted most effectively from generation to generation."[7] Judaism, that is to say, "resists mixed marriage because it weakens the fabric of family relationship and the survival potential of the Jewish community, and because it makes it more difficult to establish the *mikdash me'at* [sanctity] that should be the goal of every Jewish marriage."[8] These words carry a special weight for us as rabbis. The purpose of our rabbinical function, our teaching, counseling, and leadership, is to help our people make *Jewish* choices, build *Jewish* homes, and ensure the transmission of *Jewish* life and identity to our children. Mixed marriage tends to frustrate the achievement of these ends. For these reasons our Conference has resolved its "opposition to participation by its members in any ceremony which solemnizes a mixed marriage." It is true that a significant number of Reform rabbis do officiate at mixed marriages (under widely varying circumstances, requirements, and limitations), and the resolution itself notes that members of the Conference "continue to hold divergent interpretations of Jewish tradition."[9] Yet those rabbis who officiate at mixed marriages do so out of the hope that officiation will encourage the non-Jewish spouse to help build a Jewish home, to help raise Jewish children, and to one day make the choice to become a Jew. To put it differently, we Reform rabbis are not indifferent to the marriage choices of our people. On the contrary: we want them to make the choice for Jewish marriage, which by definition is a marriage between Jews. We do not in the least regret our welcoming attitude toward the mixed married and our efforts at outreach to them. But we should never forget that the ideal toward which we rabbis strive, teach, and lead is that Jews should marry Jews. Since one of the ways in which we convey our teaching is through personal example, a rabbi's life and home should embody this ideal.

It might be argued that our position here contradicts that which we enunciate in another responsum, where we suggest that a Jew should not be disqualified from teaching in a Reform religious school solely because he or she is married to a non-Jew.[10] If it is conceivable that a religious school teacher, who instructs his or her students in Judaism, may be a partner in a mixed marriage, why do we set different expectations for the rabbi, who is also a teacher of Judaism? The answer is that the religious school teacher and the rabbi play two very different roles in the life of our community. Most of our religious school teachers are drawn from the ranks of our congregants, and they teach our children on a part-time basis. Our rabbis, by contrast, like our cantors and our Reform Jewish educators, have accepted upon themselves (and are properly expected by our community to live up to) higher standards of Jewish learning and observance than those that we demand of others. It is true that none of us, including those of us who are rabbis, achieves these higher standards with perfection. It is also true, however, that we and the people we serve continue to hold us accountable to them. We therefore conclude, as we write in that responsum, that "a Jewish religious professional, whose very life is dedicated to setting an example of Jewish commitment to which our people should aspire, cannot serve as a 'positive Judaic role model' if he or she is married to a non-Jew."

We have no doubt that the individual who prompted this *sh'eilah* is a committed and caring Jew. Her desire to enter the rabbinate testifies to her commitment and to what we can only imagine has been a long and involved religious journey that has brought her to this point. Someday, perhaps, her husband will come to share that commitment to Judaism; should that happen, she might wish to consider once again a career in the rabbinate. Until such time, though the rabbinate is not yet a proper career choice for her, we hope that she will find fulfillment in the many opportunities for Jewish life and learning that are afforded her as a member of a Reform Jewish community.

NOTES

1. On the training and qualifications of rabbis, see section 2 of *Reform Responsa for the Twenty-first Century*, no. 5759.3, vol. 1, pp. 319–29. There, we note that as a matter of technical Jewish law no formal ordination is required in order that an individual may acquire the title "rabbi." On the other hand, it has become the widespread *minhag*, or customary observance in our community to require that an individual seeking to function as a rabbi successfully complete a course of study at a recognized rabbinical school or yeshivah.

2. These rules are spelled out in section 6 of the "Policy and Consent Form" that each applicant for admission to HUC-JIR must fill out and submit to the National Director of Admissions and Recruitment. That section reads: "It is the policy and practice

of Hebrew Union College–Jewish Institute of Religion that any student currently engaged, married, or partnered/committed to a person who is not Jewish (conversion is acceptable) will not be ordained or invested by HUC-JIR. Therefore, no person currently in the aforementioned circumstance shall be accepted to the Rabbinical or Cantorial program of HUC-JIR. Any applicant who is in a significant relationship with someone who is not Jewish (even if that person intends to or is already working towards conversion) should contact the National Director of Admissions and Recruitment to discuss how the policy may affect his/her application."

3. This prohibition is rooted in Deut. 7:1–4. Although the Torah text explicitly mentions the seven Canaanite nations, the Rabbis interpret the passage so that the prohibition applies to all gentiles (BT *Kiddushin* 68b). The Talmudic passage cites two midrashim, or derivations, in support of this extension. The first is the Torah's statement in 7:4, "for they [the members of the seven nations] will turn your children away from Me to worship other gods"; this, says the Talmud, comes to include *all* those who are capable of turning your children away, and that includes all non-Jews. The other derivation is based upon the permit to maintain a female captive taken during war (Deut. 21:10–14). The key phrase is verse 13, "after that you may come to her and possess her." The Talmud understands "after that" to mean "after she converts to Judaism"; thus, prior to her conversion, marriage is prohibited.

4. Deut. 7:3 declares *lo titchatein bam*, which might be translated as "do not marry them." The Talmud (BT *Kiddushin* 68b), however, reads it as "there shall be no legal institution of marriage between you and them" (see Rashi ad loc., s.v. *lo titchatein bam*). As Maimonides puts it, "When one marries [*m'kadeish*] a non-Jew, no valid marriage [*kiddushin*] exists" (*Yad, Ishut* 4:15). See also *SA, EHE* 44:8 (gentiles do not belong to the category of those individuals who can contract valid *kiddushin*).

5. In the words of one such survey, "The Jewish taboo on mixed marriage has clearly collapsed." The findings indicate that 50 percent of the respondents "agree" with the statement "It is racist to oppose Jewish-gentile marriages." Still again, 56 percent of the respondents are either "neutral" (40 percent) about marriage between a Jew and a gentile or see such marriages as a "positive good" (16 percent). See *Responding to Intermarriage: Survey, Analysis, Policy* (American Jewish Committee, Department of Contemporary Jewish Life, January 2001).

6. See www.urj.org/outreach.

7. Simeon J. Maslin, ed., *Gates of Mitzvah* (New York: CCAR Press, 1979), 36.

8. Ibid., 37.

9. For the text of the resolution, see *CCAR Yearbook* 83 (1973): 97. On the history of the CCAR's attitude toward mixed marriage, see *Rabbi's Manual* (New York, CCAR Press, 1988), 242–43.

10. See *Reform Responsa for the Twenty-first Century*, no. 5758.14, vol. 1, pp. 275–79.

CHOSHEN MISHPAT:
THE LIFE OF THE COMMUNITY

Minimal Dues for Congregational Membership
5764.5

Sh'eilah

A family in my congregation has refused, claiming financial hardship, to pay even a token amount toward synagogue dues. Although we offer dues relief to households that cannot afford our standard assessments, in most cases we do ask that they pay a small amount toward their membership. We do not doubt that this family has experienced difficult financial circumstances. Still, they do not seem to be in worse straits than other households that do pay some amount, however small, in synagogue dues. What should be our approach toward this family? (Rabbi Ellen Lewis, Washington, New Jersey)

T'shuvah

This case, as described to us, involves a family that despite its difficult economic condition *can* pay a small amount toward synagogue dues but chooses not to do so. Our task is to evaluate this sort of choice from the perspective of Jewish tradition. We therefore frame the question in this way: is an individual or a household entitled to refuse to pay obligations assessed by the Jewish community? And if the answer to that question is "no," are there circumstances under which we might make an exception to the general rule?

1. THE INDIVIDUAL'S OBLIGATIONS TO THE COMMUNITY[1]

Jewish tradition teaches that every Jew is obligated to contribute his or her fair share toward the welfare of the community.[2] For example, *tzedakah*, support for the poor, is a mitzvah, a religious duty, and not a matter of choice.[3] This duty is incumbent upon every individual; "even the poor person who is supported by *tzedakah* is obligated to contribute *tzedakah* from what he himself is given."[4] The poor are exempt from the normal requirement to contribute *tzedakah* if that gift will drive them below the poverty line.[5] If, however, the community (traditionally, the *beit din*) should determine through a fair appraisal[6] that an individual ought to contribute a particular amount, that person may not refuse to pay less than the assessment. Should he or she fail to meet that obligation, community authorities are empowered to collect it through coercive legal means if necessary.[7] The community is also empowered to coerce its members to build and to support its synagogue.[8] Some authorities, indeed, consider support for the synagogue to take precedence over *tzedakah* for the poor.[9]

The lesson is clear: support for the synagogue is understood as a tax, a legally enforceable contribution from which only the most destitute citizens are exempt. While our Diaspora Jewish communities no longer wield the power to levy taxes or to coerce individual Jews to contribute to vital communal needs and institutions, the language of "coercion" indicates just how seriously we take these moral obligations. This is especially true with regard to the synagogue, the primary institution through which we nowadays organize ourselves as a community. It is the synagogue, more than any other agency, that brings us together for prayer, Torah study, Jewish fellowship, social and political action—in short, the synagogue enables us to live successful Jewish lives in the fullest sense of that expression. It is therefore a mitzvah for each one of us to contribute to its support.

In the *sh'eilah* before us, the family in question does not appear to be destitute. To repeat, the family *can* contribute a small amount to the synagogue but chooses not to do so. As we have seen, this is not a valid and acceptable Jewish choice. Were the situation otherwise—if, for example, the family simply could not contribute toward the synagogue without risking its solvency—we would hold them exempt from the requirement to contribute, just as the halachah exempts the very poor from the obligation of *tzedakah*. Every synagogue with which we are familiar offers dues relief to families under financial duress and will either suspend or waive the dues requirement entirely in cases of dire need. In this case, however, the synagogue authorities have determined that this family can in fact afford "to pay a small amount toward their membership." Assuming that this is a fair evaluation of the circumstances,[10] the family has no valid basis in Jewish law to protest the synagogue's decision. We might add that in joining the synagogue, the family stipulated its acceptance of the congregation's rules and procedures, including the financial obligations of membership. The family, in other words, has agreed in advance that it cannot remain a "member" of the synagogue without making an appropriate contribution toward dues.

2. THE COMMUNITY'S OBLIGATION TO PROVIDE JEWISH EDUCATION

There is, however, another perspective from which our tradition might view this question. Suppose that this family has children of religious school age: should the congregation admit the children to its school even if the parents refuse to pay their minimum dues assessment? Jewish education, as we know, is of critical importance to our future as a people; shall we deny it to these children, who are certainly not at fault in this matter? Might we say that the goal of transmitting Torah knowledge and Jewish identity to the next generation takes priority over the strict enforcement of our financial rules and regulations? To be sure, our tradition holds the father (we today would say "parent") primarily responsible for teaching Torah to his child[11] or for hiring a teacher to do so.[12] Yet the community has long realized an essential problem with this system: "If one does not have a father, one will not learn Torah." For this reason, Y'hoshua ben Gamla, a High Priest who lived in the first century C.E., enacted a decree (*takanah*) that "teachers of children be placed in every town."[13] That *takanah*, in turn, was adopted by all Jewish communities,[14] which have acknowledged that the funding of Jewish education is a public responsibility as well as a private, familial one.[15] Perhaps this congregation and all others should accept this responsibility, making sure that a Jewish education is available to all

Jewish children, even if their parents do not fulfill their own duty under the terms of this mitzvah.

We would not, however, want to impose this as a requirement upon the congregation. The *takanah* of Y'hoshua ben Gamla "never was intended to release parents from the obligation that the Torah imposes upon them, but rather to make it easier for them to fulfill it."[16] Were the congregation to bear the entire cost of education for the children of parents who refuse to pay their fair share, it would send the message that parents are somehow permitted to shirk their duty toward their children and toward the community. It would, additionally, place an unfair burden upon those members of the congregation who *do* pay toward the upkeep of the synagogue and the school. It is indeed unfortunate that some children are denied a Jewish education as a result of their parents' inadvertent or willful neglect of their responsibility to help provide it. It is vital that our communities develop outreach and funding initiatives that would allow Jewish education to reach the children of unaffiliated families. But it is simply wrong to expect the synagogue, an organization that depends for its survival upon the fair-share contributions of its members, to compensate for the refusal of members who can—but won't—accept their financial responsibility toward the institution.

CONCLUSION

One of the most fundamental principles of Jewish communal life is that no Jew should be denied the opportunity to affiliate with the community and no Jewish child should be denied a Jewish education out of inability to pay dues and fees. The synagogue, as the central unit of Jewish association in our communities, bears the moral obligation to make membership affordable to all Jews. Yet because the synagogue is a membership organization, it can exist and function only so long as its members meet their duly assessed financial obligations toward it. A congregation has no duty to provide membership and education services to households that refuse to pay, in the words of our *sh'eilah*, "even a token amount toward synagogue dues." Such a refusal is evidence,

not of poverty, but of a set of priorities that devalues the importance
of synagogue membership and Jewish education. The refusal, in other
words, stems from an economic choice on the part of the family.[17] They
cannot expect the congregation to validate that choice by granting
them a free membership, a benefit denied to those who are willing to
contribute their fair share to the life and sustenance of the synagogue.

NOTES

1. See, in general, Contemporary American Reform Responsa, no. 138, pp. 202–4
(http://data.ccarnet.org/cgi-bin/respdisp.pl?file=138&year=carr), and section 1 of
Reform Responsa for the Twenty-first Century, no. 5758.1, vol. 1, pp. 311–18.

2. *SA, CM* 163:1, and Isserles ad loc.: a community is empowered to require its citizens
(literally, "the citizens may coerce [*kofin*] each other") to contribute to "all the needs of
the city." The chapter as a whole is a treatise on Jewish public law, the rules concerning
our obligations toward the communities in which we live. See *M. Bava Batra* 1:5; BT
Bava Batra 7b–8b; and *Tosefta, Bava M'tzia* 11:18–23.

3. "It is a positive mitzvah to give *tzedakah* in accordance with one's means" (*SA, YD*
247:1), an affirmative formulation of the Talmudic dictum (BT *K'tubot* 68a and *Bava
Batra* 10a) that "when one ignores the duty to give *tzedakah*, it is as though he has
committed idolatry."

4. BT *Gittin* 7b; *Yad, Matanot Aniyim* 7:5; *SA, YD* 248:1.

5. *Siftei Kohein, YD* 248, n. 1. See also Isserles, *YD* 251:3: "One is not obligated to give
tzedakah until he has the wherewithal to support himself [*ad sh'yehei lo parnasato*]."
By "normal requirement," we refer to the customary amounts stated in the sources
(one-fifth or one-tenth of his annual income; see *SA, YD* 249:1); on the other hand,
even the poorest of the poor is expected to make *some* sort of *tzedakah* contribution,
albeit less than that amount (*Bayit Chadash, Tur, YD* 248; *Aruch HaShulchan, YD*
248:3).

6. "Fair appraisal" means that a community may not demand from an individual a
higher amount than he should properly give (BT *Bava Batra* 8b; *Yad, Matanot Aniyim*
7:11; *SA, YD* 248:7.

7. BT *K'tubot* 49b and *Bava Batra* 8b; *Yad, Matanot Aniyim* 7:10; *SA, YD* 248:1. The
power to coerce an individual to give *tzedakah* is the subject of some controversy in the

halachah. There is a Talmudic rule (BT *Chulin* 110b) that "the *beit din* does not enforce the observance of a positive commandment when the Torah specifies a reward for the keeping of that commandment." Since we are told that God will bless us for helping the poor (Deut. 15:10), we ought not to be able to coerce over matter of *tzedakah*. *Tosafot* (*Bava Batra* 8b, s.v. *achpeh*) notes this contradiction and offers various resolutions of it. Perhaps the best resolution of all comes from R. David ibn Zimra (sixteenth-to seventeenth-century Egypt), in his commentary to *Yad, Matanot Aniyim* 7:10. *Tzedakah*, he writes, differs from other positive commandments in that the welfare of the poor depends upon it. It is considered, moreover, a debt owed by the individual, and just as a creditor may take legal action to collect from the debtor, so may the court force an individual to pay his *tzedakah* obligation.

8. *Tosefta, Bava M'tzia* 11:23; *Yad, T'filah* 11:1; *SA, CM* 163:1.

9. Provided that the poor are not in a life-threatening situation. See *SA, YD* 249:16, relying upon a decision of R. Yosef Kolon (fifteenth-century Italy), *Resp. Maharik*, no. 128. See also R. Avraham Danzig, *Chochmat Adam* 145:7. The wording "some authorities" (*yeish mi sh'omer*) in the *Shulchan Aruch* passage indicates that not every authority agrees with the setting of priorities, and see *Biur HaGra* to YD 249:20. As the remainder of the passage indicates, however, the issue is linked to the role of the synagogue in helping to fulfill the mitzvah of Torah study, which occupies the summit of priorities in Rabbinic Judaism (*talmud Torah k'neged kulam* [M. *Pei-ah* 1:1].

10. See above at note 6.

11. This responsibility is derived from Deut. 11:19 ("and you shall teach [these words] to your children"). See BT *Kiddushin* 29a–b; *Yad, Talmud Torah* 1:1; *SA, YD* 245:1.

12. *Yad, Talmud Torah* 1:3; *SA, YD* 245:4. *Hagahot Maimoniot* to *Yad, Talmud Torah* 1:1, cites R. Meir of Rothenburg (thirteenth century) to the effect that this requirement is simply a logical outgrowth of the mitzvah to teach Torah; if one cannot perform that task personally, one must hire an agent to do so. The requirement, moreover, can be enforced by the *beit din*.

13. BT *Bava Batra* 21a.

14. *Yad, Talmud Torah* 2:1; *SA, YD* 245:7.

15. See Isserles, *SA, CM* 163:3, end: if the parents of the children cannot pay the fee for Torah teachers, the community must raise the money by taxing its members according to their ability to pay. The Gaon of Vilna (*Biur HaGra* ad loc.) notes that this is simply one of the "needs of the city" that the citizens are required to fulfill (see note 1).

16. R. Chaim David Halevy (twentieth-century Israel), *Resp. Aseh L'cha Rav* 5:23, at p. 172. See also *Aruch HaShulchan*, YD 245:9: the community taxes itself to provide education "for the poor and for the orphans." The father, meanwhile, is coerced if necessary to pay for the education of his son; he is not released from this duty by the fact that the public is also involved in the education of children.

17. There are, of course, other possible explanations. A refusal to pay dues may be the result of a dispute over this or that synagogue policy, anger over perceived mistreatment, and the like. Our responsum presumes that the refusal to pay dues does not stem from such a factor but reflects an economic decision on the part of the family.

SYNAGOGUE DUES RELIEF AND INCOME TAX RETURNS
5765.3

Sh'eilah

Our congregation is considering requiring tax forms before granting relief on dues and fees—a practice that we understand most or many other synagogues undertake. How would the Responsa Committee advise us on this suggestion? (Rabbi Marc Belgrad, Buffalo Grove, Illinois)

T'shuvah

As we have written elsewhere,[1] the individual Jew is required to pay his or her fair share to support the institutions of the Jewish community. Support for the synagogue, in particular, is regarded as *tzedakah*, and *tzedakah* is a mitzvah, a religious obligation.[2] It is, moreover, an obligation that is set according to one's ability to pay, and our tradition vests the community with the power to appraise each household's economic capacity and to set its level of *tzedakah* contribution accordingly. As Maimonides expresses the law, "One who does not wish to contribute according to the amount that is proper for him can be coerced by the *beit din* [the communal authorities] to give the amount at which he was appraised." This "coercion" might take the form of court action: the authorities would attach an individual's income or confiscate his property in order to pay off his debt to *tzedakah*.[3] The point is that our tradition understands *tzedakah* as a tax, one of the financial obligations of community membership. When even the poor are required to give *tzedakah* according to their limited means,[4] individual synagogue members cannot claim that tradition grants them a "right" to refuse to pay their fair share in support of the congregation. There are, of course, limits to the community's power to set the levels of contribution. An individual is not required to give *tzedakah* unless he is able to support himself financially.[5] Moreover, the halachah explicitly condemns *tzedakah* collectors (*gabaim*) who use tactics of pressure and shame to force individuals into giving *more* than their fair share.[6] Yet so long as it meets the demands of fairness and so long as it takes care not to transgress against the dignity of the individual, the community is entitled to take vigorous action to collect the obligations that its members owe to it.

Let us consider our *sh'eilah* in light of these Jewish teachings. A member household, claiming financial need, seeks reduced dues from the congregation. The synagogue committee charged with acting on this request wishes to know whether the claim comports with the facts: does the request for dues relief reflect real financial distress, or is it based upon the relatively low priority that the household assigns to synagogue membership? In some cases, it is obvious that a member or a family has encountered economic hardship. At other times, such hardship is not apparent from the member's observable lifestyle. In those cases, given that our tradition requires that the community appraise an individual's proper level of *tzedakah* contribution, the community may use all appropriate means in making that assessment. In theory, therefore, the congregation is entitled to demand that members seeking relief furnish evidence that will document their financial hardship. Income tax returns, we should note, are far from perfect in this regard; they do not necessarily afford a full and accurate picture of the financial pressures acting upon a particular household. Still, provided that they are read with the requisite care, tax returns can offer evidence that the synagogue committee will want to see before making its decision.

On the other hand, the demand to see a member's private financial information will likely provoke a negative reaction. For this reason, the Central Conference of American Rabbis and the Union for Reform Judaism recommend against asking congregants for their tax returns as part of the dues relief process: "Trust is the key element in creating a sensitive and welcoming process for dues adjustments. Requesting written documentation of a person's financial situation in the form of tax returns or similar material often strikes the person as an affront and an invasion of privacy, which only serves to reinforce the stereotype that synagogues are concerned solely about money."[7] In saying this, our movement gives expression to another central Jewish value, the respect for the privacy or the dignity of the individual.[8] As we have written in another context, "There are aspects of our existence which are and must remain off-limits to the eyes and tongues of those among whom we live, and we are therefore under no moral or religious obligation to share with them information about ourselves that they have no legitimate reason to know. This conclusion drawn from our law may not be the exact equivalent of the 'right to privacy' in other legal systems. But it does express, in language too clear to permit of misunderstanding, a commitment to the proposition that all of us, created in the divine image, are possessed of a dignity which at some critical point requires that all others leave us be and let us alone."[9] Jewish tradition, in other words, empowers a synagogue to enforce its legitimate financial demands, but this power must be balanced against the concern for the essential dignity and privacy of its members.

How do we draw the line between these two conflicting values? The answer lies in what lawyers call the "reasonable expectation of privacy." Although Jewish tradition vests communal organizations with coercive powers to collect financial obligations, today's Jewish community enjoys no such quasi-governmental authority. Our synagogue members will tend to view a demand to submit sensitive financial information to the congregation's leaders as an unjustifiable trespass upon their privacy. Thus, even if the synagogue technically enjoys the power to make that demand, in the contemporary context such an action is likely to be counterproductive and damaging to the synagogue's reputation.

None of this means that a synagogue must automatically grant a member's request for a dues adjustment. It is vital that every synagogue member pay his or her fair share to the sustenance of the congregation. When a household experiences financial reverses and is forced to seek dues relief, we must respond positively to its request in a caring and compassionate manner. There will, however, be instances when such a request does not reflect true financial need but simply the relatively low priority that the household assigns to synagogue affiliation. In such instances, we are entitled to refuse the request, for to accede to it would be to increase unfairly the monetary burden shouldered by the rest of our members. The challenge for the congregation is to design a dues adjustment process that is both fair and compassionate, one that asserts the congregation's legitimate financial requirements while demonstrating sensitivity to its members' economic needs and personal dignity. The CCAR and the URJ believe that we can meet this challenge, even if we do not demand that members submit their tax returns as part of the process.[10]

NOTES

1. See *Reform Responsa for the Twenty-first Century*, no. 5764.5, vol. 2, pp. 277–83.

2. "It is a positive mitzvah to give *tzedakah* in accordance with one's means" (*SA, YD* 247:1), an affirmative formulation of the Talmudic dictum (BT *K'tubot* 68a and *Bava Batra* 10a) that "when one ignores the duty to give *tzedakah*, it is as though he has committed idolatry."

3. *Yad, Matanot Aniyim* 7:10. This is Rambam's interpretation of the Talmudic precedents at BT *Bava Batra* 8b and *K'tubot* 49b. There is a controversy among the *rishonim*, the "early" halachic authorities, over this issue; some rule that coercion is not allowed in order to collect *tzedakah*. For discussion, see our responsum no. 5764.5 (see note 1, above) at note 7. As we read the issue, Rambam and his supporters have the better case: the halachah does allow the community to take coercive action in order to collect *tzedakah*.

4. BT *Gittin* 7b; *Yad, Matanot Aniyim* 7:5; *SA, YD* 248:1.

5. *Siftei Kohein, YD* 248, n. 1. See also Isserles, *YD* 251:3: "One is not obligated to give *tzedakah* until he has the wherewithal to support himself [*ad sh'yehei lo parnasato*]." By "normal requirement," we refer to the customary amounts stated in the sources (one-fifth or one-tenth of his annual income; see *SA, YD* 249:1); on the other hand, even the poorest of the poor is expected to make *some* sort of *tzedakah* contribution, albeit less than that amount (*Bayit Chadash, Tur, YD* 248; *Aruch HaShulchan, YD* 248:3).

6. See Jer. 30:20: "I will punish all who oppress them." The midrash says: this refers to *tzedakah* collectors who demand too much from the people (BT *Bava Batra* 8b; *Yad, Matanot Aniyim* 7:11; *SA, YD* 248:7).

7. Rabbi Renni Altman, ed., *Money Matters: Compassionate Guidelines for Talking Dues* (New York: URJ-CCAR Commission on Outreach and Synagogue Community and the URJ-CCAR Commission on Synagogue Management, revised edition, 2003), p. 10, par. 7 (http://urj.org//cong/finance//?syspage=document&item_id=14855 (accessed August 19, 2009).

8. Jewish tradition does not speak of a "right to privacy," but it does contain rules and principles that protect us from the prying eyes of our neighbors, from gossip and slander, and from public humiliation. For sources and discussion, see of *Reform Responsa for the Twenty-first Century*, no. 5763.7, vol. 2, pp. 307–13, section 2.

9. *Responsa for the Twenty-first Century*, no. 5756.2, vol. 1, pp. 331–42, section 2.

10. For a suggested dues adjustment process, see Altman, *Money Matters*.

Sh'eilah

What are proper and/or acceptable methods for dealing with situations in which congregants and former congregants refuse to pay their debts to the congregation? We already have in place systems for reducing dues and fees, as well as for people making payments over time. We are interested in knowing what further steps we might take, including the sending of dunning notices from an outside service; the use of a collection agency, including credit reporting; and the filing of a lawsuit. (Rabbi Marc J. Belgrad, Buffalo Grove, Illinois)

T'shuvah

"The very fact that the question is asked reveals a feeling that it is wrong to bring Jewish religious disputes to the secular courts." Thus begins a responsum issued by the CCAR Responsa Committee in 1961, dealing with the question of whether a congregation may use legal processes to collect delinquent building pledges.[1] The *t'shuvah* rules that the resort to such processes "is contrary to both the letter and the spirit of Jewish legal tradition" and bases its conclusion primarily upon three points:

1. A building pledge is best understood as a document of gift (*sh'tar matanah*), "which cannot legally (in the eyes of Jewish law) be dealt with by the non-Jewish courts."

2. A long tradition in Jewish law denounces resort to gentile courts.

3. To bring intra-communal disputes of this nature to the secular courts is a *chilul HaShem*, an action that "profanes God's holy name."

This Committee, however, disagrees substantially with the reasoning upon which our predecessors based their decision. Specifically, we take issue with each of the three major points of their 1961 ruling. Although we are most reluctant to see synagogues resort to lawsuits and other legal action in order to collect obligations owed to them, and although we believe that such steps may well be destructive to the ethos of the synagogue and the purposes for which it exists, these measures should be available to congregations as a last resort, when all others have failed.

1. COLLECTION OF DEBTS IN NON-JEWISH COURTS

The 1961 responsum cites a single source (*SA, CM* 68:1) to support its contention that the halachah forbids the resort to gentile courts in order to enforce "Jewish documents of gift." Yet a careful reading of that text shows that, in fact, it speaks to the opposite situation: the validity of a *gentile* document of gift in a *Jewish* court.[2] The *Shulchan Aruch* adopts the ruling of Maimonides,[3] who declares that a document of gift processed by a gentile court is invalid under Jewish law and is therefore not enforced by the judges of a Jewish court (*beit din*).[4] This rule does not address the question before us, and it therefore does *not* prohibit a synagogue or other Jewish institution from asking a secular court to enforce a monetary pledge that, as the 1961 responsum notes, is considered valid and enforceable under Jewish law.[5]

2. THE PROHIBITION AGAINST RESORT TO GENTILE COURTS

The halachah, to be sure, does record a general prohibition upon Jewish litigants from bringing actions in gentile courts,[6] and the 1961 responsum cites this "long tradition in Jewish law" as a major justification for its decision. We, however, find the reliance upon this prohibition to be puzzling, for several reasons. First, the earlier responsum acknowledges that this requirement is waived in the event that one of the litigants refuses to appear before or accept the judgment of the Jewish tribunal. If the other litigant finds that he cannot recover his property through the processes of Jewish law, which is certainly the case in the question before us, he may seek redress in the gentile courts.[7] In other words, while the halachah demands allegiance to the Jewish legal system, its overriding concern is *justice*: Jewish individuals and institutions must be able to protect their legal rights, and they are therefore permitted to bring suit before whichever court is empowered to grant that protection. The 1961 responsum, by contrast, suggests that we are somehow less than entitled to this legal redress. Second, as historians and halachists have written, Jewish courts have lost their juridical autonomy and powers of enforcement during the modern period, and it has therefore become customary for Jews to take their monetary disputes to the civil courts.[8] The 1961 responsum, ironically, would deny to Reform synagogues a legal tool that other Jews, including those in the Orthodox community, accept as normal procedure.[9] Finally, the traditional prohibition simply does not speak to our present-day political situation. We Jews who are full citizens of our nation, who participate in the making and the administration of its law, and who expect and demand equal protection under that law simply do not regard its court system as foreign and alien to us. These are not "gentile" courts, but *our* courts, belonging to "us" just as surely as to "them." To suggest that Jews should not avail themselves of our nation's courts on the grounds that they are "secular" or "gentile" tribunals is to imply that our legal position in this society is not that of equal citizenship. We ought to avoid any such implication.[10]

3. CHILUL HASHEM

The Torah (Lev. 22:32) forbids us to act in such a way as to profane the holy name of God. What sorts of acts are contemplated by this prohibition? Jewish thought over the centuries has offered several distinct answers to this question.[11] In one familiar usage, this prohibition means that a Jew should not act in such a way as to bring disrepute upon the name of God and upon the people of Israel in the eyes of the nations of the world.[12] Adopting this interpretation, the 1961 responsum suggests that synagogues not bring disputes before the civil courts, for to do so is to invite scandal and, therefore, *chilul HaShem*. Once again, we would dissent from the reasoning in that responsum. Although we do not make light of its concern, we think that it reflects an earlier period in American Jewish life, when genteel anti-Semitism was rampant, and Jews, as a result, were *excessively* fearful of presenting a negative image to the general public. Today, thankfully, we are more confident of our position in society. American Jews today can stand up for their rights without fear that doing so will invite scandal. In the contemporary context, to argue for our rights before a court of law is *not* to court public humiliation or to "wash our dirty linen in public." It is, rather, to demand the justice to which we are entitled according to the law of the land and according to the dictates of our Torah and tradition. We need not be dissuaded from seeking justice for ourselves on account of our fears as to what others might think of us.

There is, however, another interpretation of *chilul HaShem*, one that makes a much more powerful demand upon us. In both biblical[13] and Rabbinic teaching,[14] various types of behavior are said to profane the divine name because they are sharply inconsistent with the moral standards expected of us as a people covenanted with God. These actions are not necessarily "sins"; they do not necessarily violate any explicit prohibitions of the Torah.[15] Nor are they to be avoided primarily because of the negative impression they might make upon gentile observers. They are "wrong" purely and simply because of the impression they ought to make upon *us*, because those who strive to be holy should not behave in such a manner. Viewed in this light, our issue takes on a very different cast. The question the congregation should ask itself prior to taking legal action to collect on members' obligations is not whether such action is *permitted* under Jewish law (for it manifestly *is* permitted) but rather whether it accords with our vision of what a synagogue ought to be and of its role in Jewish life.

This question admits of no easy answers. Like all other institutions, a synagogue budgets for its expenses on the basis of projected revenue. Like all other voluntary associations, the contemporary synagogue depends for its revenue upon the willingness of its members to meet their financial obligations. When a member who has the ability to pay a freely accepted obligation to the synagogue refuses to meet that pledge, it is neither "illegal" nor "immoral" for the congregation to take legal action against that individual's breach of faith.[16] Yet the synagogue is *not* like all other institutions. It is first and foremost a community of Jews bound together by ties of faith, affection, and mutual concern. These values, which define the synagogue's mission and form the basis of its spiritual strength and institutional prestige, stand fundamentally at odds with the strife and contention that characterize our overly litigious society. When a synagogue initiates legal action against one of its members, whatever its justification for that action, it embarks upon a course of conduct that is by its nature a bitter and divisive exercise, destructive of the core values that define the synagogue's mission and purpose. It does something that the synagogue, as the institutional embodiment of our covenant with God, ideally should not do. And for that reason, it may constitute an example of *chilul HaShem*.

CONCLUSION

Jewish tradition permits a synagogue to undertake legal action to collect debts owed to it by its members. We are not prohibited from seeking justice on these matters in the civil courts. Yet because we are lessened as a religious community when we take such steps, we should engage in legal action only as the absolutely last resort, when all other available remedies have been tried and have failed.[17] The choice rests in the hands of the synagogue's leaders; ultimately, it is for them to decide whether the financial benefit of enforcing a member's obligations justifies the spiritual price the synagogue shall pay in collecting it.

NOTES

1. *American Reform Responsa*, no. 17; *CCAR Yearbook* 72 (1961): 127–29.

2. This issue begins with the Mishnah's declaration that "all documents processed by gentile courts, even though their signatories are gentiles, are valid, with the exception of documents of divorce and manumission" (*M. Gittin* 1:5). The Talmud (BT *Gittin* 10b) objects that this rule cannot apply to a document of gift (*sh'tar matanah*). Unlike a

document of sale (*sh'tar m'chirah*), which serves merely as evidentiary evidence that a sale has taken place (and was effected through some other instrument, such as money, physical possession, etc.), a document of gift is itself the instrument through which the transaction was effected. How then can a Jewish court accept and enforce such a document if it was processed in a gentile court? Two possibilities are suggested. The *Amora* Sh'muel says, "The law of the state is valid law" (*dina d'malchuta dina*): that is, our courts *do* accept such documents as valid. The anonymous voice (*s'tam*) of the Talmud, however, prefers to emend the text of the Mishnah's rule: "All documents…are valid, with the exception of documents *like* those of divorce, etc." In other words, if a document processed by a gentile court is in itself the instrument through which a legal transaction is effected (as is the case with divorce, which is effected by the document [*get*] itself), a Jewish court will not accept that document as valid and will not enforce it; see Rashi, ad loc., s.v. *tanei chutz*.

3. *Yad, Malveh V'Loveh*, 27:1, based upon the Talmudic discussion cited in the preceding note.

4. See *Magid Mishneh* to *Yad*, ad loc.: like Rashi (see note 2), Rambam holds that unlike a deed of sale, which serves a purely evidentiary function, a deed of gift is itself the instrument of transaction and, if it originates in a gentile court, is therefore invalid under Jewish law. The *Sefer Mei-irat Einayim*, CM 68:3, gives a similar explanation to the identical ruling in the *Shulchan Aruch*.

5. A pledge to *tzedakah* is considered a vow (*neder*; SA, YD 257:3). See also YD 248:1: the obligation to give *tzedakah* is enforceable by the court.

6. BT *Gittin* 88b, a saying of Rabbi Tarfon, based upon a midrash on Exod. 21:1: "These are the laws you shall place before *them*"—that is, and *not* before gentile courts. The prohibition, as enunciated by Maimonides (*Yad, Sanhedrin* 26:7) and the *Shulchan Aruch* (CM 26:1), declares, "Whoever brings his case before the gentile courts is a wicked man, whose action amounts to blasphemy and violence against the Law of Moses, our teacher."

7. This rule is found in the Maimonides and *Shulchan Aruch* passages cited in the preceding note. The commentaries to those passages (and see also *Beit Yosef* to *Tur*, CM 26) tend to identify BT *Bava Kama* 92b as the Talmudic source of this rule. Originally, the halachah specified that a Jew might have recourse to a gentile court only upon receiving prior permission from the Jewish court. Recently, however, this situation has changed; see the responsum by Kluger in the following note.

8. Among the historians, see especially Menachem Elon, *Jewish Law: History, Sources, and Principles* (Philadelphia: Jewish Publication Society of America, 1994), 1575–84. Elon posits that the loss of Jewish juridical autonomy accounts for the lack

of significant development in Jewish monetary law (*dinei mamonot*) over the past several centuries. Among the halachists, see R. Solomon B. Freehof, *Reform Responsa* (Cincinnati: Hebrew Union College Press, 1960), 7–8: Jewish civil law is now neglected by almost all Jews. "People who surely consider themselves Orthodox have simply ceased to resort to rabbinical courts in business matters" (p. 8). Ironically, R. Freehof is the principal author of the 1961 CCAR responsum that urges a *Reform* synagogue to observe the prohibition against resorting to non-Jewish courts. The clearest Orthodox halachic statement concerning this is perhaps the ruling by R. Sh'lomo Kluger (nineteenth-century Galicia), *Resp. Ha'elef Lecha Sh'lomo, CM*, no. 3. R. Kluger notes that it has become the "widespread custom" (*minhag pashut*) for Jews to resort to non-Jewish courts even without the prior permission of a *beit din*, "especially because under the law of the land [*dina d'malchuta*], Jewish courts are unable to enforce their decisions."

9. The most interesting example is the prenuptial agreement signed by some Orthodox couples, under which the groom undertakes, in the event of civil divorce, to provide maintenance of his wife at the level set according to Jewish law. This agreement serves as an inducement to the husband to issue a Jewish document of divorce (*get piturin*) to his wife, who would otherwise be forbidden to remarry under Orthodox auspices, since it is only upon religious divorce that he would be free of the obligation of maintenance. Significantly, this agreement is drawn up as a contract enforceable in a civil court. In other words, at the outset of marriage the couple enter into an agreement that explicitly contemplates the resort to a non-Jewish court, if necessary, in order to secure justice for the wife. See Elyakim Ellinson, "*Seruv Latet Get,*" *Sinai* 69 (Sivan–Tamuz, 5731/1971): 135–68; J. David Bleich, "Modern-Day *Agunot*: A Proposed Remedy," *Jewish Law Annual* 4 (1981): 167–87; J. David Bleich, *Contemporary Halakhic Problems* (New York: Ktav/Yeshiva, 1977), 1:154–59; and Reuven P. Bulka, *The RCA Lifecycle Madrikh* (New York: Rabbinical Council of America, 1995), 69–75. A similar procedure is utilized by some liberal Jewish communities in Europe.

10. We do not mean to disparage the possibility that Jews in our society might choose to order their affairs through the processes of Jewish law. Some Jews do submit their disputes to a *beit din*, a rabbinical court that operates according to halachah, and they agree in advance to accept the decision of that court as binding. There are good reasons, in fact, to recommend such a course, not the least of which is our desire that the long and honored tradition of Jewish civil law be developed and brought up to date through its application to contemporary issues in the areas of torts, obligations, property, and the like. All we are saying here is that we Jews who reside in democratic societies should not regard the civil courts of our country as "gentile" courts that do not belong to us.

11. One of these, not directly relevant to our *sh'eilah*, is provided by Maimonides, *Yad, Y'sodei HaTorah* 5:10: any Jew who violates any mitzvah out of his own free choice simply in order to demonstrate his rejection of its authority (*l'hachis*) is guilty of *chilul HaShem*.

12. See *Encyclopedia Talmudit* 15:351–56. Among the many examples of this line of interpretation, see the commentaries of Nachmanides to Num. 14:13 and of Abraham ibn Ezra (both the "long" and the "short" versions) to Exod. 32:12. In these cases, Moses dissuades God from destroying Israel with the argument that such an action would be destructive to God's reputation in the eyes of the nations. See also Rabban Gamliel's *takanah* forbidding Jews from making use of the stolen property of gentiles on the grounds of *chilul HaShem* (JT *Bava Kama* 4:3, 4b).

13. See Amos 2:7, concerning the maltreatment of the poor as well as sexual immorality, and Jer. 34:16, concerning the people's failure to honor the obligation (called a covenant) to set free their indentured servants.

14. See BT *Yoma* 86a, where the sage Rav declares that he would commit *chilul HaShem* were he to fail to pay his debts to shopkeepers in a timely fashion. See also Rashi to Num. 25:14. The classic statement of this approach to *chilul HaShem* is *Yad, Y'sodei HaTorah* 5:11.

15. See *Yad, Y'sodei HaTorah* 5:11: when a person known for his righteous behavior commits an act that causes the community to doubt his righteousness, even though that act is not a "sin" per se, he has profaned God's holy name.

16. Consider, for example, what would happen were the synagogue to fail to pay its own financial obligations. It is most unlikely that the synagogue's vendors would refrain from taking legal action to collect on those obligations merely because the synagogue is a religious institution.

17. A number of these remedies exist. The congregation can alert other synagogues in the community that this member has broken faith, so that he or she should not be invited to join any institution within the Jewish community until all past obligations are paid. Similarly, we can tell our members that acceptance of their children to religious school, admission to High Holy Day services, and the scheduling of certain life-cycle events are contingent upon payment of financial obligations or the making of acceptable arrangements to do so. Obviously, these steps do not guarantee that financial obligations will be met; still, they are less difficult, divisive, and contentious than legal action to collect those obligations.

SOLICITATION OF SYNAGOGUE MEMBERS BY OTHER JEWISH ORGANIZATIONS

5763.1

Sh'eilah

In many communities, organizations such as Chabad, Aish HaTorah, and others either directly or indirectly solicit members of existing congregations for programs, activities, worship, and financial support. Are these practices ethical according to Jewish tradition? Does such solicitation or even ministering to members of existing congregations transgress the prohibition of *hasagat g'vul*? (Rabbi Ned Soltz, Fullerton, California)

T'shuvah

Our canons of professional practice, as embodied in the CCAR's *Code of Ethics for Rabbis*, expressly forbid us from rendering "pastoral attentions to members of other congregations, *havurot*, and other religious institutions" if such attentions would harm collegial or institutional relationships. A rabbi, moreover, "should neither solicit nor sanction efforts to solicit members of another congregation."[1] It is clear, therefore, that by our own *takanah*, or authoritative legislative enactment, it would be wrong for rabbis and synagogues to engage in the practices described in our *sh'eilah*. The problem, of course, is that the *Code of Ethics* is binding only upon members of the CCAR; it does not apply to other rabbis or to organizations such as Chabad and Aish HaTorah. Hence, our *sho-eil* asks whether such solicitation is prohibited by traditional Jewish law and ethics, that is, by standards that are independent of our own rabbinical community and that other religious Jews would find persuasive and compelling.

In particular, our *sh'eilah* points to the principle of *hasagat g'vul*, a term drawn from the Torah's prohibition against removing the boundary markers that separate one's property from that of one's neighbor (Deut. 19:14 and 27:17). Although the biblical sources do not apply this concept to matters outside the realm of property law, it does receive such an interpretation in the classical midrash and the geonic literature.[2] By the late medieval period, halachic authorities use the phrase *hasagat g'vul* to describe unauthorized economic competition, that is, transgression against an individual's legally valid claim to the control of a particular office or market.[3] Might we utilize this principle in our case? When another Jewish organization asks our members for financial support or seeks their participation in its programs or activities, does it "violate the boundaries" that define and protect our synagogue community?

To answer this question requires that we make two judgments, one quantitative and one qualitative. On the quantitative side, we should keep in mind that the prohibition of *hasagat g'vul*, when applied to issues like those raised in our *sh'eilah*, is an economic concept; its purpose is to protect the livelihood of individuals and businesses against ruinous competition. Under certain conditions, Jewish law allows an existing business to restrain the entry into its market of a potential competitor, on the grounds that the competitor would destroy the livelihood (*mekape'ach et parnasato*) of the existing business. If the level of competition is not "ruinous"—that is, if the entry of the competitor would not necessarily drive the existing merchant or artisan out of business—this restriction does not apply.[4] As a qualitative matter, restrictions against competition are generally not invoked against those, like *m'lamdim* (teachers of Torah to children) and communal rabbis, whose business involves mitzvot.[5] The Talmud justifies this free competition on the principle *kinat sofrim marbah chochmah*, literally, "jealousy among scribes increases wisdom,"[6] essentially, "free intellectual competition is good for Jewish life." There are, of course, exceptions to this rule.[7] The rabbinate, for example, has become a salaried profession, and rabbis can qualify for the same protections accorded to other professionals.[8] Still, Jewish tradition in general frowns upon actions that artificially restrict competition and free market entry in matters related to Torah and mitzvot, particularly when this competition is not "ruinous."

How do we apply these judgments to cases such as the one described in our *sh'eilah*? Are these other Jewish organizations, when they enter our "market," guilty of *hasagat g'vul*? True, they "compete" with us for funding from the community and for participation by our members in their programs and activities. In the vast majority of cases, however, this competition is far from "ruinous"; the financial stability of our synagogue is not called into question. Moreover, precisely because these organizations perform mitzvot, we want our members to be involved in their programming. The goal of our own activity, after all, is to help produce good and caring Jews, and such people *should* be involved with other Jewish organizations that fulfill needed and vital tasks. Obviously, we do not want their involvement to lessen the amount of support they give to our synagogue, but on this point, we think, we have little to fear. A Jew who becomes active to the fullest extent in the life of the community will likely be more rather than less conscientious in contributing to the life of our congregation. At any rate, we suffer when we assume a narrow perspective on Jewish community life. When we actively discourage the participation of our own members in the work of other Jewish organizations (and, indeed, in the work of agencies in the general community that feed the hungry and care for the needy), we declare that our congregation is somehow isolated from the concerns that those groups address. A good synagogue, one that is truly committed to the cause of Torah, mitzvot, *g'milut chasadim*, and *tikkun haolam* would not send such a message to its own members and to the community at large.

Does this approach change when our "competitors" are Chabad, Aish HaTorah, or other Orthodox groups?[9] Such organizations might be construed as "inimical to Reform Judaism," thereby forfeiting any claim to our active support.[10] We need not, however, directly oppose their activity on grounds of *hasagat g'vul*. First of all, Jewish tradition does not absolutely forbid a group of individuals within the community from leaving a congregation to form their own synagogue, especially when the new congregation follows a different liturgical ritual (*nusach*) from the old one, which would certainly be the case here.[11] Moreover, the competition these groups pose to us is hardly "ruinous"; it is highly doubtful that their activity will drive our congregations into insolvency. Nor do we fear exposing our members to their point of view. On the contrary: as liberal Jews, committed to the concept of Jewish religious pluralism, we welcome the vigorous discourse and debate that these groups might introduce into our community. If this should awaken the intellectual curiosity of our members and make them question long-held assumptions about their Judaism, then *mah tov*, so much the better. Our knowledge of and confidence in our own approach to Jewish belief and practice can only benefit and be strengthened by such encounters. As Reform Jews, open to the intellectual currents of modernity and ready to wrestle with the challenges they present to us, we therefore embrace that ancient dictum: *kinat sofrim marbah chochmah.* Good argument is good for the Jews.

CONCLUSION

Although we Reform rabbis have resolved not to solicit members from other congregations, the traditional principle of *hasagat g'vul* would not prevent other Jewish organizations from soliciting our members to participate in their programs. We should meet these organizations, even if we consider them "competitors," in a spirit of friendly discussion and argument, with confidence that our own position is right for us. On the other hand, we are under no obligation to provide any assistance to organizations we deem to be "inimical to Reform Judaism."

NOTES

1. Central Conference of American Rabbis, *Code of Ethics for Rabbis*, adopted in convention assembled, June 1991, and as amended in 1993, 1998, 2001, 2003, and 2004, http://ccarnet.org/documentsandpositions/ethics (accessed on March 10, 2010). See sec. II.C.3–4.

2. In *Sifrei D'varim* (to 19:14) the prohibition is applied to "one who exchanges the rulings of R. Eliezer with those of R. Y'hoshua"; i.e., one who cites the ruling of one sage in the name of the other. Rav Sherira Gaon learns from the verse that "one should

not transgress against accepted communal custom [*minhag*]," the "boundaries" drawn up by "previous generations" (the responsum is collected in *Resp. Shaarei Tzedek*, no. 20 and cited in *Tur*, CM 368). The same interpretation is applied to the very similar verse in Prov. 22:28; see *Midrash Mishlei* (ed. Buber), 22:28, and Rashi to the verse.

3. For example, R. Sh'lomo Luria (sixteenth-century Poland) rules that when an individual has contracted with the local ruler to collect taxes, one who supplants that individual (by offering a higher sum to the ruler) violates the rule of *hasagat g'vul*. Luria concedes that the prohibition in Deut. 19:14 applies strictly to violations of real property rights; nonetheless, the repetition of the prohibition in Deut. 27:17 extends its terms to other aspects of commerce and economic life. See *Resp. Maharshal*, no. 89. Luria's contemporary, R. Meir Katznelbogen, applies the rule to competition among merchants (*Resp. Maharam Padua*, no. 41).

4. BT *Bava Batra* 21b–22a; *Yad, Sh'cheinim* 6:8ff.; *SA, CM* 156:5ff. The rules concerning "ruinous competition" (*hayored l'omanut chaveiro*) are exceedingly complex, and this area of the law is filled with *machloket*, points of dispute. This is because the halachah wishes to strike a careful if complicated balance between two important interests. It wishes to protect the livelihood of merchants and artisans; at the same time, it does not oppose free competition, and it recognizes the value of such competition to the economy and to consumers.

5. BT *Bava Batra* 21b; *Yad, Talmud Torah* 2:7; *SA, YD* 245:22.

6. Rashi, *Bava Batra* 21b, s.v. *umodeh Rav Huna*, explains that as a result of this "jealous" competition, the teachers "will be careful to do their work well, since they are wary of each other." Rambam (*Yad, Talmud Torah* 2:7) does not mention this explanation, but substitutes it with Isa. 42:21, that is, God wishes that "Torah be increased and glorified"; hence, competition in the field of mitzvot is a good thing.

7. For example, halachic authorities have permitted the granting of copyright to the printers and publishers of sacred texts, even though such a monopoly is difficult to square with traditional Jewish legal doctrine, on the grounds that without the protection that copyright affords them, these individuals would never assume the financial risks involved in bringing editions of the Talmud and the *Mishneh Torah*, among other works, to market. Thus, copyright is a matter over which the community has no real choice. See R. Moshe Isserles, *Resp. Rema*, no. 10; and R. Moshe Sofer, *Resp. Chatam Sofer, CM*, no. 41. On another matter, the Rambam rules that a *mohel* who interferes with another *mohel's* expected income is guilty of *hasagat g'vul*; *Resp. HaRambam* (ed. Blau), no. 273. Note, however, the author's language: the offending *mohel* interferes with the set livelihood (*parnasah k'vuah*) of a poor, God-fearing Jew

(*ani ben Torah*). In other words, this is a case of "ruinous competition," not competition pure and simple.

8. This position, which applies the doctrines of *hasagat g'vul* and "ruinous competition" to the rabbinate, is a departure from the more traditional position perhaps best expressed by the fifteenth-century German authority R. Yisrael Isserlein, in *Resp. T'rumat HaDeshen* 2:128: the fact that we rabbis receive an income for performing our communal function is an embarrassment to us, so much so that we cannot justify a claim of entitlement to that income and protection from competition. The economic situation of the rabbinate clearly has changed, as is noted in *Resp. Chatam Sofer, CM*, no. 21: rabbis now accept the reality that they are salaried professionals and are not embarrassed to demand they be treated with the same respect as is accorded to other professionals. In the North American Reform rabbinate, issues of "ruinous competition" are regulated in the *CCAR Code of Ethics for Rabbis*, section II.C.

9. We distinguish here between *Jewish* organizations, even though they disagree with our own approach to Judaism, and *apostate* groups such as Jews for Jesus or Messianic Jewish congregations. Our approach to apostates is one of "strict separation tempered with openness." See *Reform Responsa for the Twenty-first Century*, no. 5761.2, vol. 2, pp. 241–46, at notes 1–4. Apostasy, unlike Orthodoxy, is not a legitimate Jewish religious choice. We take no position in this responsum on the question of the messianism present in the doctrine of Chabad Chasidism or on the question of whether, given the messianic claims raised by many members of Chabad for their late Rebbe, Chabad has "crossed the line" from legitimate Judaism to apostasy. A powerful argument that it *has* crossed that line is raised by Professor David Berger, an Orthodox Jewish scholar, in his *The Rebbe, the Messiah, and the Scandal of Orthodox Indifference* (London: Littman Library, 2001). The matter therefore deserves our attention, and any contacts between Reform rabbis and the Chabad Movement should be maintained with the utmost caution.

10. See *Contemporary American Reform Responsa (CARR)*, no. 25, and *Questions and Reform Jewish Answers (QRJA)*, no. 92.

11. We make no determination here that either Chabad or Aish HaTorah is "inimical" to our interests as a Reform Movement; we note simply that the local rabbi must make that judgment and is entitled to act accordingly.

12. The word "absolutely" indicates that this, too, is a complex question. On the one hand, Jewish tradition favors large congregations over small ones and would discourage individuals from leaving an established synagogue on that account; for sources, see *TFN*, no. 5752.12, pp. 3–6, at notes 2–5. On the other hand, if an individual finds that

he cannot pray with *kavanah* (intention and concentration) in an existing synagogue because of discord between him and the other members, he should pray elsewhere (R. David ibn Zimra [sixteenth- to seventeenth-century Egypt], *Resp. Radbaz* 3:472, and R. Avraham Danzig [eighteenth- to nineteenth- century Germany/Lithuania], *Chayei Adam* 17:5). R. Yitzchak bar Sheshet (fourteenth-century Spain/North Africa) rules that individuals have the unfettered right to leave an existing synagogue to form their own congregation (*Resp. Rivash*, no. 331). Although some authorities limit this right in cases where the split would cause significant financial loss to the existing congregation, there is no opposition to the formation of a new synagogue that follows a different *nusach* from the old one. For discussion, see Zalman Druck, *Mikdash M'at* (Jerusalem, Wagshal, 1973), 10–15.

Sh'eilah

Jewish organizations often request that a synagogue share its membership list with them, in order that those organizations may reach a wider audience for their work. Is it ethical for the synagogue to provide its membership list to these organizations without the express consent of each member? (Rabbi Larry Englander, Mississauga, Ontario)

T'shuvah

This *sh'eilah* requires that we consider the balance between communal authority and personal privacy. Our tradition bestows upon the community a great deal of power to do good, to see to it that its members perform mitzvot, the duties and obligations of Jewish life. It also evidences deep concern for the dignity of the individual, protecting him or her from the unwarranted interference of the community and the unwanted gaze[1] of the other. When these two values clash, how shall we draw the line between them?

1. THE JEWISH COMMUNITY AND ITS AUTHORITY

We Jews, in the view of our tradition, find meaning first and foremost not as individuals but as members of *Am Yisrael*, the Jewish people. The covenant, the eternal bond between God and Israel, was made with the community as a whole and is expressed in communal language: we are to be "a kingdom of priests and a holy nation" (Exod. 19:6), and it is the "entire congregation of Israel" that hears the commandment that "you shall be holy" (Lev. 19:2).[2] The liturgy of our prayer book (siddur) expresses the essentially corporate nature of our existence and destiny. Our prayers are written in plural language, so that even when a Jew prays privately, he or she speaks of the God "who has sanctified *us*," praises the God "who in love has chosen *the people Israel*" for divine service, and implores God to "heal *us* and *we* shall be healed." The tradition teaches us that it is better to pray in the midst of a congregation than to do so privately[3] and provides that certain parts of the liturgy, those having to do with the sanctification of God, may be recited *only* in the midst of a congregation, for "I will be sanctified *in the midst of* the people of Israel" (Lev. 22:32).[4] In other words, we most truly uphold the covenant and sanctify the name of God when we become "Israel," the Jewish community.

Given its emphasis upon the centrality of community, it is not surprising that Jewish tradition speaks hardly at all about "individual rights." Jewish law, after all, proceeds from the mitzvot of the Torah, the obligations imposed upon the people by their covenant with God. When we study our sacred texts, we are much more likely to read of "duties" than of "rights."[5] To put this differently, the Torah does not proclaim a libertarian philosophy. Our lives, our bodies, and our property are not our own, to do with as we please so long as we do not interfere with the rights of others; they belong rather to God, who has given them to us for safekeeping and to whom we owe an ultimate account for the way we use them.[6] It follows that when we see another Jew transgressing against the Torah, each of us is entitled (and even required) to take action to ensure that he or she abides by the Torah's dictates.[7] Talmudic law allows the proper authorities to coerce an individual to perform a variety of mitzvot that are incumbent upon him or her: to fulfill a vow,[8] to issue a divorce,[9] to give *tzedakah*,[10] and others.[11] Indeed, the organized community exercises the same authority as that possessed in Temple times by the Sanhedrin, the great *beit din* (rabbinical court), to enforce its decrees upon its citizens.[12]

From the above, we might well draw the conclusion that the community, in this case the synagogue, ought to allow other Jewish organizations to solicit its members to participate in and to contribute to their programs. Many of these organizations—local federations, day schools, Zionist groups, facilities for senior citizens, social action agencies, and numerous others—serve vital Jewish purposes, and since the community is traditionally empowered to enforce the performance of mitzvot, it would follow that the synagogue board is authorized to aid these organizations in the achievement of their goals. This, perhaps, is what Hillel had in mind when he instructed us, "Do not separate from the community" (*M. Avot* 2:4): when the community is engaged in Torah and mitzvot, "this is truly the crown of God's glory," and it is unworthy of any of us to stand aside.[13] One could therefore make a strong argument that the synagogue, the present-day embodiment of the Jewish community of old, ought to provide its membership list to these organizations, for to do so would strengthen and enrich the community as a whole.

2. THE PRIVACY OF THE INDIVIDUAL

Against this argument, however, stands our concern for the privacy and the dignity of the individual synagogue member. Although, to repeat, Jewish tradition does not speak in terms of "rights," including a "right" to privacy, it does impose upon us the corresponding duty to refrain from infringing upon a person's essential dignity. A homeowner, for example, may take action to protect the household against the prying eyes of neighbors, for "damage caused by visibility" (*hezeik r'iyah*) is an actionable tort under Jewish law.[14] The Torah and halachah forbid gossip and slander (*r'chilut*) as damaging to a person's reputation,[15] and they prohibit us from saying or doing anything that causes embarrassment (*halbanat panim*) to others.[16] Significantly, although as we have seen the halachah allows the community to coerce individuals to give *tzedakah*, we are forbidden to shame them in public.[17] Taken together, these and other provisions of Jewish law proclaim that the life of the individual is not a completely open book, that at some point the community must cease their efforts to intervene into what are, at bottom, matters that are none of its business. As we have written in another context: "There are aspects of our existence which are and must remain off-limits to the eyes and tongues of those among whom we live, and we are therefore under no moral or religious obligation to share with them information about ourselves that they have no legitimate reason to know. This conclusion drawn from our law may not be the exact equivalent of the 'right to privacy' in other legal systems. But it does express, in language too clear to permit of misunderstanding, a commitment to the proposition that all of us, created in the divine image, are possessed of a dignity which at some critical point requires that all others leave us be and let us alone."[18]

This concern for individual privacy counsels *against* a synagogue's sharing its membership list with other agencies in the absence of the individual's express consent, or in the absence of a duly adopted provision in the synagogue's bylaws permitting such an action. The question has to do with what lawyers would call a "reasonable expectation of privacy." In our day, when the Jewish community no longer enjoys the coercive powers described above, individuals who join our synagogues expect that their membership information will remain the confidential property of the synagogue. To act in a manner contrary to that expectation, to grant other organizations access to membership information without the member's consent, would be a violation of the halachic prohibition of fraud and deception (*g'neivat daat*).[19] True, our tradition has permitted the rare act of deception for the sake of a "higher" purpose,[20] and the organizations that seek our mailing lists undoubtedly believe that they represent such purposes. We think, however, that they face a high burden of proof if they wish to set aside Judaism's protection of individual privacy and prohibition of deceptive conduct.

CONCLUSION

The community enjoys a high standing in Jewish law, particularly as an agency for aiding (or even coercing) individuals to do that which is right and good. In our own time, the community does not enjoy the coercive powers it once possessed. It still has the duty, however, to encourage its members to perform mitzvot. On the other hand, Jewish tradition shows a deep regard for the dignity and privacy of the individual. In our case, individual members of a synagogue have a reasonable expectation that the synagogue will not share their names and other personal information with other organizations without the express consent of the member or in the absence of a clear statement in the congregation's bylaws permitting the sharing of this information. Whether the synagogue should adopt such a policy is a decision for its members to make.

NOTES

1. See Jeffrey Rosen, *The Unwanted Gaze: The Destruction of Privacy in America* (New York: Random House, 2000).

2. See Rashi ad loc., quoting the *Sifra* to Lev. 19:2: the mitzvot in this section of the Torah were spoken in the presence of the entire community because they contain the essence of the Torah itself.

3. BT *B'rachot* 7b–8a. As Maimonides expresses the idea, "The prayer of the community is always accepted.... Therefore, one should strive to join the community, and one should not pray privately if one is able to pray with a congregation" (*Yad, T'filah* 8:1).

4. See M. *M'gillah* 4:3; BT *M'gillah* 23b; *Yad, T'filah* 8:5–6; and *SA*, OC 69:1: "matters having to do with sanctification" (*kol davar sh'bikedushah*) must be recited in the presence of a congregation (*eidah*) consisting of no less than ten adult Jews. These "matters" include the liturgical rubrics *Kaddish, K'dushah, Bar'chu,* and the reading of the Torah (*Mishnah B'rurah*, OC 55:2).

5. See Haim Cohn, *Human Rights in Jewish Law* (New York: Ktav, 1984), 18: "The particular structure of Jewish law qua religious law—with God as the central object of love and veneration, and the worship and service of God as the overriding purpose of all law—postulates a system of duties rather than a system of rights." See also R. Elliot N. Dorff, *To Do the Right and the Good: A Jewish Approach to Modern Social Ethics* (Philadelphia: Jewish Publication Society, 2002), 17–26.

6. This idea, found throughout our sources, is perhaps best expressed in the traditional prohibitions against suicide and against doing physical harm to our bodies. Jewish tradition is *not* neutral when it comes to these so-called "victimless" crimes, for the individual is not the owner of his or her own life and body to do with them as he or she pleases. For sources and discussion, see *Teshuvot for the Nineties* (*TFN*), no. 5754.14, pp. 337–63, especially at notes 3 and 4, and no. 5752.7, pp. 127–32. See also *Reform Responsa for the Twenty-first Century*, no. 5759.4, vol. 1, pp. 357–64.

7. For example, Lev. 19:17 enjoins us to "reprove your kinsman, so that you not incur guilt on his account," and our tradition adds that "whosoever has it in his power to protest against sin and does not do so is implicated in that very sin, inasmuch as he could have issued a rebuke" (*Yad, Dei-ot* 6:7, from BT *Arachin* 16b). The well-known Talmudic saying *kol Yisrael arevim zeh bezeh*, which is usually translated as "all Jews are responsible for one another," in fact declares that each of us bears a duty to intervene when we see a fellow Jew committing a sin (BT *Sh'vuot* 39a and *Sanhedrin* 27b).

8. BT *Bava Batra* 48a and *Arachin* 21a; *Yad, Maaseh HaKorbanot* 14:16.

9. BT *Bava Batra* 48a and *Arachin* 21a; *Yad, Geirushin* 2:20; *SA, EHE* 134:5 and 154:21. See, in general, *TFN*, no. 5754.6, pp. 209–16.

10. BT *Bava Batra* 8b (and *Tosafot* ad loc., s.v. *achpeh*); *Yad, Matanot Aniyim* 7:10; *SA, YD* 248:1.

11. For example, should a *mohel* refuse to circumcise a baby boy, the *beit din* may coerce him to do so if there is no other *mohel* available (*Resp. Rashba* 1:472; *SA, YD* 461). How, precisely, could such "coercion" take place in a way that is safe for the child? See *Pitchei T'shuvah, YD* 261:4: the *beit din* is permitted to trick the recalcitrant *mohel*, to promise him an exorbitant fee and to renege on the offer following the circumcision.

12. Although the Talmud never states that the community (*kahal*) may employ coercion to enforce its decrees, the medieval authorities recognized such a power. The equation of the *kahal* to the Sanhedrin is most associated with R. Sh'lomo b. Adret (Rashba; d. 1310) of Barcelona; see his *Responsa* 5:126, 1:729, 3:411, and 3:417. See also R. Asher b. Yechiel (d. 1327), *Resp. HaRosh* 6:5, 6:7, who extends the "majority rule principle" (*acharei rabim l'hatot*) from its original context (i.e., that a court's verdict is determined by the majority of its judges) to apply to all matters of public (*rabim*, i.e., community) concern. Other scholars derived this communal power from other sources. See *Reform Responsa for the Twenty-first Century*, no. 5758.1, vol. 1, pp. 311–18.

13. See the commentary of R. Yonah Gerondi to *M. Avot* 2:4, included in the standard printed editions of the Babylonian Talmud.

14. *M. Bava Batra* 3:7; BT *Bava Batra* 2b–3a; *Yad, Sh'cheinim* 2:14; *SA, CM* 54.

15. Lev. 19:16; *Yad, Dei-ot* 7:1–2. For sources and discussion on the prohibition of gossip in general, see *TFN*, no. 5750.4, pp. 187–90.

16. The prohibition is derived from Lev. 19:17; see *Sifra* to the verse and BT *Arachin* 16b. See also *Yad, Dei-ot* 6:8, and *Sefer HaChinuch, mitzvah* 240.

17. BT *Bava Batra* 8b; *Yad, Matanot Aniyim* 7:11; *Tur, YD* 248; *SA, YD* 248:7.

18. *Reform Responsa for the Twenty-first Century*, no. 5756.2, vol. 1, pp. 331–42, section 2.

19. BT *Chulin* 94a; *Yad, Dei-ot* 2:6 and *M'chirah* 18:1ff.; and *SA, CM* 228:6.

20. For example, in Gen. 18:13 God intentionally misquotes to Abraham Sarah's remark in verse 12, in order to spare him embarrassment and to preserve peace between husband and wife. See BT *Bava M'tzia* 87a and the final chapter of Tractate *Derech Eretz Zuta*. See Nachmanides to Gen. 18:13 for a less daring but essentially similar evaluation of God's report. In addition, see at note 11, above.

A Sex Offender in the Synagogue*
5765.4

Sh'eilah

A young man was sexually molested at a synagogue day camp program by a junior counselor. The perpetrator was convicted, spent about a year in juvenile detention, and was recently released. The victim's family has gotten a restraining order that prevents the perpetrator from being near the victim's home, school, and synagogue.

1. If the judge had not allowed the synagogue to be included in the restraining order, should we have allowed the perpetrator to attend services or religious school and under what conditions?

2. During the hearings, it came out that the perpetrator's mother was aware that her son had previously molested other children and she had not informed the director of education, who was in charge of the camp program. Given this circumstance, is there any reason to deny the mother access to the synagogue? (The victim's mother, due to her anger, cannot tolerate being in the same place as the perpetrator's mother.)

T'shuvah

This *sh'eilah* presents us with two separate cases. The first is a hypothetical one: should the synagogue have denied access to the perpetrator had the court not done so?

1. READMITTING THE OFFENDER?

The Mitzvah of Repentance. The perpetrator, who seeks access to the synagogue and to its programs, might argue that he has met the terms of the punishment administered for his crime. For the synagogue to deny him entry would be to add to his punishment, to make it more severe than required by law, and such a course, he might say, does him an injustice. The wrong, he might further argue, is compounded by the fact that he is a minor, whom the law does not hold totally responsible for his actions, and by the fact that he can claim that his tendency toward sexual abuse is the product of social and psychological factors that lie largely beyond his control. Expulsion from the synagogue, therefore, might cause him real psychological harm and be counterproductive to his successful reintegration into the community. It would run counter to a fundamental goal and norm of Judaism: the encouragement of repentance (t'shuvah), the process by which the sinner turns away from evil. Our sources, as we all know, speak at length of the overriding importance of t'shuvah.[1] We read, in particular, that "great is repentance, because it annuls the verdict [g'zar din] rendered against a person."[2] T'shuvah, in other words, expunges the record of our sins,[3] so that "even one who is wicked throughout his lifetime may do t'shuvah at the very end, and not a single fact of all his evil will be remembered against him."[4] God therefore does not desire the punishment of the sinner but rather that he or she turn away from wickedness.[5] And do the Rabbis not tell us, with deep insight into human character, that the repentant sinner is more to be admired than a purely righteous person, because the former, unlike the latter, has experienced and overcome the temptation to do evil?[6]

In ancient times, the Temple and the sacrifices were the means by which Israel achieved atonement for sin. Today, when repentance is the only avenue remaining for atonement,[7] it is the task of the synagogue—the "Temple in miniature"[8]—to provide a locus for the work of t'shuvah. The perpetrator thus might argue that to exclude any Jew from the synagogue on the grounds that he or she is a sinner is to frustrate the performance of this task. To exclude this Jew, a young man for whom rehabilitation is surely not yet an impossible dream, would send the message that we do not truly believe in the possibility of t'shuvah and that the synagogue is no longer a place in which those who truly seek to repent can work toward personal redemption.

2. READMITTING THE OFFENDER? THE MITZVAH TO PROTECT OURSELVES FROM DANGER

Responding to all this, those who would deny access to the perpetrator would argue that no individual possesses an unlimited right of membership in the community and of access to its institutions. Jewish tradition, indeed, permits the community to exclude an individual from membership and participation for sufficient cause.[9] The ban or excommunication (*cherem* or *nidui*) served in medieval times as a principal means by which the community enforced its decrees on taxation and other rules. To be sure, such expulsion is difficult to square with our modern temperament. We should, in general, avoid taking such a drastic step to express our displeasure with any member of a congregation. As R. Solomon B. Freehof puts it, "Much more, it would seem, could be accomplished by bringing the Jew of ill repute under the influence of the synagogue and its teachings."[10] Nonetheless, the halachah does recognize that *cherem* can be a legitimate expression of communal power, and as the institutional embodiment of our community, the synagogue is entitled to determine just who shall be a member and who shall *cease* to be a member of the congregation.

Moreover, while there is no denying the centrality of *t'shuvah* to our Judaic value system, it can be argued that "repentance" is an inappropriate category with which to approach this question. As Maimonides puts it: "What is true repentance? When a person has the opportunity and capacity to repeat that particular transgression but refrains from doing so, not on account of fear or weakness but because he has repented of that sin."[11] In our case, this is a standard that cannot be met. This "sinner," we must remember, is a sex offender, one who has committed an act of sexual abuse against another young person. It is, to say the least, far from obvious that an individual who displays tendencies to this sort of behavior can ever be rid of them or bring them under full control. All that we know about the etiology of sexual abuse suggests that this perpetrator, should he be permitted to take part in the life of the synagogue, may well pose a continued danger to the safety and well-being of its children.[12] And our tradition also teaches that we are obligated to remove from our property any factor that poses danger to the life, health, or property of others.[13] Hence, we might say that it is our duty to deny this young perpetrator access to our synagogue and that, should we allow him entry and should he repeat his abusive behavior, it is *we* who must do *t'shuvah*.

3. THE COMMITTEE'S OPINION

It is never an easy thing to decide between two moral or religious values that seem to pull us in opposite directions. In this case, however, it is clear to us that our first duty, the obligation that takes precedence over all others, is to ensure that our synagogues and schools are places of safety for those who enter them. While the convicted sex offender is right to look upon the synagogue as a place of spiritual healing, that right pertains to *all* of its members, its families and their children. Their sense of security and well-being can be threatened by the presence of a sex offender in the midst of the congregation. In the case that prompted this inquiry, the court agreed that the danger was real and issued its restraining order. In the hypothetical case posed by our *sh'eilah*, the danger might be no less real, and it is reasonable to presume that the offender's presence would be deeply disturbing to his victim as well as to others. It is their synagogue, too, and the congregation's leadership bears the overriding duty to reassure all its members that the synagogue is a safe place and that this safety extends to all congregational functions. The congregation is therefore under no Judaic religious obligation to admit this young person, a convicted and (hopefully) recovering sex offender, onto its grounds or into its programmatic activities.

4. THE OFFENDER'S MOTHER

The second part of this *sh'eilah* is not hypothetical: should the mother of the perpetrator, who did not inform the congregation of her son's history of sexual abuse, be denied access to the synagogue? We sympathize with those who say yes. The mother's failure to notify the synagogue, however she attempts to explain or to justify it, is inexcusable. Unlike her son, she is an adult, and we hold her fully culpable for this shocking lapse of moral responsibility. Yet we think that it would be inappropriate for the congregation to deny her access, for two reasons. First, she poses no threat to the safety of congregants. Second, she, too, must do *t'shuvah*, and she must do it in the synagogue, the very place where she committed her transgression. She must ask the forgiveness of those against whom she has sinned: her son's victim, the victim's family, and, for that matter, the entire congregation.[14] We recognize, as our *sh'eilah* emphasizes, that to allow her to return to the congregation will lead to tension and to personal distress, particularly to the victim's mother. Yet this is no argument in favor of banishment. On the contrary: the victim's mother bears her own responsibility in this process of *t'shuvah*. It is her duty— and the duty of the congregation as a whole—to *accept* the repentance of the perpetrator's mother, if and when she offers it fully and sincerely.[15] That task will be difficult, but it is what our tradition requires.

5. A PARTIAL DISSENT

One member of this Committee, though agreeing with the broad trend of the decision, believes that the congregation should be encouraged to find appropriate means of allowing those who have committed sexual offenses to participate in synagogue life. To this end, we could benefit from the experience of a number of Christian churches that have developed protocols stipulating the precise conditions under which a sex offender might be allowed entry and participation in the community.[16] These may include restricted access to the synagogue building(s) and grounds; a requirement that while on synagogue grounds the offender be accompanied at all times by a family member or by an individual designated by the synagogue; a prohibition of access to the school and nursery areas of the synagogue facility; and so forth. The synagogue might require that the offender and (if he/she is a minor) the offender's family sign an agreement expressly accepting these restrictions, and it might require them to report from time to time to an appropriate committee concerning their adherence to these guidelines. In addition, the synagogue might require the perpetrator to make a statement acknowledging the pain he or she has caused the victim. Such an open acknowledgment of responsibility, called a *vidui*, is perfectly consistent with our tradition's conception of repentance.[17] Taking these or similar measures will allow us to reach out in love and concern to one of the most marginalized and, frankly, one of the most despised segments of our Jewish population. This member agrees, however, that should these protocols prove impractical to administer and enforce, or should they fail to reassure the congregants that they and their children are truly safe while at the synagogue, the congregation is entitled to deny access to the perpetrator, on the grounds that its overriding duty is to make the synagogue a safe place for *all* who make up its community.

NOTES

*The Responsa Committee gratefully acknowledges the assistance provided by Rabbi Ruth Alpers, the Jay Stein Director of Human Relations at the Hebrew Union College–Jewish Institute of Religion, in the preparation of this *t'shuvah*.

1. See, for example, the praises to repentance (*g'dolah t'shuvah*) in BT *Yoma* 86a–b: "Great is *t'shuvah*" because it brings healing to the world, lengthens the span of our days, hastens the final redemption, and because "when one person repents of sin, the entire world finds forgiveness."

2. BT *Rosh HaShanah* 17b.

3. Cf. Isa. 1:18: "Though your sins be red as crimson, they shall become white as snow."

4. BT *Kiddushin* 40b; *Yad, T'shuvah* 1:3.

5. Ezek. 18:23, 18:32, and 33:11. See as well BT *B'rachot* 10a, where B'ruriah, the wife of R. Meir, subjects Ps. 104:35 ("May sinners perish from the earth") to a creative re-reading. By deftly altering the vocalization (*nikud*) of the word *chataim*, she changes the meaning of the verse: God desires the death of *sin*, not the death of sinners. Reform and repentance must take precedence over punishment.

6. BT *B'rachot* 34b: *b'makom shebaalei t'shuvah omdin, tzadikim g'murim einam omdin.* See *Yad, T'shuvah* 7:4.

7. *Yad, T'shuvah* 1:3.

8. BT *M'gillah* 29a, on Ezek. 11:16.

9. BT *B'rachot* 19a; *Yad, Talmud Torah* 6:14; *SA*, YD 334:43.

10. *American Reform Responsa*, no. 16.

11. *Yad, T'shuvah* 2:1.

12. This does *not* mean that we believe that a sexual offender cannot be successfully treated. As the American Psychiatric Association puts it, "Few perpetrators are 'untreatable'"; see *Dangerous Sex Offenders: A Task Force Report* (Washington, DC: American Psychiatric Association, 1999), 164, which raises questions as to the reliability of recidivism statistics for sex offenders. It means, rather, that such treatment can be an involved and difficult process and that its success can hinge on a number of factors. One such factor, for example, is the offender's desire to effect a change in his life. "No evidence supports the notion that persons with paraphilias can be treated successfully without their cooperation" (ibid., 175). Moreover, the sponsoring organization of that task force report concedes that "unlike the successful treatment outcomes for most other mental illnesses, the outlook for successful treatment and rehabilitation of individuals with pedophilia is guarded. Even after intensive treatment, the course of the disorder usually is chronic and lifelong in most patients" (American Psychiatric Association, *Fact Sheet: Pedophilia*, http://www.medem.com/medlb/article_detaillb.cfm?article_ID=ZZZUZRUZGLC&sub_cat=355, accessed Aug. 19, 2009). It also means that the definition of "success" must be a realistic one. In the words of one group of therapists, a sex offender is comparable to an alcoholic in that he should never consider himself cured. "He has a behavioral and thinking handicap that he can keep within acceptable limits only by continuing to practice a series of controls. As he demonstrates increasing internal controls, external controls can be cautiously relaxed" (Michael A. O'Connell et al., *Working with Sex Offenders: Guidelines for Therapist Selection* [Newbury Park, CA: Sage, 1990], 105). Treatment, in other words, is hard, slow work that takes a long time, and in the meantime, we do not know that the offender will not repeat his offense when he has the opportunity to do so.

13. The halachah derives this rule by extending the Torah's requirement that the homeowner construct a parapet or guardrail for his roof (Deut. 22:8). Thus, one is forbidden to keep a vicious dog or an non-sturdy ladder on one's property (BT *K'tubot* 41b and *Bava Kama* 15b; *Yad, Rotzei-ach* 11:4; *SA*, CM 427:7–10.

14. "Yom Kippur effects atonement for sins one has committed against God. For sins one has committed against another person, however, Yom Kippur does not effect

atonement until the sinner has conciliated the offended party" (*M. Yoma* 8:9; *Yad, T'shuvah* 2:9).

15. "[The offended party] should not act cruelly and refuse to be reconciled...but rather, when the sinner requests pardon, the offended party should pardon him with sincerity and with a willing spirit" (*Yad, T'shuvah* 2:10, based on *M. Bava Kama* 8:7).

16. Some of the suggestions found in the text can be found in Carol J. Adams, *When the Abuser Is Among Us: One Church's Response to a Perpetrator* (Seattle: Center for the Prevention of Sexual and Domestic Violence, 1994), and in Peggy Halsey, "When the Abuser Is One of Us," *The Interpreter* (a publication of the United Methodist Church), September 2001, 24–25. On the need to set "clear rules and boundaries" for a sex offender seeking admission to the community, see Kathy MacDonald et al., *Counselling for Sexual Abuse* (Oxford: Oxford University Press, 1995), 279.

17. BT *Yoma* 86b; *Yad, T'shuvah* 2:2.

Sh'eilah

A Jewish woman from a nearby congregation recently contacted me.
Her congregation does not currently have a rabbi, so she asked me to
perform a baby-naming ceremony for her daughter. She then informed
me that although her husband is not Jewish, the rabbi who performed
their wedding had "given him a Hebrew name," and she asked that this
name be included on her daughter's naming certificate. Because I regard
a Hebrew name to be a symbol of Jewish commitment to the covenant
at Sinai, it is not my custom to assign Hebrew names to non-Jewish
spouses. On the other hand, the rabbi who did assign the Hebrew name
to this man is my colleague. If another rabbi has set the precedent of
giving a Hebrew name to a non-Jew, is it my obligation to honor that
act? (Rabbi Geoffrey Dennis, Flower Mound, Texas)

T'shuvah

Your question touches upon a classic conflict in Reform Jewish practice
between two deeply felt religious principles. On the one hand, we are
firmly committed to the idea of rabbinical autonomy. Each Reform rabbi
functions, in his or her congregational community, as the *mara d'atra*,
the local religious authority. This status, to be sure, does not grant
the rabbi autocratic power to decide questions of religious practice. In
our movement these are resolved cooperatively between the rabbi and
the congregation. Yet within this cooperative model the rabbi enjoys a
certain sphere of authority over issues of practice. When we speak of
"rabbinical autonomy," we mean that no other rabbi has the right to
interfere in the recognized prerogatives of the rabbi of the congregation.
The Central Conference of American Rabbis (CCAR), our rabbinical
association, recognizes the autonomy of its members over questions of
religious observance. Although the Conference may adopt resolutions

that formulate a communal rabbinical position on these matters, these resolutions are seen as nonbinding upon its members. The individual Reform rabbi retains the freedom to determine his or her own standards of religious practice.[1] Thus, from this standpoint, you are entitled set your own policy concerning the assignment of Hebrew names in your congregation regardless of the policies adopted by other rabbis.

On the other hand, the Reform rabbinate is more than an aggregation of isolated individuals. We are a community; as you pointedly note in your *sh'eilah*, we regard each other as *colleagues*, as fellow practitioners, as co-workers in a common enterprise. We therefore accept that our individual rabbinical autonomy is limited to some extent by a sense of collegial responsibility, the desire to honor and respect the actions of our colleagues in the exercise of their legitimate rabbinical functions. For this reason, you quite rightly feel an obligation to affirm your colleague's decision concerning the granting of a Hebrew name to the non-Jewish spouse.

This conflict between personal autonomy and collegial responsibility is difficult to resolve. We cannot simply choose one side and reject the other out of hand, because we believe quite strongly in both. Yet we think there is a way of successfully negotiating between these opposing commitments. This path is pointed out by the Jewish legal tradition. The halachah, too, is beset by a tension between rabbinical freedom of decision and deference to communal standards. How Jewish law deals with this tension may suggest to us a method of dealing with our own.

In classical Jewish legal thought, the Babylonian Talmud is the supreme source of halachic authority. This is the case, writes Maimonides, because all Israel accepted or ratified the Talmud as their binding legal standard. It follows that the post-Talmudic legal decisors—Maimonides uses the term *geonim* to describe them all—enjoy no such authority. The halachic scholar is free to rule in accordance with his own reading of the Talmudic sources, even if this ruling is contradicted by the view of other authorities.[2] In this respect, we can say that the Jewish legal tradition recognizes a high degree of rabbinical autonomy in the interpretation of Torah and halachah. Yet the tradition also contains an opposing view, that of R. Avraham b. David of Posquierres (Rabad; twelfth century), who holds that the rulings of the *geonim* have now attained the status of decided law; "we no longer have the authority to dispute their rulings on the basis of our own interpretation, unless the matter is a *kushya m'fursemet*," that is, a long-standing controversy in the legal literature. In the absence of such a controversy, says Rabad, when there is a legal consensus among the post-Talmudic scholars, we are obligated to accept that position even when we disagree with the legal reasoning that supports it.[3] This idea, in turn, is criticized by R. Asher b. Yechiel (Rosh; thirteenth to fourteenth century), who upholds the doctrine of rabbinical autonomy in no uncertain terms. He writes, "If the contemporary scholar disagrees with the words of the *geonim* and if he can bring persuasive Talmudic evidence to support his view, then 'Jepthah in his generation is equivalent to Samuel in *his* generation,'[4] that is, on any matter that is not decided in the Talmud, a judge may argue as he sees fit, even if he disputes the words of the *geonim*."[5] The pendulum swings back by the sixteenth century with the creation of the *Shulchan Aruch*, the legal "code" whose authors, R. Yosef Caro and R. Moshe Isserles, declare the halachah according to the consensus view among earlier scholars.[6] Yet even that great compendium did not bring an end to rabbinical independence; halachists continue to this day to modify, adjust, and alter the Jewish legal consensus by writing commentaries, compendia, and responsa.[7]

This back-and-forth debate between autonomy of decision and the constraint of consensus exists because both principles are indispensable. It is in the nature of Jewish law that the interpretation of the legal sources is the prerogative of the individual scholar, who must declare the truth as it appears to him or (nowadays) her, regardless of the opinion of others. Yet no rabbi is an island; the study and practice of Torah are a communal concern. When scholars derive conclusions from halachic texts, they do so not for themselves alone but for an entire community, to whom they are ultimately responsible. The accepted, "consensus" standards of ritual and ethical observance are not merely the opinions drawn by rabbis through a purely intellectual investigation of the texts. They belong to the people; they are the lines and the parameters by which the members of the community define themselves as Jews and within which they live their Jewish lives. Rabbis should be careful not to challenge this consensus in the absence of good and sufficient reason, for the members of the community are entitled to expect that the substance of their Judaism will remain reasonably consistent over time. Rabbis must therefore continually seek a proper balance between their freedom to interpret the Torah as they see fit and the reasonable expectations of the community that looks to them for guidance.

The same applies to Reform rabbis. We, too, cherish our freedom, but we know that our rabbinate is a communal practice. We as individuals do not define what a rabbi is and what a rabbi does. That is the task of the Jewish community and tradition, which delineate our roles and empower us to serve as "teachers in Israel." We are "rabbis," in other words, only to the extent that we act in a manner coherent with the tradition that has created the term and that gives it meaning. Our autonomy must therefore fit within the life of community and tradition; it must be balanced against the reasonable expectations of the colleagues with whom we work and of the people to whom we render our service.

Just what are those "reasonable expectations"? Since we are Reform rabbis, our colleagues and people are entitled to expect that we will conduct ourselves as members of that distinct and identifiable rabbinical community. Since our rabbinate, like all others, is a communal enterprise (i.e., since we cannot function as "rabbis" except in association with our colleagues in that endeavor), we can be expected to make every effort to honor and respect the actions our colleagues perform in the discharge of their rabbinical duties, even when those actions do not reflect our own standards of practice. Yet precisely because we are *Reform* rabbis, our colleagues and people know that we can and frequently do disagree among ourselves over important matters of religious practice. That is the nature of Reform Judaism and of the Reform rabbinate. We cannot reasonably be expected to alter our practice simply because a colleague "does it differently," especially when the disagreement is a *machloket l'shem shamayim*, one that rises to the level of high principle.

How do we distinguish between those cases in which we can be expected to compromise and those in which we cannot? Here, the Rabad's notion of *kushya m'fursemet* is helpful. When a particular dispute over an issue of deep significance has been identified as a "long-standing controversy" within Reform rabbinical practice, a rabbi is entitled to adhere to one side or the other as a matter of religious principle. In such a case, although the rabbi may choose to alter or modify his or her principled stance in the name of collegiality, there can be no reasonable expectation that he or she will do so. In a similar way, although resolutions of the CCAR and the responsa issued by this Committee exert no obligatory power over the religious practice of the individual Reform rabbi, such statements and rulings serve to inform our community as to the standards of practice that they can "reasonably expect" of the rabbi. Thus, if the Conference or this Committee has endorsed a particular practice, the rabbi is fully entitled to adopt that standard as his or her own and cannot be reasonably expected to compromise that position out of a sense of collegial responsibility to a rabbi whose standard differs. The following hypothetical cases may serve to illustrate our point.

CASE 1

A person converts to Judaism under the guidance of Rabbi A, who does not require *t'vilah* (ritual immersion) as part of the conversion procedure. The Jew-by-choice then joins the congregation of Rabbi B, who does require *t'vilah* for conversion. Rabbi B should accept this individual as a true proselyte, because there is a consensus of practice within the American Reform Movement to accept converts even if they do not undergo the traditional rites of circumcision and immersion.[8] This stance has been affirmed by this Committee, even though our responsa have tended to encourage Reform rabbis to insist upon these rites,[9] as well as by the Conference as a whole in its "Guidelines for Rabbis Working with Prospective *Gerim*," adopted in 2001, even though that document encourages rabbis to educate potential Jews-by-choice concerning the traditional rites.[10] A conversion has the status of a *maaseh beit din*, a "court action";[11] each Reform rabbi is expected to give "full faith and credit" to such actions performed by other Reform rabbis.

CASE 2

Rabbi A is scheduled to officiate at a wedding ceremony between a Jew and a non-Jew. At the last minute, the rabbi is called out of town and asks Rabbi B to officiate in his place. Rabbi B does not officiate at mixed marriages, and while she may agree to help Rabbi A in this instance, she is under no collegial obligation to do so. It is well-known that Reform rabbis are deeply divided over the propriety of officiating at mixed marriages. The Conference and this Committee are both on record as opposing the practice,[12] and it is the consensus among us that the Reform rabbi has every right as a matter of religious principle to refuse to officiate at a mixed marriage. Thus, a colleague or congregant cannot reasonably expect that a rabbi who does not officiate at mixed marriages will change that position out of collegial considerations.

CASE 3

A family has scheduled a bar mitzvah service at the congregation of Rabbi A, who takes the view that non-Jews are not called to the Torah. The family at one time lived in another community, whose rabbi permitted such participation to non-Jews, including this family's own non-Jewish relatives at the bat mitzvah service of their older child. Since it is well-known that issues of synagogue policy are matters of local custom and rabbinical prerogative, the family cannot reasonably expect Rabbi A to alter this practice, whether out of a sense of collegiality toward the other rabbi or out of a desire not to "discriminate" between the two children.

The foregoing helps to shape our thinking concerning your *sh'eilah*. The issue you face—the Hebrew name given by a colleague to a non-Jewish spouse—is not the private business of this man and his family. As you correctly note, there is really no such thing as a "Hebrew" name. The names we bestow are *Jewish* names; they testify to our membership in the Jewish people and to our participation in the covenant. This is not, in other words, a matter of little consequence but rather of high religious principle; it is precisely the sort of question on which you can be reasonably expected to take a principled stance and upon which you *cannot* be reasonably expected to change your practice for collegial reasons. In addition, this Committee has recently issued a responsum that supports your position in full: the "Hebrew" name we bestow is a *covenantal* name and not a biological one, and it is therefore inappropriate to grant such a name to a person who remains outside the covenant.[13]

For these reasons, the action of your colleague, while lying within his own prerogative, does not serve as a binding precedent upon you. The woman who has contacted you has every reason to expect that you will maintain your current practice. You are under no communal or collegial obligation to change it.

NOTES

1. See, for example, the section entitled "Historical and Halachic Notes" in *Rabbi's Manual* (New York: CCAR Press, 1988), 220: "The Notes do not establish or create a new Reform Halacha; rather, they aim to inform the rabbi of prevailing practice based on the historic continuities and discontinuities of Reform. From the beginning, Reform Judaism has been fed by two streams: by the authority of tradition and the freedom of the individual. These Notes are designed as a guide to our colleagues so that they may reach their decisions on the basis of both contemporary requirements and traditional practice." In other words, while the rabbi's decision ought to be informed by historical communal considerations, the decision ultimately rests in the rabbi's own hands.

2. *Yad*, Introduction.

3. Rabad's comment originates in *Katuv Sham* (ed. Jerusalem [1990], 198), his *hasagot* (critical notes) to the *Sefer HaM'orot* of R. Zerachyah Halevy. It is cited by R. Asher b. Yechiel, *Hil. HaRosh, Sanhedrin* 4:6.

4. See BT *Rosh HaShanah* 25b, on Deut. 17:9.

5. *Hil. HaRosh, Sanhedrin* 4:6.

6. On the codificatory work of Caro and Isserles, see Menachem Elon, *Jewish Law* (Philadelphia: Jewish Publication Society of America, 1994), 1309–66. While both Caro and Isserles utilize halachic consensus as the key to determining the authoritative law, each follows his own method of identifying that consensus. Caro announces that he will accept the majority view from among the three great "pillars of halachic judgment"—Alfasi, Maimonides, and R. Asher b. Yechiel—unless the predominant practice follows a different view; see the introduction to his *Beit Yosef.* Isserles uses the rule *hilch'ta k'vatra-ei*, "the law follows the latest authorities"; i.e., he rules in accordance with the consensus view among the German and Eastern European scholars (his own teachers) of the fifteenth and early sixteenth centuries; see the introduction to his *Darchei Moshe.*

7. For a detailed argument that the contemporary halachist retains the discretion to rule as he/she sees fit, even in contradiction to the *Shulchan Aruch*, see Joel Roth, *The Halakhic Process: A Systemic Analysis* (New York: Jewish Theological Seminary, 1988), 81–113. See as well Moshe Zemer, *Evolving Halakhah* (Woodstock, VT: Jewish Lights, 1999).

8. The CCAR declared in 1892 that Reform rabbis are permitted to perform conversions "without any initiatory rite, ceremony, or observance whatever" (*CCAR Yearbook* 3 [1893]: 94–95; *American Reform Responsa*, no. 68, pp. 236–37).

9. See *Reform Responsa for the Twenty-first Century*, no. 5756.13, vol. 1, pp. 99–120, which is largely taken up with a detailed critique of the reasoning cited in support of the 1892 resolution, at notes 35 and 36. There, too, we state the following: "In general, the tendency of this Committee is to urge in the strongest terms that all proselytes undergo the traditional rites for entry into the covenant. We do so not because we suppose that Orthodox Jews will recognize the validity of our conversions, but because we regard these practices as a positive *Jewish* standard that applies to us as it does to all other Jews. This testifies to our conviction that when we accept a *ger* or *giyoret* into our midst, we convert him or her to *Judaism.* Although we presume that our proselytes will remain firm in their commitment to a Reform approach to our faith and tradition, we do not require that they do so; we do not make their conversion contingent upon their staying within our fold. We are not in the business of creating a separate sect, cut off from the rest of our Jewish family. Rather, when we accept a proselyte, we admit this person into *Am Yisrael*, the Jewish community as a whole, a living and historical enterprise of which we are an organic part. We therefore believe that it is appropriate

and preferable to mark the moment of conversion not simply with liturgy of our own creation but precisely with those rituals that are and have been for centuries employed by the Jewish community as a whole."

10. The "Guidelines" are available at http://ccarnet.org/glgerim7.html. On the traditional rites, see section 8b; on the acceptance of conversions performed by colleagues, see section 10.

11. *SA, YD* 268:3.

12. *CCAR Yearbook* 83 (1973): 97; *Rabbi's Manual*, 242–43; *American Reform Responsa*, no. 147.

13. *Reform Responsa for the Twenty-first Century*, no. 5760.6, vol. 2, pp. 85–91, at notes 14–17.

WITHHOLDING PATERNITY INFORMATION FROM A FATHER
5760.8

Sh'eilah

A single Jewish woman is pregnant by a gentile man she has known for a short time. The pregnancy was unplanned, but she is happy about it and plans to raise the child. However, she does not wish to tell the child's father. They remain friendly, but she does not want to share custody. They are not currently involved in a relationship; in fact, the man is now in a relationship with another woman, which may result in marriage. She plans to tell the child about his/her father only when the child is old enough to ask directly. She wonders, however, if withholding this information is a Jewishly proper thing to do. (Rabbi Faedra L. Weiss, Indianapolis, Indiana)

T'shuvah

We assume that this woman will consult an attorney to determine her duty under the law to share this information with her child's father. The rules governing parental obligations fall under the category of *dina d'malchuta dina*, the principle by which Jewish law accepts as valid and binding the legitimate acts of the civil government.[1] While the law of the state will ultimately dispose of this matter, the task before us is to consider how Jewish law and tradition would speak to it. On that score, we believe the answer is unequivocal: this woman has a moral obligation to inform the father of her child of the fact of his paternity.

We base our answer upon the following considerations:

1. Judaism teaches us that it is forbidden to deceive other people, even when the deception arguably would not result in palpable harm to them.[2] True, the tradition recognizes that there are times

when an overriding value, such as peace within a marriage or a family, justifies a certain measure of deceptive behavior.[3] Yet those instances are rare; surely the general standard of conduct as taught by Jewish tradition is that honesty and truthfulness ought to guide our actions. One who wishes to act deceptively must satisfy a high burden of proof that this case is serious enough to warrant a departure from that standard.

2. We do not think that our case justifies such a departure. Indeed, it seems that the only value served by withholding information from the father is the mother's desire not to share custody of the child with him. Yet under Jewish law she is not entitled to do this. The Mishnah speaks of *mitzvot haben al haav*, obligations that the father owes to his son.[4] The Talmud[5] lists these as follows: the requirement to have his son circumcised,[6] to perform the mitzvah of *pidyon haben*,[7] to teach him Torah,[8] to find him a wife, and to teach him a trade. These texts refer in part to religious obligations that apply only within a Jewish context, and they reflect distinctions in gender roles that no longer make sense to us as Reform Jews. It is our practice to read such texts in an egalitarian way and in a way that does not make invidious distinctions between Jews and non-Jews in determining ethical duties, responsibilities that we as human beings bear toward other human beings. When we read the texts in this manner, they teach us that a parent is obligated to provide for his or her child's basic needs, to help educate that child so that he or she may become a responsible member of human society. This duty is expressed as well in the halachah's rules concerning the custody of children. In a situation where the minor child does not live together with both parents, each parent owes certain personal and financial obligations toward him or her.[9] These obligations are ultimately adjudicated by the *beit din*, the Jewish court, in accordance with the best interests of the child, yet it must be kept in mind that *both* parents figure into the court's deliberations.[10] In other words, the father as well as the mother owes duties of care and support to this child, and it would

be wrong to deny him the opportunity to meet those duties and thereby to fulfill his obligations as a parent.

What if the child's father does not wish to share custody of or provide financial support for his child? He may renounce his obligations through the process of adoption, by which all parental duties are transferred to the adoptive parent or parents.[11] This renunciation, however, must be intentional. A father who does not know of the birth of his child cannot be said to have renounced his obligations toward that child. To put this another way: the mother is not entitled to be a "gatekeeper," the sole arbiter who will determine whether the biological father can be a true father to the child he has helped to create.

3. The Mishnah also speaks of *mitzvot haav al haben*, obligations owed by a child to his or her parents.[12] These obligations are summarized under the heading of the mitzvot concerning the honor and reverence that one must show toward one's parents.[13] Obviously, a child cannot fulfill these mitzvot unless he or she knows the identity of the parent; it is therefore wrong to withhold that information from the child. In our case, the mother "plans to tell the child about his/her father only when the child is old enough to ask directly." This approach places the mother's needs before the child's and creates an atmosphere of secrecy and shame for the child that is not the child's responsibility. To withhold the father's identity until the child is ready to verbalize a request for it is to withhold information that is vital to the child's self-understanding. Each of us creates a narrative for ourselves, a story that expresses in the most personal sort of way our conception of our origin and place in the world. We begin this journey of self-explanation at a most early age. Children learn at a very young age that everyone is "supposed" to have a father and a mother. While there are many legitimate different family constellations, it is critical that the mother acknowledge and talk about this child's situation, so that its particular situation will be a natural part of his/her own self-understanding and personal narrative. To do otherwise requires the

child to invent or imagine a story, and the child will get a message that there is a secret around his or her origins. We think, therefore, that it is essential for the mother to communicate this information to her child as soon as possible.

4. The mother may, of course, argue that withholding information from the father serves her child's best interests. We think, however, that in most cases the opposite is true. It is better for the child's long-term emotional health when he or she has the opportunity to know both parents. We suspect, moreover, that the mother's desire to withhold this information from the father has less to do with her child's best interests than with her own unresolved issues concerning her relationship with him. As our prophets teach us (Jer. 31:28–29 and Ezek. 18:2ff.), it is wrong to make children suffer for the sins of their parents.

NOTES

1. For a discussion of this principle, see *Reform Responsa for the Twenty-first Century*, no. 5757.1, vol. 1, pp. 347–56. We argue that the validity of *dina d'malchuta* rests upon the fact that those who dwell in the "kingdom," by virtue of their residence there, imply their willingness to accept the kingdom's laws. This is especially true for those of us who are citizens of democratic political systems, who enjoy political rights and equality with all other citizens. Since the citizens of such a state make its laws, they accept in advance the validity of all legislation that falls into the purview of the state's legitimate legislative power. While some laws, such as those that unfairly discriminate among citizens or that impede the free exercise of their civil and political rights, would not be accepted as "legitimate" under this doctrine, regulations concerning the legal obligations between parents and children are widely accepted as a valid exercise of the community's power and jurisdiction.

2. The concept is *g'neivat daat*, literally the "theft of the mind." See BT *Chulin* 94a; *Yad, Dei-ot* 2:6 and *M'chirah* 18:1ff.; and *SA, CM* 228:6.

3. For example, in Gen. 18:13 God intentionally misquotes to Abraham Sarah's remark in verse 12, in order to spare him embarrassment and to preserve peace between husband and wife. See BT *Bava M'tzia* 87a and the final chapter of tractate *Derech Eretz Zuta*. Nachmanides to Gen. 18:13 offers a less daring evaluation of

God's report, although he acknowledges that God's statement does not reveal the whole truth.

4. *M. Kiddushin* 1:7.

5. BT *Kiddushin* 29a.

6. *Yad, Milah* 1:1; *SA, YD* 260:1.

7. *Yad, Bikurim* 11:1; *SA, YD* 305:1.

8. *Yad, Talmud Torah* 1:1; *SA, YD* 245:1.

9. See BT *K'tubot* 65b; *Yad, Ishut* 12:14, and *SA, EHE* 71:1. The father is obligated under Torah law to provide maintenance for his children until they reach the age of six, even if their mother has the means to support them. From that point on, the obligation is continued under Rabbinic law, as an aspect of the general requirement to give *tzedakah*: the *beit din* can coerce the father to provide maintenance, just as it is empowered to coerce an individual to pay *tzedakah* according to his or her means.

10. See *SA, EHE* 82:7. Custody of the child usually resides with the mother. The father, however, may demand custody of his son when the boy reaches the age of six; this derives from the father's duty to teach Torah to his son (see at note 8). On the other hand, the *beit din* can decide that the child's welfare demands an alteration of any of these arrangements (Isserles ad loc.). This "best interests of the child" rule is rooted in a responsum by R. Sh'muel di Medina (sixteenth-century Salonika; *Resp. Maharashdam, EHE*, no. 123).

11. On adoption, see *Teshuvot for the Nineties (TFN)*, no. 5753.12, pp. 201–7.

12. *M. Kiddushin* 1:7.

13. BT *Kiddushin* 29a; Exod. 20:12; Deut. 5:16; Lev. 19:3. On the extent and the limitations of the mitzvah to render honor and reverence, see *TFN* no. 5753.12, pp. 201–7.

COPYRIGHT AND THE INTERNET
5761.1

Sh'eilah

According to Jewish law, is it right to download files (music, games, etc.) from the Internet without the creator's consent or monetary compensation? (Rabbi Eric Gurvis and the ninth grade religious school class, Temple Shalom, Newton, Massachusetts)

T'shuvah

The easiest way to answer this question is to refer it to the civil authorities. Jewish law contains the principle of *dina d'malchuta dina*,[1] which recognizes the validity of the law of the state or the general government. This law is valid and binding upon us because the citizens of the commonwealth have agreed in advance to abide by the laws that pertain to the government's accepted legislative power.[2] Our question is one of property rights, specifically the issue of ownership of what we call "intellectual property," and this clearly falls into the category of those matters that the state may properly regulate through its legal system. Jewish law would recognize as valid the decision reached on this question by the legal system under which we live, whatever that decision might be.

Yet this "easy" answer does not really address the question we have been asked. Our *sho-eil* wants to know how *Jewish* law would resolve the issue, were it not a matter to be adjudicated by the civil courts. That is, according to the tradition of legal and religious thought known as the halachah, what is our ethical duty with respect to materials we download from the Internet? Are we permitted to access these materials freely? Or do we violate the rights of their creators and owners if we download them without their permission or do not pay them compensation? If we were dealing with a question of tangible property (real estate or chattel), our response would be obvious. Taking or borrowing the property of another person without that person's consent is tantamount to theft. But we are dealing instead with the ownership of intellectual property, a set of rights called "copyright." Does Jewish law recognize copyright? And if so, does copyright protection extend to material available over the Internet?

"Copyright"[3] as a legal principle does not enter the halachic literature, or the law in general, until the invention of printing. Prior to that time, there were no mechanical means to make multiple copies of written texts. The advent of the printing press led to the creation of a new industry in which many workers were employed and in which considerable money was spent in the production of books and other printed materials. Since it was now relatively easy to make copies of these texts and to distribute them on a mass scale, authors and publishers sought to protect their investments from encroachment by competitors.[4]

The first case we encounter in Jewish law concerns the printing of an edition of the *Mishneh Torah*, the law code of Maimonides, by R. Meir of Padua and a gentile printer in Venice in 1550. A competitor thereupon published the same work, pricing it somewhat lower than the first edition. R. Moshe Isserles, one of the authors of the *Shulchan Aruch*, issued a ban against the competitor's edition, on the grounds that its publication wrongfully injured the livelihood of R. Meir and the first printer.[5] This ruling was controversial, since the relevant Talmudic passage seems to allow free economic competition.[6] Isserles apparently reads the passage to say that, while competition is permitted, the competitor may not destroy the livelihood of the established business.[7] The printer has a copyright upon the book, therefore, because free competition in this case would drive him from the market and deprive him of any chance to recoup his investment. Some later authorities were reluctant to accept this view. The Torah, they argued, belongs to all of us, and the study of the Torah is a central religious duty. How can anyone claim property rights over sacred texts, literature produced in fulfillment of a mitzvah?[8] This objection, however, was countered by the very practical concern that, without some sort of protection allowing him to realize a profit, no printer would undertake the financial risks necessary to publish works of Torah learning. Our devotion to the mitzvah of Torah study therefore requires that we recognize the property rights of the publishers of sacred literature.[9] In addition, those who expressed doubts about copyright did so with respect to printers who published works written by others. These authorities were much more willing to recognize that the *author* of a work of Torah scholarship had a right to profit from his own book.[10]

Jewish law, in other words, accepts that the author of a text enjoys a copyright over his or her work, as a matter either of principle (the creator of a text is its rightful owner)[11] or of pragmatism (without copyright protection, few would venture to publish such works). If this is true of sacred literature, where one could object that there should be no such thing as a copyright over words of Torah, it is certainly true of other written works, where that objection does not apply. And if the authors of written texts deserve copyright protection, there is no reason why we should not extend that protection to other forms of intellectual property, which like written texts are created by authors who invest time and resources into their creation in the hope of earning a livelihood and of achieving a return on their investment. These works should not be copied or reproduced without the consent of their authors, the authors' legal representatives, or those to whom the authors have transferred legal title.[12]

Does the new technology change these conclusions in any substantial way? The development of the Internet and the World Wide Web has dramatically transformed the publishing marketplace during the past decade, making it possible to reproduce literary and artistic materials and to distribute them instantaneously to an audience that circles the globe. Some contend that this new technology has radically altered the notion of copyright as well. Since it is so easy to download files and to share texts, the argument runs, the authors of these materials cannot reasonably expect to control their sale and distribution. Some go further, claiming that in this new "information age," where the rapid sharing of data has become the norm, it is wrong as well as impractical to try to impede the free distribution of knowledge and information.[13]

It seems to us, however, that while information technology has become more sophisticated, the ethical issues that led to the creation of copyright laws remain the same. If it is wrong to print a book or to copy a painting without obtaining the permission of its creator, it is just as wrong to download literary and artistic creations as files without the consent of those who authored them or who own the rights to them. It is true that the "Internet age" confronts us with fundamentally new realities. It may also be true that existing copyright laws are insufficient to respond to these new realities. But it is *certainly* true that we continue to shoulder a duty, under Jewish tradition as well as under the law of the state, to honor, protect, and safeguard the rights of authors and publishers to the works they create.

It is therefore wrong, from the standpoint of Jewish law, to download files from the Internet unless one has obtained permission from the authors of those files to do so.

NOTES

1. This principle, enunciated by the *Amora* Sh'muel, is found four times in the Babylonian Talmud (BT *N'darim* 28a; *Gittin* 10b; *Bava Kama* 113a–b; *Bava Batra* 54b–55a). A similar concept is found as well in tannaitic literature, although it is given no explicit legal formulation there; see *M. Gittin* 1:5.

2. The agreement is called a stipulation (*t'nai*), in effect a contract or compact into which the members of the community have entered. Note the language "accepted legislative power": the principle of *dina d'malchuta dina* does not entail that *all* the acts of the general government are accepted by Jewish law as valid and binding. On the theory and the limits of *dina d'malchuta dina*, see *Reform Responsa for the Twenty-first Century*, no. 5757.1, vol. 1, pp. 347–56.

3. We follow the definition of "copyright" as set forth in *Corpus Juris Secundum* (St. Paul: West Publishing Co., 1990) 18:2 (94): the right of literary property as recognized

and sanctioned by positive law; the exclusive right of printing or otherwise multiplying copies of an intellectual production and of publishing and vending the same; and the right of preventing all others from doing so.

4. For the historical background see J. A. L. Sterling, *World Copyright Law* (London: Sweet and Maxwell, 1998), 7ff. The granting of publication monopolies was a well-established practice in the printing center of Venice for nearly one hundred years prior to the case involving the *Mishneh Torah*.

5. *Responsa Rema* (R. Moshe Isserles), no. 10.

6. See BT *Bava Batra* 21b: may a competitor from the immediate community or from outside the community open a similar business there, or can the existing artisan or merchant prevent him from doing so? Most early authorities rule that the competitor must be allowed to do business, inasmuch as a similar business already exists within the community (*Yad, Sh'cheinim* 6:8; Alfasi to *Bava Batra* 21b; *Hil. HaRosh, Bava Batra* 2:12). On the other hand, R. Mordechai b. Hillel (*Sefer HaMordechai, Bava Batra*, chap. 516) writes that the competitor may be prevented from setting up his business in a spot where all the potential customers will pass by his establishment without seeing that of the existing merchant or artisan, thereby depriving the latter of business.

7. Isserles uses the term *bari hezeka* ("the damage is clear and palpable"; see also his *Darchei Moshe* to *Tur, CM* 155:4). R. Moshe Sofer (eighteenth- to nineteenth-century Hungary) explains Isserles' point as follows: the existing business has no right to prevent the entry of a competitor when the competition will result in a lessening of the existing business's income. But if the competition would destroy the existing business, the latter has the right to prevent the entry of the competitor (*Resp. Chatam Sofer, CM*, no. 79).

8. As one *poseik* put it: if Moses himself taught Torah without receiving payment, how can we demand the right to profit from publishing sacred texts (see BT *N'darim* 30a, on Deut. 4:5)? R. Yitzchak Schmelkes (nineteenth-century Galicia), *Resp. Beit Yitzchak, YD* 2:75.

9. *Resp. Chatam Sofer, CM*, no. 57.

10. *Resp. Beit Yitzchak* (see note 6); *Resp. Sho-eil Umeshiv* (R. Shaul Natanson, nineteenth-century Galicia), 1:44; and *Resp. Meshiv Davar* (R. Naftali Zvi Y'hudah Berlin, nineteenth-century Lithuania), 1:24.

11. This argument is put forth by R. Berlin in *Resp. Meshiv Davar*, ibid. See also R. Shimon Shkop, *Chidushei R. Shimon Y'hudah HaKohein, Bava Kama*, no. 1: "It is an

accepted principle in Torah law that one who creates a thing is the owner of all rights to and over it."

12. This statement is a simplification of a complex legal and ethical situation. The law of the state generally allows an individual to make limited "fair use" of copyrighted material for certain specific purposes. There is no requirement to obtain the author's consent to use the materials for these purposes. The problem emerges when one reproduces literary and artistic materials for purposes other than "fair use."

13. For a look at some of these arguments, see Ron Coleman, "Copycats on the Superhighway," *American Bar Association Journal* 81 (July 1995): 68–70.

THE SYNAGOGUE AND ORGANIZED LABOR
5761.4

Sh'eilah

Our congregation is in the process of cost estimating some new construction to our synagogue facility. Our cost estimators suggested that we can save some three hundred thousand dollars by using nonunion as opposed to unionized labor. Do Jewish law and ethics offer us guidance in making this decision? (Rabbi Stuart Gershon, Summit, New Jersey)

T'shuvah

Jewish tradition does offer guidance toward answering your question. That guidance is divided, however, between the affirmation of two conflicting concerns. On the one hand, Jewish law supports the right of workers to organize into unions in order to protect and further their economic and social interests. In our Reform Jewish tradition, this support is very warm indeed. On the other hand, consumers also have interests that deserve protection. One of these is the legitimate desire to reduce costs by spending less for goods and services. Our goal in this responsum is to examine both of these concerns and to propose a way to resolve their conflict in a reasonable manner.

1. ORGANIZED LABOR AND JEWISH LAW

We read in the Talmud, "The residents of a community [*b'nei ha-ir*] are entitled to establish the community's units of measurement, the prices of commodities, and the wages paid to workers; they are also entitled to punish those who violate these rules."[1] This passage is a major source of the Jewish law of *takanot hakahal*, the power of the community to govern itself by adopting legislation on a wide variety of matters.[2] The Talmud makes clear, moreover, that the term *b'nei ha-ir* (the residents of a community) applies not only to the local citizenry but also to the members of specific commercial or trade group. Thus we read in a related passage that the butchers of a certain town adopted a rule that prohibited any one of them from doing business on a day that had been reserved for another.[3] Workers in other trades possess similar powers.[4] Medieval halachah, indeed, recognized that "any group whose members share a common economic interest" is endowed with the power of the b'nei ha-ir to legislate concerning wages, competition, and working conditions.[5] The regulations adopted by these groups are binding upon their members in much the same way as the laws adopted by the b'nei ha-ir are binding upon all the residents of the community.[6] This position was affirmed by leading twentieth-century poskim, who rule that the halachah permits workers to organize in support of their economic interests.[7]

Some authorities go farther. In their view, Jewish law does not merely permit workers to form unions; it positively encourages them to do so. In the words of R. Avraham Yitzchak HaKohein Kook, unionization partakes of the Torah's insistence upon justice (tzedek), righteousness (yosher), and the betterment of society (tikkun olam). The existence of nonunion labor lowers the general wage rate and leads to inferior working conditions; therefore, such labor causes financial loss to all workers.[8] R. Ben Zion Ouziel regards unionization as a matter of simple justice and common sense. If workers were forbidden to organize, the individual worker would find himself isolated and alone, left to the mercy of market caprice, forced to hire himself out at starvation wages to the detriment of himself and his family. Halachah empowers workers to unionize, because it is through the power of organization that they can achieve decent wages, secure their economic dignity, and create institutions for cultural advancement and social support.[9] Our own Central Conference of American Rabbis has taken a similar stand. Frequently during our history we have resolved to support the right of labor to organize, to bargain collectively, and to secure fair wages and humane working conditions. As early as 1921, we resolved that "under the present organization of society, labor's only safeguard against a retrogression to former inhuman standards is the union."[10] We have endorsed progressive legislation, such as the Wagner National Labor Relations Act in the United States, that guarantees workers the right to form unions.[11] We have supported the unionization of social workers serving Jewish communal agencies.[12] In particular, we have championed the cause of farm workers, urging that they be allowed to organize to secure a decent standard of living and future for their children.[13] Summarizing this long history of support for organized labor, we declared in 1985 that "Trade Unionism traditionally is important to the well-being of America as a whole, and to minorities, including the Jewish community in particular. Primarily concerned with the large working class, it is perforce one of the strongest supports and most secure foundations of our democracy.... The CCAR reiterates its traditional support of organized labor and calls upon its members to help establish local conferences of religion and labor, and to remind their congregants of the importance of a strong, effective, and responsible labor movement to the health of American society. The CCAR calls upon the constituent agencies of the Reform movement and upon the Union of American Hebrew Congregations to give consideration to the establishment of programs and projects to further these ends."[14]

The language of this resolution requires that we as Reform Jews work to put the expressed ideals of our movement into concrete practice. This, too, is but a matter of simple justice and common sense. We who have championed the cause of organized labor for so many decades can hardly exempt our own institutions from the ethical standards we would impose upon others. When our "constituent agencies" hire nonunion labor in preference to union workers, we thereby help to depress the level of wages and deal a setback to the cause for which workers organize. We cannot in good conscience do this. If we believe that unionization aids the cause of workers by raising their standard of living and allowing them a greater say in their conditions of employment—and our resolutions clearly testify to this belief—then our support for unionized labor must begin at home. The synagogue bears an ethical responsibility to hire unionized workers when they are available.

2. FAIR PRICE AND JEWISH LAW

The question we face, however, is not as simple as that. Jewish tradition considers the interests of the consumer as well as those of the worker. This consideration is expressed through the law of *onaah* (price fraud), which specifies that buyers and sellers are entitled either to compensation or to annul a sale when the amount paid diverges more than a specified amount from the fair market price for the object or service in question.[15] Unionized labor can be said to distort the market by forcing consumers to pay significantly more for labor than they would otherwise do. To be sure, the laws of *onaah* do not as a matter of technical halachah apply to wages paid to hired workers.[16] Still, the halachah displays a general tendency to supervise the stability of prices in the market place,[17] and it looks askance upon factors that upset this stability to the detriment of consumers. Some authorities, in fact, limit the power of trade groups to set prices and wages, since in the absence of controls these unions might cause unfair economic loss to the community.[18] Consumers, in other words, are entitled to protection against unreasonable economic demands from merchants and from workers. If such protection is not afforded them by the communal government, the consumers may boycott the providers of the goods and services, even when these pertain to religious observance, until the prices come down to appropriate levels.[19] Jewish law, in other words, recognizes that consumers have a valid interest in maintaining a reasonable level of prices for goods and services, including the cost of labor.

To this, we may add the Talmudic principle that "the Torah protects the property of Israel" (*haTorah chasah al mamonam shel Yisrael*).[20] That is, Jewish law seeks to spare us unnecessary expense in the observance of mitzvot. This principle motivates *poskim* toward finding leniencies in the law when a more stringent conclusion would involve significant financial loss.[21] It should be noted that this principle is not absolute. It is balanced by the counter-principle "there is no poverty in a place of wealth" (*ein aniyut b'mekom ashirut*): that is, price should be no object when it comes to the Torah and to determining the proper observance.[22] Various authorities over the centuries have sought to resolve the apparent conflict between these two principles.[23] At any rate, the fact that our tradition will at times take financial loss into account in assessing the precise level of religious duty suggests that we should be careful before demanding that a congregation incur a large expense when alternatives are available.

3. *TZEDAKAH*: THE DEMANDS OF SOCIAL JUSTICE

How then shall we attempt to reconcile the conflict between these two values, the one favoring unionization, the other protecting the consumer? The answer, it seems to us, rests with the demand of our Torah and our tradition that we do *tzedakah*. This word, usually associated with "charity," is better translated according to its Hebrew root as "social justice." As justice, *tzedakah* is obligatory conduct, not a voluntary contribution; thus, the court can require an individual to contribute an amount that the court has determined is proper for that person.[24] To put this more bluntly, *tzedakah* is expensive. It is the nature of *tzedakah* that it costs money. If we want to work for social justice, we have to be prepared to invest of our time and our substance. And while there are limits to the amount that can be demanded of any person,[25] no Jew—and, we would add, no Jewish institution—can escape the duty of *tzedakah* on the grounds that it involves financial expense.

With this in mind, we can put our conflicting values into perspective. First, let us consider the concept of *onaah*. We noted above that a transaction may be canceled when its price exceeds by a specified amount the "fair market value" of the product in question. On this basis, we might conclude that if the cost of hiring organized labor significantly exceeds the cost of engaging nonunion workers, the "union price" is an example of *onaah* and we have no ethical obligation to pay our workers at that rate. We reject this conclusion. If, as we believe and as we have resolved on numerous occasions, unionization is an indispensable means of securing justice for workers in our society, then our dedication to *tzedakah* requires that we not set the "fair market value" of labor according to the wage level for nonunion workers. On the contrary: it is the nonunion wage rate that qualifies for the label *onaah*, for that rate depresses the market, lowering the wages and the standard of living that workers would otherwise achieve. Justice rather demands that we measure the "fair market price" for labor according to the accepted cost for *union* labor in a particular locale. In would be unjust and injurious to all workers were we to set the standard for "fair wages" according to lower, nonunion scale.

Similarly, the demand to do *tzedakah* modifies our understanding and application of the principle "the Torah protects the property of Israel." All that principle means is that financial considerations *may* be relevant in determining how we are to perform a mitzvah. It does not mean that we are exempt from performing the mitzvah merely because it is expensive.[26] Again, once we determine that nonunion labor frustrates the mitzvah of social justice, it becomes clear that our own value commitments require that our institutions show a decided preference for hiring union labor.

We acknowledge the existence of other visions of *tzedakah* than the one we have sketched here. We are aware that some will argue that nonunion labor in fact serves the cause of "social justice" for all by reducing the overall cost of goods and services and that lower wages mean that more jobs will be available for unemployed workers. We will not contest these issues here. Suffice it to say that a general concept such as "social justice" can be meaningless in the absence of some substantive vision that gives it content. Our particular vision of social justice, the understanding of that term that makes the most sense to us, is the vision put forth by the CCAR and by the prominent *poskim* whose words we have cited. It involves the empowerment of workers to control their destiny and to achieve goals (higher wages and benefits, better working conditions, a more secure future for workers and their families) that all of us want for ourselves and our children. This is the vision of "social justice" that the Reform Movement has proclaimed for many years. If we believe what we preach, it is our duty to practice the same.

In short, although Jewish tradition does recognize the legitimate interests of consumers, it does not teach us that consumers are always entitled to the lowest possible price for goods and services. Rather, it teaches that the interests of all of us are best served when we work together to build a just society. Our synagogues are indeed consumers of goods and services, but in their buying and selling, they ought to remember the higher purposes for which synagogues are established in the first place.

CONCLUSION

In the final analysis, we cannot tell your congregation what it "must" do. It is easy for us, who do not have to raise the three hundred thousand dollars of which you speak, to tell you that you must incur that expense. We recognize, too, that your decision must be based upon local factors of which we are unaware. For example, it is sometimes the case that labor unions act in an unfair (to say nothing of an illegal) manner. Like all institutions, they can be corrupt, rapacious, or discriminatory. There are times, in other words, when cooperation with a labor union may *not* serve the public interest and the cause of *tzedakah*. All we can tell you is that, *in general*, Jewish tradition and our Reform Jewish interpretation of that tradition perceive unionization as an indispensable tool in the long struggle for social justice and the rights of workers. For that reason, your congregation should make every effort to hire union labor for your construction project.

NOTES

1. BT *Bava Batra* 8b and Rashi ad loc.

2. *Yad, M'chirah* 14:9; SA, CM 231:27. On the subject of *takanot hakahal*, see *Reform Responsa for the Twenty-first Century*, no. 5758.1, vol. 1, pp. 311–18, at notes 4–7.

3. BT *Bava Batra* 9a.

4. *Tosefta, Bava M'tzia* 11:12.

5. R. Sh'lomo b. Adret, *Resp. Rashba* 4:185 (*sh'kol chaburah sh'hem benei inyan echad harei hem ke-ir bifnei atzmah*...). R. Asher b. Yechiel, *Hil. HaRosh, Bava Batra* 1:33,

writes that "craftsmen" (*baalei omanut*) are empowered to set the regulations governing their trade, as does R. Yitzchak b. Sheshet, *Resp. Rivash*, no. 399. The law is codified in *SA, CM* 231:28.

6. One difference between laws adopted by the citizenry as a whole and laws adopted by professional groups is that the latter are considered binding upon the group's members only if they meet with the approval of an *adam chashuv*, a "distinguished public figure" (BT *Bava Batra* 9a). The definition of this term, which in that Talmudic passage is applied to the *Amora* Rava, is the subject of some controversy. Some require that this person be a Torah scholar who serves as a leader in the local government (*parnas al hatzibur*; R. Yosef ibn Migash and R. Yonatan HaKohein of Lunel, cited in *Shitah Mekubetzet, Bava Batra* 9a; R. Menachem HaMeiri, *Beit HaB'chirah, Bava Batra* 8b; *Magid Mishneh, Hil. M'chirah* 14:11; *SA, CM* 231:28). Others do not require that this communal leader be a Torah scholar (*Resp. Rashba* 4:185). On the other hand, where there is no *adam chashuv* in place, the professional group may adopt whatever rules it sees fit and enforce them on its members. And at least one authority holds that the consent of the *adam chashuv* is required only to approve measures taken by the association that involve fines and penalties against its members; all other rules, including the setting of wages and salaries, may be adopted without such approval (R. Moshe Feinstein, *Resp. Ig'rot Moshe, CM* 1:58). In our own legal environment, of course, the secular authorities, who regulate union-management relations through legislation, fulfill this function.

7. Among these *poskim* are R. Avraham Yitzchak HaKohein Kook, *N'tivah*, 11 Nisan 1933; R. Ben Zion Ouziel, *Resp. Piskei Ouziel B'she'elot Hazeman*, no. 46 ("It is beyond all dispute that our Sages recognize the rules adopted by unions of craftsmen or laborers and by professional organizations"), and R. Moshe Feinstein, *Resp. Ig'rot Moshe, CM* 1:58 ("There is no basis in halachah for outlawing the formation of labor unions"). R. Eliezer Y'hudah Waldenberg, *Resp. Tzitz Eliezer* 2:23, permits the formation and functioning of unions on the basis of local custom (*minhag ham'dinah*): laws governing labor-management relations are matters of communal authority, and the community is entitled through legislation to recognize labor unionization. See also R. Katriel P. Tekhursh, *Keter Efraim*, no. 19, and R. Chaim David Halevy, *Aseh L'cha Rav*, 2:64.

8. See note 7.

9. See note 7.

10. *CCAR Yearbook* (CCARY) 31 (1921): 44.

11. *CCARY* 45 (1935): 79; *CCARY* 50 (1940): 104, 105.

12. *CCARY* 46 (1936): 78.

13. *CCARY* 83 (1973): 109; *CCARY* 86 (1976): 68; *CCARY* 89 (1979): 102.

14. *CCARY* 95 (1985): 239–40.

15. See *M. Bava M'tzia* 4:3–7; *Yad, M'chirah* 12; and *SA, CM* 427. The amount of divergence is set at one-sixth of the accepted market price for the object or service. If the price charged exceeds the market price by one-sixth, the buyer is entitled to a refund of the overcharge; similarly, if the price falls below the market price by one-sixth, the seller is entitled to compensation in that amount. Should the price charged diverge by *more* than one-sixth of the market price, the sale may be invalidated entirely.

16. *SA, CM* 227:33 (and see 227:29), derived from *M. Bava M'tzia* 4:9.

17. BT *Bava Batra* 89a; *Yad, G'neivah* 8:20 and *M'chirah* 14:1; *SA, CM* 231:2.

18. R. Menachem HaMeiri, *Beit HaB'chirah, Bava Batra* 9a; R. Yom Tov ben Ishbili, *Chidushei HaRitva, Bava Batra* 9a; R. Nissim Gerondi, *Chidushei HaRan, Bava Batra* 9a. The "controls" spoken of here refer to the concept of *adam chashuv* (see note 6). The "distinguished public figure" functions as an arbiter between the conflicting economic demands of labor and management or of merchants and consumers. A number of authorities suggest that all labor disputes must be submitted to the approval of the *adam chashuv*, in the form of a rabbinical *beit din* or a specially appointed court of arbitration, provided that such an agency exists within the community. These include R. Ben Zion Ouziel (see note 7), R. Chaim David Halevy (see note 7); R. Shaul Yisraeli, *Amudim*, Nisan 5726 (1966), 223; and R. Sh'lomo Daichovsky, *HaTtzofeh*, 9 Tevet 5733 (1973), 3.

19. See *M. K'ritot* 1:7. R. Menachem Mendel Krochmal (seventeenth century; *Resp. Tzemach Tzedek*, no. 28) cites that mishnah in permitting a consumer boycott against local fishmongers.

20. BT *Chulin* 49b and parallels. Rashi ad loc., s.v. *hatorah chasah*, links the principle to the *Sifra* on Lev. 14:36. See also *M. N'gaim* 12:5.

21. For example, R. David Zvi Hoffmann (*Resp. Melamed Leho'il* 1:91) permits a Jew who owns stock in a restaurant to retain ownership of his shares, even though the restaurant remains open during Pesach and the Jewish stockholder therefore will profit from the sale of *chameitz*. He seeks a lenient answer, in part, "because the Torah protects the property of Israel."

22. See BT *M'nachot* 89a and parallels.

23. The most comprehensive summary of these discussions is R. Chaim Chizkiah Medini's nineteenth-century *S'dei Chemed*, 1:128, p. 44. Among other passages, he cites R. Moshe Sh'lomo ibn Habib's seventeenth-century work *Sh'mot BaAretz* (section *yom t'ruah*, on BT *Rosh HaShanah* 27a). There, we read that the halachah does *not* determine in advance the conditions under which either principle must apply. That decision is rather left to the discretion of the sages in every generation.

24. BT *K'tubot* 49a; *Yad, Matanot Aniyim* 7:10; *SA, YD* 248:1.

25. See *SA, YD* 249:1–2 for the ideal and practical levels of giving.

26. The responsum cited in note 21 is not an argument against this point. While R. Hoffmann explained the search for a lenient answer on the grounds that *haTorah chasah al mamonam shel Yisrael*, that principle did not in and of itself justify the answer. The particular halachic question there was whether a stockholder in a corporation can be said to "own" its *chameitz* and therefore be found in violation of the Torah during Pesach. Hoffmann argues that the owning of stock in a company does not constitute "ownership" in that sense. If, on the other hand, he had concluded that stock shares do constitute "ownership," he would have required that the stockholders sell those shares despite the financial loss incurred.

Sh'eilah

For many years, our congregation has rung the bell for the Salvation Army on December 24. The money raised from this effort goes to support their outreach ministries. This past year, the Salvation Army agreed to offer benefits to domestic partners and then, after much pressure, rescinded this position. A member of our community has asked whether we should continue to support the Salvation Army in this effort, given the position of Reform Judaism toward benefits for domestic partners. (Rabbi Bruce Kadden, Salinas, California)

T'shuvah

The action that your member suggests is akin to an economic boycott, the decision by a community to refrain from doing business with a particular merchant or group of merchants in order to pressure them into meeting the community's demands. Jewish tradition permits economic boycotts for just cause. One famous example is found in a responsum of R. Menachem Mendel Krochmal (seventeenth-century Moravia).[1] In that case, the fishmongers of a certain town, who knew that the local Jews bought fish every week to serve at their Sabbath meals, had raised their prices to an unreasonable level. The Jewish residents adopted an ordinance (*takanat hakahal*)[2] to the effect that "no person shall buy fish for two months." The issue before Rabbi Krochmal was this: given that by long-standing custom (*minhag*) the Jews served fish "for the honor of the Sabbath" (*l'chvod Shabbat*), did their boycott transgress against the obligations to honor and to delight in the seventh day?[3] Rejecting these concerns, he permitted the boycott by way of an analogy to *M. K'ritot* 1:7, which recounts that Rabban Shimon b. Gamliel introduced a leniency into the halachah in order to lower the unconscionable prices that merchants were charging for sacrificial animals. Rabbi Krochmal reasons as follows: if the quest for economic justice permitted Rabban Shimon b. Gamliel to depart from the accepted understanding of a matter of Torah law (*davar d'oraita*),[4] the same end surely permits Jews to refrain from buying fish, especially since there are other ways for Jews to render honor to the Sabbath. If so, your congregation is just as surely permitted to engage in a boycott in this case. The Central Conference of American Rabbis has resolved that same-sex couples ought to "share fully and equally in the rights of civil marriage"[5]; this means that, for us, it is a matter of economic justice that businesses and organizations offer domestic partner benefits to their employees. So long as your congregation can find other ways to assist the poor and the hungry who would otherwise benefit from your participation in the December 24th project, it has every right to boycott the Salvation Army in the name of social justice.

We as the Responsa Committee, however, cannot say whether your congregation *ought* to take this step. The decision to undertake an economic boycott is a matter of social policy rather than principle. A principle is a concept to which we are devoted because it is the right and proper thing to do. Economic justice for same-sex couples is such a principle. A policy, on the other hand, is a tool that a community might—or might not—use to achieve its principles. A policy decision must be evaluated by its effectiveness as a means toward reaching a desired end. Such an evaluation may, in some cases, dissuade us from pursuing a policy that we might otherwise think is a good idea. For example, it is possible that an economic boycott will backfire. Boycotts are sometimes said to cause a degree of harm to the employees of the targeted businesses that outweighs the good they might accomplish. In this instance, you might decide that your refusal to participate in the Salvation Army drive will have negative results—a loss of funds for the poor and hungry of your city, the creation of an unacceptable degree of community strife—that would convince you to seek other, less harmful means by which to accomplish your goal. On the other hand, you might decide that since there are other ways to help feed the hungry and to house the homeless, there is no overriding need for you to join forces with the Salvation Army in particular. And it may be that the positive statement this decision would make on behalf of the rights of domestic partners would more than balance any negative effects it might have.

Your decision, therefore, is one of policy: which choice is the most effective and least counterproductive means of achieving the goal of economic and social justice in your community? The Responsa Committee, precisely because we are neither empowered nor specifically qualified to answer questions of policy, cannot advise you as to which choice to make. Our task is to issue decisions based upon principle, upon the interpretation and application of the Jewish legal tradition to the question at hand. As we understand it, Jewish tradition *permits* us to undertake boycotts in pursuit of social justice, but it does not *require* that we do so if we determine that a boycott would be ineffective or otherwise disadvantageous. The decision ultimately requires a careful judgment of all the facts that apply to this particular case. That judgment must be left to the discretion of your congregation.

Our answer would be different were the CCAR to adopt a formal resolution calling upon our congregations to boycott organizations that do not offer domestic partner benefits to their employees. In that case, we would be dealing with a question of "law," a *takanah* adopted by our Conference. Yet while the Conference has endorsed such benefits, it has not to this point advocated boycotts of groups such as the Salvation Army that do not provide them.[6] Boycotts and similar actions remain matters of policy, undertaken at the discretion of our members when they believe that such tools are effective means for achieving our principles and larger goals.

CONCLUSION

Your congregation is perfectly entitled to discontinue its support of the Salvation Army because of that organization's refusal to award domestic partner benefits to its employees. It is not, however, required to do so. The decision rests squarely with the congregation. So long as our Conference has not formulated a stance on this particular issue, neither Jewish law nor Reform Jewish principle dictates your answer. It is therefore not the place or function of this Committee to tell you what it should be.

NOTES

1. *Resp. Tzemach Tzedek*, no. 28.

2. On the subject of *takanot hakahal* as a source of Jewish law, see the discussion in section 1 of *Reform Responsa for the Twenty-first Century*, no. 5758.1, vol. 1, pp. 311–18.

3. On the duties of "honoring the Sabbath" (*k'vod Shabbat*) and "delighting in the Sabbath" (*oneg Shabbat*) see *Yad, Shabbat* 29:1 and 30:1ff., as well as Mark Washofsky, *Jewish Living* (New York: UAHC Press, 2001), 73–74 and 377.

4. There is another interpretation of Rabban Shimon's action: namely, that insistence upon the preexisting strict standard of the law, precisely because it led to higher prices, would cause individuals to violate the law at its most basic level. See Rashi, BT *K'ritot* 8a, s.v. *nichnas l'veit din*. Thus, "economic justice" is not necessarily the root cause of Rabban Shimon's decision. Nonetheless, the plain sense of the mishnah does seem to support the economic justice interpretation. R. Krochmal, too, sees the desire to lower unreasonable prices as the motivating factor in that decision.

5. Resolution "On Gay and Lesbian Marriage," adopted by the 107th Annual Convention of the Central Conference of American Rabbis, March 1996 (http://data .ccarnet.org/cgi-bin/resodisp.pl?file=gl&year=1996).

6. See ibid. This element distinguishes the present *sh'eilah* from the question we consider in our responsum no. 5761.4, "The Synagogue and Organized Labor" (*Reform Responsa for the Twenty-first Century*, vol. 2, pp. 345–54). There, we rule that a synagogue ought to hire union workers rather than nonunion workers for its construction job. Given the CCAR's frequent endorsement of organized labor over the years, it seemed to us that this was a matter of "law" as well as "policy": it would be hypocritical for a Reform synagogue not to strive to award the job to unionized workers. Even there, however, we wrote that the congregation needs to make these decisions in full awareness of its own local situation and its own economic condition. Thus, while we tried to offer some general guidance, based upon Jewish and Reform Jewish tradition, we did not feel entirely comfortable with requiring of the congregation a specific decision in a concrete case.

Inheritance: How Much to Leave to a Child?

5765.10

Sh'eilah

I received a call from a temple member who is rewriting his will and would like some guidance from Jewish tradition regarding disposition of his assets upon his death. He has two children and three grandchildren and is concerned about leaving so much to them that they might not lead productive lives. He seeks some kind of formula on how his wealth should be divided between charitable bequests and gifts to his family. His philanthropy occupies an ever-increasing amount of his semi-retirement time. (Rabbi Stephen S. Pearce, San Francisco, California)

T'shuvah

For a comprehensive treatment of the Jewish law of inheritance, as well as for a consideration of a question quite similar to the one you ask, we refer you and your congregant to a *t'shuvah* of our colleague and teacher R. Walter Jacob.[1] The issue dealt with the distribution of the estate: may the normal order of inheritance be "rearranged from the standard recommendation and favor one child over another," to compensate for that child's "bad luck" or inability to take care of him- or herself? Unfortunately, as Rabbi Jacob notes, "in the lengthy discussions of wills and estates, which took place in traditional literature, there is little which deals with the question which you have asked." The same might be said for the present *sh'eilah*. The tradition offers no specific formula of the kind that your congregant seeks. Still, it offers guidance as to how a parent should think about these issues, and from that guidance we might be able to formulate a general approach, if not a specific formula. We therefore turn to a consideration of those aspects of the Jewish law of inheritance relevant to your question. Once again, a fuller analysis may be found in Rabbi Jacob's *t'shuvah*. This responsum relies upon many of the sources he cites and accordingly should be read as a supplement to his work.

Your congregant seeks to rewrite his will so as to limit the amount of
his estate that he leaves to his children and grandchildren. The difficulty
with this course of action, from a traditional Jewish perspective, is that
the Torah sets forth the order of inheritance in strict and specific fashion.
Property is inherited by sons, not by daughters (unless there are no sons);
the firstborn son receives a double portion of the estate; and so forth.
No "will" is valid at Jewish law that deviates from the Torah's order of
testamentary succession.[2] In fact, Jewish law does not recognize a "will"
per se, since the "last will and testament" familiar in our contemporary
legal systems takes effect only upon the death of the testator (i.e., the one
who issues the will), and according to the Jewish legal tradition a gift
made after the death of the donor is invalid (*ein sh'tar l'achar mitah*).[3]

None of this means that an individual is powerless to affect the ultimate
distribution of his property. He may do so in any way he wishes,
provided that he does it in the form of a gift executed while he is still
alive. The gift may be made while he is perfectly well (*matanat bari*)
or when he is on his (presumed) deathbed (*matanat sh'chiv m'ra*). In
some cases, the Rabbis encouraged a father to make such gifts as a
means of rectifying the perceived inequities of the inheritance laws.[4] In
theory, then, so long as he executes valid acts of gift prior to his death,
therefore, a father can create his own order of "inheritance," transferring
his estate to anyone he wishes.

Does this mean that a father may effectively disinherit one or more
of his children under Jewish law? Not exactly. Although he is legally
empowered to make gifts prior to his death, "the Sages are displeased"
with the one who "gives his property to others and leaves his children
with nothing," even if his children are not of good character.[5] The
reason given for this is that, even if one's child does not act properly,
how does one know that the child's son will not be worthy?[6] One should
therefore leave intact the Torah's order of succession rather than try to
influence one's children's behavior from beyond the grave. True, one
authority suggests that "the Sages" would not be "displeased" with such
a gift so long as the donor reserves a symbolic (if small) amount for his

legal heirs.[7] Others, however, approve of this device only when the donor has no children and would be inherited by other relatives; if he has children, they insist, the principal part of his estate (*ikar iz'vono*) must go to them.[8] It follows that, while Jewish law enables parents to transfer their estate away from their children, it prefers that they not do so.

The tradition also teaches that it may be unwise for parents to attempt to control the behavior of their adult children. The Talmud, for example, forbids a father from exerting physical discipline upon his adult son, on the grounds of the commandment "Do not place a stumbling block before the blind" (Lev. 19:14): that is, the discipline might cause the son to lash out in resentment or to bear a grudge against his father and thereby violate the commandment "Honor your father and your mother."[9] There is a time, in other words, when overt acts of discipline or "education" toward our children become inappropriate and counterproductive. While it is understandable, therefore, that this parent wishes to influence his children in a positive direction, Jewish tradition would counsel him (and all of us) to seek a proper balance between actions that express legitimate parental concerns and those that, however well-intentioned, would be perceived as intrusive or punitive.

Let us now consider our *sh'eilah* in light of both our Jewish tradition and the particular perspective that we Reform Jews bring to bear upon it. What sort of guidance does it offer our *sho-eil*? First, we would note that as Reform Judaism insists upon gender equality in matters of religious or legal obligation, it makes no difference whether the testator is a father or a mother, and it is irrelevant whether the heir is a son or a daughter. The rules of inheritance ought to be the same in either case. Second, we see nothing objectionable in the tradition's strong preference that the children receive "the principal part" of the estate. At the same time, we think that parents on occasion may have a legitimate interest in determining that their estates are distributed in a manner other than that specified in the classical Jewish order of inheritance. The power to disburse the estate through gifts made prior to death can be an effective means of performing acts of *tzedakah* and social justice, and it is a tool through which unfortunate consequences might be avoided. Third, although we agree that parents should not distribute their estate in a way that the children will see as "punitive," there is no reason why they cannot set reasonable, nonpunitive terms to govern the estate's distribution. We suspect, in other words, that "the Sages" would not be "displeased" if a parent sought to establish reasonable controls upon the distribution of the estate to adult children who, in her considered judgment, would use it to negative ends. For example, while the tradition offers your congregant no "formula" of the kind he seeks, it would permit him to stipulate that the inheritance be distributed in stages. He might establish a trust fund that would ensure his children and grandchildren receive a certain level of income even though they are not permitted to access the principal. He might also stipulate the purposes for which funds may be withdrawn from the trust: to pay tuition and other educational expenses, to assist the children and grandchildren in entering business or professional life, to make donations to *tzedakah*, and so forth. Given that these purposes allow either the father or his heirs to perform mitzvot, such stipulations do not in our opinion qualify as punitive in nature. They serve rather as proper expressions of a parent's wish that his children and grandchildren might leave, as our *sh'eilah* puts it, "productive lives."

The children and grandchildren, of course, might disagree with this assessment and regard restrictions of this type as "punitive" indeed. For this reason, among others, it is obviously the better course for your congregant and his heirs to resolve their differences while he is still alive. Surely both sides would wish to avoid the unpleasantness that all too often erupts among families over provisions in a deceased person's will. If, however, such a resolution proves impossible to achieve, your congregant is entitled according to the letter and spirit of Jewish tradition to dispose of his estate along the lines that we have suggested.

NOTES

1. *Questions and Reform Jewish Answers* (*New American Reform Responsa*), no. 239.

2. The father may, however, direct his entire estate to one legitimate heir among the others; M. *Bava Batra* 8:5; *Yad, Nachalot* 6:2; *SA, CM* 281:1. This is the case only when he is *sh'chiv m'ra*; see below.

3. See BT *Bava Batra* 135b; *Yad, Z'chiyah Umatanah* 8:12; *SA, CM* 250:18.

4. One famous example of this is the *k'tubat banin dichrin* (M. *K'tubot* 4:10), an obligation that the Rabbis imposed upon the groom at the time of marriage. The groom was to stipulate that upon his death his wife's sons would inherit the entire value of their mother's *ketubah*; they would not be required to share that sum with sons that their father may have had by other wives. The purpose of this obligation was to encourage the bride's father to make a gift of property to her prior to marriage ("that he would transfer property to her as he would do to his son"), which he would be more likely to do if he knew in advance that the property she brought into the marriage would be passed down through her (and her father's) family line (BT *K'tubot* 52b). The practical effect of this was to ensure that the daughter "inherited" a fair share of the father's estate, though this was done as a gift rather than as a formal inheritance.

5. M. *Bava Batra* 8:5; BT *Bava Batra* 133b; *Yad, Nachalot* 6:11; *SA, CM* 282:1; *Resp. Maharashdam* (fifteenth-century Salonika), *CM*, no. 311.

6. BT *K'tubot* 53a; *Beit Yosef* to *Tur, CM* 282; *Sefer Mei-irat Einayim* to SA, *CM* 282.

7. R. Shimon ben Tzemach Duran (fifteenth-century Algiers), *Resp. Tashbetz* 3:147.

8. *Resp. Chatam Sofer, CM*, no. 151; *Aruch HaShulchan, CM* 282:3.

9. BT *Mo-eid Katan* 17a and *Yad, Mamrim* 6:9. In general, the commandment "You shall not place a stumbling block before the blind" is understood to forbid us from leading another person into sin unwittingly; see BT *P'sachim* 22b.

Preventive War
5762.8

Sh'eilah

Does our tradition countenance preemptive military action when there is suspicion, but no prima facie evidence exists, that a perceived enemy will attack? My question presupposes that innocent lives will be lost in the event of such action. I would also note that Israel engaged in such an action when it bombed the Iraqi Osirak nuclear facilities in 1981. (Rabbi Benno M. Wallach, Houston, Texas)

Teshuvah

We received this *sh'eilah* and composed our answer during a time of fierce national debate in the United States over the wisdom of initiating a war against Iraq. The goal of such a war would be to depose Saddam Hussein, the ruler of that country. The stated justification for this war is that Saddam Hussein's regime either possesses or is in the process of developing nuclear, chemical, and/or biological weapons of mass destruction, that it poses a threat to its neighbors, and that it someday may come to endanger the security of the United States itself. At the moment, as our *sho-eil* suggests, there is no prima facie evidence that Iraq is actively contemplating or planning a military attack upon any of its neighbors, much less the United States.

We should note that the question does not ask for our opinion as to the advisability of a military strike against Iraq. That is understandable, for we rabbis hardly qualify as experts in diplomacy and defense policy. We have been asked rather to discuss the teachings of Jewish tradition on the general (and hence more abstract) question of the permissibility of initiating a war under these circumstances. While rabbis are professionally competent to address that subject, it poses some serious difficulties of its own. Although Jewish tradition has much to say about the conduct of war, our sacred texts tend to speak to the political context of the ancient Jewish commonwealth (*malchut Yisrael*) under the leadership of a Davidic monarch. It is instructive that Maimonides in his *Mishneh Torah* codifies the Talmudic discussions of the rules of war under the heading *Hilchot M'lachim Umilchemoteihem*, "The Laws of Kings and Their Wars," and that the very first law he mentions is the biblical commandment "to appoint a king over Israel."[1] We could conclude that the traditional Jewish law of government and war bears no relevance at all to our question, which deals with a non-Jewish government that is not ruled by a king, Davidic or otherwise. We do not, however, draw that conclusion. We believe in a *Torat chayim*, a living Torah. Though the literary sources of our tradition were written long ago in a very different time and place, we affirm that these texts, through proper and prayerful interpretation, address us as well, yielding teachings that have direct bearing upon our own day and our own lives. It is in this spirit that the ancient Jewish law of government and war has been applied to the contemporary context of the State of Israel.[2] It is in this spirit as well that we Reform Jews have historically looked to the Bible and our other sacred texts for guidance in responding to the pressing social issues that face us today.

Let us consider, then, what our tradition has to say about the waging of a preventive war, one that is not fought in an immediate situation of national self-defense. Let us ask whether the lessons it teaches have a substantial application to situations such as that faced, at this writing, by the United States in its dealings with Iraq.

1. COMMANDED AND DISCRETIONARY WARS

According to Maimonides,[3] the king of Israel is permitted to fight two distinct kinds of war. The first category is "commanded war" (*milchemet mitzvah*), which includes war against the seven Canaanite nations, war against Amalek, and wars fought "to assist the Jews against enemies who have attacked them." Only when he has completed these military tasks is he permitted to engage in "discretionary war" (*milchemet har'shut*), a war he fights "against other nations to expand Israel's borders and to enhance his greatness and reputation."[4] These wars differ from each other not only in their strategic purpose but also with respect to the rules that govern them. First, the king must consult with and receive the approval of the Sanhedrin before fighting a discretionary war; no such confirmation is required for a *milchemet mitzvah*, which the king "wages on his own initiative."[5] In addition, soldiers who participate in a *milchemet mitzvah* are exempt from the obligation to perform any positive commandment that may interfere with their military responsibilities; those fighting in a *milchemet har'shut* enjoy no such exemption.[6] Finally, an individual might avoid service in a discretionary war if he qualifies for one of the exemptions mentioned in Deut. 20:5–8 (one who has built a new home but has not yet lived in it; one who has planted a vineyard but has not yet redeemed it for his own use;[7] one who has betrothed a woman but has not yet consummated the marriage; one who is excessively fearful of battle). In the case of a commanded war, however, these exemptions do not apply; rather, all must go out to fight in a *milchemet mitzvah*, "even the groom from his chamber and the bride from her *chuppah*."[8]

Many of these laws and teachings do not apply to our day and time. The seven Canaanite nations no longer exist,[9] and Amalek is today a homiletical device, a symbol of irrational hatred and evil rather than the name of an actual people. Yet the third kind of "commanded war"—the war "to assist the Jews against enemies who have attacked them"—sadly retains its relevance, reminding us that threats against our national existence continue to plague us. It also teaches us that our tradition rejects pacifism as a policy of national defense. The Torah does not expect us to submit to armed aggression, to stand silently and passively when others seek to conquer and dominate us. The people of Israel have the right to defend themselves from attack. Indeed, we are commanded to do so: the obligation to defend and preserve our lives overrides virtually every other religious duty.[10] Though the word *mitzvah* has a particularly Jewish connotation, there is no reason to believe that the Jews are the only people that is entitled to self-defense. Every nation must possess the right to take up arms if necessary to protect itself and its citizens against military attack.

2. DISCRETIONARY WAR IN OUR TIME

Discretionary war, too, is still with us, for states continue to fight wars in order to expand their borders and their power, "to increase their greatness and reputation." Given that Jewish law, as we have seen, permits the state to fight discretionary wars, we might draw the conclusion that it is morally justifiable for governments to wage such wars in our own day and time. We believe that this conclusion is erroneous, for two principal reasons.

First, although the Torah allows the king to engage in war for reasons other than national defense, it most certainly does not advocate that he do so. Indeed, the opposite is the case. Jewish law offers but grudging approval of the state's military regime,[11] and it places significant roadblocks in the path of the king who wishes to embark upon a discretionary war. Consider, for example, that he must obtain the permission of the Sanhedrin before initiating such a conflict. This requires him to appear before a prestigious legislative-judicial institution to make a compelling case for his war, and it raises the possibility that this case will fail to persuade. Consider, moreover, the exemptions from military service that are granted in a discretionary war. This means that the king must fight his war with a significantly reduced army, forcing him to think again about the advisability of initiating the conflict. These regulations, which make it much less likely that the king will engage in war unless it is absolutely necessary to do so, act as a significant brake upon his militaristic impulses.[12]

Second, although the Torah permits the state to resort to arms, it does not glorify war. Again, the opposite is the case. Peace, and not war, is our primary aspiration; we are commanded to seek peace and pursue it (Psalm 34:15). Our tradition teaches us that shalom, "peace," is the name of God and the name of the Messiah.[13] It informs us that God does not rejoice at the downfall of the wicked; therefore, the angels were forbidden to join in the song that celebrates Israel's deliverance from the Egyptians.[14] It reminds us that war's weapons are incompatible with the Temple and the worship of God.[15] Our biblical history recounts that King David, whose military career offers us the very paradigm for "discretionary war,"[16] was not permitted to build the Temple because "you have shed much blood and fought great battles; you shall not build a House for My name for you have shed much blood on the earth in my sight" (I Chron. 22:8).[17] To put this another way, David's aggressive nature was incompatible with the teaching that "one who saves a single human life has saved an entire world."[18] In its abhorrence of bloodshed, the Torah instructs that before undertaking any war, commanded or discretionary, we must reach out to our foes and offer them peace.[19] All this, we are taught, is because the blessing of peace is equal to all other blessings combined.[20]

From the Torah's exaltation of peace as a predominant social value and from the strict limitations it places upon the conduct of *milchemet har'shut*, we learn a somber lesson: war is at best a necessary evil, "necessary" perhaps but "evil" all the same. This lesson in turn leads us to conclude that the Torah's permit for the king to engage in war "to increase his greatness and reputation" is a political justification of such a policy but not a *moral* justification of it. This concession to the *realpolitik* of the ancient Near East cannot blind us to the reality of war as it is fought today, to the horrific price it exacts of soldiers and noncombatants alike, and to the prospect of massive and unfathomable destruction that its armaments have placed in our hands.[21] If the Torah's teaching of peace means anything to us, in the context of our time, it means that such is too high a price to pay for the enhancement of a state's material interests.[22] On the contrary: we are morally justified in waging war only when war is absolutely necessary and unavoidable. A war fought *today* for anything other than defensive purposes must therefore be viewed as an *un*necessary evil, as a transgression of the message of the Torah, and as a repudiation of our most cherished values and commitments.

3. PREVENTIVE WAR

On the other hand, so long as it has made every sincere effort to reach a peaceful solution, a nation has every moral justification to take up arms for defensive purposes. We do not restrict "defensive purposes" to the nation's own defense. Governments may enter into mutual security pacts in which each pledges to come to the aid of the other if attacked. And at times—though all too infrequently—major powers go to war to protect smaller countries or helpless populations under attack from aggressor governments. Such wars are quite reasonably understood as wars fought for "defensive purposes" and are therefore morally justifiable.[23] A war undertaken in response to a direct attack by an enemy power is undoubtedly a "commanded" war. At issue here is whether a preventive war is included in this category. We want to distinguish between *preventive* war and a *preemptive* military strike, such as that initiated by Israel in 1967. A preemptive strike, as we use the term, is one launched against an enemy that has mobilized or is engaged in obvious and active preparation for war. As our *sho-eil* would put it, there is clear prima facie evidence that the enemy is planning to attack. Given this state of affairs, national security is definitely threatened, and it serves no moral purpose for the nation to wait for the enemy to strike before undertaking measures of self-defense. A preemptive strike can in fact shorten the war and thus save many lives that would have been lost in a protracted conflict. Our concern is with the preventive war, initiated against a nation that may plausibly pose a threat to us in the future, even though it poses no immediate or near-term threat and is not currently planning to attack us or, for that matter, any other nation. Can we understand a war such as this as a case of *milchemet mitzvah*, a war that a nation is morally entitled to fight?

The halachic response to this question begins with *Mishnah Sotah* 8:7. Following an extensive treatment of the rules concerning the exemptions from service in warfare (Deut. 20:5–8), the text presents the following dispute:

> These exemptions apply to the case of discretionary war [*milchemet har'shut*]. In a commanded war [*milchemet mitzvah*], however, all

must go to the front, even the groom from his wedding chamber and the bride from her *chuppah*.

Rabbi Y'hudah says: these exemptions apply to the case of commanded war [*milchemet mitzvah*]. In an obligatory war [*milchemet chovah*], however, all must go to the front, even the groom from his wedding chamber and the bride from her *chuppah*.

The Talmud (BT *Sotah* 44b) offers two explanations as to the nature of this disagreement. According to Rabbi Yochanan, the dispute between the two opinions is purely a linguistic one: Rabbi Y'hudah uses the term *mitzvah* to describe what the anonymous opinion (in the Talmud's language, that of "the Sages") calls a "discretionary" war and the term *chovah* to describe what the Sages call a "commanded" war. Rava, on the other hand, sees the dispute as more substantive:

Both opinions [in the mishnah] agree that Joshua's wars of conquest were obligatory [*chovah*] and that David's wars of expansion [*r'vachah*] were discretionary [*r'shut*]. They disagree, however, over the case of a war fought to weaken the gentiles so that they will not attack. One view calls this *mitzvah*, and the other calls it *r'shut*. The difference is that, if this war is one of mitzvah, the soldier who fights in it is exempt from the obligation to perform other mitzvot.

In Rava's view, Rabbi Y'hudah adds a third, "middle" category to the classification of wars. In between the wars that we *must* fight and the wars that we *may* fight is the type of conflict that we call preventive war, an offensive launched against another nation or nations to forestall the possibility of future attack. Rabbi Y'hudah does not regard preventive war as "obligatory"; therefore, those normally exempt from military service are also exempt from serving in this war. At the same time, he does not regard preventive war as entirely "discretionary," for it might play an important role in the defense policy of the nation. In this sense, he sees preventive war as serving the purpose of mitzvah, so that those who do take part in it are exempt from the obligation to perform other mitzvot that might interfere with their military service. (This exemption is based on the rule that "one who is engaged in the performance of a mitzvah is exempt from the obligation to perform other mitzvot."[24]) The Sages, for their part, do not add a "middle" category to the classification of war. They define preventive war as a form of discretionary war, as *milchemet har'shut*; exemptions from military service apply, and those who *do* serve in the war are not exempt from the performance of other mitzvot.

Although this text is not free of difficulty,[25] it is clear that the Sages do not view preventive war as an instance of "commanded" war. Maimonides rules accordingly.[26] In this, he follows the well-known decision-making principle that the halachah is determined according to the majority position in a Talmudic dispute.[27] His ruling is also consistent with the substantive message of our tradition. The Torah, as we have seen, seeks to make it difficult for the state to wage wars that are not absolutely necessary. While a war fought in direct self-defense is clearly necessary and therefore "commanded," a war initiated against a nation that *might* attack some day does not fall into this category.[28] It is a "discretionary" war, a war that the Torah grudgingly allows the king to fight, but a war that, in the context of the history of our time, cannot be justified on moral grounds.

4. THE PRESENT SITUATION

How does all this illuminate the choices that the United States faces as it considers an offensive against Iraq? If we perceive a military strike against that nation as a case of "preventive" war, then the weight of our tradition would counsel against it. Yet it is not at all clear that this is the category we should apply in considering an attack against the Iraqi regime. Let us suppose that the arguments being made in favor of such an attack are in fact correct. Let us suppose that intelligence experts are fairly certain that Saddam Hussein's regime is building and stockpiling weapons of mass destruction. No hard evidence may exist to prove this assertion, but let us posit that the experts have good reason to believe that it is true. If this is the case, then there is also good reason to believe that this regime, which has compiled a record of aggression against other countries and against its own citizens, continues to harbor aggressive intentions. We would therefore judge Iraq to be a threat to peace and security, if not today or tomorrow then surely at some point in the realistically near future. Under these circumstances, we would be justified in viewing an attack upon Iraq as a *preemptive* war, as a strike against a real enemy engaged in the early stages of a planned military offensive, rather than as a *preventive* war against a nation that *might* one day pose a threat but that does not do so now. As we note above, a preemptive strike in the legitimate cause of self-defense more closely resembles a commanded war than a discretionary one. We deem such a strike to be morally justifiable.

We repeat: morally "justifiable," not necessarily morally *justified*. As rabbis, we are in no better position than anyone else to evaluate the military and diplomatic arguments for and against this contemplated war. Based upon what we know as we write these words, it lies beyond our competence to determine whether a strike against Iraq would fall into the category of preemptive rather than preventive war. We do not say that the war is justified but simply that it *can* be justified, that a case *can* be made that such an offensive is necessary for the defense of this nation and of others. The government has the right, and indeed the duty, to make this case. As our tradition calls upon the king to consult with the Sanhedrin before embarking upon any war other than a *milchemet mitzvah*, so it is essential that the leaders of the American government consult with the Congress and with the representatives of other governments in order to convince them that this war is clearly necessary for the defense of this nation and of others.

We concede that it may be impossible for the government to prove its case beyond a reasonable doubt. We recognize that its decision may be based largely upon intelligence reports that cannot be revealed to the public. We know that there can be honest differences of opinion over the evaluation of evidence. We also know that governments are liable to make cynical use of the rhetoric of self-defense in order to justify

wars that are in truth fought for other purposes. We cannot escape
the shadows of uncertainty when considering questions of this nature.
For example, to cite the case presented by our *sho-eil*, we may never
know with precision just how close Iraq had come to building a nuclear
bomb before Israel's air force destroyed the reactor at Osirak. All we
can say is that *if* the Iraqis were building a bomb there, then Israel was
morally justified in attacking the facility in the name of national defense.
When diplomacy fails, when our foes spurn the offer of peace that our
tradition bids us to make them, when they are clearly bent upon their
aggressive course, then the time to initiate preemptive action is sooner
rather than later.[29] Ultimately, history will judge the morality of that
action. In the meantime, we can demand that our leaders do not lie to
us; if they cannot tell us everything they know, let them make their case
as completely and as honestly as they can. Human beings assume a high
moral responsibility when they propose to lead nations into war; let
them accept that responsibility with the utmost seriousness.

CONCLUSION

Jewish tradition distinguishes between "commanded" and
"discretionary" wars; while urging us to refrain from the latter, it
permits us to engage in the former. A "commanded" war is a war fought
in the name of national defense, against an enemy who is attacking us
now or is engaged in plans to attack us in the future. While *preventive*
war, war launched against a nation that *might* some day pose a threat,
cannot be morally justified, a *preemptive* strike against a clear foe that
is presently arming itself can be a legitimate act of self-defense. If the
leader of a nation determines that a particular contemplated offensive is,
in fact, an example of a preemptive rather than a preventive strike, and
when that leader also determines that there is no way to avert the danger
through nonviolent, diplomatic means, then he or she must justify that
assessment to the public, to the deliberative bodies of that country, and
to the nations of the world. An attack may be morally justifiable, but the
government bears the responsibility to do all that it can to make the case
that it is in the right.

It also bears a heavy responsibility for its conduct of the war, no matter how justified that war may be. In the words of a former chief rabbi of the Israel Defense Forces, "Even though the mitzvah to fight wars is laid down in the Torah, we are commanded to show mercy to the enemy. Even during wartime, we are permitted to kill only in self-defense or in pursuit of legitimate military objectives. We are forbidden to harm a noncombatant population, and we are surely prohibited from striking at women and children who take no part in battle."[30] We know that civilian deaths are inevitable in war, no matter how carefully it is waged. That inevitability, however, does not exempt those who prosecute war from the task of keeping its collateral damage to the absolute minimum.

May the One who makes peace in the highest heavens grant peace to us, to all Israel, and to all the world.

NOTES

1. Deut. 17:15; *Yad, M'lachim* 1:1. By reading this verse as a mitzvah, a commandment, Rambam follows the opinion of Rabbi Yosei and Rabbi Y'hudah in BT *Sanhedrin* 20b: "Three commandments were imposed upon Israel as they entered their land: to set a king over them, to destroy Amalek, and to build the Temple." Another *baraita* in the text preserves an opposing view: "R. N'horai said, 'This passage was stated only because of the complaints of the Jews,'" i.e., the people would one day demand to be ruled by a king so that they could resemble all the other nations (I Sam. 8:5–6; see Rashi ad loc., s.v. *lo ne'emrah parashah zo*). In other words, the people were permitted, but not commanded, to appoint a king. These positions appear with some minor variations in *Tosefta, Sanhedrin* 4:2.

2. Rabbi Avraham Yitzchak Kook provides a famous example of such halachic reasoning. He suggests that, in the absence of a Davidic monarch (*melech*), the powers of the monarch (*malchut*) do not disappear but rather revert to the people of Israel. The people can thereupon bestow those powers upon any person or institution they choose; that person or institution thus exercises the full governmental authority of the king (*Resp. Mishpat Kohein* 144:14). On the basis of this insight (*chidush*), Rabbi Shaul Yisraeli develops a halachic constitutional theory that authorizes the establishment and proper functioning of a modern, sovereign Jewish state (*Resp. Amud Hayemini*, chaps. 7–9).

3. *Yad, M'lachim* 5:1.

4. See *M. Sotah* 8:7 and BT *Sotah* 44b. The Talmud, quoting Rava, offers illustrative examples of these two kinds of war: "All opinions regard Joshua's wars of conquest as *mitzvah,* and all opinions regard David's wars of expansion [*r'vachah*] as discretionary." Rambam apparently derives his illustrations of *milchemet mitzvah* directly from the biblical text, which explicitly commands Israel to wage war against the Canaanites (Deut. 7:1–2 and 20:17) and Amalek (Deut. 25:19). On the other hand, the Torah never explicitly commands us to wage war "to assist the Jews against enemies who have attacked them." R. Sh'lomo Goren, in his treatise *Meishiv Milchamah* 3:372, derives the Toraitic basis for such a war from Lev. 19:16, "Do not stand idly by the blood of your neighbor," which the Rabbinic tradition interprets as a positive duty to save the life of one who is in danger (BT *Sanhedrin* 73a).

5. *Yad, M'lachim* 5:2, from *M. Sanhedrin* 1:5 and 2:4.

6. BT *Sotah* 44b. The principle here is "one who is engaged in the performance of a mitzvah is exempt from the performance of other mitzvot" (BT *Sukkah* 25a and 26a, but the concept exists elsewhere, as with the exemption of the bridegroom from the requirement to recite the *Sh'ma* on his wedding night; see BT *B'rachot* 11a and 16a).

7. See Lev. 19:23–25.

8. *Yad, M'lachim* 7:1–4, from *M. Sotah* 8:1ff.

9. See *M. Yadayim* 4:4: Sennacherib, the king of Assyria, long ago destroyed the nations and blurred the ancient boundaries between them.

10. The rule of self-defense is derived from a number of citations in our literature. See principally BT *Yoma* 85b, where we learn that the saving of life (*pikuach nefesh*) takes precedence over the observance of Shabbat and sets aside its prohibitions. On the specific issue of defensive warfare on Shabbat, see BT *Eiruvin* 45a; *Yad, Shabbat* 2:22; and *SA, OC* 329:6–7.

11. In I Samuel 8, we read that the people demand that the prophet Samuel anoint a king "to rule over us, like all the other nations." Samuel (vv. 11ff.) informs the people of what they are truly asking, listing a number of oppressive measures, such as the creation of armies, that a king might undertake. He calls this *mishpat hamelech,* "the royal constitution." The people accept it, despite Samuel's attempts to dissuade them. The Talmud preserves two important Rabbinic opinions on this passage (BT *Sanhedrin* 20b). One view holds that "the king is permitted all powers enumerated in Samuel's list." Another suggests that Samuel's enumeration was intended solely to intimidate the people, to dissuade them from demanding a king. These two

viewpoints are, at bottom, not at all contradictory: yes, the king legitimately exercises all the powers enumerated in Samuel's "royal constitution" (*Yad, M'lachim* 4:1 and *Kesef Mishneh* ad loc.), but woe to the people whose king engages in warlike behavior. For an aggadic description of the decision-making process leading to discretionary war, see BT *B'rachot* 2b.

12. A conclusion drawn explicitly by R. Chaim David Halevy, the late Sephardic chief rabbi of Tel Aviv–Yafo, in his *Resp. Aseh L'cha Rav* 3:58 (at pp. 320–22). He writes, "We learn from this that those who believe that the Torah of Israel is militaristic are in serious error. On the contrary: in a world that was entirely militaristic, in which all problems were addressed by recourse to the sword, the Torah came to teach us that we must restrain such aspirations."

13. Tractate *Derech Eretz Zuta, perek* "Hashalom."

14. "My creatures are drowning in the sea and you want to sing?" (BT *M'gillah* 6b and *Sanhedrin* 39b). The question arises: if the angels were not permitted to rejoice, why did Israel celebrate the destruction of the Egyptians with the Song at the Sea? One explanation is that Israel did *not* sing. The verse (Exodus 15:1) begins with the words *Az yashir Mosheh*, "Then Moses sang," etc. The verb, however, is written in the imperfect or future tense, allowing the midrash to speculate that the song was in fact not sung at that time but will be sung in the world-to-come (*Tanchuma*, ed. Buber, to Exod. 15:1; see also BT *Sanhedrin* 91b).

15. Exod. 20:22 (the prohibition against carving the stones of the altar with iron implements). Rashi ad loc., from the *M'chilta*: the altar was created to lengthen our lives, while iron comes to shorten them. It is therefore improper to allow iron to contribute to the building of the altar. The *Rokeach* (twelfth- to thirteenth-century Ashkenaz) writes that this is the source of the custom to cover the knife during the recitation of *Birkat HaMazon*, since the table is compared to the altar (BT *Chagigah* 27a).

16. See BT *Sotah* 44b, where "David's wars of expansion" are cited as the example par excellence of *milchemet har'shut*.

17. See the commentary of R. David Kimchi (Radak) to the verse. He suggests that the blood referred to here recalls the innocent people (like Uriah) whom David executed or conspired to have killed. Nonetheless, Radak also points to the plain sense of the text, namely that David was a man of war and the Temple, by contrast, is a place of peace. Rambam, in his commentary to *Mishnah Avot* (*Sh'monah P'rakim*), chap. 7 (Kafach ed., p. 394), writes that although David's wars may have been justified, his military

exploits were evidence of a streak of cruelty in him that made him unworthy to build the Temple.

18. M. Sanhedrin 4:5. Some manuscripts of this Mishnaic text read "whoever saves a single *Jewish* life [*nefesh achat m'Yisrael*]," while others omit the word *m'Yisrael* so that the meaning is "a single human life" without national distinction. See the *hashlamot* by R. Chanoch Albeck to his *Mishnah*, vol. 4, p. 445, and *Dikdukei Sof'rim, Sanhedrin* 37a. We think that the reading in our text is superior, not only because of its substance, but also because the proof text cited on behalf of this statement (Gen. 4:10) as well as the words of the Mishnah that immediately follow the citation of this verse ("therefore, only one human was created at the beginning...") suggest a universal context and not to a particularly Jewish one.

19. Deut. 20:10, according to the interpretation of Rambam (*Yad, M'lachim* 6:1), although the *Sifrei* to the verse restricts the commandment to discretionary war. Nachmanides, in his commentary to the verse, offers a strategy for reading the *Sifrei* as speaking to both commanded war and discretionary war.

20. Rashi to Lev. 26:6, from the *Sifra*.

21. "When God created the first human, God took him and showed him all the trees of the Garden of Eden. God said to him, 'Look at my creations! See how beautiful and pleasing they are! All this have I created for your sake. Take care, therefore, that you do not set upon a course of evil. Take care that you do not destroy My world. For if you destroy it, there is no one who can repair the damage you inflict'" (*Midrash Kohelet Rabbah* to Eccles. 7:13).

22. The tradition sees economic interest (*parnasah*) as the primary *causus belli* of the discretionary war. See the aggadah describing the initiation of such a war in BT *B'rachot* 2b, as well as the comment in BT *Sotah* 44b that David fought his discretionary wars for *r'vachah*, a term that encompasses "expansion" and "profit."

23. The traditional Jewish doctrine of rescue, which imposes upon us the duty to save others whose lives are in danger, is relevant here. See Lev. 19:16; BT *Sanhedrin* 73a; *Yad, Rotzei-ach* 1:14; and *SA, CM* 426:1.

24. The formal rule—*haosek bamitzvah patur min hamitzvah*—is found in BT *Sukkah* 25a and 26a.

25. For example, does Rava come to explain the words of Rabbi Yochanan, as Rashi suggests (BT *Sotah* 44b, s.v. *mitzvah d'rabanan*), or does he dispute him, as indicated by the parallel *sugya* in the *Talmud Y'rushalmi*? And if we follow Rava's explanation, why

do we not use the terms *chovah* and *r'shut* to classify all wars? Why does Rambam, in other words, refer to the wars against the Canaanites and Amalek as *mitzvah* rather than *chovah* (see *Kesef Mishneh, M'lachim* 5:1)?

26. See his commentary to M. *Sotah* 8:7 (Kafach ed., p. 185) as well as *Yad, M'lachim* 5:1, where he does not mention preventive war at all. *Lechem Mishneh* ad loc. explains that Rambam includes preventive war in the category of wars fought by the king "to enhance his greatness and reputation."

27. *Yachid v'rabim halachah k'rabim* (BT *B'rachot* 9a and many other places).

28. See JT *Sotah* 8:10 (23a): "a *milchemet r'shut* is when we attack them; a *milchemet chovah* is when they attack us."

29. To take another example, if the British and French governments had reason to suspect Adolf Hitler's aggressive intent in 1936 when he marched his troops into the Rhineland, they would have been morally justified in taking action to stop him then and there. History teaches, sadly, that they had very good reason to suspect him, and the world paid dearly for their failure to take action at that time.

30. Goren, *Meishiv Milchamah*, 1:14–16. See also R. Avraham Shapira, former chief rabbi of Israel, in *T'chumin* 4 (1983): 182.

HUNGER STRIKE: ON THE FORCE-FEEDING OF PRISONERS
5766.3

Sh'eilah

What would be the Jewish view of force-feeding (strapping somebody to a chair and putting a tube down their nose in as painless a fashion as possible) a mentally stable prisoner who desires to starve himself to death to make a political statement? (Rabbi Joel Schwartzman, Morrison, Colorado)

T'shuvah

This question arises with respect to the treatment of detainees imprisoned at the U.S. naval base at Guantanamo Bay, Cuba. These detainees were captured during military operations beginning in 2001 against the Al Qaeda terrorist organization and the Taliban government of Afghanistan. During the summer and fall of 2005, they staged a hunger strike to protest their detention and treatment. In February 2006, various news organizations reported that prison officials were force-feeding the detainees, in a manner similar to that described by our *sho-eil*, as a means of breaking the strike. Military officials justified these harsh measures as necessary to save the lives of the hunger strikers. The prisoners themselves have charged that both the restraint and the insertion of the feeding tubes were accomplished through excessive violence.[1]

We compose this responsum in the summer of 2006, a time when the "war on terror" and the invasions of Afghanistan and Iraq are subjects of intense political controversy. We seek, however, to set the politics aside and to view this *sh'eilah*, as we do all others, as a *Jewish* one, involving the interpretation and application of values central to our religious tradition. With respect to this question, those values point us in different and conflicting directions. This is not an easy question for us; the "Jewish view," as our *sho-eil* puts it, is far from obvious. We will therefore set forth as thoroughly as we can the arguments both for and against force-feeding, in the hope that our answer will encompass the valid points raised by both sides and do justice to the genuine complexity of the case.

1. ARGUMENTS IN FAVOR OF FORCE-FEEDING

Jewish tradition teaches that *pikuach nefesh*, the preservation of human life, is a mitzvah, a religious duty, and that it transcends and supersedes virtually all others.[2] The Rabbis derive this from Leviticus 18:5: "You shall keep My statutes and My laws, which a person shall perform and live by them." They interpret the words "and live by them" to mean "and not die by them."[3] Thus, "one is to perform the mitzvot in such a way that one's life is not subjected to danger."[4] The supreme value that Judaism places upon the safeguarding of life expresses itself in three related rules. First, we are forbidden to cause physical harm (*chavalah*) to ourselves[5] or to place ourselves in any unnecessary danger.[6] Second, the practice of medicine is itself a form of *pikuach nefesh* and therefore supersedes other conflicting religious obligations,[7] even such serious ones as the prohibitions surrounding Shabbat and Yom Kippur.[8] And third, we are forbidden "to stand idly by the blood" of another (Lev. 19:16): that is, we bear a positive obligation to rescue the lives of those who are in danger.[9]

These teachings raise a sharp critique of the tactics of the hunger strikers. If there is a single, uncontested feature of the "Jewish view" of this question, it is that human life is sacred and that it must be treated with the utmost reverence. Yes, there are times when our tradition would permit and even demand that one die rather than violate a mitzvah, but the circumstances in which this demand applies are strictly limited.[10] In other words, one is not entitled to choose martyrdom in order "to make a political statement."[11] All of this would lead to the conclusion that the prisoners are forbidden to endanger their lives by engaging in a hunger strike and that the prison officials, who are ultimately responsible for the health and safety of those in their custody, are justified in taking strong action if necessary to bring the strike to an end. That such action may involve force and violence is regrettable, but the blame for this unhappy result lies with the prisoners themselves. By refusing nourishment, it is they who are endangering their lives. The prison officials, by contrast, are simply following the dictates of Jewish law, which enjoins us to fulfill the obligation of *pikuach nefesh* quickly and diligently: "Whosoever delays in the performance of this mitzvah is guilty of bloodshed."[12]

2. ARGUMENTS AGAINST FORCE FEEDING

On the other hand, a case can be made that Jewish tradition does not warrant the force-feeding of prisoners who have undertaken a hunger strike. That case rests upon the following three points.

a. This is a political, not a medical question. Answers are frequently dictated by the way in which we frame the questions. If we define this question primarily as a medical one, we will tend to ask it as follows: "Under Jewish law, is a patient entitled to refuse life-sustaining medical treatment?" The answer, clearly, is "no": under the rule of *pikuach nefesh*, a patient is morally obligated to accept a remedy that consensus medical opinion regards as *r'fuah b'dukah* or *r'fuah vada-it*, one that offers a reasonably certain prospect of a successful therapeutic outcome.[13] If hunger is a disease, then food is a "sure remedy" for it. Yet we would note that the prisoners themselves do not see this as a medical question. They have chosen the hunger strike as a tactic to protest against the conditions of their captivity. Their goal is to bring pressure upon their jailers, not necessarily to kill themselves or to cause themselves irreparable physical harm. Indeed, the prison officials at Guantanamo concur in this assessment.[14] If so, then the forceful insertion of nasogastric tubes is arguably a political rather than a medical intervention, designed not to save lives but "to break the hunger strikes because they were having a disruptive effect and causing stress for the medical staff." If the strike and the attendant force-feeding both serve political goals, then the rules and principles that apply to a medical context may not be appropriate here.[15] In this connection, we would note that the prohibition against inflicting physical damage upon oneself, to which we refer above, is limited to cases in which the injury is done "in a contemptible manner" or for no good purpose.[16] Obviously, those who undertake a hunger strike in protest against prison conditions would say that the harm they inflict upon themselves does not fall into that category. We would add that a number of Orthodox rabbis participated in hunger strikes during the 1990s in protest of the Oslo peace accords between Israel and the Palestine Liberation Organization. Although the strikes were controversial, the fact that they took place suggests that they were able to distinguish, on Jewish grounds, between an action designed to endanger one's life and health (forbidden) and an action intended to "make a political statement" (permitted).[17]

b. Force-feeding is widely regarded as torture. This policy is set forth by the World Medical Association (WMA) in its "Declaration of Tokyo" concerning "torture and other cruel, inhuman or degrading treatment or punishment in relation to detention and imprisonment":[18]

> Where a prisoner refuses nourishment and is considered by the physician as capable of forming an unimpaired and rational judgment concerning the consequences of such a voluntary refusal of nourishment, he or she shall not be fed artificially. The decision as to the capacity of the prisoner to form such a judgment should be confirmed by at least one other independent physician. The consequences of the refusal of nourishment shall be explained by the physician to the prisoner.

The American Medical Association, a member organization of the WMA, has reaffirmed its endorsement of this clause of the Tokyo policy.[19] In March 2006, the British medical journal *The Lancet* published a letter of protest, signed by over 250 distinguished physicians from the United States and Europe, against the force-feeding at Guantanamo. The letter, which calls upon the U.S. government "to ensure that detainees are assessed by independent physicians and that techniques such as forcefeeding and restraint chairs are abandoned forthwith in accordance with internationally agreed standards,"[20] has garnered the support of well-known human rights organizations.[21] We take these statements with the utmost seriousness. As Jews, we are heirs to a tradition that commands us to pursue justice (Deut. 16:20) and to a Torah "whose ways are pleasantness" and "whose paths are peace" (Prov. 3:17).[22] How then can we support a tactic that much of the world's enlightened medical-ethical opinion has castigated as a form of torture? To do so is arguably to perpetrate a *chilul HaShem*, a profanation of God's name, an offense we commit whenever we behave in a manner inconsistent with the high standards that the world expects of a people that lives in covenant with God.[23]

Before we reach that conclusion, however, let us consider that the Tokyo Declaration's opposition to force-feeding is based upon two principles that enjoy a dominant—some would say a "canonical"[24]—standing in contemporary secular bioethics. The first of these is patient autonomy, which holds that a medical procedure is ethical to the extent that a competent patient makes his or her own decision regarding that procedure in an autonomous manner, free of coercion. The second is informed consent: the patient agrees to a suggested treatment only when he or she has been supplied with all material information that a reasonable medical layperson would consider significant with regard to that decision.[25] Applied to our case, these principles suggest that when a prisoner makes a rational, informed decision that he does not wish to be fed, we are not permitted to feed him against his expressed will, even though the decision may result in his death.[26] Yet as we have seen, the classical Judaic approach to questions of life and death is founded not upon the affirmation of individual autonomy but upon the commitment to the sanctity of life and the duty to heal. In the traditional Jewish view, the patient has no right to make a decision, however "informed," for suicide, and the physician, who like every person bears a positive duty to save life, has no right to sit passively and watch the patient die.[27] The Jewish physician can therefore make a powerful argument that, when

confronted by a situation such as the one described in our *sh'eilah*, his or
her ethical responsibility is to save the patient's life rather than to respect
the patient's autonomy.[28]

We do not believe that the contemporary Western model of bioethics
is any more exalted, noble, or humane than the Judaic approach.
In saying this, we do not mean to disparage modernity or its
contributions to moral thought. We mean rather that as heirs to
both the classical Jewish tradition *and* the culture of modernity, we
would not wish to live in a society that rejects *either* source of ethical
value. Thus, while we acknowledge that the modern affirmation of
the dignity of the individual human being serves in our world as a
bulwark against tyranny and oppression, particularly of the sort rooted
in religious extremism, we reject the notion that "modern, progressive,
and Western" culture enjoys a monopoly upon moral truth. On the
contrary: we believe that contemporary secular civilization can learn
a great deal from the Jewish tradition, especially in the realm of
bioethics, where the Judaic approach can yield answers that might well
be morally superior to those produced by secular thought.[29] As citizens
of Western society and participants in its culture, we cannot ignore the
fact that the predominant medical-ethical opinion in *our* society and
culture defines the force-feeding of patients as an immoral act. But as
Jews, we cannot apply the label "torture" to a procedure designed to
save the life of prisoners in our custody, even if they seem bound and
determined upon suicide.

c. Force-feeding transgresses against Jewish ethical principles. Yet
even if we view this as a medical rather than a political question, the
fact that a patient is obligated to accept life-sustaining treatment does
not necessarily mean that we may force it upon her against her will.
Here it is essential to consider just what force-feeding entails. As one
Guantanamo detainee has described the procedure:

> The head is immobilized by a strap so it can't be moved, their hands
> are cuffed to the chair and the legs are shackled. They ask, "Are

you going to eat or not?" and if not, they insert the tube. People have been urinating and defecating on themselves in these feedings and vomiting and bleeding. They ask to be allowed to go to the bathroom, but they will not let them go. They have sometimes put diapers on them.[30]

Another charges that "a lieutenant came to his isolation cell and told him that if he did not agree to eat solid food, he would be strapped into the chair and force-fed. After he refused to comply, he said, soldiers picked him up by the throat, threw him to the floor and strapped him to the restraint chair."[31] The nasogastric tubes, inserted forcibly against the prisoners' wishes, have been said to cause "unbearable pain."[32] We have no way, of course, to verify these statements, and we also know that the force-feeding has been defended by officials of the U.S. Defense Department as "compassionate" and "humane."[33] Still, it is possible that these descriptions are accurate, and it is quite plausible that harsh, violent measures would be required to compel nutrients upon a prisoner who is determined to refuse them. And it is questionable whether Jewish tradition obligates us to resort to such violence even when the treatment is necessary to save a patient's life. R. Moshe Feinstein, for example, has ruled that medical treatment, though compulsory under Jewish law, "must be administered in such a way that it does not frighten the patient. For fear, even though it be irrational, may itself cause him harm or even kill him.... It is therefore preferable that the physicians not administer treatment against the patient's will...and the physicians must consider this matter very carefully."[34] We would phrase this point somewhat differently: medical treatment can be considered obligatory only when it is *medicine*, that is, when it partakes of the mitzvah of healing (*r'fuah*). To the extent that a medical procedure causes significant harm to a patient, it may be said to lose its therapeutic value and therefore its standing as "medicine" that the patient would be obligated to accept.[35] We are, of course, in no position to draw a proper balance in this case between the "harm" caused to the detainee by the violent force-feeding and its obvious benefit of saving his life, *provided* that he was intent upon suicide in the first place. Nonetheless, the concern over the negative effects of these measures must give us pause before we assert that we are morally bound to administer them by force.

In addition, even if force-feeding could be said to have no objective and observable "negative effects," we would still have reason to oppose it. Violence against a patient, even when exercised by medical professionals convinced they are acting in the patient's best interests, is still violence.[36] It is the sort of treatment that offends against our most basic conceptions of *k'vod hab'riyot*, the essential dignity that all of us, including prisoners, possess as human beings created in the image of God.[37] Force is sometimes necessary in our dealings with others, but it should never be resorted to lightly. And when we do choose that path, we had best make sure that our actions are truly the only available means by which to achieve a vital purpose.

TOWARD A CONCLUSION

What is the "Jewish view" of force-feeding? As we have indicated, we think that there can be no simple, one-sided answer to this question. We have encountered powerful Judaic arguments both for and against the practice, arguments based upon Jewish legal and moral values that demand our respect and assent. Accordingly, our response acknowledges the wisdom of all these arguments in an effort to arrive at what we think is the most persuasive interpretation of the teachings of our tradition.

We begin from the obvious starting point: *pikuach nefesh*, the duty to preserve human life and to rescue those in danger, is the overriding Jewish moral concern. In any sort of "Jewish view," the obligation to save the life of a patient must take precedence over the desire to respect the patient's autonomously chosen decision to die. This is especially true given that a decision to embark upon a hunger strike must raise concerns as to the patient's ability to arrive at a truly rational choice based upon "informed consent."[38]

CHOSHEN MISHPAT • 389

At the same time, force-feeding by its nature is a violent, even brutal tactic that "shocks the conscience"[39] and robs the prisoner of his fundamental human dignity. Although force-feeding can under extreme circumstances be justified on medical grounds, we think that prison authorities can abuse it all too easily for nonmedical purposes, as a tool for punishment or discipline. When they do so, we fully agree with those who condemn the measure as a form of torture. It is to be avoided in all cases except when it is obviously necessary to save the life of the hunger striker.

How do we draw a proper balance between these conflicting values and concerns? We find helpful guidance, surprisingly perhaps, in the regulations regarding hunger strikes adopted by the U.S. Federal Bureau of Prisons.[40] These provide that a prisoner who embarks on a hunger strike is at first permitted to maintain that action. He is placed under careful medical supervision, and food is brought to his cell three times a day. Prison officials will make efforts to persuade him to abandon the strike, but they will not force him to do so until "a physician determines that the inmate's life or health will be threatened if treatment is not initiated immediately." The prisoner may be fed involuntarily only "if the physician is convinced to a reasonable medical certainty that there is an immediate threat to the inmate's life, or permanent damage to the inmate's health."[41] The words "immediate" and "permanent" are crucial here. They declare that the only acceptable grounds for force-feeding are medical and that those grounds must be sufficiently urgent to remove virtually all doubt that the feeding is medically necessary. These regulations, if adhered to in the case of the Guantanamo detainees, would prevent the misuse of force-feeding for other purposes, such as for maintaining prison discipline or for relieving "stress" upon the prison staff.[42]

ONE FINAL NOTE

The Bureau's rules also provide that when nasogastric tubes are inserted by force, "these events should be videotaped."[43] We cannot overemphasize the importance of this point for our *t'shuvah*. The force-feeding of prisoners must be carefully supervised, for only in that way can we hope to prevent excessive violence and other mistreatment. This supervision therefore should be performed by outside observers who do not represent the prison system or the military. Although this might interfere with the secrecy that currently surrounds the activities at the Guantanamo prison camp, we think it is the best way for the U.S. military to demonstrate its commitment to "humane" and "compassionate" treatment of the detainees in the face of severe international criticism. In so doing, they would fulfill the spirit of the Mishnah's dictum that it is essential to display our innocence in the sight of people as well as in the sight of God.[44] It would also meet the high standard set by the United States Declaration of Independence, which proclaims the American people's "decent respect to the opinions of mankind."

NOTES

1. This description is culled from the following news sources: "Force-Feeding at Guantanamo Is Now Acknowledged," *New York Times*, February 22, 2006 (http://www.nytimes.com/2006/02/22/international/middleeast/22gitmo.html?ex=129826 4400&en=7ea399aeaba6605e&ei=5090&partner=rssuserland&emc=rss); "Doctors Attack US Over Guantanamo," *British Broadcasting Corporation*, March 10, 2006 (http://news.bbc.co.uk/1/hi/world/americas/4790742.stm); "Guantanamo Force Feeding Tactics Are Called Torture," *Washington Post*, March 1, 2006 (http://www.washingtonpost.com/wp-dyn/content/article/2006/02/28/AR2006022801344.html). (Articles accessed August 21, 2009.)

2. The classical formulation of this rule is the phrase *yaavor v'al yehareg*, "one should transgress the commandment rather than be killed," in the event that a persecutor demands that a Jew either violate the mitzvah or forfeit his life. See BT *Sanhedrin* 74a and *Avodah Zarah* 27b; *Yad, Y'sodei HaTorah* 5:1ff.; *SA, YD* 157:1. On the exceptions to this rule see note 10, below.

3. BT *Yoma* 85b, *Sanhedrin* 74a, and *Avodah Zarah* 27b; *Sifra* to Lev. 18:5.

4. Rashi, BT *Yoma* 85b, s.v. *d'shmu'el leit leh pircha*.

5. BT *Bava Kama* 90b; *Yad, Chovel Umazik* 5:1. But see below in the text.

6. Derived from Deut. 4:9. *Yad, Rotzei-ach* 11:4; *SA, CM* 427:8–10. On this basis, a number of contemporary Orthodox authorities have begun to prohibit smoking. See the discussion in *Teshuvot for the Nineties (TFN)*, no. 5753.23, pp. 331–35.

7. M. *Yoma* 8:5; Nachmanides, *Torat HaAdam*, ed. Chavel (Jerusalem: Mosad Harav Kook, 1964), 41–42; *Tur* and *SA, YD* 336:1.

8. Thus, a person who rejects the instruction of a competent physician (*rofei baki*) on the grounds that the instruction involves prohibited labor on Shabbat is "a pious fool [*chasid shoteh*]. This is not an act of piety but of suicide. One is required to do what the physicians prescribe" (R. David ibn Zimra [sixteenth- to seventeenth-century Egypt], *Resp. Radbaz* 1:1139).

9. BT *Sanhredrin* 73a: "From where do we learn that one who sees his fellow drowning in the river, attacked by a wild beast, or threatened by robbers is obliged to save him? From the verse 'Do not stand idly by the blood of your fellow.'" Rambam (*Yad, Rotzei-ach* 1:14) codifies the rule as follows: "One who is able to save his fellow [from danger] and does not do so has transgressed against the mitzvah of Lev. 19:16." See also *SA, CM* 426.

10. See the sources enumerated in note 2, above. Jewish tradition requires martyrdom in three specific cases; to put this differently, there are three mitzvot that one must never violate, even at the cost of one's life. These are idolatry, the sexual transgressions enumerated in Leviticus 18, and murder. These are formulated in the sources as "exceptions" to the rule of *pikuach nefesh* established by the interpretation of Lev. 18:5. Each exception is itself derived by way of midrash (textual interpretation) or *s'vara* (logical inference); see BT *Sanhedrin* 74a.

11. See *Yad, Y'sodei HaTorah* 5:4: "If the case is one in which the Torah says, 'Transgress the commandment and save your life,' the one who chooses to die rather than transgress is culpable for his own death"; i.e., he has committed suicide. But see below in the text.

12. *SA, YD* 336:1.

13. See *TFN*, no. 5754.14, pp. 337ff., at notes 38–40.

14. According to Maj. Gen. Jay W. Hood, commander of the prison camp at the Guantanamo naval base, the hunger strikers are not suicidal but are simply protesting their confinement. "In none of these [cases] have I ever gotten the impression that these guys want to die." See Susan Okie, MD, "Glimpses of Guantanamo: Medical Ethics and the War on Terror," *New England Journal of Medicine* 353, no. 24 (Dec. 15, 2005): 2529–34.

15. "Force-Feeding at Guantanamo Is Now Acknowledged" (see note 1, above). The quotation is attributed to two "Defense Department officials." See also "Guantanamo Medics Accused of Abusive Force-Feeding," *Boston Globe*, Oct. 15, 2005 (http://www.boston.com/news/nation/articles/2005/10/15/guantanamo_medics_accused_of_abusive_force_feeding, accessed August 21, 2009), quoting Dr. Arthur Caplan, director of the Center for Bioethics at the University of Pennsylvania: "Medicine is supposed to remain neutral. When you start to become complicit in efforts to break resistance using medical expertise that should be there simply to protect the health of people, you're headed down the wrong track."

16. *Yad, Chovel Umazik* 5:1: the phrase is *derech nitzayon* (or, in some readings, *bizayon*). See *TFN*, no. 5752.7, "Cosmetic Surgery."

17. See R. Menachem Feliks, "*Ve'af al Pi Chen: Shevitat Raav*," *T'chumin* 16 (1996/5756): 291–95. Feliks contends that the halachah permits an individual to undertake a voluntary fast (*taanit yachid*) in order to protest against policies of the Israeli government that, in the individual's opinion, endanger the Jewish people and state. He would not apply his argument, obviously, to the Muslim detainees at Guantanamo. From a liberal perspective, though, the notion that one may declare a fast in service to a "higher purpose" is a principle that should not be restricted to Jews.

18. *The World Medical Association Declaration of Tokyo* (1975, 2005, and 2006), paragraph 6 (http://www.wma.net/e/policy/c18.htm, accessed August 21, 2009).

19. "AMA Reiterates Opposition to Feeding Individuals against Their Will," statement by Duane Cady, MD, chair, American Medical Association, cited by M. K. Wynia, "Should Doctors Force Feed Prisoners?" *MedGenMed* 9, no. 4 (2007): 5, http://www.medscape.com/viewarticle/563171 (accessed August 21, 2009).

20. David J. Nichol et al., "Forcefeeding and Restraint of Guantanamo Bay Hunger Strikers," *The Lancet* 367 (March 11, 2006): 9513 (http://www.thelancet.com/journals/lancet/article/PIIS0140673606683268/fulltext, accessed August 21, 2009).

21. Among these are Physicians for Human Rights (http://physiciansforhumanrights.org/library/news-2005-09-16.html) and Amnesty International (http://www.amnesty.org.uk/news_details.asp?NewsID=16898; accessed August 21, 2009).

22. Halachic authorities sometimes cite this verse as a guide for the interpretation of the Torah's laws according to its ultimate intent. Thus, Maimonides rules (*Yad, Chanukah* 4:14) that, in the event one has only enough oil either for household illumination or for the Chanukah lamp, one should use it for household illumination, "for the sake of

domestic peace" (*mishum shalom beito*). He adds, "Great is peace, for the entire Torah was given to bring peace to the world, as it is said, 'whose ways are pleasantness, etc.'"

23. For sources and discussion on *chilul HaShem*, see *Reform Responsa for the Twenty-first Century*, no. 5764.1, vol. 2, pp. 291–98, at notes 11–15.

24. The term is used by R. Hamel, "The Reign of Autonomy: Is the End in Sight?" *Second Opinion*, January 1995, 75–79.

25. These definitions reflect the formulation of American law, represented especially by the leading case *Canterbury v. Spence*, 464 F.2d 772 (D.C. Cir. 1972). The classic formulation is perhaps that of Judge Benjamin N. Cardozo in *Schloendorff v. Society of N.Y. Hospital*, 105 N.E. 92 (N.Y. 1914): "Every human being of adult years and sound mind has a right to determine what shall be done with his own body, and a surgeon who performs an operation without his patient's consent commits an assault for which he is liable in damages." See, in general, Ruth R. Faden, Tom L. Beauchamp, in collaboration with Nancy M. P. King, *A History and Theory of Informed Consent* (New York: Oxford University Press, 1986).

26. See the statement from the WMA's Tokyo Declaration at note 18, above. It is, however, not certain that the Guantanamo detainees are able to make an "informed" decision under the conditions of their incarceration. See Okie, "Glimpses of Guantanamo," 2530–31.

27. In this, Jewish tradition would dissent from the decision of the British authorities who allowed hunger-striking members of the Irish Republican Army to starve themselves to death while in prison in 1981. See Okie, "Glimpses of Guantanamo," 2530.

28. For an example of such a powerful argument, see Shimeon Glick, MD, "Unlimited Human Autonomy: A Cultural Bias?" *New England Journal of Medicine* 356 (March 27, 1997): 954–56 (http://content.nejm.org/cgi/content/short/336/13/954, accessed August 21, 2009).

29. For an example, see *Reform Responsa for the Twenty-first Century*, no. 5763.2, "Live Liver Transplantation," vol. 2, pp. 143–64, section 4 and following.

30. "Force-Feeding at Guantanamo Is Now Acknowledged" (see note 1, above).

31. Ibid.

32. "Guantanamo Force Feeding Tactics Are Called Torture" (see note 1, above).

33. "Force-Feeding at Guantanamo Is Now Acknowledged" and "Doctors Attack US Over Guantanamo" (see note 1, above).

34. *Resp. Ig'rot Moshe, CM* 2:73, part 5.

35. For a detailed analysis of this point, see *TFN,* no. 5754.14, pp. 337–63, at section 3.

36. Some of these objections, it might be argued, can be removed simply by sedating the prisoners prior to force-feeding. While it is true that, as a matter of degree, sedation would reduce the amount of violence employed in force-feeding, it would still in its essence, as a forcible transgression of the patient's will, constitute an act of violence against him. As such, the Judaic principles cited in this paragraph would continue to apply. Needless to say, moreover, the procedure would still be defined as "torture" under the Tokyo Declaration (note 18, above).

37. Although it may sound like a lofty ethical principle with little substantive content, *k'vod hab'riyot* functions as a real consideration in halachah. In its general formulation, the rule is that considerations of "human dignity" may be great enough to supersede a conflicting Rabbinic ordinance (BT *B'rachot* 19b; *Yad, Shabbat* 26:23 and *Kilayim* 10:29). In this case, of course, the conflicting ordinance is *pikuach nefesh,* which originates in the Torah (*d'oraita*), and one might argue that the saving of life surely overrides considerations of *k'vod hab'riyot.* But one leading *poseik* suggests that "dignity" (*kavod*) may in some cases override *pikuach nefesh.* See R. Sh'lomo Kluger (nineteenth-century Galicia), *Chochmat Sh'lomo* to *SA, CM* 426:1.

38. See note 26, above, as well as Glick, "Unlimited Human Autonomy, 955: "One might perhaps see forcing people to undergo lifesaving therapy as an action that does respect their autonomy and for which they may ultimately be grateful; their judgment may be temporarily compromised by irrationality, although they remain within the bounds of legally defined competence."

39. This phrase is particularly appropriate here, in that it is the definition of "torture" adopted by the U.S. Supreme Court in a case involving the seizure of evidence from a suspect by means of induced vomiting. The Court held that "the proceedings by which the conviction was obtained do more than offend some fastidious squeamishness or private sentimentalism about combating crime too energetically. This is conduct that shocks the conscience.... They are methods too close to the rack and the screw to permit of constitutional differentiation." *Rochin v. California,* 345 U.S. 165 (1952), at 172.

40. U.S. Department of Justice, Federal Bureau of Prisons, *Program Statement,* no. P5562.05, July 29, 2005 (http://www.bop.gov/policy/progstat/5562_005.pdf, accessed August 21, 2009).

41. Ibid., p. 6.

42. See above at note 15. The goal of prison population control can be met in other ways. For example, the *Statement* provides that when a prisoner undertakes a hunger strike, he or she may be isolated in "a medically appropriate locked room" (p. 3). The formal justification for this rule is medical: isolation allows for close monitoring of the prisoner's physical condition. But it also addresses the concerns surrounding discipline (i.e., preventing the hunger strike from causing disturbances among the inmate population), thereby avoiding the resort to force-feeding as a means of breaking the strike.

43. *Program Statement*, p. 7.

44. *M. Sh'kalim* 3:2, based upon Num. 32:22.

NEW RESPONSA INDEX
Volumes 1 and 2

Breinigsville, PA USA
05 April 2011
259234BV00004B/1/P

9 780881 231618